Land and Spirituality in Rabbinic Literature

The Brill Reference Library of Judaism

Editors

Alan J. Avery-Peck (*College of the Holy Cross*)
William Scott Green (*University of Miami*)

Editorial Board

Herbert Basser (*Queen's University*)
Bruce D. Chilton (*Bard College*)
Mayer I. Gruber (*Ben-Gurion University of the Negev*)
Ithamar Gruenwald (*Tel Aviv University*)
Arkady Kovelman (*Moscow State University*)
Baruch A. Levine (*New York University*)
Allan Nadler (*Drew University*)
Jacob Neusner Z"l (*Bard College*)
Maren Niehoff (*Hebrew University of Jerusalem*)
Gary G. Porton (*University of Illinois*)
Aviezer Ravitzky (*Hebrew University of Jerusalem*)
Dov Schwartz (*Bar Ilan University*)
Günter Stemberger (*University of Vienna*)
Michael E. Stone (*Hebrew University of Jerusalem*)
Elliot R. Wolfson (*University of California, Santa Barbara*)

VOLUME 71

The titles published in this series are listed at *brill.com/brlj*

Land and Spirituality in Rabbinic Literature

A Memorial Volume for Yaakov Elman ז״ל

Edited by

Shana Strauch Schick

BRILL

LEIDEN | BOSTON

Cover illustration: Jewish Tombstone from Late Antique Zoar (Zoora), Jordan. From the Collection of Yeshiva University Museum.

Library of Congress Cataloging-in-Publication Data

Names: Strauch Schick, Shana, editor. | Elman, Yaakov, honouree.
Title: Land and spirituality in rabbinic literature : a memorial volume for Yaakov Elman / edited by Shana Strauch Schick.
Description: Leiden ; Boston : Brill, [2022] | Series: The Brill reference library of Judaism, 1571-5000 ; volume 71 | Includes bibliographical references and index.
Identifiers: LCCN 2021057500 (print) | LCCN 2021057501 (ebook) |
    ISBN 9789004503151 (hardback) | ISBN 9789004503168 (ebook)
Subjects: LCSH: Judaism–Customs and practices–History–168 B.C.-135 A.D. | Jews–History–168 B.C.-135 A.D. | Rabbinical literature–History and criticism. | Excavations (Archaeology)–Israel. | Samaritan religious poetry–History and criticism. | Jewish religious poetry–History and criticism. | Elman, Yaakov. | Jewish scholars–Israel–Biography.
Classification: LCC BM700 .L235 2022 (print) | LCC BM700 (ebook) |
    DDC 296.4/9–dc23/eng/20220103
LC record available at https://lccn.loc.gov/2021057500
LC ebook record available at https://lccn.loc.gov/2021057501

Typeface for the Latin, Greek, and Cyrillic scripts: "Brill". See and download: brill.com/brill-typeface.

ISSN 1571-5000
ISBN 978-90-04-50315-1 (hardback)
ISBN 978-90-04-50316-8 (e-book)

Copyright 2022 by Shana Strauch Schick. Published by Koninklijke Brill NV, Leiden, The Netherlands.
Koninklijke Brill NV incorporates the imprints Brill, Brill Nijhoff, Brill Hotei, Brill Schöningh, Brill Fink, Brill mentis, Vandenhoeck & Ruprecht, Böhlau and V&R unipress.
Koninklijke Brill NV reserves the right to protect this publication against unauthorized use. Requests for re-use and/or translations must be addressed to Koninklijke Brill NV via brill.com or copyright.com.

This book is printed on acid-free paper and produced in a sustainable manner.

Contents

Preface   VII
List of Illustrations   XII
Contributors   XIV

PART 1
Torat Erets Yisrael

1. Rabbinic Paleontology: Jewish Encounters with Fossil Giants in Roman Antiquity   3
   Elisha Fine and Steven Fine

2. Tosefta Eduyot 1:1 On the Fear of Losing Torah and the Redaction of Tannaitic Materials   38
   Michal Bar-Asher Siegal

3. Minhag and Popular Practice in Roman Palestine   51
   Stuart S. Miller

4. The Roman Freedman and the *Ḥalal*: The Legal Models That Shaped Rabbinic Law on the Status of Converts in Marriage   63
   Yael Wilfand

5. Shimon b. Shatah, the Donkey, and the Diamond: The Treasure and the Blessing, Law and Artistry   92
   Nachman Levine

6. Whence Leprosy? An Inquiry into the Theodicies of the Tannaim   106
   Shlomo Zuckier

7. Feasting, Fasting, and the Bounty of the Land: Rituals of Sukkot in Samaritan and Rabbinic Antiquity   137
   Laura S. Lieber

8. Two Parallel Consolatory Poems for Tisha be'Av in Aramaic and Hebrew   159
   Moshe J. Bernstein

PART 2
Torat Erets Yisrael in Babylonia

9   The Motif of the Forgetting and Restoration of Law: An Inter-Talmudic Difference about the Divine Role in Rabbinic Law   175
    Alyssa M. Gray

10 The Use of Literary Considerations as a Key for Assessing the Reliability of Memrot in the Babylonian Talmud: The Case of the *Lo Shanu Ela* Traditions   208
    Barak Cohen

11 Cultural Attitudes towards Scent in the Interpretation of Isaiah 11:3   239
    Meira Wolkenfeld

12 "And God Blessed Them": Procreation in Palestinian *Halakhah* and in Babylonian *Aggadah*   260
    Shana Strauch Schick

PART 3
Tributes to Yaakov Elman

13 Remembering Yaakov Elman ז״ל   295
    Laurence H. Schiffman

14 Perpetual Motion   299
    Shai Secunda

15 Professor Yaakov Elman: A Talmud Scholar of Singular Depth and Scope   302
    Shana Strauch Schick

16 A Tribute to Professor Yaakov Elman   305
    Meira Wolkenfeld

    Photographs   307
    Bibliography of Yaakov Elman's Publications   310
    Index   319

Preface

Land and Spirit in Rabbinic Literature: Studies in Memory of Yaakov Elman ז״ל is a collection of studies devoted to the texts, traditions, and practices of the Land of Israel from the end of the Second Temple continuing through the early rabbinic period (70 CE) to the end of the first millennium.

This volume has its origins in the conference, "Land and Spirituality in Rabbinic Literature: A Day in Memory of Professor Yaakov Elman" that I organized at the Yeshiva University Center for Israel Studies in New York in 2019, where most of these papers were presented. This is the second volume dedicated to Yaakov Elman under the auspices of the Yeshiva University Center for Israel Studies. The first, *Shoshannat Yaakov: Jewish and Iranian Studies in Honor of Yaakov Elman,* edited by Shai Secunda and Steven Fine (Brill, 2012) celebrated his ongoing work; sadly, this volume is dedicated to his memory. We miss him. Professor Elman's interests were wide-ranging and diverse. His studies reflect a unique ability to synthesize information and approaches from across many disciplines and fields of knowledge; all with the goal of shedding light on the texts, intellectual history, and culture of the people whom he studied—be they rabbis, Zoroastrians, or the Qumran community.

The studies in this volume display a similarly vibrant level of diversity. A wide range of methodologies are employed, including critical textual reconstruction, literary analysis, history, and the interplay between law and narrative. These studies are united by their shared focus on traditions from the Land of Israel and their rigorous approaches, which together offer a picture of rabbinic literature and Israelite cultures—Jewish and Samaritan, that are multi-layered and complex.

The first part of the volume comprises studies on Palestinian literature that examine practices and beliefs that developed in the Land of Israel. Together these articles depict a rich and textured picture of Late Antique Palestine, which displays certain commonalities with the culture of its Roman overseers and in other ways is highly distinctive.

The collection begins with an examination of how Second Temple through later rabbinic texts understood the prehistoric past. Elisha Fine and Steven Fine excavate Josephus, rabbinic and classical sources and suggest that ancient Jews responded to fossil discoveries, imagining the bones of ancient elephants, and possibly other large mammals, to be those of the biblical *anaqim*. Drawing on recent work that has identified similar references in Greco-Roman texts, they demonstrate that what have previously been deemed fanciful passages in Josephus and rabbinic literature about giants and monstrous beings rather interpret discoveries of prehistoric fossils. Turning to how the rabbis understood their own past, Michal Bar-Asher Siegal examines both the philological aspects of Tosefta Eduyot 1 along with its content, to reconstruct its textual development, while uncovering a source of tension that existed within the rabbinic imagination. Considering previous studies devoted to this text, which appears to present a tantalizingly elusive history of the early rabbinic movement, Bar-Asher Siegal argues that Tosefta Eduyot draws on two earlier tannaitic sources, one preserved only in the Bavli, to discuss the rabbis' fear that several aspects of Torah learning may become lost in the future. This paper bolsters the evidence that the Bavli appears to preserve versions of tannaitic traditions that predate those found in extant Palestinian works.

The following articles examine aspects of extra-rabbinic factors that often helped to shape Palestinian rabbinic law, *halakhah*. Stuart Miller points to the significant impact that the popular practices of everyday Jews had upon the amoraim of the Land of Israel and the laws which they articulated. Drawing on anecdotes, discussions of *halakhot* which preoccupied the rabbis, as well as archeological evidence, Miller paints a picture of the ongoing interactions between rabbis and everyday Jews living in the Land of Israel during the amoraic period. This, he argues, contrasts with the amoraim of Babylonia who, having far less daily contact with Jews who were not part of their collegium, took a narrower approach towards *minhag* when deciding *halakhah*. Yael Wilfand looks to the Greco-Roman context of the Palestinian rabbis and the role that Roman imperial law had in the shaping of *halakhah*. She suggests that what appears to be inconsistencies in tannaitic rulings regarding the status of converts reflect Roman models of citizenship for former slaves. As opposed to earlier scholars who have understood the diverse rabbinic perspectives on the status of converts as a matter of varying levels of stringency, Wilfand argues that Roman norms, notions, and laws regarding freedmen and freedwomen served as a conceptual framework for rabbinic thinking on this issue. Nachman Levine continues the discussion of extra-halakhic elements in Palestinian texts in his literary analysis of an aggadic narrative appearing in Deuteronomy Rabbah and its parallel in the Jerusalem Talmud (Bava Metsia 2:5, 8c). He demonstrates not only the high level of literary artistry evinced in this brief account, but a meta-halakhic message on ethical behavior embedded therein. This narrative reveals a source of conflict for its author between the accepted law that one need not return a lost object to a non-Jew, and a moral imperative that one should. Levine thus points to the tensions that arise between legal principles versus ethical values, as well as law and narrative more generally. Shlomo Zuckier examines another tension between legal versus narrative texts in his study of the rabbinic discussions surrounding the cause of the biblical malady of *tsaraat*. In contrast to previous studies which have argued that early rabbinic traditions do not correlate *tsaraat* with sin, corresponding to how *tsaraat* is discussed in legal contexts, Zuckier argues that the dominant approach as evidenced in tannaitic and amoraic aggadic literature is that it is in fact a form of divine retribution, reflecting the themes of various biblical narratives concerning *tsaraat*.

Laura Lieber focuses on the neighboring Samaritan community as a point of comparison with rabbinic practices. Lieber suggests that the modern-day Samaritan observance of the holiday of Sukkot, which is significantly different from rabbinic practice, is based on different underlying interpretations of the biblical text coupled with evolving historical circumstances. Weaving together Samaritan sources from late antiquity with events that led to practices up to the present, she argues that the holiday of Sukkot was linked with the Garden of Eden and the state of purity engendered by the fast of Yom Kippur as well as the agricultural abundance experienced by the Samaritan community during the fourth through seventh centuries.

Moving to the byzantine and early Islamic period, Moshe Bernstein offers a picture of synagogue liturgical practice in Palestine during the mid-Byzantium period. Through identifying striking literary and thematic similarities between a Palestinian Aramaic lament poem devoted to the fast of the Ninth of Av and a Hebrew "expansion" poem found in the liturgy of its afternoon prayers, both from roughly the same period, Bernstein offers a new possibility as to when (and by whom) the latter might have been recited during the ninth of Av service. He thus demonstrates that Hebrew and Aramaic poetry may in fact have had similar liturgical functions, albeit for different synagogue constituencies.

The second section of the volume shifts its focus to the Babylonian Talmud, the Bavli, and how this compendium encountered, incorporated, and differed from traditions from the Land of Israel. The theme of forgetting Torah is revisited in Alyssa Grey's article, in which she offers a thorough examination of the motif of the forgetting and restoration of Torah knowledge and how it differs in the statements of Palestinian versus Babylonian rabbis. She notes significant differences not only in the greater prevalence of this motif in rabbinic texts from the Land of Israel, but in their willingness to introduce Divine oversight into the rabbinic legal process. While rabbis of the Land of Israel regard unknowing restorations of Torah as the hidden involvement of the Divine in human activities, Bavli texts describe similar restorations as the result of painstaking human endeavors. Barak Cohen turns to another instance where material appearing in the Yerushalmi is incorporated in the Bavli, analyzing instances where the Bavli reports amoraic statements found in the Yerushalmi by use of the term *lo shanu ela*, "they taught [this] only." Although the Bavli redactors reworked their sources by introducing this phrase, they nevertheless retained the original halakhic content found in the parallel Yerushalmi traditions. Arguing that we must distinguish content from language and style, Cohen makes an important contribution to the larger issue of the reliability of attributed statements in the Bavli.

No volume devoted to Yaakov Elman would be complete without a study examining Bavli texts in relation to Zoroastrian literature. Meira Wolkenfeld looks at the ways that Palestinian rabbinic texts and the Bavli interpret Isaiah 11:3's description of the messiah "smelling," and argues that their differing understandings reflect the divergent values attributed to the sense of smell in the Roman world as opposed to Sasanian Iran. Whereas texts from the Land of Israel interpret this verse metaphorically, the Bavli offers a literal interpretation which corresponds with other Bavli passages, as well as Middle Persian Zoroastrian texts, that evince a similar positive view of the sense of smell.

In the final article, the relationship between law and narrative returns in my examination of the divergent positions expressed in Palestinian versus Bavli texts concerning women's role and obligation in procreation. In both aggadic and halakhic discussions of these issues the Bavli incorporates traditions from the Land of Israel, but it reframes them in ways that conform with the approach of Babylonian sages. The interrelationship of law and narrative is highlighted by the manner in which Palestinian rulings resurface in the Bavli as narratives, thereby giving voice to a more inclusive Palestinian approach and acknowledging the challenges that the Bavli's exclusionary rulings may pose in practice.

Following these studies, we have taken this opportunity to include some of the remembrances and tributes written in the wake of Yaakov Elman's passing, from his doctoral advisor, Lawrence H. Schiffman and his doctoral students Shai Secunda, Meira Wolkenfeld, and myself. This is followed by a bibliography of his scholarly publications, which now includes several posthumously published articles.

A number of people have helped make this volume possible. At Brill, Alan Avery-Peck, editor of the series, offered early support and enthusiasm for this memorial volume, and Katelyn Chin, Erika Mandarino, and Noortje Maranus were exceedingly kind and helpful throughout the publishing process. I am grateful for the assistance of two students at Yeshiva University: David Selis, the Leon Charney Doctoral Fellow at the Bernard Revel Graduate School, helped with the images, compiled the bibliography, and contributed to the editing. Baruch-Lev Kelmn, the Dr. Joseph and Faye Glatt Research Associate of the Center for Israel Studies and now a graduate student at Revel, aided in editing, making the index, and other technical aspects. Thanks to Shulamith Z. Berger, the Curator of Special Collections and Hebraica-Judaica at the Yeshiva University Library for collecting and scanning the images of Yaakov Elman that we have included in this volume, which capture his joy in teaching.

My special thanks to Steven Fine, who invited me to organize the conference and has supported this endeavor from beginning to end. From developing the idea of the initial conference to securing funding for it and helping in all aspects of the process of editing and publishing this volume, this book would not exist without his initiative and efforts. I thank the YU Center for Israel Studies for making this project possible, and for appointing me a Leon Charney Fellow. I especially thank Mrs. Tzili Charney for her ongoing support for the Center for Israel Studies, and for helping it to become an internationally-known and respected engine of scholarship and learning.

Finally, I would like to thank all of the authors whose scholarly contributions have made this volume possible. I gained a great deal from reading their articles and am grateful for their responsiveness and eagerness to help bring this project to fruition.

Speaking for myself and all the contributors, we hope that this volume will serve as a reminder not only of the kind of scholarship that Yaakov pursued and inspired, but of his deep humanity, glowing eyes, and quick smile. For those of us who had the privilege to know him well, he will be remembered most for his kindness, which was manifest in both his life and scholarship. As he put it, "When you're a caring, thoughtful person you notice things that others tend to overlook and that really helps in scholarship." May the memory of Yaakov Elman be a blessing—and an inspiration—to us all.

Shana Strauch Schick
Jerusalem
17 Av 5781
July 26, 2021

Illustrations

Cover Illustration

Jewish Tombstone from Late Antique Zoar (Zoora), Jordan. From the Collection of Yeshiva University Museum.

1. תתניח נפשה דסארה ברת
2. פינחס דמיתת בחדסר יומין
3. בירח אדר תנאנה דשתה
4. תלתיאה דשאבועה שנת
5. תלת מה ושת[י]ן שנין לחרבן
6. בית מקדשה תאנוח על
7. משכבה שאלום

1. Rest the soul of Sarah, daughter of
2. Pinhas, who died on the eleventh day,
3. in the month of Adar II; year
4. three of the sabbatical [cycle], the year,
5. three hundred and sixty years of the destruction
6. of the Temple. May she rest in
7. her grave. Shalom

ILLUSTRATIONS XIII

Transcription and translation by Steven Fine, "'Rest the Soul of Sarah, Daughter of Pinhas': A Jewish Tombstone From Zoar, From the Collection of Yeshiva University Museum," in *Wisdom Has Built Her: A Tribute in Memory of Leah D. Adler z"l* ed. Shulamith Berger, Zvi Erenyi, Shulamis Hes, Moshe Schapiro, Richard White (New York: Mendel Gottesman Library, Yeshiva University, 2021).

In-Text Illustrations

1.1 Mammoth Molar, after Tobias Cohen, *Sefer Ma'aseh Tuvia* (Venice, 1708), Olam ha-Qatan, 77 (Steven Fine). 3
1.2 Mammoth Molars From Bethlehem, Complete M3s in occlusal (top) and lingual (bottom) views. (a–b) M18523, R; (c–d) M 18524, Natural History Museum, London. (after Rabinovich and Lister, "The Earliest Elephants Out of Africa," fig. 7). 5
1.3 Skull of Elephas Maximus, partially reconstructed, Gavur Lake Swamp, Turkey, MTA Natural History Museum, Ankara (after Girdland-Flink, Albayrak, Lister, 2018, Wikimedia Commons). 6
1.4 Goliath Ossuary, Jericho, no. 18, ins. 9a–b (courtesy of Ann Killebrew). 7
1.5 Elonei Mamre, "the Oaks of Mamre," 1st century (Wikimedia Commons). 12
1.6 Tomb of Makhpelah, Hebron, 1st century (Wikimedia Commons). 12
1.7 Prehistoric Whale Bones, Wadi Al-Hitan, Egypt (Wikimedia Commons). 20
1.8 Couch and Footstool with Bone Carvings and Glass Inlays, 1st–2nd centuries CE, reconstruction (Metropolitan Museum of Art, Gift of J. Pierpont Morgan, 1917). 22
1.9 Throne of Maximianus, 6th century CE, Ravenna (Wikimedia Commons). 23
7.1 "General view of succa of the Samaritan Community on Mount Grizim," Mark Neyman, National Photo Collection of Israel. 156

Contributors

Michal Bar-Asher Siegal
is a scholar of rabbinic Judaism. She is an associate professor at The Goldstein-Goren Department of Jewish Thought, Ben-Gurion University of the Negev, and was an elected member of the Israel Young Academy of Sciences. Her first book is *Early Christian Monastic Literature and the Babylonian Talmud* (CUP 2013). Her second book is *Jewish—Christian Dialogues on Scripture in Late Antiquity: Heretic Narratives of the Babylonian Talmud* (CUP 2019).

Moshe J. Bernstein
is Professor of Bible and Jewish History at Yeshiva University, where he holds the David A. and Fannie M. Denenberg Chair in Biblical Studies. His work on biblical interpretation in the Dead Sea Scrolls is collected in *Reading and Re-Reading Scripture at Qumran* 2 volumes (Leiden: Brill Academic Publishers, 2013). His interests in Aramaic extend to the *targumim* and Jewish Aramaic liturgical poetry of late antiquity.

Barak S. Cohen
is a Senior lecturer at the Department of Talmud, faculty of Jewish Studies, Bar-Ilan University. He has published extensively on the intellectual history, chronology, and historiography of the Babylonian Amoraim. His most recent book is *For Out of Babylonia Shall Come Torah and the Word of the Lord from Nehar Peqod* (Brill, 2017).

Elisha N. Fine
is a doctoral student in Jewish History of the modern period at the Bernard Revel Graduate School of Jewish Studies of Yeshiva University. Having recently completed his MSW at the Wurzweiler School of Social Work, his work focuses on the cultural history of death and dying.

Steven Fine
is the Churgin Professor of Jewish History at Yeshiva University and director of the Yeshiva University Center for Israel Studies and the Israelite Samaritans Project. His most recent book is *The Menorah: From the Bible to Modern Israel* (2016). In 2013 he received the Samaritan Medal for Samaritan Studies.

Alyssa M. Gray
is the Emily S. and Rabbi Bernard H. Mehlman Chair in Rabbinics and Professor of Codes and Responsa Literature at HUC-JIR in New York. She is the author of

Charity in Rabbinic Judaism: Atonement, Rewards, and Righteousness (New York and London: Routledge, 2019; paperback ed., 2020) and *A Talmud in Exile: The Influence of Yerushalmi Avodah Zarah on the Formation of Bavli Avodah Zarah* (Brown, 2005; 2nd digital edition; Brown, 2020).

Laura S. Lieber

is Professor of Religious Studies and Classical Studies at Duke University, where she directs the Duke Center for Jewish Studies. Her most recent book is *Jewish Aramaic Poetry from Late Antiquity* (Brill, 2017), and her translation of early Samaritan piyyutim, *Classical Samaritan Poetry in Context* is forthcoming with Penn State University Press.

Nachman Levine

teaches Bible and Midrash, and is currently a Fellow at the Yeshiva University's Center for Israel Studies. His interest is in the reading of Midrash in the interface of literary theory, art history, and the realia of material culture.

Stuart S. Miller

is Professor of Hebrew, History, and Judaic Studies in the Department of Literatures, Cultures and Languages at the University of Connecticut at Storrs. He also serves as Academic Director of the university's Center for Judaic Studies and Contemporary Jewish Life. His most recent book is *At the Intersection of Texts and Material Finds: Stepped Pools, Stone Vessels and Ritual Purity among the Jews of Roman Galilee* (Vandenhoeck & Ruprecht, 2015; 2nd Revised Edition, 2019).

Lawrence H. Schiffman

is the Judge Abraham Lieberman Professor of Hebrew and Judaic Studies at New York University and Director of the Global Network for Advanced Research in Jewish Studies. He was Chair of NYU's Skirball Department of Hebrew and Judaic Studies, and from 2011 to 2014 served as Vice Provost for Undergraduate Education at Yeshiva University. He specializes in the Dead Sea Scrolls, Judaism in Late Antiquity, and Talmudic literature.

Shai Secunda

holds the Jacob Neusner Chair in the History and Theology of Judaism at Bard College. His first book, *The Iranian Talmud: Reading the Bavli in its Sasanian Context* was published by University of Pennsylvania Press in 2014, and his second book, *The Talmud's Red Fence: Menstrual Impurity and Difference in Babylonian Judaism and its Sasanian Contexti* was published by Oxford University Press in 2020.

Shana Strauch Schick
is a lecturer of Talmud at Shalem College in Jerusalem and a fellow at Yeshiva University's Center for Israel Studies. Her first book is *Intention in Talmudic Jurisprudence: Between Thought and Deed* (Brill, 2021). Her upcoming monograph explores contrasting representation of women in rabbinic legal and narrative texts of Babylonia versus the Land of Israel.

Yael Wilfand
teaches Jewish history at the School of Basic Jewish Studies at Bar-Ilan University. She studies the social and cultural history of Jews who lived in the Land of Israel during the first five centuries CE with a special interest in the relationship between rabbinic sources and the Roman world. Her first book is *Poverty, Charity and the Image of the Poor in Rabbinic Texts from the Land of Israel* (Sheffield Phoenix Press, 2014).

Meira Wolkenfeld
is a doctoral candidate at the Bernard Revel Graduate School of Jewish Studies at Yeshiva University. Her dissertation examines the sense of smell in the world of the Babylonian Talmud. She has taught at Nyack College and in different Jewish communal settings.

Shlomo Zuckier
is a Research Fellow at the Notre Dame Center for Philosophy of Religion. He completed his PhD in Ancient Judaism, with distinction, at Yale University and has taught graduate courses in Jewish Studies at Yale, Yeshiva, and Touro Universities. Shlomo received MAs in Bible and Talmud at Revel, where he studied under Prof. Elman, *z"l*.

PART 1

Torat Erets Yisrael

∴

CHAPTER 1

Rabbinic Paleontology: Jewish Encounters with Fossil Giants in Roman Antiquity

Elisha Fine and Steven Fine

Now that we have written in praise and disparagement of the nature of man, we must now survey two types of humans of strange visage, both at length and in an abbreviated way. The first are the giants mentioned occasionally in [biblical] verses and also of whom authors writing about the wonders of the world wrote much. These are found in a number of places in varied climates, and I—loving brevity, will cite only those which I have seen with my own eyes. I will report to you honestly what I saw.

In 1694/5 workers excavated and released from the depths of the earth close to the city of Salonicco [Thessaloniki] a major Jewish center (עיר ואם בישראל) … and they found within the mountain, on the bank of the river, the name of which I have forgotten, a giant thirty-three cubits long (according to [the length of] our arms) and four handbreadths diameter. He remains from the remnant of the ancient Rephaites [Deuteronomy 3:11, which include Og King of Bashan—SF]. They filled the skull with twenty dry measures (שיניאקוס, Latin: *congius*) of barley, where each dry measure is two Roman liters. In truth, I saw only a large bone which is one of the two bones of the forearm and a tooth that weighs three hundred and fifty drachma. This is its image (fig. 1.1):

FIGURE 1.1

If one of the roots were not broken, it would easily weigh four hundred drachmas. It is still stored among the treasures of the master, the esteemed noble Monsieur Pierre-Antoine de Castagnère, marquis de Châteauneuf, honored ambassador of the righteous and successful king of France [to the Ottoman Sultan] ....¹

So writes Tobias Cohen (1652–1729), author of *Ma'aseh Tuvia*, an influential Hebrew medical encyclopedia written by a Jewish doctor from Poland in Edirne (Adrianopolis) in eastern Thrace. Cohen completed his work in Istanbul and it was published in Venice in 1707.² The molar that Cohen describes and illustrates belonged to a prehistoric elephant, but in his day it was thought to derive from an ancient giant (fig. 1.2).³ Tobias goes on to describe a giant's tooth owned by the Turkish Sultan, and concludes with a discussion of a particularly tall woman of his own day whom he conjectures might be a descendant of ancient giants. Ma'aseh Tuvia represented the best science of its moment, a "complex interplay of tradition and empiricism."⁴

The identification of bones of large prehistoric mammals, especially elephants (Proboscideans) with the remains of ancient giants has a very long history in western culture. Ancient Greeks and Romans unearthed, marveled over and interpreted ancient bones, and elites wrote about them. Modern academic scholars, with their modernist inclinations, have been slow to focus on reports of giants and their discovery. As Brian R. Doak put it, "the popular or even cartoonish appeal of giant or monstrous beings may have actively repelled the academy in the past, as the sheer popularity of conspiracy theories about burials of giant bones or fantastical creatures does not lend scholarly gravitas to this field of study."⁵

---

1 Tobias Cohen, *Sefer Ma'aseh Tuvia* (Venice, 1708), *Olam ha-Qatan*, 77.
2 A. Levinsohn, *Tuvia ha-Rofeh ve-Sifro Ma'aseh Tuvia*, 18–19. This text is mentioned by Slifkin, *Sacred Monsters*, 138.
3 Adrian Lister confirms that Cohen's tooth is "certainly an elephant" (email communication, March, 2020). For the Latin Christian and French tradition, see Stephens, 1989, esp. 58–97. For other early modern examples, Bondeson, *A Cabinet of Medical Curiosities* 72–95: Cohen, *The Fate of the Mammoth*, 23–40; Slifkin, *Sacred Monsters*, 138.
4 This succinct formulation is suggested by Malkiel, "The Rabbi and the Crocodile," 115. On Cohen's approach, see Ruderman, *Jewish Thought and Scientific Discovery in Early Modern Europe*, 229–255. For other early modern examples of mammoth bone discovery and interpretation, Bondeson, *A Cabinet of Medical Curiosities*, 72–95: Cohen, *The Fate of the Mammoth*, 23–40.
5 Doak, "The Giant in a Thousand Years," 14.

FIGURE 1.2   Mammoth Molars From Bethlehem, Complete M3s in occlusal (top) and lingual (bottom) views. (a–b) M18523, R; (c–d) M 18524, Natural History Museum, London
AFTER RABINOVICH AND LISTER, "THE EARLIEST ELEPHANTS OUT OF AFRICA," FIG. 7

Classical sources have been assembled and popularized by Adrienne Mayor in her *The First Fossil Hunters: Dinosaurs, Mammoths, and Myth in Greek and Roman Times*.[6] Published in 2000, this volume is important for our understanding of the classical reports of giant humans and other creatures. The bones of large prehistoric mammals, especially prehistoric elephants, discovered in jumbles across the Mediterranean world and beyond, Mayor argues, were imagined by ancients to be two legged creatures, their teeth the remains of giants.[7] Rhinoceroses and giraffes are well represented in the fossil record as well.[8] Mayor further assembles testimony that Roman period elites actively searched for the bones of "giants" to display in temples, palaces and gardens.[9] Among these authors, she briefly points to a discovery reported by Flavius Josephus.[10]

---

6   Mayor, *The First Fossil Hunters*.
7   Mayor, *The First Fossil Hunters*, 77–83.
8   Rivka Rabinovich and Adrian Lister stressed this point in email communications (March, 2021). See, for example, Pandolfia, Rivals, Rabinovich, "A New Species of Rhinoceros from the Site of Bethlehem," 48–60.
9   Mayor, *The First Fossil Hunters*, 76.
10 Mayor, *The First Fossil Hunters*, 13.

FIGURE 1.3
A partially reconstructed skull of *Elephas maximus* from Gavur Lake Swamp, Turkey, MTA Natural History Museum, Ankara
AFTER GIRDLAND-FLINK, ALBAYRAK, LISTER, 2018, WIKIMEDIA COMMONS

In this article we build on this work, exploring texts that describe the discovery, presentation and interpretation of the bones of "giants" by Jews in Roman antiquity. Beginning with Josephus' testimony, we will then turn to evidence preserved in the writings of the ancient Rabbis.

Giant Bones in Josephus and in Second Temple Period Judaism

Particularly tall people—and not only mythological giants—were worthy of note in Josephus's world—both in the larger culture and among literati.[11] Josephus, for example, mentions a "giant" sent to Emperor Tiberius as a "gift" from Artabanus, king of the Parthians. He was "a man seven cubits tall, a Jew by race named Eleazar, who on account of his size was called 'the Giant'" (Γίγας, *Antiquities* 18.103).[12] Beyond the literary evidence, the most monumental family tomb discovered in the first century Jewish necropolis at Jericho

---

11   On giants in later Second Temple period literature, see the articles assembled and edited by Goff, Stuckenbruck, and Moran, *Ancient Tales of Giants from Qumran and Turfan*. For Greek and Roman literature, Mayor, *The First Fossil Hunters*, passim.

12   Translations of Greek and Latin texts are based upon the Loeb Classical Library, occasionally with modest adjustments. Translations of the Hebrew Bible are based upon *The Oxford Annotated Bible with the Apocrypha: Revised Standard Version*, eds. Bruce M. Metzger and Herbert G. May. (New York: Oxford University Press, 1965) and of rabbinic sources are our own.

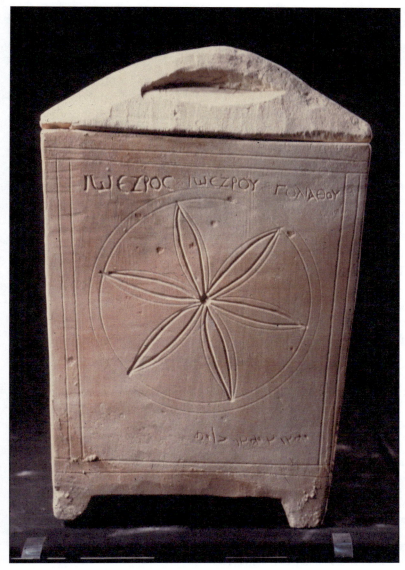

FIGURE 1.4 Goliath Ossuary. Jericho, no. 18, ins. 9a–b
COURTESY OF ANN KILLEBREW

includes ossuaries with inscriptions identifying five members of a single family as "Goliath," inscribed on three ossuaries.[13] Two of the inscriptions are bilingual, yielding גלית and Γολιάθου, "of Goliath."[14] The longest is in Greek:[15] "Salome, wife of Yoezer, of Goliath/and her son Ishmael, of Goliath and her son Yoezer." The Goliath family included very tall people for their day. Three of the male internees are described by the excavators as "tall" and one was "very tall."[16] Rachel Hachlili notes "particularly the exceptional height of the father Yeho'ezer bar Ele'azar." He stood 1.885 m. tall (6.18 ft.).[17]

Giants were a subject of fascination to Jewish authors of the Greco-Roman period, as they were to classical authors in general. These included those responsible for the Dead Sea Scrolls, where a "book of Giants" is preserved.[18] Jews in the classical world were well primed for thinking about giants by biblical tradition. Deuteronomy 3:11, for example, has it that "Og king of Bashan was the last survivor of the giant Rephaites. His bed was made of iron and was more than thirteen feet long and six feet wide. It can still be seen in the Ammonite city of Rabbah."[19] Josephus's reflection on the biblical *anaqim* falls well within this tradition, though interestingly, our author seems to downplay the size of Og—despite biblical reference to his size. Josephus writes only that "he had a size (μέγελός) and beauty such as few could boast" (*Antiquities* 4.98).

Josephus mentions giants in his portrayal of the biblical spies and their report on the "people of the land" in Numbers 13.[20] At *Antiquities* 3.305 he relates that "in Hebron they asserted that they had lit upon the descendants of giants (τῶν γιγάντων)." This follows on Numbers 13:22 and 28 and parallels, where the powerful יְלִידֵי הָעֲנָק, "descendants of the Anaq" are listed among

---

13   Hachlili, Killebrew, and Netzer, *Jericho*, 37–50, 142–154.
14   Hachlili, Killebrew, and Netzer, *Jericho*, 143, nos. 2a, b; 9a b, c; 10, 11a–c; L.Y. Rahmani, *A Catalogue of Jewish Ossuaries in the Collections of the State of Israel* (Jerusalem: Israel Antiquities Authority and Israel Academy of Sciences and Humanities, 1994), nos. 799, 800, 801. Rahmani notes that the spelling here parallels the Septuagint (no. 799, p. 243).
15   Hachlili, Killebrew, and Netzer, *Jericho*, 143, no. 10; Rahmani, *A Catalogue of Jewish Ossuaries*, no. 800.
16   Hachlili, Killebrew, and Netzer, *Jericho*, 195.
17   Hachlili, Killebrew, and Netzer, *Jericho*, 154.
18   Stuckenbruck, *The Book of Giants from Qumran*; Angel, "Reading the Book of Giants in Literary and Historical Context," 323–346.
19   The most recent and most complete study of biblical giants was carried out by Doak, *The Last of the Rephaim* (2011), esp. 112–151; idem, *The Last of the Rephaim* (2012), esp. 70–99. To this add Maeir, "Memories, Myths and Megalithics," 675–690. On Og's bed, Doak, *The Last of the Rephaim*, 137–143; Lindquist, "King Og's Iron Bed," 477–492.
20   For giants in Second Temple period literature in Greek, Tuval, "'Συναγωγὴ γιγάντων' (Prov 21:16): The Giants in the Jewish Literature in Greek," 41–57. On Josephan passages, 55–56.

the powerful people of the Land.[21] We read in Numbers 13:22: "They went up into the Negev, and came to Hebron; and Ahiman, Sheshai, and Talmai, the descendants of Anak, were there. (Hebron was built seven years before Zo'an in Egypt)." Josephus leaves out the complaint of the biblical scouts that "we were in their eyes as grasshoppers" (Numbers 13:33)—removing any taint of Israelite cowardice.[22] He later describes to his Roman audience the biblical conquest of Canaan, after the death of Joshua son of Nun, and his charge to "destroy the race of the Canaanites" (Antiquities 5.125):

Ὅθεν μετεστρατοπέδευσαν εἰς Νεβρῶνα καὶ ταύτην ἑλόντες κτείνουσι πάντας· ὑπελείπετο δὲ τῶν γιγάντων ἔτι γένος, οἳ διὰ σωμάτων μεγέθη καὶ μορφὰς οὐδὲν τοῖς ἄλλοις ἀνθρώποις παραπλησίας παράδοξον ἦσαν θέαμα καὶ δεινὸν ἄκουσμα. δείκνυται δὲ καὶ νῦν ἔτι τούτων ὀστᾶ μηδὲν τοῖς ὑπὸ πύστιν ἐρχομένοις ἐοικότα.

So they moved their camp to Hebron, took capture of that town and massacred all therein. Howbeit there remained yet a race of giants, who, by reason of their huge frames and figures in no wise like to the rest of mankind, were an amazing spectacle and a tale of terror to the ear. Their bones are shown to this day, bearing no resemblance to any that have come within men's ken.

This text expands on Joshua 11:21, "And Joshua came at that time, and wiped out the *anaqim* from the hill country, from Hebron, from Debir, from Anab, and from all the hill country of Judah, and from all the hill country of Israel; Joshua utterly destroyed them with their cities." The identification of giants at Hebron revolves around the identification of Arba of *Kiryat Arba*, "the city of Arba"— the oft-noted previous designation for Hebron.[23] Joshua 14:15 explains that וְשֵׁם חֶבְרוֹן לְפָנִים קִרְיַת אַרְבַּע, הָאָדָם הַגָּדוֹל בָּעֲנָקִים הוּא "Now the name of Hebron formerly was Kiryat Arba; he was the great man among the Anakim." Joshua 15:13b–14 adds that the son of this "great man" was called "the Anaq," "the giant":

לִיהוֹשֻׁעַ אֶת-קִרְיַת אַרְבַּע אֲבִי הָעֲנָק, הִיא חֶבְרוֹן. וַיֹּרֶשׁ מִשָּׁם כָּלֵב, אֶת-שְׁלוֹשָׁה בְּנֵי הָעֲנָק
אֶת-שֵׁשַׁי וְאֶת-אֲחִימַן וְאֶת-תַּלְמַי, יְלִידֵי הָעֲנָק,

---

21 On the definite article of יְלִידֵי הָעֲנָק, see Doak, *The Last of the Rephaim* (2011), 114, n. 85. idem, *The Last of the Rephaim* 2012, 72, n. 86.
22 See the comments of Feldman, *Flavius Josephus*, 325.
23 Beginning with Genesis 22:3.

> To Joshua, he gave Kiryat Arba, the **father of the** Anaq, that is, Hebron. And Caleb drove out from there the three **sons of the** Anaq, Sheshai and Ahiman and Talmai, **descendants of the** Anaq.

Joshua 21:11 refers to Arba as אֲבִי הָעֲנוֹק, "the father of the Anoq." The Septuagint to Joshua 15:13b intensifies the connection between the biblical giants and Hebron. The Hebrew toponym *Kiryat Arbʿa* is transliterated πόλιν Ἀρβὸκ (*polin Arbok*),[24] which assimilates the initial *alef* of *Arba*, and the *ayyin* of ʿ*Anaq*. Similarly, the Septuagint harmonizes the final letters of the Hebrew *Arba* and *Anaq*, choosing the hard *qof* over the gutteral *ayyin*. The "city of Arbok" is called the "*mother city* [μητρόπολιν] of Enak" in the Septuagint.[25] This reflects the Biblical tradition (Numbers 13:22, Joshua 14:15, 15:13–14, and Judges 1:20) that focuses upon the relationship of the *anaqim* with Hebron, while acknowledging their wider distribution west of the Jordan (Deuteronomy 9:2, Joshua 11:21).[26] Reading Josephus together with the Septuagint, Joshua destroyed the giants in their home territory. He pointedly never refers to Hebron by its "previous name" as Kiryat Arba or Kiryat Anak, and avoids calling their pre-Conquest center a "mother city," of the destroyed giants.

Josephus does not tell us who identified the large bones at Hebron as a biblical *anaq*. He simply writes that they "are shown," δείκνυται, in the sense of presentation. The fossilized bones of prehistoric elephants and other large mammals have been documented at a number of sites in the southern Levant, including at Bethlehem, approximately 21 km. north of Hebron.[27] At Revadim Quarry, in Israel's southern coastal plain (approximately 65 km. from Hebron), prehistoric elephant remains were discovered in a large open-air site.[28]

---

24 For variants, Doak, *The Last of the Rephaim* (2011), 125, n. 121; *The Last of the Rephaim* (2012), 72, n. 86.
25 See Van Der Horst, "The Site of Adam's Tomb," 251–252.
26 See Doak, *The Last of the Rephaim* (2011), 116–119; idem, *The Last of the Rephaim* (2012), 73–75.
27 Rabinovich and Lister, "The earliest elephants out of Africa," 23–42. See also Bate, "Discovery of a Fossil Elephant in Palestine,", 219; Gardner and Bate, "The Bone-Bearing Beds of Bethlehem," 431–433. On Bate and her work, Shindler, *Discovering Dorothea*; Stekelis, *Interim Report to the Wellcome Trust, The Wellcome-Marston Archeological Research Expedition*. See also Pandolfia, Luca, Florent Rivals, Rivka Rabinovich, "A New Species of Rhinoceros from the Site of Bethlehem."
28 Rabinovich, Ackermann, Aladjem, Barkai, Biton, Milevski, Solodenko, Marder, "Elephants at the Middle Pleistocene Acheulian open-air site of Revadim Quarry, Israel," 276–277 (25 October 2012), 183–197. For another recent discovery, Rabinovich, Herzlinger, Calvo, Rivals, Mischke, Beiner, "Erq el Ahmar Elephant Site," 1–18.

Josephus describes other attractions in the area of Hebron with the same verb, suggesting local sources of his information. At *War* 4.530–532 he informs us that according to the statements of its inhabitants (οἱ ἐπιχώριοι), Hebron is of greater antiquity than any other town in the country, and even older than Memphis in Egypt (Genesis 23). He continues:

> μυθεύουσι δὲ αὐτὴν καὶ οἰκητήριον Ἀβράμου τοῦ Ἰουδαίων προγόνου γεγονέναι μετὰ τὴν ἐκ τῆς Μεσοποταμίας ἀπανάστασιν, τούς τε παῖδας αὐτοῦ λέγουσι καταβῆναι εἰς Αἴγυπτον ἔνθεν. ὧν καὶ τὰ μνημεῖα μέχρι νῦν ἐν τῇδε τῇ πολίχνῃ δείκνυται πάνυ καλῆς μαρμάρου καὶ φιλοτίμως εἰργασμένα.

> **They also relate** that it was there that Abraham, the progenitor of the Jews took up his abode after his migration from Mesopotamia, and from there that his posterity went into Egypt. Their tombs **are shown** in this little town to this day, of really fine marble and of exquisite workmanship.

The monumental enclosure of the patriarchal tomb was constructed by Herod the Great or one of his immediate successors (fig. 1.6).[29] The workmanship is indeed "exquisite," though the enclosure was built of white limestone and not marble.[30] Close to Hebron, Josephus describes biblical *Elonei Mamre*, "the Oaks of Mamre" a place where a historic tree is "also shown" (Genesis 13:18, fig. 1.4):

> δείκνυται δ' ἀπὸ σταδίων ἓξ τοῦ ἄστεος τερέβινθος μεγίστη, καὶ φασὶ τὸ δένδρον ἀπὸ τῆς κτίσεως μέχρι νῦν διαμένειν.

> At a distance of six furlongs from the town is **also shown** a huge terebinth-tree, which is said to have stood there since creation.

In the area of Hebron, then, were a variety of pilgrimage sites, which Josephus identifies based upon local knowledge—from a tree dating to "creation" to the patriarchal tomb to the bones of a giant. Mamre was encompassed by an impressive Herodian compound, with pilasters similar to those constructed at the Tomb of the Patriarchs (fig. 1.5, 1.6) and on the Temple Mount retaining walls.[31]

---

29   Vincent and Mackay. *Hébron*, 145–155; Schiller, *Me'arat Ha-Makhpelah*.
30   Josephus makes a similar mistake at *War* 5.190, claiming that the stone used in the Temple portico was "marble," correcting himself at *Antiquities* 15.116 with "polished stone." See Fischer and Stein, "Josephus on the Use of Marble in Building Projects of Herod the Great," esp. 79–83.
31   Magen, "Mamre," 3: 939–941. 5: 2103; Stiebel, "A Light Unto the Nations," 219–234, especially 222–223; Fine and Schertz, "Herod's Temple," 76.

FIGURE 1.5
Elonei Mamre, "the Oaks of Mamre," 1st century
WIKIMEDIA COMMONS

FIGURE 1.6   Tomb of Machpelah, Hebron, 1st century
WIKIMEDIA COMMONS

Josephus later presents himself as a trustworthy eyewitness to the topography and architecture of Judaea and especially the events of the Jewish War of 66–74.[32] He also identifies remains of a number of other biblical sites. At *Antiquities* 1.92 he describes the display of the remains of Noah's Ark: "The Armenians call that spot Landing-place, for it was there that the ark came safe to land, and they show the relics of it to this day." At *Antiquities* 1.203 he points to the salt stone "wife of Lot," of Genesis 19:26, located on the western shore of the Dead Sea in a much more direct way than he does the Hebron sites. Josephus adds: "And I bore witness to this, for it even now still remains" (ἱστόρησα

---

32   Rajak, *Josephus*, 78.

δ' αὐτήν, ἔτι γὰρ καὶ νῦν διαμένει).³³ Josephus writes the reality of Biblical history onto the historicized landscape of the Roman world—which for him is explicit and undeniable evidence of Jewish antiquity.³⁴

Josephus's Giants in the Roman World

Josephus's interest in the bones of the Hebron giant would not have been unusual to his Roman elite readership. Sites related to heroes, giants and battles are a common feature of the Greco-Roman historical "tool box." Descriptions of the discovery of the remains of ancient battles and the bones of classical heroes and of foes, especially giants, are so widespread that a Roman reader would find Josephus's testimony reasonable—even mundane. His contemporary, Pliny the Elder (d. 79 CE) reports, for example, that:

> When a mountain in Crete was cleft by an earthquake, a skeleton [or, "body"] 46 cubits long was found, which some thought to be that of [the giant hunter] Orion and others of [the young giant] Otus. The records attest that the skeleton of Orestes dug up at the command of an oracle measured 7 cubits (*Natural History* 7.73–75).³⁵

A huge skeleton was discovered on Crete, according to Pliny, as a result of an earthquake. Pliny reports a dispute in identifying the remains. It was identified with one of two mythological giants, the huntsman Orion, others with Otus, the son of Iphimedia and Poseidon. The dispute was resolved by an oracle, which had the bones exhumed. We are not told where they were placed in the end.

Mayor assembled numerous other testimonia of this kind, the basic pattern being discovery of a "giant" followed by identification of the giant with a specific event or individual as either a hero or a foe through local knowledge or the intervention of an oracle. This is often followed by memorialization of the discovery. To cite just one more example from near the time of Josephus, Ovid (43 BCE–17 CE) writes in the *Metamorphoses* (7.443–447) that:

---

33   See Feldman, *Flavius Josephus: Judean Antiquities 1–4*, 77, and n. 631; Bar Ilan, "Meqomot Pellah be-Erets Yisrael be-Et ha-Atiqah," 229–239.
34   Note Josephus' reference to Noah's ark, which "landed in the mountains of Armenia" (*Against Apion*, 1.130). See also Josephus' enthusiastic description of a fortress built at Ecbatana in Midaea by Daniel, "preserved to this day" (*Antiquities* 10.264); Begg, *Judean Antiquities 5–7*, 30, n. 334.
35   Pliny, *Natural History, Volume I: Books 1–2*, Translated by Rackham, 553–555.

> A way lies safe and open now to Alcathoe and the Lelegeian walls, now that Sciron is no more. To this robber's scattered bones both land and sea denied a resting-place; but, long tossed about, it is said that in time they hardened into cliffs; and the cliffs still bear the name of Sciron.[36]

It is noteworthy that Josephus' *anaqim* "bear no resemblance to any that have come within men's ken." While quite sure that he had seen the bones of giants, these humans somehow do not look like other people.[37] This statement shows just how powerful the identification was, that even in the face of actual visual evidence, it remained secure. We find a similar statement in the *Astronomy* of Manilius (first century BCE). Manilius writes that the giants discovered in his time were broods of deformed creatures of "unnatural face and shape:"[38]

> He saw the earth rising up, so that he deemed all nature was being overthrown; mountains piled on lofty mountains he saw growing; he saw the stars retreating from heights which were now neighbours, heights which brought up the armed Giants, brood of a mother they tore apart, deformed creatures of unnatural face and shape.

Josephus does not say where and under what circumstances the bones of the defeated *anaqim* "are shown," and by whom. He does not suggest, though, that they were removed from their place of their discovery, from the area of Hebron. Were these bones "shown" to visitors within a cave, or perhaps along the way, on a hillside on some private or public way? The public display of giant bones was well known in the Roman world. Suetonius writes that in his palace "at Capri, on the Gulf of Naples. Augustus collected the huge skeletons of land and sea monsters, popularly known as 'Giants' Bones,' and the weapons of ancient heroes ...."[39] In 1905 the fossilized bones of ice age mammals of the type that might have been displayed in Augustus' garden were discovered under the foundation of the Grand Hotel Quisisana on the Island of Capri. They were transferred to the local Natural History Museum, Museo Ignazio Cerio, and are displayed there.[40] In *On Animals* 16.39, Aelian (ca. 170–230 CE) suggests presentation in situ:[41]

---

36 Ovid. *Metamorphoses, Volume I: Books 1–8*. Translated by Miller, Revised by Goold, 7.443–447.
37 Mayor, The First Fossil Hunters, 61.
38 Manilius, *Astronomica*. Edited and translated by Goold, 1:420–430.
39 Suetonius, *Lives of the Caesars, Volume I*, Augustus 72; Mayor, 2011, 172–175.
40 Mayor, *The First Fossil Hunters*, 172–175; https://www.centrocaprense.org/en/museum/palaeontology-geology/.
41 Aelian, *On Animals, Volume I: Books 1–5*, tr. A.F. Scholfield, 16.39.

> Historians of Chios assert that near Mount Pelinnaeus in a wooded glen there was a dragon of gigantic size who made the Chians shudder. No farmer or shepherd dared approach the monster's lair. But a miraculous event allowed the discovery of how large it really was. During a violent lightning storm a forest fire destroyed the entire region of the wooded slopes .... After the fire, all the Chians came to see and discovered the bones of gigantic size and a terrifying skull. From these the villagers were able to imagine how large and terrible the brute was when alive.

Similarly, Philostratus (ca. 200–230 CE) writes in *Heroicus* that a giant found in Sigeum, across the Dardanelles on the coast of Asia Minor, "measured 33 feet, and lay in a rocky cave, with the head inland and the body extending out to the end of the cape .... The skeleton was human" (8.3–14).[42] Others preserved the bones of giant heroes in shrines and temples. In his *Guide to Greece*, Pausanias (ca. 150 CE) reports that in Messenia:[43]

> There is also the tomb of Aristomenes here. They say that it is not a cenotaph, but when I asked whence and in what manner they recovered the bones of Aristomenes, they said that they sent to Rhodes for them, and that it was the god of Delphi who ordered it. They also instructed me in the nature of the rites carried out at the tomb. The bull which is to be offered to the dead man is brought to the tomb and bound to the pillar which stands upon the grave. Being fierce and unused to bonds he will not stand; and if the pillar is moved by his struggles and bounds, it is a good omen to the Messenians, but if the pillar is not moved the sign portends misfortune.

These examples will suffice to contextualize Josephus' *anaq* bones within the larger Roman period discourse on giant bones and their discovery.

Beyond the biblical connection of Hebron with giants, Josephus's *anaq* is part of the larger construction of Hebron as the national necropolis. The population of famous internees in the Herodian Tomb of the Machpellah, increased beyond the biblical patriarchs as Roman antiquity progressed, through a process that Isaak Heinemann called *rikuz*, the concentration of traditions.[44] The *Testaments of the Twelve Patriarchs*, likely a Jewish text, has each of the patri-

---

42 Philostratus. *Heroicus. Gymnasticus. Discourses 1 and 2*, ed. and tr, Rusten, König, 8.3–14.
43 Pausanias, *Description of Greece, Volume I: Books 1–2 (Attica and Corinth)*, tr. Jones, 4.32.3.
44 Heinemann, *Darkei ha-Aggadah*, 25–34.

archs buried in Hebron, including Joseph.[45] Adam and Eve were added, filling out the "four" of Qiryat Arba, the "city of the four" as rabbis and later Jerome understood this toponym.[46] By tannaitic times Moses was associated with the national tomb, through the literary construction of an imagined tunnel from Hebron that reached to his unknown burial site on Mt. Nebo, on the eastern side of the Jordan.[47]

> Semalyon said: "And Moses Died *there*" (Deuteronomy 34:5). From whence do you say that a tunnel reaches from the tomb of Moses to the tomb of the patriarchs? It says here "and Moses died *there*," and it says elsewhere "*There* they buried Abraham and Sarah his wife" (Genesis 49:21).

This fiction allowed Moses to literally rest with his ancestors *there*, in physical proximity to them. *Midrash Tanḥuma* (edited ca. 8th century) places Aaron his brother in the Tomb of Makhpelah,[48] and the head of Esau rests beside his father Isaac.[49] The display of the giant "bones of the *Anaqim*" adds texture to this necropolis city, concretely weaving Roman and late antique Hebron more completely into the Biblical epic—from Adam and Eve through the antediluvian *Anaqim*, the patriarchs and matriarchs, the heroes of the Exodus and finally Joshua's conquest of the Land. All of this could be imagined (and some viewed) by Jewish visitors to Hebron, a "small city" made monumental in the monumental largess of the Herodians. A short walk distant at Mamre, was the ancient tree that Josephus tells us dates to "creation." Jews and their Greek and Roman neighbors shared the myth of long dead giants wiped out in a primordial war, what Greeks called a *Gigantomachy*.[50] For Josephus, the giants displayed in Hebron were the *Anaqim* killed by Joshua during the heroic conquest of the Land—the Israelite *Gigantomachy*. The display of the "bones of the Anaqim" at Hebron is a Jewish variation on the larger Greco-Roman theme.

---

45 *The Old Testament Pseudepigrapha*, ed. Charlesworth, 1: 774–828.
46 Gafni, "Pre-Histories' of Jerusalem in Hellenistic, Jewish and Christian Literature," 5–22; Van Der Horst, "The Site of Adam's Tomb," 251–252.
47 Sifre Deuteronomy 357, ed. L. Finkelstein, p. 428. See Ish-Shalom, "The Cave of Machpela," 207–208.
48 *Midrash Tanḥuma: Ha-qadum Ve-Ha-Yashan*. ed. Buber, *Huqat* 2:132; Ish-Shalom, "The Cave of Machpela," 203–209.
49 Pirqe de'Rabbi Eliezer, ch. 39, 94a.
50 Hanfmann, "Giants," 616.

Late Antique Sources: Rabbinic Literature

Rabbis knew of large bones, which they too interpreted in terms of biblical traditions. *Babylonian Talmud, Niddah* 24b–25a preserves two purportedly tannaitic traditions of giant sightings, and discusses the implications of this evidence. These follow after a larger discussion that is a locus for reflection on rabbinic authority. In the first baraita of this group, one Abba Shaul describes the colors of bones he has seen as evidence for alcohol consumption. The text continues:

1. תניא:
2. אבא שאול אומר,
3. ואיתימא רבי יוחנן:
4. קובר מתים הייתי
5. פעם אחת רצתי אחר צבי
6. ונכנסתי בקולית של מת
7. ורצתי אחריו שלוש פרסאות
8. וצבי לא הגעתי
9. וקולית לא כלתה
10. כשחזרתי לאחור אמרו לי:
11. "של עוג מלך הבשן היתה."

1. A Tannaitic tradition:
2. Abba Shaul says,
3. and some say it was Rabbi Yoḥanan:
4. I was burying the dead.
5. Once I ran after a gazelle
6. and I entered into the thigh bone of a corpse
7. and I ran after it three parsangs
8. and I did not reach the gazelle
9. and the thigh bone did not end
10. When I returned they said to me:
11. "That was the thigh bone of Og the king of Bashan."

The second tradition reads:

12. תניא:
13. אבא שאול אומר:
14. קובר מתים הייתי
15. פעם אחת נפתחה מערה תחתי

16. ועמדתי בגלגל עינו של מת עד חוטמי.
17. כשחזרתי לאחורי אמרו:
18. "עין של אבשלום היתה"

12. A [tannaitic] tradition:
13. Abba Shaul says:
14. Once I was burying the dead
15. A cave opened under me
16. And I stood in the eye socket of a corpse up to my nose
17. Then when I returned they said:
18. "It was the eye of Absalom"

These traditions appear in no extant Palestinian collection, though the Bavli clearly assumes that they are Palestinian in origin. They tell the tale of Abba Shaul, who flourished during the mid-second century, an expert in burial.[51] The first tradition is alternatively associated with the influential third generation Palestinian amora Rabbi Yoḥanan son of Napḥa. Long cave systems are a common geological feature of Palestine, and chasing or following a gazelle into one was clearly part of the life experience of locals.[52] The Hariton Cave, in Upper Naḥal Teqoa is 3.45 km. long.[53] The Malcham cave system in Mt. Sodom is the longest salt cave system in the world at more than ten kilometers.[54] In the second tradition (lines 12–18), Abba Shaul accidentally falls into a hole "when the ground opened up beneath him." Again, this is not an unusual occurrence in the hill country of Palestine, where, crevices, and man made pits abound—often covered with thick vegetation. Rivka Rabinovich and Adrian M. Lister report that elephant teeth were first discovered "in the debris of a water hole at the town of Bethlehem in the 1930s."[55] In many areas of modern Iraq, "sinkholes and collapses," are reasonably common. By contrast, they do not exist in the Mesopotamia Plain, the area of Jewish habitation in late antiquity.[56] The confluence of caves, sinkholes and fossils in Palestine is a natural imaginative leap. Fantastic in size, this aggadic fantasy is consistent with the local knowledge of Jews familiar with Judaea, the Shephelah and the Galilee—which could, of course, include Babylonian sojourners (*neḥutai*) and immigrants. We

---

51 Lerner, "Abba Saul," 1:40.
52 Frumkin, ed. *Holy Land Atlas*.
53 Frumkin, ed. *Holy Land Atlas*, 51, 90–95.
54 Frumkin, "Discovery of the Largest Salt Cave in the World," 138–158, (Hebrew).
55 Rabinovich and Lister, "The Earliest Elephants Out of Africa," 23.
56 Sissakian, Al-Ansari and Knutsson, "Karst Forms in Iraq," 1.

are thus making no claims based on geology for the place where this story was composed, though these tales might have been all the more fantastic to a Babylonian audience for the very foreignness of the physical setting. The alienness of discovery in long and dark caves fits within the category described by Dina Stein, whereby "Geographical distancing is one of the means by which tall tales establish their quasi-veracity."[57]

Bones of dead and fossilized creatures are still discovered in Judean hills.[58] In an interesting case, in 1678, antiquities dealers attempted to sell Emperor Leopold I of Austria a giant tooth—certainly a prehistoric elephant tooth—discovered "in a deep cavern near Jerusalem." They claimed that beside the tooth was a "Chaldean"—that is, Aramaic—inscription that read "Here lies the Giant OG." True or not, discovery of such a tooth within a Jerusalem cave is completely plausible. While the convenient accompanying signage—in a Jewish language no less—strains credulity, it tracks well with our Talmudic tradition.[59]

The bones described in lines 1–11 measure three parsangs long, each parsang equaling approximately twelve Roman miles. Hyperbole to be sure, discoveries of ancient or modern whales may stand behind this tradition. Large whales do occasionally beach along the Mediterranean coast. In 1966 the discovery of a whale skeleton on the beach at Rosh ha-Niqra was reported in the press, for example.[60] Similarly, a large group of fossilized prehistoric whales has been uncovered in Wadi Al-Hitan in Egypt. Among these is a fully intact Basilosaurus, 18 m. long (fig. 1.7).[61] Pliny reports that "The skeleton of the monster to which Andromeda in the story was exposed was brought by Marcus Scaurus [ca. 58 B.C.] from the town of Jaffa in Judaea and shown at Rome among the rest of the marvels of his aedileship. It was 40 feet long, the height of the ribs exceeding the elephants of India, and the spine 1.5 inches thick."[62] Whether Marcus Scaurus was a scoundrel who fabricated large creatures for display, as Mayor suggests, is not relevant here. Pliny believed his story.[63]

---

57   Stein, *Textual Mirrors*, 62.
58   Frumkin, ed. *Holy Land Atlas*, 24, 25, 41.
59   Bondeson, *A Cabinet of Medical Curiosities*, 87, narrates this event. It is mentioned by Slifkin, *Sacred Monsters*, 138.
60   Ilan, "Sheled Leviatan Nadir Nitgalah be-Hof Rosh ha-Niqra," 1.
61   International Union for Conservation of Nature (IUCN), "First intact fossil of prehistoric whale discovered in Wadi Al-Hitan," 10 June 2015, https://www.iucn.org/content/first-intact-fossil-prehistoric-whale-discovered-wadi-al-hitan.
62   Pliny the Elder, *Natural History* 9.4.11.
63   Mayor, *The First Fossil Hunters*, 138–139.

FIGURE 1.7 Prehistoric Whale Bones, Wadi Al-Hitan, Egypt
WIKIMEDIA COMMONS

The eyewitness statements in the first-person singular place this tale firmly within a small but significant group of first person sightings and descriptions of places, events and things that are significant, or even unbelievable. In tannaitic sources it is a claim to witness, as it was for Josephus and for Roman authors. In later rabbinic sources, like this one, this form of evidence transforms into a literary trope.[64]

Another rhetorical device used in the eyewitness report genre of midrashic literature is the knowledgeable guide. At b.Bava Batra, 74b an Arab guide serves as the important and authentic non-Jewish source of local knowledge in the collection of tall tales attributed to Rabba bar bar Ḥanna:[65]

---

64   Fine, *Art, History and the Historiography of Judaism in the Greco-Roman World*, 73–74.
65   The literature on the Rabba bar Bar Hanna stories is voluminous. See most recently Grossmark, *Travel Narratives in Rabbinic Literature*, 2010; Kiperwasser, "Rabba bar bar Hanna's Voyages," 215–242, (Hebrew); Stein, "Believing Is Seeing," 9–32, (Hebrew); idem, *Textual Mirrors*, 64, 71, and the bibliography cited by each.

> He [the Arab merchant] said unto me:
> "Come and I will show you the Dead
> of the Wilderness"
> I went and saw them; and they looked as if in a
> state of exhilaration.
> They slept on their back; and the knee of one of them
> was raised,
> and the Arab merchant passed under the knee, riding on a camel
> with spear erect,
> and did not touch it

Like the tale of Abba Shaul and his encounter with the enormous bones of Og and Absalom, the tale of Rabbah bar bar Ḥannah emphasizes the enormity of the dead: "They slept on their back; and the knee of one of them was raised, and the Arab merchant passed under the knee, riding on a camel with spear erect, and did not touch it." Similarly, Abba Shaul, as reported in Bavli Niddah, consulted with unnamed informants–"they said to me: [It] was the thigh bone of Og the king of Bashan," "They said: that was the eye of Absalom." These informants serve to provide rabbis with local knowledge to explain local "discoveries."

Encounters with the enormous bones of Og, Absalom and the "generation in the desert" are consistent with rabbinic traditions that describe biblical figures of enormous size.[66] Adam is said to have been so tall that he reached the heavens. It was downhill from there. Abraham is the greatest of the giants even when compared to Og King of Bashan, the archetypal biblical giant and survivor of Noah's Flood.[67] A midrash attached at the end of tractate Soferim has it that Og was so large that he consumed "one thousand oxen daily, and every variety of animal, and he drank one thousand measures and a drop of his semen was thirty-six liters, and it was thus for all generations." Still, Abraham was "the largest among the giants." He was "taller than seventy-four men, and his eating and drinking was commensurate, as was his strength." Nonetheless, Abraham used one of the teeth of Og (identified as Abraham's servant Eliezer) to fabricate beds from it "and would sleep there. Others say [it was]

---

66   Slifkin, *Sacred Monsters*, 123–147 discusses a selection of the relevant sources. See Ginzberg, *The Legends of the Jews*, 7, s.v. Giants, Og.

67   *Masekhet Sofrim*, ed. Michael Higger, 365–367, and parallels cited there. Blank, "On Tractate Sofrim," esp. 8, n. 20. Blank notes that "among the manuscripts which include this material, two are the earliest manuscripts of Soferim (13th-century) and both happen to be copies of Mahzor Vitry-namely, British Library 655 ... and Parma 159 .... The relationship

FIGURE 1.8 Couch and footstool with bone carvings and glass inlays, 1st–2nd centuries CE, reconstruction
METROPOLITAN MUSEUM OF ART, GIFT OF J. PIERPONT MORGAN, 1917

a chair made of tooth and he would sit upon it all the days of his life." Furniture made of bone—ivory—is not unheard of in Roman antiquity, Note, for example, a reconstructed 1st–2nd century CE Roman couch, a bed inlaid with ivory (שן פיל, "elephant tooth" in rabbinic Hebrew[68]) that is preserved in the collection of the Metropolitan Museum of Art (fig. 1.8).[69] Similarly, the magnificent sixth-century ivory *Throne of Maximianus*, commissioned by Emperor Justinian himself, is preserved in the Museo Arcivescovile in Ravenna (fig. 1.9).[70] Our exercise in midrashic imagination is but one fantastic step away from the Roman period reality.

Bavli Niddah 24b–25a goes on to describe the implications of these traditions, positing the diminution of height from early tannaic times to their own in theological terms:

---

of Soferim to Mahzor Vitry, and to the literature of the school of Rashi in general, deserves closer examination."

68 Jastrow, *Dictionary of the Targumim, the Talmud Babli, and Yerushalmi, and the Midrashic Literature*, 1608.

69 Richter, *The Furniture of the Greeks, Etruscans and Romans*, 105, 106, 108, fig. 520, 531; Paul, Zanker, Seán Hemingway, Lightfoot, and Mertens. *Roman Art*, no. 43, pp. 130–130. On the rabbinic מיטה, couch or bed, see Karen Kirschenbaum, *Furniture of the Home in the Mishnah*, 142–258, (Hebrew).

70 Kitzinger, *Byzantine Art in the Making*, 94–96. On thrones and chairs in rabbinic literature, Kirschenbaum, *Furniture of the Home in the Mishnah*, 87–101.

RABBINIC PALEONTOLOGY: JEWISH ENCOUNTERS WITH FOSSIL GIANTS 23

FIGURE 1.9
Throne of Maximianus, 6th c. Ravenna
WIKIMEDIA COMMONS

19. ושמא תאמר אבא שאול ננס היה[71]
20. אבא שאול ארוך בדורותיו
21. ורבי טרפון מגיע לכתפו
22. ור׳ טרפון ארוך בדורו
23. [ור׳ עקיבא היה מגיע לכתיפו
24. ור׳ עקיב׳ גדול בדורו][72]
25. היה ור[בי][73] מ[איר] מגיע לכתפו
26. רבי מאיר ארוך בדורו היה
27. ורבי מגיע לכתפו
28. רבי ארוך בדורו היה
29. ורבי חייא מגיע לכתפו
30. ורבי חייא ארוך בדורו היה
31. ורב מגיע לכתפו
32. רב ארוך בדורו היה
33. ורב יהודה מגיע לכתפו
34. ורב יהודה ארוך בדורו היה
35. ואדא דיילא מגיע לכתפו

71 All manuscripts read היה throughout.
72 Vatican manuscripts 111, 113.
73 Lines 24–25 do not appear in the Munich manuscript 95.

36. פרשתבינא דפומבדיתא קאי ליה לאדא דיילא עד פלגיה
37. וכולי עלמא קאי לפרשתבינא דפומבדיתא עד חרציה

19. And if you were heard to say that Abba Shaul was a dwarf
20. Abba Shaul was giant in his generation[74]
21. And Rabbi Tarfon reached his shoulder
22. Rabbi Tarfon was giant in his generation
23. [Rabbi Aqiva reached his shoulder
24. Rabbi Aqiva was enormous in his generation]
25. Rabbi Meir reached his shoulder
26. And Rabbi Meir was giant in his generation
27. And Rabbi reached his shoulder
28. And Rabbi was giant in his generation
29. And Rabbi Hiyya reached his shoulder
30. And Rabbi Hiyya was giant in his generation
31. And Rav reached his shoulder
32. Rav was giant in his generation
33. And Rav Yehuda reached his shoulder
34. And Rav Yehuda was giant in his generation
35. And Ada the attendant also reached up to his shoulder.
36. And when the ruler of Pumbedita would stand next to Ada the attendant, he would reach half of his height.
37. And when all the world stands next to the ruler[75] of Pumbedita, they would reach his loins.

This discussion begins with the possibility that Abba Shaul was small, thus diminishing the size of the skeletal remains somewhat. It quickly dismisses that notion, however, thereby increasing the physical stature of this early sage, and by implication, the size of the bones that he happened upon. Lines 19–37 suggests that the generations of Rabbis were themselves "giant in their generations," though each was smaller than the generation before. For this text, the chain of tradition encodes a literal diminution of the heights of rabbis, together with their entire generations. In the conception and presumably in the minds of those that encountered traditions such as these—specific earlier Rabbis are

---

74 literally, "generations."
75 Sololoff, 2002, p. 894, s.v. פושתבינא, from the Middle Persian *puštībās*—protector, bodyguard. *Teshuvot ha-Geonim—Gaonic Responsa from Geniza MSS*, ed. Assaf, p. 82, line 22 interprets: אדם בעל כוח גבוה מכל העם, "a person with greater power than all the people." See nn. 9–10.

imbued with greater physical stature. In the manuscript traditions this chain is set off in Hebrew, even as it moves from Palestinian to Babylonian sages of the Pumbedita academy. This is obscured in the Vilna edition, which reads "Rabbi X was (הוה)" where the manuscripts read "Rabbi X was (היה)." Thus, the holy rabbis are presented in the holy tongue, while the servant and ruler, appended to the list, are in the colloquial Aramaic. The chain ends with comparison of Rav Yehudah with a non-rabbi, named Ada. The pericope concludes with an Aramaic addendum, which compares the height of Ada—now called אדא דיילא, "Ada the attendant" of Rav Yehuda,[76] to the most important Persian official in the area, the nicely rhyming לפרשתבינא דפומבדיתא, "the *parshtavina* of Pumbedita." The intention here is unclear, though it seems that it was meant to elicit a chuckle, the least important Jew of the rabbinic circle towering over the most important official of the local Persian administration. Still, the status of the rabbis is clear—while even a servant of the sages towers over this representative of the Sasanian rulers. Others reach only as high as his private parts! Bavli Niddah 24b–25a uses a tale of unearthing the giant bones of biblical villains as a jumping off point to express notions of generational decline in physical stature; sacred and temporal power.

Augustine of Hippo (d. 430 CE) reflects a similar anthropology in his *City of God* 15:9, with no correlation between height and social stature:

> ... In the same way some people refuse to believe that men's bodies were of much larger size then than they are now. It was this point that prompted their most distinguished poet Virgil to say of an enormous boundary-stone that a brave warrior of those early times caught up and, as he ran, swung around and hurled.
>
> Scarce could that stone twice six picked men uprise
> With bodies such as now the earth displays.[77]
>
> The implication is that the earth used to produce larger bodies. How much more so then was that true before that celebrated and far-famed flood when the world was younger!
>
> As far as the size of bodies is concerned, however, sceptics are generally persuaded by the evidence in tombs uncovered through the ravages of time, the violence of streams, or various other occurrences. For incredibly large bones of the dead have been found in them or dislodged from them. On the shore of Utica I myself, not alone but with several others,

---

76 Heiman, *Toldot ha-Tannaim ve-ha-Amoraim*, 1:105.
77 Aeneid 12.899–900.

saw a human molar so enormous that, if it were divided up in pieces to the dimensions of our teeth, it would, so it seemed to us, have made a hundred of them. But that molar, I should suppose, belonged to some giant. For not only were bodies in general much larger than our own, but the giants towered far above the rest, even as in subsequent times including our own, there have almost always been bodies which, few in number, far surpassed the size of the others. Pliny the Elder, a man of great learning, declares that, as the world advances more and more in age, nature bears smaller and smaller bodies;[78] and when he mentions that even Homer regretted that in his poetry, he does not ridicule such statements as poetic fictions but, speaking as a recorder of nature, assumes their historicity.[79] But, as I have said, the size of ancient bones is disclosed even in much later ages by the frequent discovery of bones, for bones are long-lasting.

Augustine assumes that his educated audience is likely to be skeptical of this discovery. For that reason he includes the essential detail that this massive tooth was shown to him, thus his eyewitness account buttressed by a tradition of giant bone discovery.[80] Augustine goes on to connect his discovery to men "*before the world-renowned deluge,*" the *anaqim* of Scripture. Augustine's testimony was so significant in later periods that the rationalist Italian scholar, Azariah de Rossi (ca. 1511–1578) cites it in the course of a critical essay on rabbinic exaggeration in aggadic texts. He calls Augustine ראש חכמי הנוצרים, "the head of the Christian sages," to give some credence to a Zohar tradition (1, 62a) whereby "Rabbi Hiyya and Rabbi Yehudah walked 300 feet on the bone of one of those [who died in] the flood."[81] The Jewish stage was thus set for Cohen more than a century later when he came upon the teeth of giants.

Rabbi Yoḥanan Ben Zakkai and Hadrian

A tradition unique to a single Spanish manuscript of Midrash Tanḥuma (ca. 8–9th century), now at the Bodleian Library of Oxford University (Ms. Huntington 74), builds on our b. Niddah tradition, taking it in a very different direction:

---

78   Cited above.
79   Iliad 5.302–304.
80   Mayor, *The First Fossil Hunters*, 155–156.
81   de Rossi, *Sefer Me'or Anayyim* (Mantua, 1573), *Imrei Bina* ch. 20, 98a.

1. "ראה החלותי תת לפניך את סיחון ואת ארצו החל רש וגו'" (דברים ב, ל"א)
2. זה שאמר הכתוב: "ואנכי השמדתי את האמורי מפניכם אשר כגובה ארזים גבהו וחסון הוא כאלונים" (עמוס ט, ב)
3. אמר ר' יוחנן:
4. קולייתו של סיחון היה בה שמונה עשרה אמות,
5. באמות בני דורו.
6. ועוג מלך הבשן?
7. אבא שאול אומר,
8. קובר מתים הייתי
9. פעם אחת רצתי אחר צבי
10. ונכנס לתוך קולית של מת,
11. ורצתי אחריו שלשה פרסאות,
12. והצבי לא הגעתי,
13. וקולית המת לא כלתה,
14. ושאלתי מי הוא,
15. ואמרו לי קולית עוג מלך הבשן היא זו.
16. אדריינוס הרשע כשכיבש את ירושלים היה מתגאה לומר:
17. כיבשתי את ירושלים בכח.
18. אמר לו רבן יוחנן בן זכאי
19. אל תתגאה, אלולי שהיה מן השמים לא כבשת
20. מה עשה רבן יוחנן?
21. נטלו והכניסו לתוך המערה,
22. והראה לו אמוריים קבורים,
23. והיה אחד מהם של שמונה עשרה אמה
24. אמרתי לו: כשהיה לנו זכות כל אלו נפלו בידינו,
25. ועכשיו על ידי עוונותינו שלטת בנו.
26. והכתוב אומר "ואנכי השמדתי את האמורי מפניכם,"
27. באיזה זכות?
28. בזכות התורה שקבלתם
29. שמתחלה: "אנכי ה' אלהיך" (שמות כ, ב).
30. בשביל "אנכי,"
31. "אנכי השמדתי את האמורי מפניכם" (דברים ב, ל"א).

1. "Behold, I have given Siḥon and his land to you; begin to take possession, that you may occupy his land" (Deuteronomy 2:31).
2. As Scripture says: "Yet I destroyed the Amorite before you, whose height was like the height of the cedars and who was as strong as the oaks; [I destroyed his fruit above, and his roots beneath]" (Amos 9:2).
3. Said Rabbi Yoḥanan:

4. The eye socket of Siḥon had within it (measured) eighteen cubits.
5. In the cubits of people of his time.
6. And Og king of Bashan?
7. Abba Shaul says:
8. I was burying the dead,
9. Once I ran after a gazelle
10. And entered the eye socket of a corpse
11. And ran after it three parsangs
12. And I did not reach the gazelle
13. And the eye socket of the dead did not end
14. And I asked who this is.
15. They told me this is the eyesocket of Og king of Bashan
16. Hadrian, the evil one, when he conquered Jerusalem, became haughty, saying:
17. "I conquered Jerusalem by my might!"
18. Rabban Yoḥanan ben Zakkai said to him:
19. "Do not be proud. Were it not [decreed from] from Heaven, you would not conquered it!"
20. What did Rabbi Yoḥanan do?
21. He took him into a cave.
22. and showed him buried Amorites,
23. and one of them was eighteen cubits in length.
24. I said to him: "When we merited it, all of these were in our hands,
25. and now owing to our sins, you rule us."
26. And the scripture says: "Yet I (*Anokhi*) destroyed the Amorite before them [whose height was like the height of the cedars and who was as strong as the oaks]" (Amos 9:2).
27. "By what merit?"
28. "By the merit of the Torah that you received,
29. Which begins: I (*Anokhi*) am the Lord your God" (Ex 20:2).
30. By the merit of *Anokhi* (that is, by my own merit).
31. "Behold, I (*Anokhi*) have given Sihon and his land to you" (Deuteronomy 2:31).

This proem is associated with Deuteronomy 2:31, and the evocation of "Siḥon and his land." Amos 9:2 and its description of the antediluvian Amorite giants, provides the connecting thread. After citing a parallel to Niddah 24b, with some ellipses and restructuring, this midrash, lines 16–31, sets out to explain the anomaly of Israel's biblical success in battle versus its colonized late antique subservience to Rome, imagining a mass burial of ancient giants, killed in the biblical *Gigantomachy*. It opens with the Emperor boasting of having destroyed Jerusalem. The pericope is a response to that claim, arguing that God allowed the destruction to happen, as he had destroyed the Amorites before him. This conversation is ascribed to Rabban Yoḥanan ben Zakkai, the heroic savior of Torah after the destruction of Jerusalem in 70, whom rabbinic sources describe having been in conversation with the then-general Vespasian. This text is a continuation of that dialog, though with the "wrong" emperor.

One could well imagine a version of the story with Vespasian as protagonist. This text, however, has it that Yoḥanan ben Zakkai was in conversation with Hadrian, clearly conflating the two emperors into a single imperial voice, and perhaps even conflating the two Jewish revolts into one extended battle (as World War I and II are often conflated today). Jews of this transition period between Byzantium and Islam were not the only ones to confuse/conflate the two. Samaritan sources make the same "mistake," identifying the destroyer of Jerusalem as Hadrian, who is married to a Samaritan woman and was a friend of the Samaritans—even giving them the huge "Andalusian doors" of the Jerusalem Temple (the legendary Corinthian gold gate of Nicanor?[82]), which were fitted to the synagogue built in Nablus by the high priest Aqbun.[83]

Hadrian has a complex presence in rabbinic sources. From the persecutor of Beitar, of whom it is said "May God grind his bones," he becomes an itinerant and even positive character in amoraic midrashim, who engages in conversation with even ordinary Jews.[84] Here Hadrian engages Rabban Yoḥanan b. Zakkai on his own turf—and is bested by him. Ben Zakkai rebuffed the "haughtiness of Hadrian" by engaging him—unlike the blasphemy of Titus, which in amoraic sources required Divine intervention to subvert through a tiny mosquito that nestled in Titus's brain.[85] Ben Zakkai is Hadrian's equal, the story inverting the colonial balance between Jews and Rome, between a foundational Rabbinic hero and a Roman god in the making.

Ben Zakkai's response is significant. He knew of a cave full of very large Amorite bones, to which he escorted Hadrian. Fanciful as this is, we are reminded of the many tombs of the Second Temple period and later periods—the most impressive at Beth She'arim—that dot the Holy Land.[86] Particu-

---

82   T.Kippurim 2:4 (ed. S. Lieberman); b.Yoma 38a.
83   E.g. *Kitāb al-Tarīkh of Abu 'l-Fatḥ*, tr. Stenhouse, 234.
84   Hasan-Rokem, *Tales of the Neighborhood*, 117–137.
85   Genesis Rabba 10:7 (ed. Theodor-Albeck), 82–83, Leviticus Rabba 20:5 (ed. Margaliot), 457–458, Pesiqta de'Rav. Kahane 36:5 (ed. Mandelbaum), 392 and other parallels cited by Shahar, "Titus in the Sanctum Sanctorum," 741–768, (Hebrew). See also Levinson, "Tragedies Naturally Performed," 349–382; Hasan-Rokem, *The Arch of Titus*, 55–62.
86   For a survey of discoveries, Fine, "Death, Burial, and Afterlife," 440–464.

larly pertinent is a cave that served as a mass burial site discovered outside Jerusalem's Jaffa Gate, believed to be Christian clergy "martyred" during the Sasanian incursion of 613 CE—according to patristic sources, by Jews.[87] This text provides a counter narrative to larger claims of Jewish defeat by the Romans, and may even respond to Christian fascination with bones as relics (which colonized Jews in the Christian Holy Land likely knew first-hand). As the sixth century Galilean synagogue liturgical poet, Yannai, put it somewhat indelicately, Christians are those "Who acquire assemblages of bone, Who moan to them on their festivals."[88]

Concluding Comments

Like other people in Roman antiquity, Jews discussed discoveries of large bones and contextualized them in terms of their received traditions. This phenomenon is attested first in Josephus' description of the bones of the giants at Hebron, which we have shown fits well within the Greco-Roman genre of giant discoveries. Bavli Niddah 24b is the locus for discussion of giant bones in rabbinic sources, which are given biblical resonance and current meaning as a kind of chain of tradition leading from biblical giants to ever shorter people, including rabbis. During the age of transition between New Rome and Islam, this Niddah text was transformed once again into a prose poem on Deuteronomy 2:31. The ultimate Rabbinic hero, Rabbi Yoḥanan b. Zakkai, was matched up against the Emperor Hadrian, and bested him—claiming that divine disfavor with his people allowed Imperial victory, and not Roman might. The proof of this is the bones of the *Anaqim*, slaughtered in the biblical *Gigantomachy*.

Jews, Muslims and Christians discuss additional discoveries through the middle ages, and into modern times. Benjamin of Tudela (d. 1173), for example, provides one of the more complex texts, describing the bones of a giant displayed in the great mosque in Damascus. He identifies it as the palace of the biblical Ben Hadad (Jeremiah 49:27, Amos 1:4):

> Here is a mosque of the Arabs called the Garni of Damascus; there is no building like it in the whole world; and they say that it was a palace of

---

87 Reich, "The Ancient Burial Ground in the Mamilla Neighborhood, Jerusalem," 111–118.
 Nagar, Taitz, Reich, "What can we make of these fragments?," 29–38; Avni, "The Persian Conquest of Jerusalem (614 Ce)—An Archaeological Assessment," 35–48.
88 *The Liturgical Poetry of Rabbi Yannai*, ed. Rabinovitz, 2: 221–222. See Fine, *Art and Judaism in the Greco-Roman World*, 117.

Ben Hadad. ... And in the court there is a gigantic head overlaid with gold and silver, and fashioned like a bowl with rims of gold and silver. It is as big as a cask, and three men can enter therein at the same time to bathe. In the palace is suspended the rib of one of the giants, the length being nine cubits, and the width two cubits; and they say it belonged to the King Anak of the giants of old, whose name was Abramaz. For so it was found inscribed on his grave, where it was also written that he ruled over the whole world.[89]

Who first identified this giant fossil as the biblical Anaq—Jews, Christians or Muslims? Benjamin doesn't say. The identification, however, follows Joshua 11:21. At Tarragona in Spain, Benjamin matter of factly mentions (according to the manuscript collected by the intrepid Marcus Nathan Adler) יונים ענקים, "buildings of Greek giants." Alternative texts read "Greeks and giants," יונים וענקים, an identification known from Classical sources as well.[90] The testimony of Tobias Cohen, with which we began this article, is an early modern example of this phenomenon.

Fossils bones should be added to the list of objects that pre-modern Jews—and not a few contemporary ones[91]—have interpreted through the lenses of their sacred texts and traditions. These stories are further examples of how even some of the most fantastic Rabbinic stories, often dismissed as flights of fancy by early modern and modern interpreters alike, are solidly based in then current understandings of the world. Investigations of massive bones by rabbis represent a kind of "rabbinic paleontology."

---

89   *The Itinerary of Benjamin of Tudela*, ed. Adler, (Hebrew), 47, p. 31, (English), p. 30.
90   ed. Adler, 2, Hebrew; 2, n. 8. Morère, "Antiquity in Benjamin of Tudela's Travel Narrative," 34, n. 52. On the association of large architectural remains with giants in earlier periods, see Maeir, "Memories, Myths, and Megalithics," and the bibliography there. A century after Benjamin, Zerahiah ben Shealtiel of Barcelona and Rome (d. 1290's) describes a giant discovery near Rome, published as "Letter from R. Kirchheim to Ignaz Blumenfeld" [Hebrew], 121–123. See also Ben-Shalom, *Mul Tarbut Notsrit*, 93–94; Malkiel, "The Artifact and Humanism in Medieval Jewish Thought," 32–33.
91   Note the contemporary ideological complexities among fervently Orthodox, *Hareidi,* Jews in dealing with these discoveries, and the complex negotiation between tradition and modernity that still absorbs some—as discussed and demonstrated by Slifkin, *Sacred Monsters.*

Acknowledgements

Many thanks to Joseph Angel, Arnon Atzmon, Leah Bierman Fine, Yaakov Fine, Baruch-Lev Kelman, Adrienne Mayor, Hannah Perlman, Shana Strauch Schick, Moshe Wilner and the late Louis H. Feldman and Yaakov Elman ז״ל for discussing this work with us at various stages. Special thanks to Adrian M. Lister and Rivka Rabinovich for freely sharing their paleontological expertise with us. In addition to our friend and teacher Professor Elman, we dedicate this study to the newest member of our family, Hannah Perlman.

Bibliography

Abu 'l-Fatḥ, *The Kitāb al-Tarīkh of Abu 'l-Fatḥ.* tr. Paul Stenhouse. Sydney: University of Sydney: Mandelbaum Trust, 1985.

Alon, Gedaliah. *Mehkarim be-Toldot Yisrael.* Tel Aviv: Hakibbutz Hameuchad, 1957.

Angel, Joseph L. "Reading the Book of Giants in Literary and Historical Context," *Dead Sea Discoveries* 21 (2014), 323–346.

Avni, Gideon, "The Persian Conquest of Jerusalem (614 Ce)—An Archaeological Assessment," *Bulletin of the American Schools of Oriental Research* 357 (2010): 35–48.

Bar Ilan, Meir, "Meqomot Pellah be-Erets Yisrael be-Et ha-Atiqah," *Judea and Samaria Research Studies* 5 (1985), 229–239.

Bate, Dorothea M.A., "Discovery of a Fossil Elephant in Palestine," *Nature* 134 (1934), 219.

Ben Meir, Shahar, "Titus in the Sanctum Sanctorum," *Josephus and the Rabbis*, eds. Tal Ilan and Vered Noam in collaboration with Meir Ben Shahar, Daphne Baratz, and Yael Fish. Jerusalem: Yad Ben-Zvi Press, 2017, 741–768, Hebrew.

Ben-Shalom, Ram. *Mul Tarbut Notsrit: Toda'ah Historit Ve-Dimuye avar e-Kerev Yehude Sefarad ve-Provans bi-Yeme ha-Benayim.* Jerusalem: Ben Zvi Institute, 2006.

Benjamin of Tudela, *The Itinerary of Benjamin of Tudela: Critical Text, Translation and Commentary*, ed. Marcus Nathan Adler, London: Henry Frowde, 1907.

Blank, Debra Reed, "On Tractate Sofrim, It's Time to Take Another Look at 'Our Little Sister' Soferim: A Bibliographical Essay," *The Jewish Quarterly Review* 90.1/2 (1999), 1–26.

Begg, Christopher, T. *Judean Antiquities 5–7, Flavius Josephus: Translation and Commentary.* Leiden: Brill, 2005.

Bondeson, Jan. *A Cabinet of Medical Curiosities: A Compendium of the Odd, the Bizarre, and the Unexpected.* New York: Norton Simon, 1999.

Charlesworth, James H., ed. *The Old Testament Pseudepigrapha* (Garden City, NY: Doubleday, 1983), 1: 774–828.

Cohen, Claudine. *The Fate of the Mammoth: Fossils, Myth, and History.* Chicago, IL: University of Chicago Press, 2002.

Cohen, Tobias. *Sefer Ma'aseh Tuvia*. Venice, n.p., 1708.

Doak, Brian R., *The Last of the Rephaim: Conquest and Cataclysm in the Heroic Ages of Ancient Israel*, Ph.D. dissertation. Cambridge MA: Harvard University, 2011.

Doak, Brian R., *The Last of the Rephaim: Conquest and Cataclysm in the Heroic Ages of Ancient Israel*. Boston: Ilex Foundation and Washington DC: Center for Hellenic Studies, Trustees of Harvard University, 2012.

Doak, Brian R., "The Giant in a Thousand Years: Tracing Narratives of Gigantism in the Hebrew Bible and Beyond," in *Ancient Tales of Giants from Qumran and Turfan: Contexts, Traditions, and Influences*, eds. Matthew Goff, Loren T. Stuckenbruck, and Enrico Morano. Tübingen: Mohr Siebeck, 2016, 13–32.

Feldman, Louis H., *Flavius Josephus: Judean Antiquities 1–4, Translation and Commentary*. Leiden: Brill, 1999.

Fine, Steven, *Art and Judaism in the Greco-Roman World: Toward a New "Jewish Archaeology,"* Cambridge and New York: Cambridge University Press, 2005.

Fine, Steven, *Art, History and the Historiography of Judaism in the Greco-Roman World*, Boston: Brill. 2014.

Fine, Steven, "Death, Burial, and Afterlife," *The Oxford Handbook of Jewish Daily Life in Roman Palestine*, ed. Catherine Hezser. New York: Oxford University Press, 2010, 440–464.

Fine, Steven and Peter Schertz, "Herod's Temple: An Ornament to the Empire," *Jewish Religious Architecture: From Biblical Israel to Modern Judaism*, ed. Steven Fine. Boston: Brill, 2019, 72–95.

Fischer, Moshe and Alla Stein, "Josephus on the Use of Marble in Building Projects of Herod the Great," *Journal of Jewish Studies* 45.1 (1994): 79–85.

Frumkin, Amos. *Holy Land Atlas: Judean Desert*. Jerusalem: Israel Cave Research Center, Magnes Press, 2015.

Frumkin, Amos. "Discovery of the Largest Salt Cave in the World," *Niqrot Zurim: Journal of the Israel Cave Research Center (ICRC)* 21 (2021): 138–158, Hebrew.

Gafni, Isaiah M. "Pre-Histories' of Jerusalem in Hellenistic, Jewish and Christian Literature," *Journal for the Study of the Pseudepigrapha*, 1.1 (1987), 5–22.

Gardner, Elinor W. and Dorothea M.A. Bate, "The Bone-Bearing Beds of Bethlehem: Their Fauna and Industry," *Nature* 140 (1937), 431–433.

Goff, Matthew, Loren T. Stuckenbruck, and Enrico Morano, eds. *Ancient Tales of Giants from Qumran and Turfan: Contexts, Traditions, and Influences*. Tübingen: Mohr Siebeck, 2016.

Ginzberg, Louis. *The Legends of the Jews*. Philadelphia: Jewish Publication Society, 1967.

Girdland-Flink, Linus, Ebru Albayrak and Adrian M. Lister, "Genetic Insight into an Extinct Population of Asian Elephants (*Elephas maximus*) in the Near East," *Open Quaternary*, 4.2 (2018), pp. 1–9.

Grossmark, Tziona. *Travel Narratives in Rabbinic Literature: Voyages to Imaginary Realms*. Lewiston: Edwin Mellen Press, 2010.

Hachlili, Rachel, Ann E. Killebrew, and Ehud Netzer, *Jericho: The Jewish Cemetery of the Second Temple Period*. Jerusalem: Israel Antiquities Authority, 1999.

Ha-Cohen, Mordekhai, *Cave of Machpelah*. Ramat Gan: Massada, 1970, Hebrew.

Hanfmann, George M.A. "Giants," *Oxford Classical Dictionary*, 4th ed. eds. Simon Hornblower and Anthony Spawforth. Oxford: Oxford University Press, 2012, 616.

Hasan-Rokem, Galit. *Tales of the Neighborhood: Jewish Narrative Dialogues in Late Antiquity*. University of California Press, 2003.

Hasan-Rokem, Galit. "A Narrative Triumph: The Rabbis Write Back to the Empire," *The Arch of Titus: From Rome to Jerusalem—and Back*, ed. Steven Fine. Boston: Brill, 2020 and New York: Yeshiva University Press, 2021, 55–62.

Heiman, Aharon M. *Toldot ha-Tannaim ve-ha-Amoraim*. London: ha-Ekspress, 1910.

Hirschfeld, Yizhar, *The Judean Desert Monasteries in the Byzantine Period*. New Haven: Yale University Press, 1992.

Ilan, Zvi, "Sheled Leviatan Nadir Nitgalah be-Hof Rosh ha-Niqra," *LaMerhav* (16 October, 1966), 1.

International Union for Conservation of Nature (IUCN), "First intact fossil of prehistoric whale discovered in Wadi Al-Hitan," 10 June 2015, https://www.iucn.org/content/first-intact-fossil-prehistoric-whale-discovered-wadi-al-hitan

Ish-Shalom, Michael. 1972. "The Cave of Machpela and the Sepulchre of Moses—The Development of an Aggadic Tradition," *Tarbiz* 41.2, 203–210, Hebrew.

Kiperwasser, Reuven, "Rabba bar bar Hanna's Voyages," *Jerusalem Studies Hebrew Literature* 22 (2007–2008), 215–242, Hebrew.

Kirschenbaum, Karen, *Furniture of the Home in the Mishnah*. Ramat Gan: Bar Ilan University Press, 2013, Hebrew.

Kitzinger, Ernst, *Byzantine Art in the Making: Main Lines of Stylistic Development in Mediterranean Art, 3rd–7th Century*. New York: Cambridge University Press, 1977.

Lerner, Myron Bialik, "Abba Saul," *Encyclopedia Judaica*. Jerusalem: Keter, New York Macmillan 1971, 1:40.

Levinson, Joshua, "'Tragedies Naturally Performed': Fatal Charades, Parodia Sacra and the Death of Titus," in *Jewish Culture and Society under the Christian Roman Empire*, eds. Richard Kalmin and Seth Schwartz (Leuven: Peeters, 2003), 349–382.

Levinsohn, A. *Tuvia ha-Rofeh ve-Sifro Ma'aseh Tuvia*. Berlin and London: Rimonim, 1924.

Lindquist, Maria. "King Og's Iron Bed," *Catholic Biblical Quarterly* 73 (2011): 477–492.

The Liturgical Poetry of Rabbi Yannai, ed. Z.M. Rabinovitz. Jerusalem: Bialik Institute, 1985–1987.

Magen, Izhak, "Mamre," *The New Encyclopedia of Archaeological Excavations in the Holy Land*, ed. Ephraim Stern Jerusalem: The Israel Exploration Society, 1993, 2005, 3: 939–941. 5: 2103.

Malkiel, David. "The Artifact and Humanism in Medieval Jewish Thought," *Jewish History* (2013) 27: 21–40.

Malkiel, David. "The Rabbi and the Crocodile: Interrogating Nature in the Late Quattrocento," *Speculum* 91 (2016), 115–148.

Manilius, Marcus. *Astronomica*. tr. G.P. Goold. Cambridge, Mass: Harvard University Press, 2006.

Mayor, Adrienne. *The First Fossil Hunters: Dinosaurs, Mammoths, and Myth in Greek and Roman Times*. Princeton, NJ: Princeton University Press, 2000.

Masekhet Sofrim: Ve-nila aleha Midrash Masekhet Sofrim Bet. ed. Michael Higger. New York: Hotsa'at "De-be Rabanan," 1937.

Maeir, Aren M. "Memories, Myths and Megalithics: Reconsidering the Giants of Gath," *Journal of Biblical Literature* 139.4 (2020), 675–690.

Midrash Shemot Rabbah, Chapters I–XIV. ed. Avigdor Shinan. Jerusalem and Tel Aviv: Dvir, 1984.

Midrash Tanḥuma: Ha-qadum Ve-Ha-Yashan. ed. Salomon Buber. Vilna: Romm, 1885.

Morère, Nuria, "Antiquity in Benjamin of Tudela's travel narrative: interpretation and meaning within the context of the history of travel," *Journal of Tourism History*, 9:1 (2017), 27–43.

Nagar, Yossi, Cecil Taitz, Ronny Reich, "What can we make of these fragments? Excavation at 'Mamilla' Cave, Byzantine Period, Jerusalem," *International Journal of Osteoarchaeology* 9,1 (1999) 29–38.

Neusner, Jacob. *Development of a Legend: Studies on the Traditions Concerning Yoḥanan Ben Zakkai*. Leiden: Brill, 1970.

The Oxford Annotated Bible with the Apocrypha: Revised Standard Version, eds. Bruce M. Metzger and Herbert G. May. New York: Oxford University Press, 1965.

Pandolfia, Luca, Florent Rivals, Rivka Rabinovich, "A New Species of Rhinoceros from the Site of Bethlehem: 'Dihoplus' bethlehemsis sp. nov. (Mammalia, Rhinocerotidae)," *Quaternary International*, 537 (30 January 2020), 48–60 (25 October 2012).

Pausania's Description of Greece, tr. W.H.S. Jones, and H.A. Ormerod, M.A., in 4 Volumes. Cambridge, MA, Harvard University Press; London, William Heinemann Ltd. 1918.

Philostratus, *On Heroes*, tr. Jennifer K. Berenson Maclean, and Ellen Bradshaw Aitken. Leiden: Brill, 2003.

Rabinovich, Rivka, O. Ackermann, E. Aladjem, R. Barkai, R. Biton, I. Milevski, N. Solodenko, O. Marder, "Elephants at the Middle Pleistocene Acheulian open-air site of Revadim Quarry, Israel," *Quaternary International*, 276–277 (25 October 2012), 183–197.

Rabinovich, Rivka and Adrian M. Lister, "The Earliest Elephants Out of Africa: Taxonomy and Taphonomy of Proboscidean Remains from Bethlehem," *Quaternary International* 445, (25 July 2017), 23–42.

Rabinovich, Rivka, G. Herzlinger, R. Calvo, F. Rivals, S. Mischke, G. Beiner, "Erq el Ahmar

Elephant Site—a mammoth skeleton at a rare and controversial Plio-Pleistocene site along the mammal migration route out of Africa," *Quaternary Science Reviews*, 221 (2019), 1–18.

Rajak, Tessa. *Josephus: The Historian and His Society*. London: Duckworth, 2003.

Reich, Ronny. "The Ancient Burial Ground in the Mamilla Neighborhood, Jerusalem." *Ancient Jerusalem Revealed*, ed. Hillel Geva. Jerusalem: Israel Exploration Society, 1994, 111–118.

Richter, Gisela M.A. *The Furniture of the Greeks, Etruscans and Romans*. London: Phaidon Press, 1966.

Rosen-Zvi, Yishai, "Seeing Is Believing: Miracles, Providence, and Reality in the Talmuds" TJT Supp 1, 2017: 87–101. esp. 89–90.

Rossi, Azariah de, *Sefer Me'or Anayyim*. Mantua, 1573.

Schiller, Eli. *Me'arat Ha-Makhpelah*. Jerusalem: Ari'el, 1976.

Shindler, Karolyn, *Discovering Dorothea: The Life of the Pioneering Fossil-Hunter Dorothea Bate*, London: Natural History Museum, 2017.

Sissakian, Varoujan K., Nadhir Al-Ansari and Sven Knutsson, "Karst Forms in Iraq," *Journal of Earth Sciences and Geotechnical Engineering*, 5.4 (2015), 1–26.

Slifkin, Natan. *Sacred Monsters: Mysterious and Mythical Creatures of Scripture, Talmud and Midrash*. Jerusalem: Zoo Torah and Gefen, 2011.

Stein, Dina. "Believing Is Seeing: A Reading of Bava Bathra 73a–75b," *Jerusalem Studies Hebrew Literature*, 17 (1999): 9–32, Hebrew.

Stein, Dina. *Textual Mirrors: Reflexivity, Midrash, and the Rabbinic Self*. Philadelphia: University of Pennsylvania Press, 2012.

Stekelis, Moshe, *Interim Report to the Wellcome Trust. The Wellcome-Marston Archeological Research Expedition*, London, 1940.

Stephens, W.E. *Giants in Those Days: Folklore, Ancient History, and Nationalism*. Lincoln: University of Nebraska, 1989.

Stuckenbruck, Loren T. *The Book of Giants from Qumran: Texts, Translation, and Commentary*, Tübingen: Mohr Siebeck, 1997.

Teshuvot ha-Geonim—Gaonic Responsa from Geniza MSS, ed. Simcha Assaf. Jerusalem: Darom Publishing, Jerusalem, 1928.

Tuval, Michael. ""Συναγωγὴ γιγάντων" (Prov 21:16): The Giants in the Jewish Literature in Greek," in: *Ancient Tales of Giants from Qumran and Turfan: Contexts, Traditions, and Influences*, eds. Matthew Goff, Loren T. Stuckenbruck, and Enrico Morano, eds. Tübingen: Mohr-Siebeck, 2016.

Van Der Horst, Pieter W. "The Site of Adam's Tomb," in *Studies Hebrew Literature and Jewish Culture. Amsterdam Studies in Jewish Thought*, eds. Martin F.J. Baasten and Reinier Munk, 12 (2007), 251–255.

Vincent, Louis-Hugues, and Ernest J.H. Mackay. *Hébron: Le Ḥaram El-Khalîl, Sépulture Des Patriarches*. Paris: Leroux, 1923.

Wikipedia, מערת מלח"ם, https://he.wikipedia.org/wiki/מערת_מלח%22ם
Zanker, Paul, Seán Hemingway, Christopher S. Lightfoot, and Joan R. Mertens. *Roman Art: A Guide through the Metropolitan Museum of Art's Collection*. New York: Scala Publishers, 2019.

CHAPTER 2

Tosefta Eduyot 1:1 On the Fear of Losing Torah and the Redaction of Tannaitic Materials

Michal Bar-Asher Siegal

The rabbinic corpus is notoriously lacking in self-reflective descriptions of the rabbinic period and its literary products.[1] Rabbinic sources rarely explain the nature of the rabbinic project: what rabbinic literature was meant to present, and why. But a few sources do give us a glimpse into the rabbis' broader ambitions. One of the most well-known of these passages is the first tosefta in tractate Eduyot:

כשנכנסו חכמים לכרם ביבנה אמרו. עתידה שעה שיהא אדם מבקש דבר מדברי תורה ואינו מוצא. מדברי סופרים ואינו מוצא. שנ' "}לכן{ הנה ימים באים נאם ייי והשלחתי רעב בארץ" וגו' "לבקש את דבר ייי ולא ימצאו". "דבר ייי" זו נבואה. "דבר ייי" זה הקץ. "דבר ייי" זה מבקש דבר מדברי תורה דומה לחבירו. אמרו. נתחיל מה לבית שמי ומה לבית הלל.[2]

When sages came together in (lit. entered into) the vineyard at Yavneh, they said: "The time is coming when a person will go looking for a teaching (lit. a word) from the words of Torah and will not find it, from the words of scribes and will not find it. As it is said, 'The time is surely coming, declares the Lord God, when I will set forth a famine upon the land; [not a famine of bread, or a thirst for water, but for hearing the words of the Lord. They shall wander from sea to sea and from north to east; they shall run to and fro,] seeking the word of the Lord, but they shall not find it (Amos 8:11–12).' 'The word of the Lord'—this is prophecy; 'the word of the Lord'—this is (knowledge of) the end; 'the word of the Lord'—this is one who seeks a teaching from the words of Torah that is similar to its fellow." They said: "Let us begin with what is of the House of Shammai and what is of the House of Hillel."

---

1 [Editor's note: See Alyssa M. Gray's article "The Motif of the Forgetting and Restoration of Law: An Inter-Talmudic Difference about the Divine Role in Rabbinic Law," that appears later in this volume, which similarly discusses the fear that the Torah may be forgotten as a concern unique to sages from the Land of Israel.]
2 Quotes according to MS Vienna.

The text's setting is famously, and unusually, specific in time and place: "when the rabbis entered Yavneh." It contains three parts: a problem ("The time is coming ..."), a biblical prooftext (Amos 8:11–12), and a solution developed by the rabbis at Yavneh ("Let us begin with ..."). In other words, the text explicitly describes a conscious change on the part of the rabbis, a moment in time when they identified a specific problem and enacted some kind of solution. This text has rightly been seen as a uniquely self-reflective depiction of the beginning of the rabbinic project.[3]

While many scholars addressed this issue, in this paper, I will leave aside the question of the historicity of the text and what, if anything, it can say about the actual Yavneh period. I shall only refer to the Tosefta's literary depiction of the origins of the rabbinic project and how it is viewed and presented in this text.

I start with the main problem in this central paragraph: The exact *nature* of the crisis described in the first part of the tosefta ("The time is coming when a person will go looking for a teaching from the words of Torah and will not find it, from the words of scribes and will not find it"), and the way in which the rabbis' actions represent a solution to this crisis, are not clearly defined. As a result, scholars have long debated these questions. Early scholars assumed that the Tosefta depicts an atmosphere of calamity in the aftermath of the destruction, which necessitated the compilation of rabbinic traditions, lest they be lost. Graetz[4] and Epstein[5] situated the story in the time of Rabban Gamaliel, while Albeck[6] and Urbach[7] preferred the time of Rabban Yoḥanan ben Zakkai.

In recent years, this passage has garnered renewed attention. Shlomo Naeh suggests reading the Tosefta in light of the oral nature of rabbinic literature.[8] He claims that the problem the rabbis are attempting to solve is not the fear that Torah will be *lost*, but rather the overabundance of traditions. There is just too much material to deal with in an oral culture, and the rabbis' solution is to organize it in a way that facilitates access to the accumulated oral tradi-

---

3   See for example, Graetz, *Divre Yeme Yisrael*, 172; Epstein, *Introduction to Tannaitic Literature*, 425–428; Albeck, *Introduction to the Mishnah*, 82–84, 257–259; Safrai, "The Decision According to the School of Hillel," 27–28; Cohen, "The Significance of Yavneh," 27–53; Weiss-Halivni, *Midrash, Mishnah and Gemara*, 38–47; Urbach, "Class-Status," 306–330; Shapira, "Bet ha-Midrash," 171–225; Naeh, "The Art of Memory," 582–586; Fraade, "Rabbinic Polysemy," 1–40; Schremer, "Avot Reconsidered," 287–311; Furstenberg, "From Tradition to Controversy," 587–641.
4   Graetz, *Divre Yeme Yisrael*, 172.
5   Epstein, *Introduction to Tannaitic Literature*, 426.
6   Albeck, *Introduction to the Mishnah*, 82.
7   Urbach, "Class-Status," 317.
8   Naeh, "The Art of Memory," 582–586.

tions. Steven Fraade adds that the rabbis were also contending with what he calls the problem of "the practical challenge of multivocality."[9] The multivocal nature of the rabbinic material itself made preserving it even more challenging, claims Fraade. The rabbis' solution, as described in the Tosefta, was "collecting and ordering the conflicting rulings ... without stripping them of their multivocality."[10] Yair Furstenberg, following Fraade, reasserted the view of the Yavneh rabbis' project as categorizing the collected rabbinic disagreements which bore only a vague relationship to one another, into the structured literary disagreements that we know as the fundamental units of rabbinic literature.[11]

Adiel Schremer takes a different approach.[12] He views t.Eduyot as a counterpoint to the first *mishnah* in Avot, in which the Oral Torah originates from Sinai: "Moses received Torah from Sinai and handed it to Joshua," and so on, all the way to Hillel and Shammai. Schremer recognizes the crisis presented in t.Eduyot as the blurring of the distinction between the teachings of the Written Torah and the Torah of the "scribes." In other words, the problem, as viewed by the composers of t.Eduyot, *is* m.Avot itself. The solution, according to t.Eduyot, is thus the act of identification: "declaring the authorship of each rabbinic teaching, so as to make its human origin as clear as possible."[13]

In this paper, I will attempt to add one more piece to the scholarly engagement with this fascinating text. I will concentrate on the philological aspects of the text and argue that the version preserved in MS Vienna holds the key to understanding the redaction process of the Tosefta here, and its relation to the parallel Talmudic text. It also, I think, tips the scale in favor of an approach that combines the readings of Schremer, Naeh, and Fraade.

I want to start with the tosefta's three parts and unpack the philological problems they present. First, in terms of content: the problem depicted in part A of the passage identifies two categories, known from elsewhere in t.Eduyot and other tannaitic sources: דברי תורה and דברי סופרים. We find these two categories opposed later in the same chapter in t.Eduyot 1:5

ר' יהושע בן קרחא או' דבר מדברי תורה הולכין אחר המחמיר מדברי סופרים הולכין אחר המיקל[14]

---

9   Fraade, "Rabbinic Polysemy," 21.
10   ibid, 19.
11   Furstenberg, "From Tradition to Controversy," 587–641.
12   Schremer, "Avot Reconsidered," 287–311.
13   ibid, 311.
14   MS Vienna.

R. Yehoshua ben Qorḥa says: "[In the case of] a teaching from words of Torah, we follow the stringent approach; in matters of the words of the scribes, we follow the lenient view."

These categories are also known from other tannaitic passages such as m.Sanhedrin 11:3, where several commandments are compared regarding these categories:[15]

.... חומר בדברי סופרים מדיברי תורה

There is greater stringency with regard to words of the Scribes than with regard to words of Torah.

m.Yadiyim 3:2

... אין דנין דברי תורה מדברי סופרין ולא דברי סופרים מדברי תורה ולא דברי סופרין מדברי סופרין.

The words of the Torah may not be argued from the words of the Scribes, nor may the words of the Scribes be argued from the words of the Torah, nor may the words of the Scribes be argued from [other] words of the Scribes.

In one Toseftan saying quoted in a few parallels,[16] the difference between the two categories is defined as:

... זה מדברי תורה ודברי תורה אין צריכין חזוק. וזו מדברי סופרים ודברי סופרים צריכין חזוק.

We learn this from the words of the Torah and the words of the Torah do not need reinforcement. And we learn this from the words of the Scribes and the words of the Scribes do need reinforcement.

So, these two categories, דברי תורה and דברי סופרים, are also used elsewhere in tannaitic literature. However, part B of the Tosefta we are dealing with, the *derashah* that represents the scriptural basis for the problem in part A, identifies three different categories: קץ, נבואה and דברי תורה. In other words, instead of

---

15 But see also m.Parah 11:6; t.Parah 11:5; t.Tvul Yom 1:10; Sifra Behar 3:2; Sifre Numbers 72.
16 T.Yevamot 2:4; t.Ta'anit 2:6.

two categories, we now see three categories, and three different ones, that have only the "Words of the Torah," דברי תורה, as a shared category. What's more, the proposed solution, that we begin with Hillel and Shammai, found in part C of the Tosefta, ignores the various categories completely!

Naeh and Schremer address these problems in two different ways. They both turn to a baraita in b.Shabbat 138b, which parallels parts A and B of the tosefta:

ת"ר. כשנכנסו רבותינו לכרם ביבנה אמרו עתידה תורה שתשתכח מישראל. שנא' "הנה ימים באים נאם יי'י והשלחתי רעב בארץ לא רעב ללחם ולא צמא למים כי אם לשמוע את דבר יי'י". וכתי' "ונעו מים עד ים ומצפון ועד תימן ישוטטו לבקש את דבר יי'י ולא ימצאו". "דבר יי'י". זו הלכה. "דבר יי'י". זו הקץ. "דבר יי'י". זו נבואה[17]

> When our sages entered the vineyard at Yavneh, they said: "The time is coming when Torah will be forgotten from Israel. As it is said, 'The time is surely coming, declares the Lord God, when I will set forth a famine upon the land; not a famine of bread, or a thirst for water, but for hearing the words of the Lord.' And it says 'They shall wander from sea to sea and from north to east; they shall run to and fro seeking the word of the Lord, but they shall not find it' (Amos 8:11–12). 'The word of the Lord'— this is *halakhah*; 'the word of the Lord'—this is (knowledge of) the end; 'the word of the Lord'—this is prophecy."

In this Talmudic passage, the problem at hand is explicitly stated: that Torah will be forgotten. Here also, the scriptural prooftext from Amos 8 is clearly and simply connected to the verses' plain, apocalyptic meaning.

Relying on this Talmudic parallel, Naeh suggests erasing from the Tosefta text the words "דבר יי'י" זה הקץ "דבר יי'י" זו נבואה "דבר יי'י".[18] He claims that they were mistakenly copied here from the Bavli (השתרבבו). This suggestion eliminates the problem of the mixing of categories, as there is no more נבואה or קץ; just דברי תורה ודברי סופרים in parts A and B of the tosefta. Naeh's reading, based on MS Erfurt, states as follow:

משנתכנסו חכמים בכרם ביבנה אמרו עתידה שעה שיהא אדם מבקש דבר מדברי תורה ואינו מוצא מדברי סופרים ואינו מוצא. שנ' "לכן הנה ימים באים נאם יי והשלחתי רעב לארץ לא רעב ללחם ולא צמא למים כי אם לשמע דברי יי" ונעו מים ועד ים ומצפון ועד מזרח ישוטטו לבקש את דבר יי ולא ימצאו" "דבר יי'י" זו נבואה "דבר יי'י" זה הקץ "דבר יי" שלא יהא דבר מדברי תורה דומה לחבירו. אמרו נתחיל מהילל ומשמאי.

---

17   MS. Oxford 366.
18   Naeh, "The Art of Memory," 597, n. 187.

TOSEFTA EDUYOT 1:1 ON THE FEAR OF LOSING TORAH

As can be seen, this suggestion makes clear the reason that Naeh prefers the reading of MS Erfurt for this passage. According to this version, the continuation of the third דבר יי now states: שלא יהא דבר מדברי תורה דומה לחבירו, "no teaching from the Torah will be similar to its fellow." The choice to rely on MS Erfurt and to remove these words, sets up Naeh's reading of the rabbis' proposed solution to the problem in part C of the tosefta: the rabbis will create the missing similarities by organizing rabbinic sayings and thus making the breadth of oral teachings accessible.

Schremer, on the other hand, dismisses the whole of part B, the prooftext from Amos, as influenced by the Talmudic parallel:[19]

כשנכנסו חכמים לכרם ביבנה אמרו. עתידה שעה שיהא אדם מבקש דבר מדברי תורה ואינו מוצא. מדברי סופרים ואינו מוצא. שנ׳ ״{לכן} הנה ימים באים נאם ייי והשלחתי רעב בארץ״ וגו׳ ״לבקש את דבר ייי ולא ימצאו״. ״דבר ייי״ זו נבואה. ״דבר ייי״ זה הקץ. ״דבר ייי״ זה מבקש דבר מדברי תורה דומה לחביריו. אמרו. נתחיל מה לבית שמיי ומה לבית הלל.

Schremer's suggestion removes the third reading of דבר יי, on which Naeh relies:

שנ׳ ״{לכן} הנה ימים באים נאם ייי והשלחתי רעב בארץ״ וגו׳ ״לבקש את דבר ייי ולא ימצאו״. ״דבר ייי״ זו נבואה. ״דבר ייי״ זה הקץ. ״דבר ייי״ זה מבקש דבר מדברי תורה דומה לחבירו.

Moreover, Schremer, unlike Naeh, prefers the reading in MS Vienna, because of the phrasing of the solution in part C: אמרו. נתחיל מה לבית שמיי ומה לבית הלל, "They said: 'Let us begin with what is of the House of Shammai and what is of the House of Hillel.'" The choice to rely on MS Vienna and remove this part in its entirety, aligns with Schremer's reading of the proposed solution to the crisis as one of identifying and classifying rabbinic disagreements and clarifying which of the *halakhot* are words of Torah and which are words of the Scribes.

I think that Schremer is correct in choosing MS Vienna as his textual basis. To understand why, let's turn to another difficulty in the text of the Tosefta: the syntax of the line ״דבר ייי״ זה מבקש דבר מדברי תורה דומה לחבירו. Unlike the first two *derashot* on the words דבר יי, this rabbinic interpretation is not a single word (נבואה, קץ) but rather a full sentence, which breaks the literary symmetry. In addition, the phrasing of זה followed by מבקש etc. is awkward. In MS Erfurt, the difficulties are smoothed out: This line is still stylistically different from the

---

19 Schremer, "Avot Reconsidered," 307–308, n. 68.

first two, single-word *derashot*, but the sentence here reads: שלא יהא דבר מדברי מבקש, and the word זה omits the word ms Erfurt's reading .תורה דומה לחבירו beginning instead with the negation שלא.

However, we should notice that the reading in ms Vienna is the *lectio difficilior* and actually preserves a stronger connection to the broader Tosefta passage. First, the word זה preserves the structural parallel between all three *derashot* (זה נבואה, זה הקץ). In addition, the word מבקש here connects to part A of the text: **עתידה שעה שיהא אדם מבקש דבר מדברי תורה**. ms Vienna repeats this exact phrasing again here: מבקש דבר מדברי תורה.

Therefore, I wish to suggest that the more difficult reading in ms Vienna in fact preserves the moment of "stitching," or the moment of the redaction of this passage in the Tosefta. The basis of the tosefta (red below) was a passage that contained the categories of דברי תורה ודברי סופרים. Part B in the Tosefta derives from an original tannaitic source, which is also preserved in the Babylonian Talmud (in bold below). In other words, the fact that the Talmudic *braita* has a parallel in our Tosefta is not the result of a "later addition" based on the Talmudic text. Rather, the same original source, which includes the *derashah* on Amos 8:11–12 ("דבר יייי. זו הלכה. "דבר יייי. זו הקץ. "דבר יייי. זו נבואה), was preserved independently in both the Tosefta and in the Talmud.

The composers of the Tosefta likely chose to include this source (bold) in this context, combined with the local one (red) because the two *baraitot* share a similar beginning, discussing Yavneh and predicting a future crisis using the word עתידה:

כשנכנסו חכמים לכרם ביבנה אמרו. עתידה שעה שיהא אדם מבקש דבר מדברי תורה ואינו מוצא. מדברי סופרים ואינו מוצא. מבקש דבר מדברי תורה דומה לחבירו. אמרו. נתחיל מה לבית שמיי ומה לבית הלל

ת"ר. כשנכנסו רבותינו לכרם ביבנה אמרו. עתידה תורה שתשתכח מישראל. שנא' "הנה ימים באים נאם יייי והשלחתי רעב בארץ לא רעב ללחם ולא צמא למים כי אם לשמוע את דבר יייי". וכת' "ונעו מים עד ים ומצפון ועד תימן ישוטטו לבקש את דבר יייי ולא ימצאו". "דבר יי'י." זו הלכה. "דבר יי'י". זו הקץ. "דבר יי'י". זו נבואה.

↓

כשנכנסו חכמים לכרם ביבנה אמרו. עתידה שעה שיהא אדם מבקש דבר מדברי תורה ואינו מוצא. מדברי סופרים ואינו מוצא. שנ' "{לכן} הנה ימים באים נאם יייי והשלחתי רעב בארץ" וגו' "לבקש את דבר יייי ולא ימצאו". "דבר יייי" זו נבואה. "דבר יייי" זה הקץ. "דבר יייי" זה מבקש דבר מדברי תורה דומה לחבירו. אמרו. נתחיל מה לבית שמיי ומה לבית הלל

However, when combining this *derashah* (bold) with the second tannaitic source that forms the basis of the tosefta (red), they did so in a way that collated the various categories presented in the two readings of the passage from Amos. Specifically, a phrase that includes דברי תורה, from the second source (red), replaces the original category of הלכה in the baraita (bold).

In support of the "red-ish" basis of the tosefta, as mentioned above, later in the same chapter (t.Eduyot 1:5), we see the Tosefta's practical use of these same categories of דברי תורה ודברי סופרים.

The reason I believe that this awkward stitching together of the two sources occurred at the stage of the Tosefta's redaction, rather than during a later, mistaken insertion of the baraita under the influence of the Bavli, is due to the ordering of the three *derashot* in the final version of the Tosefta. The original order of הלכה, קץ, נבואה, found in MS Oxford 366, and Modena BE Ebr. 158[20] as well as the printed editions of the Talmudic baraita, shifts in the Tosefta; הלכה is moved to the end and replaced with the local source's categories for הלכה (red): דברי תורה ודברי סופרים.[21] This replacement, I suggest, is the seam that reveals the stitching together of the two tannaitic sources.

However, MS Vatican ebr. 108 does not align with my suggestion: it has the order of the Tosefta קץ, נבואה, הלכה so the הלכה is situated at the end. I am inclined to view this order as secondary and influenced by the need to situate the הלכה as the last of the three categories, in line with the famous tosefta's order. Nevertheless, it is also possible that it represents the original order, in which case, the replacement of the הלכה with the local דברי תורה ודברי סופרים in the final version of the Tosefta would have more easily been done.

In any case, according to my reading, MS Vienna is the preferred text from which to glean the creation of the passage from its different sources. Markedly, it preserves a number of the elements of the source text—the original זו and the local מבקש דבר מדברי תורה, serving as remnants to the redaction process that took place in creating this tosefta. This philological situation in which the words remained, however, resulted in a more difficult sentence syntactically.

If my reconstruction is correct, then we can identify more clearly the editorial intent of the Tosefta's creator: to insert the categories of דברי תורה ודברי סופרים into the words of the baraita. The baraita (bold) talks about forgetting the Torah, but the reason for the crisis is inserted into it, by using these categories from the local tosefta (red).

---

20 There is a gap where קץ was supposed to appear, but the order is the same.
21 MS Moscow is unreadable in this part, and Munich 95 does not have this line at all.

However, the change brings with it a change in meaning. This, in fact, reinforces Schremer's reading of the tosefta. Schremer surveys the rabbinic sources where these categories appear and shows convincingly that דברי סופרים, "the words of the scribes," is used "to designate a halakhic teaching known to be of *rabbinic* origin," in contrast to דברי תורה, "words of Torah," which designates "a halakhic teaching considered to be of *biblical* origin."[22] Schremer then proceeds to read the tosefta as focusing on the division between Biblical and rabbinic traditions and understands the crisis described in it as the inability to differentiate between the two categories.

I think that my reading of this text and its process of composition, as described above, supports Schemer's reading. The final creation of the tosefta's editor indeed describes such a crisis. However, while Schremer removes the sentence זה מבקש דבר מדברי תורה דומה לחבירו, I believe that this line is crucial to our understanding of the text and demonstrates, as I have argued, the organic textual connection between parts A and B of the tosefta. *However*, by leaving this sentence intact, I come closer to the viewpoint of the scholars who read categorization into the solution of the text, such as Naeh and Fraade.

Let me explain. If we set aside the scriptural prooftext, then what is the nature of the crisis described in the MS Vienna text?

כשנכנסו חכמים לכרם ביבנה אמרו. עתידה שעה שיהא אדם מבקש דבר מדברי תורה ואינו מוצא. מדברי סופרים ואינו מוצא. מבקש דבר מדברי תורה דומה לחבירו.

> When sages came together in the vineyard at Yavneh, they said: "The time is coming when a person will go looking for a teaching from the words of Torah and will not find it, from the words of scribes and will not find it. One who seeks a teaching from the words of Torah that is similar to its fellow."

The Yavneh rabbis describe a man searching for and failing to find Torah teachings of biblical origin and Torah teachings of rabbinic origin. He also looks for teachings of Biblical origin that are grouped together based on certain similarities. According to this reconstruction, Schremer correctly identifies the importance of the two categories of teachings—Biblical and rabbinic—that a person will have difficulty finding. However, Schremer leaves out the last line of the passage in MS Vienna: מבקש דבר מדברי תורה דומה לחבירו. A person will *also* look for similar teachings grouped together.

---

22   Schremer, "Avot Reconsidered," 306–307.

Indeed, both of the scholarly readings of the Tosefta identify salient aspects of the crisis described by the Yavneh rabbis in the final edited version of the tosefta (bold plus red): inability to identify traditions according to their Biblical or rabbinic origin, per Schremer, AND the loss of organized groupings of similar sources, as suggested by Naeh and Fraade. מבקש דבר מדברי תורה ואינו מוצא מדברי סופרים ואינו מוצא as Schremer pointed out, and מבקש דבר מדברי תורה דומה לחבירו as Naeh and Fraade stressed.

In other words, understanding the redactional history of the text, as suggested here, allows us to choose its better version (Vienna), composed of *both* elements. The rabbis depict the loss of Torah as the absence of *both* identification AND organization of the material. These apparently opposing scholarly readings of the tosefta, are in fact *equally valid* readings of two different *parts* of the text. These two parts were combined from the local source along with the baraita preserved also in the Talmud, to create the final version that holds both parts.

I want to stress that my reconstruction of the redactional process of t.Eduyot here does not mean that I agree with Naeh and others who claim that the baraita preserved in the Talmud is fundamentally different from the one in the Tosefta. Naeh erases what he sees as a later interpolation into the Tosefta from the Bavli, because in his reading, the passage in the Bavli is projecting fear, specifically the fear of a future loss of various forms of divine teaching. Naeh wants to read the problem posed in the Tosefta as one of over-abundance rather than of loss.

However, in this respect I agree with Steven Fraade who argues that Naeh exaggerates the difference between the two sources.[23] Even if the Tosefta's problem is indeed the excessive quantity of rabbinic teaching and the difficulty of providing access to it all, the ultimate consequence of that over-abundance, if left unaddressed, is the same. If one cannot access rabbinic knowledge, it is bound to be lost! *So* both the Tosefta and the Talmudic baraita project the same fear of losing rabbinic knowledge. If there is a difference between the baraita and the Tosefta, it is in the fact that the first does not distinguish between teachings of Biblical and rabbinic origin and uses only one term, *halakhah*, while the Tosefta makes this distinction and replaces *halakhah* with terms describing these two constituent parts.

Thus, my reconstruction of the editorial process of t.Eduyot acknowledges that both original sources (red and bold) address the fear of losing rabbinic knowledge. The tannaitic baraita preserved in the Talmud and drawn on

---

23 Fraade, "Rabbinic Polysemy," 18, and see n. 52 there.

by the editor of the Tosefta (bold), describes the fear of the loss of Torah based on a reading of Amos 8:11–12, which identifies three categories of lost knowledge: נבואה קץ והלכה. In the composition process, this baraita was combined with the base text of the Tosefta (red), which describes the loss of the ability to identify the origin of traditional sources (part A), as well as the fear that sources will be lost if they are not grouped in similar categories (part B).

To put it another way, the editor of t.Eduyot 1:1 draws on sources that distinguish between two primary categories of rabbinic knowledge: דברי תורה ודברי סופרים (red). However, these categories are **superimposed** upon a tannaitic *derashah* (from the baraita also preserved in *b. Shabbat*) that is framed around three different categories: נבואה קץ והלכה (bold). The editor of our passage replaces הלכה in the *derashah* with the categories that are of primary concern to him, distinguishing between teachings of rabbinic versus Biblical origin.

This reading might even suggest that the baraita preserved in the Talmud (bold) is actually a representation of an *earlier* stage of rabbinic sources, prior to the creation of the distinction between rabbinic and Biblical traditions (*pace* Schremer, who thinks that the Talmudic baraita is a later reworking of the Tosefta). In this case, the Tosefta reworks this earlier source (bold) in order to present the division it is trying to promote, between traditions of Biblical and rabbinic origin. Alternatively, the baraita might preserve a unifying view of *halakhah* as one group, similar to the position presented in m.Avot, which Schremer claims the Tosefta is opposing.

To conclude, I have argued that a philological examination of the two manuscript versions of t.Eduyot 1:1, which identifies their respective textual difficulties, alongside a higher criticism approach that addresses the substance of the different parts of the Tosefta, might contribute to a more nuanced understanding of this rabbinic source. Such an examination has led me to offer MS Vienna as the superior text for this section of the Tosefta, at least. This version preserves the *lectio difficilior*, which still shows signs of the redactional seams, smoothed out in MS Erfurt, where the text's redactor joined two originally separate sources. This conclusion, on the single local source, supports Lieberman's comparative assessment of the two manuscripts in his Tosefta edition,[24] against Zuckermandel's preference for MS Erfurt,[25] which has been echoed recently in Robert Brody's work on the Tosefta.[26]

---

24   Lieberman, *Tosefta Ki-feshuṭah*.
25   Zuckermandel, *Tosephta Based on the Erfurt and Vienna Codices*.
26   Brody, *Mishnah and Tosefta Studies*; Brody, *Mishnah ye-tosefta Ketubot*.

According to my reconstruction, the Tosefta draws on two different tannaitic sources to discuss the rabbis' fear that the Torah may be lost at some point in the future. The perceived threats include both the blending of all rabbinic teachings without careful marking of their origin—biblical or rabbinic— and the absence of a careful organizational system that groups together similar traditions in a manner that facilitates their use. My reading thus combines multiple scholarly suggestions alongside a new philological examination.

Importantly, such a reading restores the status of the baraita found in b.Shabbat as one that preserves a tannaitic teaching, not a later Talmudic reworking of the Tosefta. The Talmudic baraita, in fact, preserves the third part of the original tannaitic trio: נבואה קץ והלכה, which the Tosefta subsequently alters. This is worth emphasizing again, when all the scholars who have dealt with these sources have assumed the opposite. The Bavli, can, on occasion, preserve an earlier version of a tannaitic source, and can even, with careful examination and scrutiny, help us reconstruct the editorial process of other tannaitic sources.

Whether this source may tell us about Yavneh itself and what the rabbis were trying to do there, it can certainly offer insight into what the composers of this text felt was the important driving force behind the rabbinic project as a whole. We learn about the emphasis they placed on categorizing halakhic teachings based on their origins, biblical or rabbinic, as well as the importance of organizing and grouping traditions. We also learn more about how they drew upon different sources to construct a text that conveyed their viewpoint. Finally, we learn something, along the way, about the layers and literary building materials that these early composers used.

Bibliography

Albeck, Hanoch. *Introduction to the Mishnah*. Jerusalem: Mosad Byaliḳ, 1959.

Brody, Robert. *Mishnah and Tosefta Studies*. Jerusalem: Hebrew University, Magnes Press, 2014.

Brody, Robert. *Mishnah ye-tosefta Ketubot*. Magnes Meḥkar ye-'iyun, 2015.

Cohen, Shaye J.D. 'The Significance of Yavneh: Pharisees, Rabbis and the End of Jewish Sectarianism', *HUCA*, 55 (1984), 27–53.

Epstein, Jacob Nahum. *Introduction to Tannaitic literature: Mishna, Tosephta and Halakhic Midrashim*. Jerusalem: Magnes; Tel Aviv: Devir, [1957], 425–428.

Fraade, Steven. "Rabbinic Polysemy and Pluralism Revisited: Between Praxis and: Thematization," *AJS Review*, 31 (2007), 1–40.

Furstenberg, Yair. "From Tradition to Controversy: New Modes of Transmission in the Teachings of Early Rabbis," *Tarbits* 85 (2018), 587–641.

Graetz, Heinrich. *Divre Yeme Yisrael*, Vol. 2. Tel-Aviv: Izreel, 1946, p. 172.

Lieberman, Saul. *Tosefta Ki-feshuṭah: Be'ur Arokh La-Tosefta*. New York, 1955.

Naeh, Shlomo. "The Art of Memory, Structures of Memory, and Forms of Text in Rabbinic Literature," [Hebrew] in *Mehqerei Talmud III, Part 2: Talmudic Studies Dedicated to the Memory of Professor Ephraim E. Urbach*, ed. Y. Sussmann and D. Rosenthal. Jerusalem, 2005, 582–586.

Safrai, Shmuel. "The Decision According to the School of Hillel in Yavneh," *Proceedings of the Seventh World Congress of Jewish Studies: Studies in the Talmud, Halacha and Midrash*. Jerusalem, 1981, 27–28.

Schremer, Adiel. "Avot Reconsidered: Rethinking Rabbinic Judaism," *JQR*, 105 (2015), 287–311.

Shapira, H. "Bet ha-Midrash (House of Study) during the Late Second Temple Period and the Age of the Mishnah: Institutional and Ideological Aspects," PhD diss., Hebrew University of Jerusalem, 2001, 171–225.

Urbach, Ephraim. "Class-Status and Leadership in the World of the Palestinian Sages," *The World of the Sages*. Jerusalem: Magnes 1988, 306–330.

Weiss-Halivni, David. *Midrash, Mishnah and Gemara*. Cambridge, MA and London 1986, 38–47.

Zuckermandel, Moses Samuel. *Tosephta Based on the Erfurt and Vienna Codices with Parallels and Variants*. Jerusalem, 1963.

CHAPTER 3

Minhag and Popular Practice in Roman Palestine

Stuart S. Miller

In my 2006 book *Sages and Commoners in Late Antique 'Erez Israel*, I picked up on an argument made long ago by Israel Ta-Shma that the authority invested in *minhag* in the Talmud Yerushalmi is far greater than in the Bavli. Most notably, the notion "custom annuls *halakhah*" (*minhag mevattel halakhah*), which does not appear in the Bavli, reflects an entirely different approach taken by the amoraim of *Erets* Israel.[1] While Ta-Shma was interested in demonstrating how this perspective influenced halakhic sources in medieval Ashkenaz, a view subsequently challenged by Haym Soloveitchik, I further developed Ta-Shma's assessment of *minhag* in the Yerushalmi.[2] My sense is that the Bavli and Geonic sources reined in the perspective of the Yerushalmi, most notably by insisting that the influence of *minhag* was limited to civil matters (*mamon*) and, as Menachem Elon claims, to liturgical and ritual matters that did not involve a biblical prohibition (*'issur*).[3]

According to the turn of the ninth-century C.E. Babylonian Pirqoi ben Baboi, R. Yehudai Gaon of Sura had harshly criticized the Jews of *Erets* Israel for faulty practices, including ritual slaughter and "other commandments that were not [done] in accordance with *halakhah* but rather according to customs appropriate [only] during a period of persecution (*keminhag shemad*)." Pirqoi continues that the Palestinians rejected the criticism and responded, "custom annuls *halakhah*."[4] Aside from the ritual slaughter matter, Pirqoi singles out the Palestinians' use of *piyyut*, their circumcision rite, and their inclusion of the Shema in the *qedushah*. What is notable is that these matters are decid-

---

1 See y.Bava Metṣia. 7, 11b; and y.Yevamot. 12, 12c. I discuss these two passages, which are central to the debate concerning *minhag mevattel halakhah*, in *Sages and Commoners*, 383 f., and, more extensively, in my, "'All Law Begins with Custom:' Rabbinic Awareness of Popular Practice," 372–377. Incidentally, "All law begins with custom" is a quote from Bederman, *Custom as a Source of Law*, 3. Its relevance here will soon be apparent.
2 See Ta-Shma, *Early Franco-German Ritual and Custom*, 61–68 [Hebrew] and cf. Soloveitchik, *Collected Essays*, 29–69. Also, see Miller, *Sages and Commoners*, 379–385.
3 Elon, *Jewish Law* 2:903 n. 27; 909–911. Elon also states that a *minhag* could annul a ritual practice if it resulted in a stricter practice.
4 ובשביל כל המצוות שנוהגין בהן שלא כהלכה אלא כמנהג שמד ולא קבלו ממנו ושלחו לו מנהג מבטל הלכה See Ginzberg, *Genizah Studies*, 2:550–560, and Lewin, *Otzar ha-Gaonim: Megillah*, 139.

edly not issues of *mamon*. Nor are they all liturgical in nature. The association of *minhag mevattel halakhah* with the Jews of *Erets* Israel evidently persisted long after the closure of the Talmud Yerushalmi in the fourth century C.E., even if another post-Talmudic source, Soferim 14:16, insists that the principle applied only when the custom can be shown to have originated among "(pious) ancients" (*vatiqin*), thereby suggesting that it was derived *by them* from the Torah. Both Soferim 14:16 and the ben Baboi tradition undeniably testify to the greater recognition *minhag* once enjoyed in *Erets* Israel in all areas of *halakhah*.[5]

By refraining from reading the relevant Yerushalmi sources in light of the Bavli and later halakhic sources, a distinct chapter in the history of *minhag* emerges, one that arguably takes its cue from the Mishnah and perhaps, not surprisingly, parallels roughly contemporaneous attempts by the Romans to grapple with the role of *mos maiorum* ("the custom of the ancestors") within their legal system. Indeed, in both rabbinic Judaism and Roman law, the notion of a *binding* customary law does not begin to crystallize until Late Antiquity.[6]

My interest, however, is *not* in rabbinic law *per se*. Rather, I suggest that much insight can be gained about the everyday practices of the Jews of Roman Palestine once we move beyond formal legal systems and questions of normativity and consider literary and, especially, material evidence. Roberta Rosenthal Kwall has suggested that "cultural analysis" can be useful in such inquiries because it emphasizes the importance of "blending the top-down and bottom-up approaches to lawmaking." It thereby "gives a voice to the creations and practices of those who were or are inferior in social status or lost in historical struggles."[7] Galit Hasan-Rokem similarly emphasizes that folk narratives embedded in rabbinic literature afford a glimpse of those who lived in the "shadow of the sages" and, therefore, of "everyday life."[8]

This is precisely my motive in focusing on the *behaviors* of non-rabbinic "commoners" that are often reflected in rabbinic anecdotes and on seemingly related behaviors suggested by the archaeological record. While this approach will undoubtedly provide a better understanding of where the rabbis were coming from, what they were doing, and why it is that, with time, they would be able

---

5 Miller, *Sages and Commoners*, 383–384. and, in greater detail, "'All Law Begins with Custom:' Rabbinic Awareness of Popular Practice," 381–383. See too my discussion below of the "intra-rabbinic" view of *minhag*.
6 For Roman law, see Thomas, "Custom and Roman Law" and my lengthier treatment in "'All Law Begins with Custom:' Rabbinic Awareness of Popular Practice," 358–362.
7 Kwall, *The Myth of the Cultural Jew*, 1–28, esp. 7–11.
8 Hasan-Rokem, *Web of Life*, 6–8.

to forge their specific brand of "Jewish law," what I have in mind is very much a bi-directional, top-down and especially bottom-up approach that redirects our attention to the real-life situations, practices, rites, and usages of the people amongst whom the sages lived. Aside from references to *minhag* and *minhag 'avoteikhem* ("custom of your fathers"), the amoraim of *Erets* Israel frequently introduced what people "practiced" or, more semantically precise, what they were "*accustomed* to do" (*nahagu ha'am, nahagin, nehigin* etc., from the same root as *minhag*: *n/h/g*) into their halakhic deliberations. This heightened attentiveness encompassed the activities of commoners who were members of the rabbis' more expansive households, such as "those of the house of Rabbi Yannai" (*devei rabbi Yannai*), whose agricultural and household activities are frequently introduced in the Yerushalmi, often with some form of *nahag*, but who are treated in the Bavli exclusively as a rabbinic school with halakhic viewpoints.[9] This awareness on the part of the amoraim of *Erets* Israel also included the doings of those less directly, if at all, engaged with the rabbis, such as the benei/anshei *'ir* X ("people of town X") or even the *'ammei haarets*.[10] All of this speaks mouthfuls about a larger, complex "Jewish" world to which the rabbis not only belonged but also very much needed to navigate in order to achieve self-definition.[11]

Thus much more can be learned once *minhag* is wrested from the usual emphasis on its place in the history of *halakhah*, which tends to regard it in purely intra-rabbinic terms.[12] The traditional approach regards the authority of *minhag* as ultimately deriving from the rabbis. Accordingly, "what people are accustomed to do" represented legal decisions that had been made long ago but forgotten.[13] This approach is at odds with how groups of people, already

---

9   Miller, *Sages and Commoners*, 339–386.
10 Miller, *Sages and Commoners*, 163–177 and 301–338.
11 My re-formulation of E.P. Sander's "common Judaism" as "complex common Judaism" is discussed in a number of my works, including: *Sages and Commoners*, 21–28 and 462–463; "Stepped Pools, Stone Vessels, and other Identity Markers of 'Complex Common Judaism;'" "The Study of 'Talmudic Israel' and/or Roman Palestine: Where Matters Stand;" and *Intersection*, chapters eight and eleven.
12 Aside from the already cited Soferim 14:16, where the *vatiqin* may be understood as earlier authorities, see the earlier story of Hillel in t.Pesaḥim 4:13–14, y.Pesaḥim 6, 33a–b, and b.Pesaḥim 66a, in which Hillel first learns a ritual practice from "Israel," whom he considers to be the "sons of prophets" but then is reminded that he learned the relevant *halakhah* from his more authoritative teachers, Shemaiah and Avatalyon. See Elon, *Jewish Law* 2:882, esp. n. 8; and 901–902.
13 See Elon, *Jewish Law* 2:883, who cites Alfasi and Nahmanides. Cf. Lifshitz, "'Minhag' and Its Place in the Normative Classification of 'Oral Law,'" 157–165 and 175–179; and Broyde, "Custom as a Source of Jewish Law," 1038.

in antiquity, more usually arrived at socially acceptable practices that enabled them to function as a society. As Carleton Kemp Allen has observed, "… custom must not be conceived as being purely a creation of judicial technique … The relation between indigenous customary law and technical treatment of it is one of action and reaction."[14] Lawrence Schiffman captures this exact dynamic when he notes that the rabbis were familiar with pre-existing "legal formulary of the Ancient Near Eastern and Greco-Roman world" and states, "… it is clear that in some cases the tannaim envisaged other procedures, and that the rabbis were discussing common practices and their legal implications, not legislating them."[15]

In thinking of "minhag" in the fulsome sense suggested here, we shall hopefully perceive some of the "action and reaction" that Kemp refers to among the ordinary Jews and the amoraim of *Erets* Israel. By looking beyond explicit references to *minhag* and even beyond "what people were accustomed to do" in the Yerushalmi and instead considering rabbinic statements and anecdotes, indeed whole narratives, that reflect, comment upon, or reproduce what apparently were quotidian behaviors, we stand to gain a more informed appreciation of the nature and evolution of these practices. At the same time, what I am suggesting is very much a two-way street that avoids privileging the writings of the rabbis and indeed reads their narratives against the grain to learn much about what Robert Cover refers to as the "nomos," i.e., the ideal normative world, that the rabbis envisioned—and the very real world to which they belonged.[16] Drawing upon a few illustrations pertaining to ritual purity from my 2015 (rev. 2019) book *At the Intersection of Texts and Material Finds …*, I would like to demonstrate the extent to which literary and archaeological evidence sheds light upon rabbinic awareness of common practices, which in turn enables us to reassess aspects of both the development of rabbinic Judaism and the larger community of Jews who resided in Roman Palestine.

There is some evidence for the continued concern for impurity stemming from contact with a corpse after the destruction of the Temple in 70 C.E., but defilement arising from sexuality, specifically from male and female genital

---

14   Allen, *Law in the Making*, 149. Allen, 112–151, discusses at length the role of jurists in determining customary law.
15   Schiffman, "Reflections on the Deeds of Sale from the Judaean Desert in Light of Rabbinic Literature," 186.
16   Cover, "Nomos and Narrative." My thanks to Naomi Graetz, who in the question-and-answer period, reminded me of the relevance of Cover's work to the direction I am taking. I pursue this further in "'All Law Begins with Custom:' Rabbinic Awareness of Popular Practice."

emissions, was a particular concern of the rabbis and of non-rabbinic commoners into Late Antiquity and beyond.[17] The Mishnaic order Tohorot provides ample testimony to the determination of the tannaim to keep alive and regulate at least select purity practices. The inclusion of tractates dedicated to *miqva'ot*, vessels, and to the ramifications of the menstrual state should not be seen as either a reflection of the past when the Temple was the focal point of Jewish life or a last ditch effort by an emerging rabbinic movement to encourage at least the fastidious amongst its followers, perhaps members of *ḥavurot*, to preserve whatever they could of the ritual purity laws.[18] The introduction of "stepped pools" used for ritual immersion and of chalkstone vessels, which, at least according to the rabbis, protected food substances from impurity were, notably, developments that took place long before the Destruction and the emergence of a rabbinic movement. We now know, of course, that ritual baths and chalkstone vessels remained in widespread use until roughly the Bar Kokhba revolt (132–135 C.E.), especially in Judaea. And even recognizing the subsequent diminution in the quantity of both, there are significant finds, particularly of ritual baths, that take us into the Byzantine period, when there appears to have been an efflorescence of pools, at least in some villages and towns, as suggested especially by those uncovered at Khirbet Susiya.[19]

Ample comments attributed to tannaim and amoraim of *Erets* Israel testify to the awareness of popular ritual purity rites that sometimes went beyond what the rabbis themselves required. The late second-century C.E. tanna R. Simeon ben Eleazar appears to have had in mind his own times, when he reportedly proclaimed, "Come and see the extent to which purity has spread,"[20] a reference to the prevalence of concerns about menstrual and other sexual impurities that affected the preparation of *profane* food.[21] *Midreshei halakhah* repeatedly assert that the most difficult legal cases were those involving *tum'ah* and *tohorah*.[22] Indeed, we even hear that questions pertaining to impurities were the major concern of Moses when Jethro advised him how to handle his

---

17 See especially, Miller, *Intersection*, chapter eight (210–248): "Domestic Judaism and the 'Well-Ordered Bayit:' Who Bathed/Immersed in the Stepped Pools at Sepphoris and Why?" Also, see, Miller, "New Directions in the Study of Ritual Purity Practices."
18 Cf. Miller, *Intersection*, 221, n. 43.
19 See Amit and Adler, "The Observance of Ritual Purity after 70 C.E.;" and cf. Miller, *Intersection*, 22–29.
20 T.Shabbat 1:14 (ed. Lieberman, 2:3–4): אמ' ר' שמעון בן לעזר בוא וראה עד היכן פרצה טהרה.
21 For a different view of the period to which R. Simeon is referring, see Adler, "Tosefta Shabbat 1:14—'Come and See the Extent to Which Purity Had Spread.'" Cf. Miller, *Intersection*, 27 f.
22 See Miller, *Intersection*, 213.

case load in Exodus 18.[23] This projection upon the past undoubtedly stemmed from an awareness of a popular preoccupation with ritual purity matters in the time of the tannaim, which is especially reflected by the many cases (*ma'asim*) regarding menstruation brought before the rabbis in the Mishnah and the Tosefta.[24]

Not surprisingly, the rabbis take for granted the existence of artificial pools and, perhaps more importantly, *natural* venues that were readily available to all for immersion, both of which they regarded as "miqva'ot."[25] What remained for the rabbis was the prescription of what constitutes pure or sufficient quantity of rainwater (or, in the case of stone vessels, the situations in which they protect substances from becoming impure). Biblically prescribed or derived laws for purification following sexual emissions as well as popular fears of miasma are the most compelling explanations for the emergence of artificial pools, not only near vineyards, graves, and synagogues, but especially, at Sepphoris and elsewhere, in domestic settings, where special care, again, suggested or indicated by biblical sources, was apparently taken with regard to food preparation and consumption.[26]

The rabbis are quite revealing when it comes to popular practices and perceptions. In a series of anecdotes presented in the third chapter of Yerushalmi Berakhot (6c), we hear that R. Yose ben Ḥalafta, the second century Sepphorean tanna, attempted to persuade his donkey driver not to jeopardize his life when he insisted on immersing at night in a dangerous locale. The donkey driver was insistent because he had had sexual relations with a married woman who was also a menstruant. Although this account emphasizes the donkey driver's lack of character, who aside from his deeds fails to listen to a prominent rabbi and forfeits his life, it also testifies to a profound, popular dread of impurity. The same may be said of another account in this passage this time involving R. Yose

---

23   Mekhilta de'Rabbi Yishmael, Yitro, Amaleq 2.
24   Goodman, *State and Society in Roman Galilee*, 94–96. Cf. Miller, *Intersection*, 213–214.
25   See m.Miqva'ot. 1:1, which discusses six grades of *miqva'ot*, most of which are natural collections of water. The rabbis considered natural running water, that is, *mayim ḥayyim* ("living water") as having purification benefits exceeding those of artificial pools. *Mayim ḥayyim* does not include pools constructed by humans, despite modern-day misconceptions. Indeed, the artificial immersion pool was still evolving in the early centuries C.E., at least from the perspective of the Tannaim. In later periods, including our own, students of Talmudic sources have tended to project the notion of a fixed, artificial *miqveh* onto many a passage that has the more general and technically accurate usage in mind. See Miller, *Intersection*, 32–44 and 308–309, esp. n. 5.
26   Miller, *Intersection*, 207–208, and 223–240. See too my, "New Directions in the Study of Ritual Purity Practices."

ben Yose, a fourth-century amora, and a fellow passenger on a ship. The rabbi pleaded with the man, who apparently was a *ba'al qeri* (one who suffered a seminal emission), not to endanger his life by lowering himself into the sea to immerse. The *sugya* also reports that the guardian of a vineyard and a married woman were once deterred from an adulterous assignation because passersby appeared, making it impossible for the couple to discreetly locate an apparently natural, outdoor pool in which they could immerse afterwards!

Although these stories might suggest that the rabbis were only interested in relating popular ritual purity practices that they regarded as strict and absurd, the following observation attributed to the early third-century R. Yannai in the same *sugya* reveals that they were cognizant of the existence of a wide range of rites, many of which met with their approval: "I heard that some are lax [with regard to immersion after a seminal emission] and some are strict. Those who are strict increase their days in goodness. Those who are lax wash in drawn water (*she'uvin*) and those who are strict immerse in 'living water' (*mayim ḥayyim*, i. e., which are most efficacious for removing impurities)."[27]

Most importantly, it is obvious that the rabbis were not responsible for establishing many of the practices and rites that they describe. Popular perceptions of the purifying characteristics of water existed in the ancient Near East long before the rabbis and led, among the Jews—whether the Dead Sea Sect, the Hasmoneans, some belonging to the Herodian house, or others living in Judaea—to the introduction of stepped pools that the rabbis would later include in their typology of collections of water that constituted *miqva'ot*. The fact that the rabbis of *Erets* Israel were hard pressed to justify immersion following sexual relations and the washing of a *ba'al qeri* in advance of prayer or study of Torah, which they attributed to Ezra, is not surprising.[28] After all, these were popular practices that had appeal long after 70 C.E., as we know not only from the Geonic "List of Differences between the Babylonians and *the People of Israel (benei EY)*" but also from Christian sources contemporaneous to the rabbis.[29]

---

27   See Miller, *Intersection*, 234 n. 96 on the textual variants. Cf. b.Berakhot 22a.
28   Full immersion in advance of the Tefillah, the Shema, and/or grace after meals: M.Berakhot 3:4–6 and t.Berakhot 2:13. For the connection with Ezra see: y.Yoma' 8, 44d; y.Ta'anit 1, 64c; y.Megillah 4, 75a; and b.Berakhot 22b. Only b.Bava Qamma 82b specifies that the immersion was in preparation for the study of Torah. See Miller, *Intersection*, 224, n. 59.
29   See Didascalia Apostolorum 6:21 (ed. Stewart-Sykes, 251); John Chrysostom, Hom. in Matthew 15:1 (MPG 58, 516); and Margaliot, ed., *The Differences between the Easterners and the People of the Land of Israel*, 108–111. Cf. my discussion in *Intersection*, 210–241, esp. 234–236. Also, see Blidstein, *Purity, Community, and Ritual*, 55 and 193–197.

In sum, the rabbis were not the official mediators of ritual purity practices, many of which originated long before they were on the scene. The plunge pools in the *frigidaria* of Roman bathhouses that the rabbis considered as possibly suitable "miqva'ot" were being used by well-meaning commoners for ritual immersion, much as in medieval Egypt women had their own rite of "pouring" and in the Lower East Side of the early 20th century some immersed in pools situated in Turkish baths.[30]

The evolution of the synagogue provides a similar, instructive phenomenon. The synagogue is an institution that arose from communal, i.e., popular needs—and its origins also predate the rabbis. Neither its liturgy nor its architecture was determined by the rabbis, although they certainly had much to say about how they believed prayer should be conducted. Similarly, the rabbis relate little about the physical structure that constitutes an artificial *miqveh*. They are more preoccupied with the purity, quality, and amount of its rainwater which, at least according to them, could not be "drawn" by human hands. The sages were interested in the function of space and place—not in the actual construction or form of either ritual baths or synagogues.[31] Their self-perceived role was one of regulating *practices* that in many instances already existed.

In any event, the interest of the rabbis of *Erets* Israel in what everyday persons did and thought when it came to ritual purity very much conforms with their respect for "custom" in all its senses and applications. Much can obviously be learned if we think of "minhag" less as a legal category that affected the derivation of *halakhah* and more as a window into the world that enabled the rabbinic movement in *Erets* Israel to emerge and in many ways define itself. And while the comments and anecdotes of the Palestinian rabbis who incorporated *minhag* into their deliberations reveal their indebtedness to the everyday practices of the Jews among whom they lived, they also testify to the persistence, development, and transformation of some observances that outlasted the destruction of the Temple and survived despite the challenges of life among the Romans.

In conclusion, the amoraim of *Erets* Israel routinely noted and took into consideration preexisting popular practices, something that is evident not only from their specific references to "what people were accustomed to do" or to local *minhagim*, but also from the anecdotes they tell about non-rabbinic commoners. In some instances, external material and documentary evidence exists supporting this assessment, as we have seen with regard to stepped pools used

---

30 See Miller, *Intersection*, 34, 40–43, and 297–306. Also, cf. now Krakowski, "Maimonides' Menstrual Reform in Egypt," esp., 253 f.

31 Ibid., 46. Cf. Schwarzer, "The Architecture of Talmud."

for ritual immersion and, as I demonstrate elsewhere, marital rites.[32] From the Talmud Yerushalmi we get the distinct impression that Palestinian amoraim were inclined to grant substantial authority to the practices of everyday persons, certainly more than their counterparts in Babylonia would allow. This becomes increasingly evident in the Geonic period, as Pirqoi's remarks indicate.

It is likely that the rabbis of Roman Palestine were compelled to consider the practices of commoners in all relevant spheres of *halakhah* because they were more engaged with non-rabbis than their counterparts in Babylonia. As Richard Kalmin has demonstrated, the Babylonian amoraim are depicted as less invested in and physically distant from non-rabbinic commoners. They tended to view the world from the *bet midrash* and, consequently, regarded Jewish life as revolving around and emanating from their way of life.[33] To be sure, the amoraim of Babylonia regarded custom as vital to the halakhic process, but they more precisely circumscribed and articulated its authority. Their efforts would ultimately lead to the fuller conceptualization of "minhag" found among the Geonim and later halakhic authorities.[34] Nevertheless, a bottom-up approach to custom in Babylonia would undoubtedly also be revealing, despite the limited availability of archaeological materials, as it would similarly provide fresh insights into the lives of ordinary Babylonian Jews. Especially interesting would be an inquiry into how precisely the inclination of the Babylonian amoraim to disallow the influence of *minhag* in instances involving a biblical prohibition affected the formulation and presentation of pertinent anecdotes and narratives in the Bavli—and how that colors our perspective of life beyond rabbinic circles in Babylonia.

Certainly, thinking about popular practices from the perspective advocated here affords a glimpse into the world of the very people among whom the rabbis of *Erets* Israel lived and undoubtedly hoped to attract to their way of life. A comment of the eminent legal scholar, Sir John William Salmond, captures the dynamic that I have attempted to describe:[35]

> Custom, is to society what law is to the state ... Nothing, therefore, is more natural than that, when the state begins to evolve out of the society, the

---

[32] See "'All Law Begins with Custom:' Rabbinic Awareness of Popular Practice," 389–394, and Miller, "Why Sheva Berakhot?"

[33] Kalmin, *The Sage in Jewish Society of Late Antiquity*, 27–50; and Kalmin, *Jewish Babylonia between Persia and Roman Palestine*, 37–86.

[34] Here see especially Libson, "Halakhah and Reality in the Gaonic Period," and Lifshitz, "'Minhag' and Its Place in the Normative Classification of 'Oral Law'," 190–241.

[35] Salmond, *Jurisprudence*, 144–145.

law of the state should ... be in great part modelled upon and coincident with the customs of the society.

This is precisely the point of *Soferim* 14:16 when it states ונהגו כן העם שאין הלכה נקבעת עד שיהא מנהג: "And so the people practiced, *since a halakhah cannot be determined unless it has been a custom.*"

Acknowledgements

This article presents an overview of my fully documented and detailed discussion, "'All Law Begins with Custom:' Rabbinic Awareness of Popular Practice and Its Implications for the Study of the Jews of Roman Palestine," which I completed while a Fellow of the University of Connecticut Humanities Institute in 2018–2019. I am honored to have been included in a conference and volume in memory of Professor Yaakov Elman *z"l*, whose collegiality, insights, and frequently noted *menschlichkeit* I have much appreciated and benefited from over the years. We especially shared an interest in looking behind Talmudic narratives to the larger culture that enables us to make better sense of them, making this article a fitting contribution to this volume.

Bibliography

Allen, Carleton Kemp. *Law in the Making*, 7th ed. Oxford: Clarendon, 1964.

Adler, Yonatan. "Tosefta Shabbat 1:14—'Come and See the Extent to Which Purity Had Spread,' An Archaeological Perspective on the Historical Background to a Late Tannaitic Passage." In *Talmuda De-Eretz Israel: Archaeology and the Rabbis in Late Antique Palestine*, edited by Steven Fine and Aaron Koller, 63–82. Berlin: De Gruyter, 2014.

Amit, David and Adler, Yonatan. "The Observance of Ritual Purity after 70 C.E.: A Reevaluation of the Evidence in Light of Recent Archaeological Discoveries." In *"Follow the Wise": Studies in Jewish History and Culture in Honor of Lee I. Levine*, edited by Zeev Weiss, Oded Irshai, Jodi Magness, and Seth Schwartz, 121–143. Winona Lake, IN: Eisenbrauns. 2010.

Bederman, David J., *Custom as a Source of Law*. Cambridge: Cambridge University Press, 2010.

Broyde, Michael J. "Custom as a Source of Jewish Law: Some Religious Reflections on David J. Bederman's *Custom as a Source of Law*." *Emory Law Journal* 61 (2012): 1037–1045.

Blidstein, Moshe. *Purity, Community, and Ritual in Early Christian Literature*. Oxford: Oxford University Press, 2017.

Cover, Robert. "Nomos and Narrative." In *Narrative, Violence, and the Law: The Essays of Robert Cover*, edited by Martha Minow, Michael Ryan, and Austin Sarat, 95–172. Ann Arbor: University of Michigan Press, 1992.

Elon, Menachem. *Jewish Law: History, Sources, and Principles*, trans. B. Auerbach and M.J. Sykes, 4 vols. Philadelphia, PA: Jewish Publication Society, 1994.

Ginzberg, Louis, *Genizah Studies in Memory of Doctor Solomon Schechter II*. Geonic and Early Karaitic Halakah. New York: Jewish Theological Seminary, 1929. [Hebrew]

Goodman, Martin. *State and Society in Roman Galilee, AD 132–212*. Totowa, NJ: Rowman & Allanheld, 1983.

Hasan-Rokem, Galit. *Web of Life: Folklore and Midrash in Rabbinic Literature*. Stanford: Stanford University Press, 2000.

Kalmin, Richard. *The Sage in Jewish Society of Late Antiquity*. London: Routledge, 1999.

Kalmin, Richard. *Jewish Babylonia between Persia and Roman Palestine*. Oxford: Oxford University, 2006.

Krakowski, Eve. "Maimonides' Menstrual Reform in Egypt." *Jewish Quarterly Review* 110:2 (2020): 245–289.

Kwall, Roberta, Rosenthal. *The Myth of the Cultural Jew: Culture and Law in Jewish Tradition*. Oxford: Oxford University, 2015.

Lewin, Benjamin, Manasseh. Otzar ha-Gaonim: *Thesaurus of the Gaonic Responsa and Commentaries following the order of the Talmudic Tractates*. 13 vols. Haifa, 1928–Jerusalem, 1944. [Hebrew]

Libson, Gideon. "Halakhah and Reality in the Gaonic Period: Taqqanah, Minhag, Tradition and Consensus: Some Observations." In *The Jews of Medieval Islam: Community, Society and Identity*, edited by Daniel H. Frank, 67–100. Leiden: Brill, 1995.

Lifshitz, Berachyahu. "'Minhag' and Its Place in the Normative Classification of 'Oral Law'," *Annual of the Institute for Research in Jewish Law* 24 (2007):123–264. [Hebrew]

Margaliot, Mordechai, ed. *The Differences between the Easterners and the People of the Land of Israel*. Jerusalem, 1937. [Hebrew]

Miller, Stuart S. "'All Law Begins with Custom:' Rabbinic Awareness of Popular Practice and its Implications for the Study of the Jews of Roman Palestine." In *From Scrolls to Tradition: A Festschrift Honoring Professor Lawrence H. Schiffman*, edited by Stuart S. Miller, Michael D. Swartz, Steven Fine, Naomi Grunhaus, and Alex P. Jassen, 350–397. Leiden: Brill, 2021.

Miller, Stuart S. *At the Intersection of Texts and Material Finds: Stepped Pools, Stone Vessels and Ritual Purity among the Jews of Roman Galilee. Journal of Ancient Judaism Supplements Series*. 2nd revised edition, Göttingen: Vandenhoeck & Ruprecht, 2019.

Miller, Stuart S. "New Directions in the Study of Ritual Purity Practices: Implications of the Sepphoris Finds." In *Sepphoris III: The Architecture, Stratigraphy, and Artifacts of the Western Summit of Sepphoris*. 2 vols., edited by Eric M. Meyers, Carol L. Meyers, and Benjamin D. Gordon, 1:445–475. University Park, PA: Eisenbrauns, 2018.

Miller, Stuart S. *Sages and Commoners in Late Antique 'Ereẓ Israel: A Philological Inquiry into Local Traditions in Talmud Yerushalmi*. Tübingen: Mohr-Siebeck, 2006.

Miller, Stuart S. "Stepped Pools, Stone Vessels, and other Identity Markers of 'Complex Common Judaism,'" *JSJ* 41 (2010): 214–243.

Miller, Stuart S. "The Study of 'Talmudic Israel' and/or Roman Palestine: Where Matters Stand." In *The Faces of Torah: Studies in the Texts and Contexts of Ancient Judaism in Honor of Steven Fraade*, edited by Christine Hayes, Tzvi Novick, Michal Bar-Asher Segal, 433–454. Vandenhoeck & Ruprecht, 2017.

Miller, Stuart S. "Why Sheva Berakhot?—From the Inclusion of 'New Faces' to an 'Act of Loving Kindness'—or Vice Versa?" *Tradition*. (Spring, 2018): 8–34.

Salmond, John W. *Jurisprudence*, 5th ed. London: Stevens and Haynes, 1916.

Schiffman, Lawrence, H. "Reflections on the Deeds of Sale from the Judaean Desert in Light of Rabbinic Literature." In *Law in the Documents of the Judaean Desert*, edited by Ranon Katzoff and David M. Schaps, 185–203. Leiden: Brill, 2005.

Schwarzer, Mitchell, "The Architecture of Talmud." *Journal of the Society of Architectural Historians* 60 (2001): 474–487.

Soloveitchik, Haym. *Collected Essays*. Oxford: Littman Library of Jewish Civilization, 2014.

Ta-Shma, Israel. *Early Franco-German Ritual and Custom*. 3rd ed. Jerusalem: Magnes, 1999. [Hebrew]

Thomas, J.A.C. "Custom and Roman Law." *Tijdschrift voor Rechtsgeschiedenis* 31 (1963): 39–53.

CHAPTER 4

The Roman Freedman and the *Ḥalal*: The Legal Models That Shaped Rabbinic Law on the Status of Converts in Marriage

Yael Wilfand

The Hebrew Bible (Tanakh) does not contain a notion of conversion, which is to say, a procedure that enables outsiders to undergo an immediate change in status to become Israelites.[1] Despite the existence of de facto ways to join Israel in the Tanakh (through marriage, for example), there is no biblical law regulating such a process. Consequently, this realm of rabbinic legislation cannot be derived directly from biblical instruction. The usage of the Hebrew word *ger* (pl. *gerim*; fem. sing. *giyoret*) reflects these changes: in the Hebrew Bible, *ger* denotes a stranger or a resident alien,[2] whereas in rabbinic literature, this word often refers to a proselyte or a convert.[3] By the second-third century CE, conversion was established and certain norms, such as the prohibition against female converts marrying priests, seem to have become standard among Jews.[4] Yet, in the absence of explicit biblical directives and given the contrasting attitudes toward *gerim* in rabbinic literature, different legal models were applied to define their position. This article examines tannaitic approaches to converts' eligibility for marriage within Jewish society. The Mishnah and Tosefta each list groups within the Jewish people that are based on lineage. In that hierarchy, priests have the highest standing, followed by Levites and Israelites. The

---

1 Even though a lengthy process may have preceded conversion, rabbinic literature envisions a transformative moment, after which that individual is considered a Jew.
2 According Koehler and Baumgartner, *Lexicon*, 201, *ger* is defined as "a man who (alone or with his family) leaves village and tribe because of war, famine, epidemic, blood guilt etc. and seeks shelter and residence at another place, where his right of landed property, marriage and taking part in jurisdiction, cult and war has been curtailed." Cf. Na'aman, "Sojourners."
3 On Qumran, see, for example, Berthelot, "La notion de גר"; Harrington, "Keeping Outsiders Out," 193–194, 196–197; Palmer, *Converts in the Dead Sea Scrolls*.
4 The prohibition against priests marrying female converts probably became well established during the Second Temple period, as some scholars understand from Philo, *Special Laws*, 1.111 and Josephus, *Against Apion*, 1.31; by the mid-second century, this restriction seems to have become a given. On Josephus and marital conditions for priests, see, for example, Schwartz, "Doing like Jews," 99–105.

lowest strata include the offspring of adulterous women and those who do not know their parents' identity. These passages detail the permissibility of marriage between their members. The question I examine is where are converts situated within this ranking?

Scholars have explained these varying rabbinic stances through prisms of stringency and leniency; I argue that they may be attributed to different legal approaches. The sources for these diverse rabbinic perspectives on the status of converts have been analyzed extensively, most notably by Shaye J.D. Cohen, Gary G. Porton, and Christine Hayes;[5] yet this material has not typically been considered in light of distinct legal frameworks, particularly Roman models. Moreover, until recently, the status of converts in rabbinic *halakhah* was rarely examined in comparison to Roman law and attitudes toward new citizens (although this direction is suggested by Moshe Lavee).[6] I investigate this theme by examining how two legal positions, which originated in Israelite tradition and Roman law respectively, may have contributed to rabbinic understandings of proselytes.[7] These approaches reflect distinct methods for defining status: The Roman model often views status within the law of persons as a matter of legal or social fact; therefore, it is ascribed rather than essential, and not heritable. Its default position is to recognize full legal personhood. The Israelite model by contrast regards persons to be imbued with an essential status that is derived from their lineage and is affected by both their ancestors' sexual histories as well as their own physical conditions. Thus, matters such as bodily integrity are seen as contributing factors to an inherent reality; cases that cannot be readily interpreted according to genealogical standards are sometimes resolved via analogous or related examples.

The relationship between rabbinic *halakhah* and Roman law has been discussed by scholars who recognize a "conceptual similarity between the Roman and the rabbinic systems."[8] Yet this subject is highly contested. On one end of

---

5 Cohen, *Beginnings of Jewishness*, 308–340 (although he considers the Roman law of persons in association with other legal sources and issues, as on pages 293–298, Cohen does not treat the topics discussed here in that context); Porton, *The Stranger*, 18–21; 76–78; 155–165; Hayes, *Gentile* Impurities, 164–192; Hayes, "The other," 243–269, 254–255; Hayes, *Divine Law*, 215–218.
6 According to Lavee, "No Boundaries," 100: "It is possible that the concept we find in Palestinian sources, and maybe also the original motivation for this legislation is close in nature to Greco-Roman legal perception of citizenship and kinship." He broadly discusses several similarities between Greek and Roman laws and Jewish conversion in Lavee, "A Convert is Like a Newborn Child," 275–279, but without addressing the parallels presented in this paper.
7 I have proposed this approach in recent articles: Wilfand, "Freedwomen"; Wilfand, "Roman Concepts of Citizenship."
8 Cohen, *Beginnings of Jewishness*, 295; Cohen, *Jewish and Roman Law*, 155–158; and, in Cohen,

the spectrum are scholars who reject the influence of Roman law on *halakhah*. For example, Ronan Katzoff writes: "I have not yet seen a single convincing argument for any particular instance of reception of Roman law into Jewish law."[9] Moshe Simon-Shoshan clarifies how these scholars explain parallels between the two legal systems:

> ... the similarities between the Mishnah and Roman legal texts are the results of the parallel development of two legal cultures that operated in the context of similar historical and cultural forces. These two bodies of work might best be viewed as products of a common experience of life in the Mediterranean world during the centuries around the turn of the Common Era.[10]

This perspective does not address the realities of the empire, its power and influence. In that context, the similarities between Roman law and rabbinic *halakhah* cannot be simply attributed to a shared Mediterranean experience. Indeed, at the opposite end of the spectrum are scholars who identify direct Roman impact on *halakhah*, often in relation to the Roman concept of citizenship and, particularly, Roman laws on civil status. For instance, on the standing of captives, Orit Malka and Yakir Paz write:

> ... legal principles of Roman law not only had an impact upon rabbinic norms and legal reasoning but also permeated and reshaped the very foundations of rabbinic jurisprudence, including, most strikingly, the fundamental relation between Jewish law and its subjects.[11]

"The Judaean legal tradition," 127, he adds: "It is easy to draw parallels and contrasts between mishnaic law and the law of the Hellenistic and Roman Empires, but it is not easy to determine influence or borrowing in either direction." See also Jackson, "Roman Influence on the Halakha," 170–203; on page 170, he writes: "And we may expect that Jews involved in local administration [...] will be familiar with some aspects of Roman public law, especially in matters of citizenship." Mélèze-Modrzejewski, "Filios Suos Tantum," 111 suggests: "In spite of certain differences between the Roman jurists and the Rabbis, a 'conceptual similarity' between the rabbinic and the Roman systems cannot be denied." For a general survey of studies on the relationship between Roman law and *halakhah*, see Rosen-Zvi, "Is the Mishnah a Roman Composition?" 487–490.

9   Katzoff, "Children of Intermarriage," 286.
10 Simon-Shoshan, *Stories of the Law*, 82.
11 Malka and Paz, "*Ab hostibus captus*," 170. See also Hayes, "Genealogy," 73–89; Wilfand, "A Proselyte."

This debate stems in part from the lack of consensus on how to define "influence" among legal systems (here, Roman law on *halakhah*). In this study, I apply a broad approach, arguing that influence does not necessarily signify imitation of every detail of a Roman law (namely its adoption "as is"), nor does it require access to written law, incorporation of Latin or Greek terminology, or acceptance of the legal or social reasoning that motivated Roman legislators. Rather, in the case discussed here, Roman norms, notions, and laws may provide a conceptual framework for rabbinic thinking on converts. As inhabitants of the Roman Empire, the sages were aware that non-Roman individuals could be granted Roman citizenship, whether in theory or from personal experience (rabbis who were active circa 212 CE, when Roman citizenship was granted to the free inhabitants of the empire, certainly had first-hand knowledge of a change in status from being Israelite to becoming both Roman and Israelite). The sages were also familiar with Roman laws regarding freed slaves who could become citizens upon manumission. The rabbis integrated these standards into their readings of the Tanakh, thereby formulating new categories and regulations when classifying the status of converts.

In this article, I present a dynamic whereby competing models are suggested by different sages. The impact of one—the model of the Roman freedman—increased over time, while the other—the model of the *ḥalal*—was eventually rejected. Rabbinic *halakhah* imported select aspects of Roman treatment of freed slaves, adapting and implementing them according to its needs. The sages then applied these elements to their interpretations of certain verses from the Tanakh that did not originally mention converts. Before analyzing the central tannaitic material—especially from Mishnah Qiddushin, Chapter Four and Tosefta Qiddushin, Chapter Five—a survey of the biblical instruction that they discuss is essential.

Biblical Background

Deuteronomy enumerates persons and peoples that are prohibited from acceptance in Israel:

(2) לֹא-יָבֹא פְצוּעַ-דַּכָּא וּכְרוּת שָׁפְכָה, בִּקְהַל ה'.

(3) לֹא-יָבֹא מַמְזֵר, בִּקְהַל ה'. גַּם דּוֹר עֲשִׂירִי, לֹא-יָבֹא לוֹ בִּקְהַל ה'.

(4) לֹא-יָבֹא עַמּוֹנִי וּמוֹאָבִי, בִּקְהַל ה'. גַּם דּוֹר עֲשִׂירִי, לֹא-יָבֹא לָהֶם בִּקְהַל ה' עַד-עוֹלָם. (5) עַל-דְּבַר אֲשֶׁר לֹא-קִדְּמוּ אֶתְכֶם, בַּלֶּחֶם וּבַמַּיִם, בַּדֶּרֶךְ, בְּצֵאתְכֶם מִמִּצְרָיִם; וַאֲשֶׁר שָׂכַר עָלֶיךָ אֶת-בִּלְעָם בֶּן-בְּעוֹר, מִפְּתוֹר אֲרַם נַהֲרַיִם—לְקַלְלֶךָּ. (6) וְלֹא-אָבָה ה' אֱלֹהֶיךָ, לִשְׁמֹעַ אֶל-בִּלְעָם, וַיַּהֲפֹךְ ה' אֱלֹהֶיךָ לְּךָ אֶת-הַקְּלָלָה, לִבְרָכָה. כִּי אֲהֵבְךָ, ה' אֱלֹהֶיךָ. (7) לֹא-תִדְרֹשׁ שְׁלֹמָם, וְטֹבָתָם, כָּל-יָמֶיךָ, לְעוֹלָם.

(2) No one whose testicles are crushed or whose penis has been severed shall enter the congregation of the Lord.

(3) No *mamzer* shall enter the congregation of the Lord. Even to the tenth generation, none of their descendants shall enter the congregation of the Lord.

(4) No Ammonite or Moabite shall enter the congregation of the Lord. Even to the tenth generation, none of their descendants shall enter the congregation of the Lord, (5) because they did not meet you with food and water on your journey out of Egypt, and because they hired against you Balaam son of Beor, from Pethor of Mesopotamia, to curse you. (6) Yet the Lord your God refused to heed Balaam; the Lord your God turned the curse into a blessing for you, because the Lord your God loved you. (7) You shall never promote their welfare or their prosperity as long as you live. (Deuteronomy 23:2–7; verses 1–7 in NRSV, slightly modified)

This passage conveys three criteria that limit entry to God's congregation (*qahal*)—two concern individuals and the third specifies nations. The word *qahal* (pl. *qehalim*) has several definitions, most notably: community; those who gather for specific purpose; and, an assembly of select Israelites, particularly adult males or representatives. Scholars debate the exact meaning of the recurrent phrase "he shall not enter (*lo yav'o*) the congregation (*qahal*) of the Lord" (verses 2–4). Some explain that these laws aim to identify who can participate in Israelite assemblies and, therefore, have full membership in Israel (including holding positions of formal leadership and serving as judges). Others read this section as a description of who may take part in the cult. However, it has also been suggested that the term *"yav'o b-..."* could signify marriage (as in 1 Kings 11:1–2). Moreover, it has been argued that the placement of these laws, immediately after listing prohibited sexual relations, implies that those who are not included in God's *qahal* cannot wed Israelites.[12]

While several interpretations are suggested for this prohibition against entering "the congregation of the Lord," the sages consistently read this phrase in Deuteronomy 23 as inherently related to marriage or cohabitation.[13] Indeed, in the rabbinic texts presented below, it is not always clear whether marriage, cohabitation or sexual relations are being discussed. In some sources, we find the root *n-ś-'* which, in that context, means "to wed." But others use the phrase *"lavo ze ba-ze,"* literally "to enter each other," which may be translated as: "to marry each other," "to cohabit with each other" or "to have sexual relations." Where applicable, I offer more than one option; yet, in some cases, the ambiguity remains.

For our discussion of converts, let us look briefly at the prohibitions that address Israelites who cannot have full membership in Israel (Deuteronomy 23:2 and 3). The first applies to men whose genitals were crushed or mutilated, probably eunuchs. This ban is related to a physical condition. The second exclusion uses the term *mamzer*, whose etymology is unclear; it is rendered "born of an illicit union" in NSRV and "misbegotten" in JPS. In rabbinic texts, *mamzer* is defined as one who was born to an adulterous woman or from incestuous sexual contact. This transgression damages the status of the child and any offspring from this line, thereby incurring a lasting impact on their lineage. While Deuteronomy states that this prohibition affects even the "tenth generation" of *mamzerim*, some commentators understand this phrase to mean "forever."[14] Following the rabbinic reading of "enter the congregation of the Lord" in relation to marriage, restrictions are imposed on these two categories with respect to matrimony and sexual conduct, nevertheless they are considered Jews who are fully required to practice the commandments.[15] Before

---

12   The literature on the definition of *qahal* is extensive, among them: Falk, "Those Excluded from the Congregation"; Cohen, *Beginnings of Jewishness*, 248–252; Tigay, *Deuteronomy*, 564–565. See also Koehler and Baumgartner, *Lexicon*, 1079.
13   Falk, "Those Excluded from the Congregation," 343; Cohen, *Beginnings of Jewishness*, 249.
14   See Sifre Deuteronomy 248–249 (Finkelstein edition, pages 277–278); Tigay, *Deuteronomy*, 567.
15   See examples in Tosefta Berakhot 5:14; Rosh Hashanah 2:5; Megillah 2:7; Menaḥot 10:13.

THE ROMAN FREEDMAN AND THE ḤALAL

investigating whether or not a convert may be included in the *qahal*, let us survey tannaitic classifications of groups within Israel, determined by their pedigree.

Israelite Groups Based on Lineage

Tannaitic literature lists at least ten categories that are based on ancestry within the Jewish people:

עשרה יחסים עלו מבבל. כהני לויי ישראי׳ חללי גירי חרורי ממזירי ונתיני שתוקי ואסופי.

> Ten genealogical classes (*yoḥasim*)[16] came up (to the Land of Israel) from Babylonia:
> priests, Levites, Israelites, *ḥalaley* (offspring of priests and women who were ineligible to marry into the priesthood), converts, *ḥarurey* (freed slaves), *mamzerey* (offspring of an adulterous woman or one born from an incestuous sexual union), *netiney* (category unclear), *shtuqey* ("silenced ones": those whose fathers' identities are unknown), and *'asufey* (those who know neither their fathers' nor mothers' identities). (Mishnah Qiddushin 4:1)

This mishnah envisions ten classes among the Israelites that returned from Babylonia.[17] As noted explicitly in the Jerusalem Talmud (Qiddushin 4:1, 65a), the idea of examining the genealogical lineage (*yoḥasim*, from the root *y-ḥ-s/ś*) of those who came from Babylonia originates in Nehemiah:

וַיִּתֵּן אֱלֹהַי אֶל־לִבִּי, וָאֶקְבְּצָה אֶת־הַחֹרִים וְאֶת־הַסְּגָנִים וְאֶת־הָעָם לְהִתְיַחֵשׂ; וָאֶמְצָא, סֵפֶר הַיַּחַשׂ הָעוֹלִים בָּרִאשׁוֹנָה, וָאֶמְצָא, כָּתוּב בּוֹ.

> My God put it into my mind to assemble the noble, the prefects, and the people, in order to register them by family (*lehityaḥes*). I found the

---

16 Koren, "Look through Your Book," 419, translates "ten *yoḥasim*" as "ten types of lineage."

17 Cohen, *Jewish and Roman Law*, 130, suggests a Roman context for this classification: "In M. Qiddushin IV:1, we read that עשרה יוחסין עלו מבבל ["Ten genealogical classes (*yoḥasim*) came up from Babylonia"], which classifies persons in ten different categories with respect to their status concerning marriage. Gaius, in the *Institutes* similarly discusses the legal effect of matrimony between Romans, Latins, *dediticii*, *peregrini*, slaves and freedman." Compare Satlow, *Jewish Marriage*, 150–151.

genealogical register (*sefer hayahas*) of those who were the first to come up, and there I found written: [...] (7:5; JPS).

Mishnah Qiddushin 4:1 assumes that these "classes" or *yohasim* were maintained long after the Israelites' return from Babylonia.[18] Thus, rather than being single-generation designations, these descriptors also applied to future offspring. Status was broadly transmitted from a father to his children yet, according to Mishnah Qiddushin 3:12, if the parental union is not valid or involves a transgression, the lower status applied.[19] I will return to Mishnah Qiddushin 4:1 with a detailed analysis below; here I present an overview of these groups to facilitate our examination of the status of converts:

1) Priests: The highest class in Israel; they were considered descendants of Moses's brother Aaron (a subset of the tribe of Levi). Jewish priesthood was transmitted from father to son.
2) Levites: Descendants of the tribe of Levi. Alongside the priests, they also served in the Temple.
3) Israelites: Ranked beneath the priests and the Levites; they were also descendants of Jacob.
4) *Halalim* (sing. *halal*; sing. fem. *halalah*): The children of priests whose mothers were disqualified from marrying priests, following Leviticus 21:7. A *halalah* may not marry a priest.
5) Converts: As mentioned above, the procedure for conversion to Judaism developed during the Second Temple period and had been fully established by the final stages of the tannaitic period (second-third centuries CE). Some scholars trace the roots of conversion to the Babylonian exile, while others suggest that it originated in the Hasmonean period or even later.[20] Thus, even though this mishnah lists converts among the classes

---

18 As Koren, "Look through Your Book," 435, notes: "It seems that the mishna echoes Nehemiah by introducing the list of returnees with the term יחסים. This mishna thus naturally places the topic of genealogy (יחסים) in the historical framework of the return from Babylonia."

19 On the categorization of m.Qiddushin 3:12 and Roman concepts that may have influenced this text, see Cohen, *Jewish and Roman Law*, 133–136; Cohen, *Beginnings of Jewishness*, 273–276, 293–298; Furstenberg, "The Rabbis and the Roman Citizenship Model," 183–185. Not all sources and opinions follow this rule; see, for example, t.Qiddushin 5:2: "A male convert and a freedman are (lit. is) permitted to [marry] (or to cohabit with) a *mamzeret*, and the child [of that couple] is a *mamzer*."

20 On this issue, see Bamberger, *Proselytism*, 13–27. Compare with Chapter Four in Cohen, *Beginnings of Jewishness*; Novak, "Gentiles," 660; Schwartz, "Doing like Jews or Becoming a Jew?"

that came from Babylonia after the exile, it is unlikely that conversion as a mechanism for joining the Israelite community existed at that stage; otherwise we would expect more references to this practice in Second Temple biblical literature.

6) Freed slaves: According to rabbinic literature, servitude within a Jewish household offered an avenue for non-Jews to join Judaism. For male slaves, circumcision was a prerequisite for service in a Jewish household (following Genesis 17:12 and Exodus 12:43–44).[21] Yet conversion was completed only after a slave had been manumitted.[22] This process resembles the Roman practice whereby former slaves of Roman citizens often received Roman citizenship following their release.[23] Therefore, it has been suggested that rabbinic laws for manumitting non-Jewish slaves reflect this Roman model.[24] Indeed, the possibility that foreign slaves could become part of Israel after being freed does not appear in the Tanakh, for that source does not envision their manumission.[25]

7) *Mamzerim*: As mentioned above, according to Mishnah Yevamot 4:13 and Qiddushin 3:12, *mamzerim* were born to adulterous women or from incestuous sexual contact (most of the prohibitions are listed in Leviticus 18–20).[26]

8) *Netinim* (sing. *natin*): In the book of Ezra, *netinim* are listed among those who came from Babylonia: "All the *netinim* and the descendants of Solomon's servants were three hundred ninety-two" (Ezra 2:58). According to the Jerusalem Talmud Qiddushin 4:1, 65b and Babylonian Talmud Yevamot 78b–79a, *netinim* are descendants of the Gibeonites mentioned in Joshua, Chapter Nine. The Talmud attributes the origin of this designation to Joshua 9:27: "But on that day Joshua made them (*va-yitnem*) hewers of wood and drawers of water for the congregation and for

---

21 Urbach, "*Halakhot* regarding Slavery," 162. For similarities between converts and freedmen, see Dohrmann, "Manumission," 59; 252 notes 52, 54.
22 Hezser, *Jewish Slavery*, 36–39.
23 Gaius, *Institutes*, 1.16–17. Gardner, *Being a Roman Citizen*, 8–11.
24 Hezser, "Slaves and Slavery," 134; Dohrmann, "Manumission," 56, 61: "The big picture of enfranchisement of alien slaves is in the end most plausibly explained by Roman influence."
25 Exodus 21:2–11, Leviticus 25:39–46, and Deuteronomy 15:12–18 present laws regarding slavery. These passages primarily focus on Hebrew slaves. Only Leviticus 25:44–46 discusses non-Israelite slaves and differentiates Israelite slaves, who are ultimately freed (the timeframe for manumission varies in these biblical passages), from non-Israelite slaves, whose servitude is permanent.
26 For a survey of scholarly treatment of *mazerim*, see Monnickendam, "The Exposed Child," 10–11, note 54.

the altar of the Lord, to continue to this day, in the place that he should choose." In rabbinic texts, the *natin* is often paired with the *mamzer* on issues related to marriage.²⁷

9) *Shtuqim* ("silenced ones"): The paternity of these individuals is unknown.
10) *'Asufim* (sing. *'asufi*): These individuals do not know the identity of either parent. The origin of this term is based on Psalms 27:10: "Though my father and mother abandon me, the Lord will take me (*ya'asfeni*)." In rabbinic texts, this Hebrew root (*'-s-f*; "to gather" or "to be picked up") refers to those who were abandoned by their parents.²⁸

Whereas the first three categories—priests, Levites and Israelites—are undoubtedly included in "the congregation of the Lord," and *mamzerim* (following Deuteronomy 23:3), *netinim, shtuqim*, and *'asufim* are excluded, the status of converts is debated in our sources.

Who Belongs to "the Congregation of the Lord"?

Tosefta Qiddushin 5:1 presents two opinions on the status of converts:

(A) גירי וחרורי ממזרי ונתיני שתוקי ואסופי וכל האסורין לבא בקהל מותרין לבוא זה בזה דברי ר׳ מאיר

(B) ר׳ יהודה אומ׳ ארבעה קהלות הן קהל כהנים קהל לוים קהל ישראל קהל גרים והשאר מותרין לבא זה בזה

(C) וחכמים אומ׳ שלש קהלות הן קהל כהנים קהל לוים קהל ישראל

A) Converts, *ḥarurey* (freed slaves), *mamzerey, netiney, shtuqey*, and *'asufey*, and all those who are forbidden from marrying (or cohabiting; lit. "to enter"; *lavo*) into the congregation (*qahal*) are permitted to marry each other (or to cohabit; *lavo ze ba-ze*).²⁹ [These are] the words of Rabbi Meir.

B) Rabbi Yehudah says: "There are four congregations (*qahalot*): a congregation of priests (*qahal kohanim*), a congregation of Levites (*qahal leviyim*), a congregation of Israelites (*qahal israel*), a congregation of converts

---

27 On the differentiation between *netinim* in biblical and rabbinic sources, see Koren, "Look through Your Book," 436. See also Baumgarten, "The Exclusion of Netinim." For a survey of scholarly literature on *netinim*, see Monnickendam, "The Exposed Child," 11, note 55.

28 More on this category in Monnickendam, "The Exposed Child," 9–14.

29 Koren, "Look through Your Book," 419, translates "are permitted *lavo ze ba-ze*" as "are permitted to cohabit with each other."

(*qahal gerim*), and the rest are permitted to marry each other (or to cohabit; *lavo ze ba-ze*)."

C) But the sages say: "There are three congregations: a congregation of priests (*qahal kohanim*), a congregation of Levites (*qahal leviyim*), [and] a congregation of Israelites (*qahal israel*)." [...]

This passage from the Tosefta offers two competing views regarding the status of converts within Israel. The source is probably a composite of two units since sections B+C—without "and the rest are permitted to marry (or to cohabit with) each other"[30]—appear as a single unit in both Sifre Deuteronomy 247 and y.Qiddushin 4:1, 65c. Although Section A does not focus on converts per se, its juxtaposition with Sections B+C contextualizes it within a discussion concerning whether converts belong to the *qahal* and, particularly, if they are allowed to wed those who "shall not enter the congregation of the Lord." I would posit that these two contrasting opinions—one attributed to both Rabbi Meir and the sages (A and C), and the other to Rabbi Yehudah—are based on a distinct legal perspective for explaining the status of the *ger*.

Rabbi Meir, a fourth-generation tanna who was active in the mid-second century, draws on the biblical phrase: "[He] shall not enter (*lo yavo*) ... to the congregation (*qahal*) of the Lord" (Deuteronomy 23:2). From this verse, he incorporates the root *b-w-'* and the word *qahal* in a ruling that bans several groups (that are not mentioned in Deuteronomy) from the ability to "enter" (marry or cohabit; *lavo*) "into the congregation." He permits converts (and freed slaves) to marry or cohabit with those whom members of the *qahal* cannot wed. Thus, like the sages (C), Rabbi Meir places proselytes outside the congregation. However, whereas Rabbi Meir focuses on those who are excluded from the congregation, Rabbi Yehudah and the sages emphasize those who are included and, as a result, cannot wed *mamzerim, netinim, shtuqim, 'asufim* or men whose genitals were damaged.

Rabbi Yehudah, a fourth-generation tanna who was active in the mid-second century, enumerates four *qahalot*: congregations of priests, Levites, Israelites, and converts (B); in contrast to Rabbi Meir, who discusses the congregation as a *qahal*, in the singular form.[31] Despite the differences in their status (for exam-

---

30 This phrase may have been added to (B) to connect the quotation from Rabbi Meir (A) with the rulings by Rabbi Yehudah and the sages (B+C).

31 The sectarian community described in the Damascus Document is also comprised of four groups: priests, Levites, the children of Israel (*bney Israel*), and converts (*ha-ger*; CD XIV, 3–6; the word *qahal* does not appear in this passage). On variants of this text and their dating, see Hempel, *The Laws of the Damascus Documents*, 134–135; Palmer,

ple, priests have more stringent marital boundaries), together they comprise God's congregation. For Rabbi Yehudah, converts are part of the *qahal* and, therefore, may not marry those who are banned from it. The sages (C), however, do not include converts in the *qahal*, which they define as priests, Levites, and Israelites; in that framework, converts may marry persons from the lower classes.

This dispute between Rabbi Yehudah and the sages also appears in Sifre Deuteronomy 247,[32] which expounds on Deuteronomy 23:2: "No one whose testicles are crushed or whose penis has been severed shall enter the congregation of the Lord" (verse 1 in NRSV):

בקהל ה׳. ר׳ יהודה או׳. ארבע קהילות הן. קהל כהנים קהל לויים קהל ישראל וקהל גרים. וחכמים אומ׳ שלשה.

"The congregation of the Lord" (Deuteronomy 23:2). Rabbi Yehudah says: "There are four congregations: a congregation of priests (*qahal kohanim*), a congregation of Levites (*qahal leviyim*), a congregation of Israelites (*qahal israel*), and a congregation of converts (*qahal gerim*)." But the sages say: "[There are] three."

The sages permit a female convert to marry or cohabit with a man whose genitals were visibly damaged; therefore, they exclude converts from the "congregation of the Lord." When, however, the Mishnah rephrases this position, it speaks of a single *qahal* and does not mention debates over whether it has four or three *qehalim*:

... פצוע דכא וכרות שפ׳ מותרין בגיורת ובמשוחררת ואינן אסורין אלא מלבוא בקהל. שנ׳ "לא יבוא פצוע דכא וכרות שפ׳ בקהל יי׳".

[...] One whose testicles are crushed or one whose penis has been severed is (lit. are) permitted to [marry or cohabit with] a female convert (*giyoret*) and freedwoman (*mesuhreret*) and is (lit. are) only forbidden

---

Converts in the Dead Sea Scrolls, 62–63. While scholars debate the meaning of the word *ger* in sectarian sources from Qumran, this text—which discusses an assembly of members of the camps, not marriage—seems to refer to proselytes. See more in, Hempel, *The Laws of the Damascus Documents*, 131. On prohibitions against marrying converts in legal documents from Qumran, see Harrington, "Keeping Outsiders Out," 193–194, 196–197.

32 Finkelstein edition, p. 276.

from marrying (lit. "to enter"; *lavo*) into the congregation (*qahal*), for it is stated [in Scripture]: "No one whose testicles are crushed or whose penis has been severed shall enter the congregation of the Lord" (Deuteronomy 23:2). (m.Yevamot 8:2)

This mishnah characterizes female converts and freedwomen as being outside of the *qahal*, and by disregarding Rabbi Yehudah's position, it follows the sages' point of view (and, like Rabbi Meir in Tosefta Qiddushin 5:1, refers to the *qahal* in the singular form). What is more, Rabbi Yehudah's perspective on the inclusion of converts in the *qahal* is not even acknowledged.

On the basis of these texts and other tannaitic material, I would suggest that this argument over the inclusion of converts in "the congregation of the Lord"—along with other passages which we will see where Rabbi Yehudah and Rabbi Yose disagree on the eligibility of a convert's daughter for marriage to a priest—originated from two legal models that provided frameworks for the position of proselytes in Israel: the *ḥalal* and the Roman freedman/freedwoman.

The *Ḥalal* Model

In its presentation of the marital restrictions imposed on priests, Leviticus 21:7 prescribes: "They shall not marry a prostitute or a *ḥalalah*;[33] neither shall they marry a woman divorced from her husband. For they are holy to their God."[34] According to rabbinic interpretation, the offspring of priests and women from any of these prohibited categories are defined as *ḥalalim*.[35] A *ḥalal* transmits this status to his offspring, and a *ḥalalah* is banned from marrying a priest. In addition, the daughter of a priest, Levite or Israelite who had sexual intercourse (by choice or by force) with a man who was disqualified from marriage into the priesthood was banned from marrying priests.[36] Such a woman is also defined as a *ḥalalah*. Although she has become disqualified from marrying a priest, she may wed a Levite or Israelite. However, a *ḥalal* may wed the daughter of a priest, Levite or Israelite. Neither men nor women with this status may marry those who "shall not enter the congregation of the Lord"; therefore, they

---

33 The NRSV renders *ḥalalah* as "a woman who has been defiled."
34 Also, Ezekiel 44:22 states: "They shall not marry a widow, or a divorced woman, but only a virgin of the stock of the house of Israel, or a widow who is the widow of a priest."
35 Sifra Emor, parashah 2, pereq 2 [95a].
36 T.Yevamot 8:1; t.Niddah 6:1; y.Yevamot 7:5, 8b.

are considered members of the *qahal* despite the defect in their lineage that restricts marriages between a *ḥalalah* and a priest.

It seems that Rabbi Yehudah equates converts to *ḥalalim*: both belong to "the congregation of the Lord" and cannot marry lower groups, such as *mamzerim*. Moreover, males may marry daughters of priests, Levites, and Israelites and, although females cannot marry priests, they may marry Levites and Israelites. Indeed, Rabbi Yehudah draws an explicit parallel between converts and *ḥalalim*, as in this discussion of the permissibility for a daughter (or other female descendant) of converts to marry a priest:

בת חלל זכר פסולה מן הכהונה לעולם.
ישרא׳ שנשא חללה בתו כשירה לכהונה. וחלל שנשא בת ישראל בתו פסולה מן הכהונה.
ר׳ יהודה או׳. בת גר זכר כבת חלל זכר.

A daughter of a male *ḥalal* is disqualified (*psulah*) from [marriage into the] priesthood for eternity.

An Israelite who married a [female] *ḥalalah*—his daughter is suitable (*ksherah*) for [marriage into the] priesthood, but a [male] *ḥalal* who married an Israelite woman (lit. a daughter of Israel)—his daughter is disqualified (*psulah*) from [marriage into the] priesthood.

Rabbi Yehudah says: "The daughter of a male *ger* is equivalent to the daughter of a male *ḥalal*." (m.Qiddushin 4:6)

And in Tosefta Qiddushin 5:3:

בת חלל זכר פסולה מן הכהונה לעולם.
ר׳ יהוד׳ אומ׳. בת גר זכר כבת חלל זכר ופסולה מן הכהונה.

A daughter of a male *ḥalal* is disqualified (*psulah*) from [marriage into the] priesthood for eternity.

Rabbi Yehudah says: "The daughter of a male *ger* is equivalent to the daughter of a male *ḥalal* and she is disqualified (*psulah*) from [marriage into the] priesthood."[37]

---

37   See also Sifra Emor, parashah 2, pereq 2 [95a].

While Rabbi Yehudah assesses the status of converts according to the *ḥalal* model, his view of freed slaves is less clear. Although he does not include them in the *qahal*, in Tosefta Qiddushin 5:2, he locates them with converts and *ḥalalim*:

ר׳ יהודה או׳ [...] גר ועבד משוחרר וחלל מותרין בכהנת

Rabbi Yehudah says: "[...] A convert and a freedman and a *ḥalal* are permitted to marry a priest['s daughter]."

Given the prohibition on marriage between female converts and priests, the *ḥalal* model enables Rabbi Yehudah to elevate converts into "the congregation of the Lord."

The Freedman/Freedwomen Model

If manumitted properly, Roman freed slaves became Roman citizens.[38] Such integration of former slaves was unique in the ancient world. While freed men and women were on par with long-standing citizens in most areas of life, some differences pertained to their position in marriage.[39] With respect to the lower social strata, Roman citizens were prohibited from marrying certain people (such as prostitutes and pimps)[40] but former slaves were not subjected to

---

38   Not every freed slave became a citizen, as Mouritsen, "Manumission," 406 notes: "During the Republic several different forms of manumission developed, which modern scholarship tends to divide into 'formal' and 'informal', the important distinction being that the former led to enfranchisement while the latter did not. 'Formal' manumission included the freeing of slaves *vindicta*, 'by the rod', through registration in the census and by testament, while slaves could be freed informally *inter amicos* and *per litteras*. Informal manumission carried no official recognition, although the liberty of those freed in that way enjoyed the protection of the urban praetor." On other ways to become a Roman citizen before 212 CE, see Lavan, "The Spread of Roman Citizenship"; Besson, "Fifty Years before the Antonine Constitution."

39   Other differences that were not related to marriage include: relations with and obligations toward their former master (now patron); and, limitations on holding positions of authority. I plan to address these topics in future research.

40   At least from the reign of Augustus, Roman law banned the freeborn (but not freed slaves) from marrying "prostitutes, pimps, procuresses, and persons convicted of adultery or caught in the act" (McGinn, *Prostitution*, 93, see the discussion on pages 85–94). The primary source for this prohibition is *Tituli ex corpore Vlpiani* 13.1–2; on problems with this text, see McGinn, *Prostitution*, 91–92. Indeed, Gardner, *Being a Roman Citizen*, 124–125,

these standards. Concerning the upper strata of society, a statute by Augustus proscribed Roman freed slaves from marrying senators and at least three generations of their male descendants.[41] Thus, select marital restrictions were imposed on freed slaves. However, they were only applied to the first generation, not to the offspring of freed slaves. As Henrik Mouritsen has written: "The underlying premise that the slave identity could be 'inherited' by individuals who had no personal experience of servitude seems incompatible with Roman perceptions of slavery."[42] Roman freed persons were in a liminal position: they were new citizens, albeit with particular limitations and liberties in relation to marriage; yet, "from a legal point of view," their children "were *ingenui* on a par with any other Roman born to free parents. Their citizenship was in principle equal to that of other Romans."[43]

The Roman freedman/freedwoman model seems to have been instrumental for developing perspectives on Jewish converts, especially as freed persons were limited in marriage with the upper echelon of society but had more flexibility in marriage with the lower strata. Indeed, rabbinic legal texts often pair converts with freed slaves.[44] While scholars have explained that the legal status

---

writes: "It has been observed also that in Ulp. *Reg.* 13.2 prostitutes are included in the list of marriage partners banned to senators, and missing from the list of those banned to other freeborn Romans." She notes that "women taken in adultery" are similarly prohibited only from marrying senators. The exact categories listed in this source notwithstanding, it was more acceptable for freed persons than the freeborn—by law and social norms—to marry members of lower societal strata.

41   On this prohibition, see Dio 54.16.2; 56.7.2; *Digest* 23.2.44 pr. (Paulus, *libro primo ad legem Iuliam et Papiam*); *Tituli ex corpore Vlpiani* 13.1–2; McGinn, *Prostitution*, 72, 91–94; 120–123; Perry, *Gender*, 8–9, 134–135; Gardner, *Women in Roman Law*, 32–33; Moreau, "Loi Iulia de maritandis ordinibus." Not only were senators barred from betrothing or marrying freed slaves, but this prohibition applied to their male and female offspring as well: "… in the male line, grandsons, granddaughters, great-grandsons, and great-granddaughters" (McGinn, *Prostitution*, 72). Cf. Moreau, "Loi Iulia de maritandis ordinibus," 5.1 who argues that this restriction was only applied to three generations of a senator's descendants. As Mouritsen, *The Freedman*, 21, explains, this legislation forbade: "… senators and their descendants from marrying freedwomen, actresses, or *infames*, whose taint apparently was considered to be of a similar nature. Again the ban reflected a perceived need to prevent 'contamination' of the citizen body in general and of the highest order in particular." Cf. the explanation by Gardner, *Being a Roman Citizen*, 39; Gardner, *Women in Roman Law*, 32–33.

42   Mouritsen, *The Freedman*, 265.

43   Mouritsen, *The Freedman*, 264.

44   See, for example, m.Ma'aser Sheni 5:14; m.Bikkurim 1:5; m. Qiddushin 4:1, 7; m.Zavim 2:1; t.Qiddushin 4:15; 5:2; t.Bava Qamma 3:4; 4:6; 9:20; t.Bava Batra 7:1. Numerous scholars have remarked on this association, for example: Cohen, *Jewish and Roman Law*, 146: "In most respects the legal status of the freedman was similar to that of the proselyte"; Hezser, *Jew-*

of converts was applied to freed persons who had served in Jewish homes, for they too became Jewish upon manumission, I propose a more complex and, at times, inverse dynamic: Roman laws and concepts regarding freedmen and freedwomen offered a legal framework that influenced certain elements of rabbinic *halakhah* concerning converts. Elsewhere I have shown that the Roman status of freed slaves provided the sages with a model for regulating the legal status of female converts.[45] As a new citizen with certain marital limitations due to the absence of a family pedigree and an assumed sexual history (before manumission), the legal position of the Roman freedwoman served as a conceptual template for considering female converts, who also had matrimonial restrictions and were without lineage. Thus, the apparent clustering of converts and freedmen in rabbinic texts may not only indicate that freedwomen were deemed similar to converts (as both groups became Jewish), but that female converts were affected to some extent by the legal and social standing of freedwomen.[46] Here, I suggest more broadly that Roman treatment of freedmen and freedwomen provided a conceptual approach for defining the status of converts in rabbinic law. Although this model was not accepted by all tannaim, I would argue for its gradual influence, which culminated in the Jerusalem Talmud which I discuss below. While the paradigm of Roman freedman/freedwoman was never copied with all its details into *halakhah*, it influenced the rabbinic view of converts.

Converts in Mishnah Qiddushin 4:1

The opening sentence of this mishnah, which lists ten genealogical classes, is cited above. Now let us look at how it regulates marriage between these groups, with special attention to converts:

(A) עשרה יחסים עלו מבבל. כהני לויי ישרא׳ חללי גירי חרורי ממזירי ונתיני שתוקי ואסופי.

(B) כהני לויי וישראל[י] מותרין לבוא זה בזה.

(C) לויי וישראל׳ חללי גירי וחרורי מותרין לבוא זה בזה.

(D) גירי חרורי ממזירי ונתיני שתוקי ואסופי מותרין לבוא זה בזה

---

ish Slavery, 109; Dohrmann, "Manumission," 59; Kahana, *Sifre on Numbers*, vol. 2, 86; Ophir and Rosen-Zvi, *Goy*, 377, note 125: "The status of freed slaves is systematically equated in rabbinic literature to that of converts, thus revealing the same dialectic."

45 See Wilfand, "Freedwomen."
46 See, for example, t.Qiddushin 4:15; 5:1–2. Compare, Porton, *The Stranger*, 29–30.

A) Ten genealogical classes (*yohasim*) came up (to the Land of Israel) from Babylonia: priests, Levites, Israelites, *halaley*, converts, freed slaves, *mamzerey, netiney, shtuqey,* and *'asufey*.
B) Priests, Levites, and Israelites are permitted to marry each other (*lavo ze ba-ze*).
C) Levites, Israelites, *halaley*, converts, and freed slaves are permitted to marry each other (*lavo ze ba-ze*).
D) Converts, *harurey, mamzerey, netiney, shtuqey,* and *'asufey* are permitted to marry each other (*lavo ze ba-ze*).

This passage does not use the term *qahal*, which appears in Tosefta, Sifre Deuteronomy and the Jerusalem Talmud. This difference in language is not surprising for, as noted above, the Mishnah makes no mention of the argument between Rabbi Yehudah and the sages over how many *qahalim* constitute "the congregation of the Lord." Rather, this mishnah delivers its ruling in an anonymous voice which conveys authority. Indeed, the Jerusalem Talmud Qiddushin 4:1, 65c notes that this mishnah rules against Rabbi Yehudah:

אמ' ר' חנינה. מתנית' דלא כר' יודה. דר' יודה אמ'. ארבע קהילות הן, קהל כהנים קהל לויים קהל ישראל קהל גרים. [...] ורבנין אמרין: שלשה קהילות הן, קהל כהנים קהל לויים קהל יש'. ...

Rabbi Ḥanina said: The mishnah does not follow (lit. is not like) Rabbi Yehudah. For Rabbi Yehudah said: "Four congregations are [included in the] congregation: a congregation of priests (*qahal kohanim*), a congregation of Levites (*qahal leviyim*), a congregation of Israelites (*qahal Israel*), [and] a congregation of converts (*qahal gerim*)." [...] The sages say: "[There are] three congregations: a congregation of priests (*qahal kohanim*), a congregation of Levites (*qahal leviyim*), [and] a congregation of Israelites (*qahal israel*)."

Mishnah Qiddushin 4:1 associates converts with freed slaves, while assigning them a unique position within Israel: they are banned from marrying priests but permitted to wed Israelites, Levites, and *halalim* (the rest of the congregation) as well as the lower groups: *mamzerim, netinim, shtuqim,* and *'asufim*, "who are not allowed to marry into the congregation." Although this source conceptualizes social relations without using the term *qahal*, by implication, this ruling places converts outside of the congregation (for they are free to wed those who are prohibited from its members), yet they are permitted to marry into the *qahal* (except for priests).⁴⁷ This mishnah is compatible with the position attributed to Rabbi Meir and the sages in Tosefta Qiddushin 5:1 (although this tosefta only addresses marriage between converts and those "who are not allowed to marry into the congregation").⁴⁸

The liminal position of converts and freed slaves resembles the station of Roman freedmen and freedwomen. These new Romans were not permitted to wed senators but they were eligible to marry other Romans, including those that freeborn citizens were proscribed from marrying. These restrictions and leniencies had legal force and reflected social norms. It is telling that the Mishnah situates the freed man and woman in the same category with converts. However, whereas Roman law views the children of freed slaves as equal to other Roman citizens in all respects, this mishnah seems to suggest that the status of both converts and freed slaves is hereditary and, therefore, immutable. As other passages in Mishnah Qiddushin, Chapter Four show, the status of converts' offspring was contested. Among the sages, Rabbi Yose seems to further the freedman/freedwoman model by applying it to the next generation.

---

47 This mishnah does not differentiate between male and female converts on this issue.
48 On the relationship between Mishnah Qiddushin 4:1 and Tosefta Qiddushin 5:1, and the possibility that the Mishnah draws on and presents a more refined version of material from this tosefta, see Friedman, *Tosefta Atiqta*, 50. Since the closing line of this mishnah (D) is almost identical to Rabbi Meir's teaching in the Tosefta, it has been claimed that the Mishnah follows Rabbi Meir:

Mishnah Qiddushin 4:1	Tosefta Qiddushin 5:1
גירי חרורי ממזירי ונתיני שתוקי ואסופי מותרין לבוא זה בזה	גירי וחרורי ממזירי ונתיני שתוקי ואסופי **וכל האסורין לבא בקהל** מותרין לבוא זה בזה **דברי ר׳ מאיר**
Converts, *ḥarurey*, *mamzerey*, *netiney*, *shtuqey*, and *'asufey* are permitted to marry each other (or to cohabit; *lavo ze ba-ze*).	Converts, *ḥarurey*, *mamzerey*, *netiney*, *shtuqey*, and *'asufey*, **and all those who are forbidden from marrying into the congregation (*qahal*)** are permitted to marry each other (or to cohabit; *lavo ze ba-ze*). **[These are] the words of Rabbi Meir.**

Rabbi Yehudah and Rabbi Yose

Rulings by Rabbi Yose and Rabbi Yehudah on converts' status in marriage appear in our chapter from the Tosefta:

> גר ועבד משוחרר מותר בממזרת והולד ממזר דברי ר׳ יוסה
> ר׳ יהודה או׳ גר לא ישא את הגיורת (הממזרת) גר ועבד משוחרר וחלל מותרין בכהנת

> "A male convert and a freedman are (lit. is) permitted to [marry] (or to cohabit with) a *mamzeret* and the child [of that couple] is a *mamzer*." [These are] the words of Rabbi Yose.
>
> Rabbi Yehudah says: "A male convert (*ger*) will not marry a female convert (*giyoret*; or a *mamzeret*). A male convert and a freedman and a *ḥalal* are permitted to marry a priest['s daughter]." (t.Qiddushin 5:2)

Rabbi Yose follows the sages' position: he groups the convert and the freedman together, and permits them to marry (or cohabit with) a *mamzeret*; however, the child of that couple will be defined as a *mamzer*. By accepting such unions, Rabbi Yose lowers the status of converts within Israel, reflecting the sages' stance that converts do not belong to the *qahal* (t.Qiddushin 5:1 and parallels) and their treatment of converts and freed slaves as analogous categories (m.Qiddushin 4:1).

Rabbi Yehudah deems a male convert, a freedman, and a male *ḥalal* qualified to marry a priest's daughter. However, the intention of the opening phrase of his teaching is less evident: "A male convert (*ger*) will not marry a female convert (*giyoret*)." Saul Lieberman suggests that this passage should read: "A male convert (*ger*) will not marry a *mamzeret*."[49] Indeed, a parallel baraita in the Babylonian Talmud, Qiddushin 72b reads *mamzeret* instead of *giyoret*:

> תנו רבנן:
> גר נושא ממזרת והולד ממזר. דברי ר׳ יוסי.
> ר׳ יהוד׳ או׳. גר לא ישא ממזרת. אחד גר ועבד משוחרר וחלל מותרין בכוהנת״.

---

49 Lieberman, *Tosefta Ki-Feshutah*, 8:966. Nonetheless, Lieberman, The tosefta, 3:293 did not include this term in his edition. He noted that the word *mamzeret* only appears in the printed edition of the Tosefta and in b.Qiddushin 72b.

The rabbis have taught [in a tannaitic tradition]:

"A male convert may marry a *mamzeret* and the child is *mamzer*." [These are] the words of Rabbi Yose.

Rabbi Yehudah says: "A male convert (*ger*) will not marry a *mamzeret*. The same [applies] to a male convert, a freedman, and a male *ḥalal*: they are [each] permitted to marry a priest['s daughter]."

Even if the word *mamzeret* does not appear in Rabbi Yehudah's ruling in Tosefta Qiddushin 5:2, the previous tosefta clearly demonstrates that he prohibits marriages between converts and *mamzerim*.

As all opinions agree (including Rabbi Yehudah's), this prohibition does not apply to freed slaves; thereby, they do not belong to the "congregation of the Lord," so they may marry those who are excluded from it. Thus, Rabbi Yehudah distinguishes between converts, who are members of the *qahal*, and freed slaves, who are not.[50] Yet freedmen, male converts, and *ḥalalim* may marry the daughters of priests. By comparison to Rabbi Yose, Rabbi Yehudah seems to elevate the status of converts by equating them with *ḥalalim* and situating them within the "congregation of the Lord."

Mishnah Qiddushin 4:6–7: Marriage between Converts' Daughters and Priests

The contrast between Rabbi Yose and Rabbi Yehudah also appears in the Mishnah. While scholars have often considered their positions on the eligibility of converts' daughters to marry priests in terms of stringency and leniency,[51] as stated above, I view the differences between these sages in relation to distinct legal models:

(A) בת חלל זכר פסולה מן הכהונה לעולם. ישרא' שנשא חללה בתו כשירה לכהונה. וחלל שנשא בת ישראל בתו פסולה מן הכהונה. ר' יהודה או'. בת גר זכר כבת חלל זכר.

(B) ר' אליעזר בן יעקב אומ'. ישר' שנשא גיורת בתו כשירה לכהונה וגר שנשא בת ישרא' בתו כשירה לכהונה. אבל גר שנשא גיורת בתו פסולה מן הכהונה. אחד גירים ואחד עבדים משוחררים אפילו עד עשרה דורות. עד שתהא אימן מיש'.

(C) ר' יוסה אומ'. אף גר שנשא גיורת בתו כשירה לכהונה.

---

50 Lieberman, *Tosefta Ki-Feshutah*, 8:964.
51 For example, Hayes, *Gentile Impurities*, 173: "The most stringent view is attributed to R. Yehudah ..."

A) A daughter of a male *ḥalal* (the offspring of a priest and a woman who was ineligible to marry into the priesthood) is disqualified (*psulah*) from [marriage into the] priesthood for eternity. An Israelite who married a [female] *ḥalalah*—his daughter is suitable (*ksherah*) for [marriage into the] priesthood, but a [male] *ḥalal* who married an Israelite woman (lit. a daughter of Israel)—his daughter is disqualified (*psulah*) from [marriage into the] priesthood. Rabbi Yehudah says: "The daughter of a male *ger* is equivalent to the daughter of a male *ḥalal*."

B) Rabbi Eliezer ben Ya'aqov says: "An Israelite [man] who married a *giyoret* (female convert)—his daughter is suitable (*ksherah*) for [marriage into the] priesthood. And a *ger* (convert) who married an Israelite woman (lit. a daughter of Israel)—his daughter is suitable (*ksherah*) for [marriage into the] priesthood. But a *ger* who married a *giyoret*—his daughter is disqualified (*psulah*) from [marriage into the] priesthood. One [rule applies to] *gerim* and [the same] one [applies to] freed slaves, even up to ten generations: [they shall not marry into the priesthood] unless their mother is an Israelite (lit. from Israel)."

C) Rabbi Yose says: "Also a *ger* who married a *giyoret*—his daughter is suitable (*ksherah*) for [marriage into the] priesthood."

This mishnah presents opinions by three second-century sages on the marriage of a proselyte's daughter with priests. Rabbi Yehudah's teaching (discussed above) equates the status of a convert's female offspring to the standing of a *ḥalal's* daughter; therefore, she is not allowed to marry a priest. Yet the daughter of a *giyoret* who married an Israelite may legitimately marry a priest.

The second view in our mishnah is attributed to Rabbi Eliezer ben Ya'aqov, who contends that having one Israelite parent (namely, one parent is a *ger* and the other is an Israelite) is sufficient for a woman to marry a priest.[52] However, if both parents are *gerim*, their daughter cannot marry a priest. This applies not only to a daughter of two converts but to their progeny, for up to ten generations.[53] Thus, for full integration into Israel—with respect to marriage into a priestly family—a convert had to wed an Israelite. The alternative required a

---

52 Cf. Katz, *Jerusalem Talmud*, 243. Two tannaim were known as Rabbi Eliezer ben Ya'aqov: the first was active during the Second Temple period and had priestly relatives (m. Middot 1:2); the other was active in the second century CE. We cannot be certain which one is cited here and whether he came from a priestly family but, since the other two sages mentioned in these passages (Rabbi Yehudah and Rabbi Yose) were active in the second century CE, the later Rabbi Eliezer ben Ya'aqov is probably quoted here.

53 See Sifre Deuteronomy 248 (Finkelstein edition, pages 277–278).

centuries-long (if not endless) wait. This provision also applies to freed slaves, and it is another example where converts and freed slaves are paired in tannaitic *halakhah*. This sage accepts neither the *ḥalal* framework nor the Roman standard which, as discussed above, places no restrictions on the children of freed slaves (in contrast to their parents)—or, needless to say, the children of new citizens—to wed senators. The comparison to senators is meaningful here, for they represent the upper stratum of Roman society, analogous to Israelite priests with respect to lineage. Of course, significant factors distinguished Roman senators from Jewish priests: whereas priestly status was exclusively transmitted from father to son, the senatorial order was not heritable and became increasingly open to new members, eventually including individuals with non-Italian lineage. Nonetheless Jewish and Roman law each monitored the marriages of their societal elites with scrutiny.

The third position is attributed to Rabbi Yose, who states that a woman may marry a priest even if her parents are both converts. According to this teaching, daughters of *gerim* are considered Israelite without qualification, even for entering this most restrictive marital bond. For this sage, no biological association with a well-established Jewish parent is required for a second-generation convert to have Israelite lineage. This approach seems to follow the Roman pattern of regarding status as no more than an ascribed legal or social designation. Moreover, even though freed men and women are not mentioned by Rabbi Yose, I suggest that his opinion is modeled after the Roman treatment of manumitted slaves discussed above. Just as Roman freedwomen were prohibited from marrying into the senatorial order while their children had no such limitation, so too a female convert is barred from marrying a priest whereas her daughter may marry a priest, even if her father is also a proselyte.

However, not only does Rabbi Yose permit daughters of two converts to marry priests but, like the sages in m.Qiddushin 4:1, he approves of marriages between proselytes and *mamzerim*. Bernard Bamberger, in trying to make sense of Rabbi Yose's stance toward converts, struggled to reconcile these two rulings.[54] This alleged inconsistency disappears if Rabbi Yose's position was shaped in correspondence with the status of Roman freed slaves who had certain limitations and liberties in relation to marriage, but whose offspring were legally equal to long-standing citizens. The respective legal models that Rabbi Yehudah and Rabbi Yose use to define the status of converts are therefore fundamental for understanding proselytes' standing in tannaitic *halakhah*. Indeed, assessing the positions of these two sages within the stringency-leniency

---

54   Bamberger, *Proselytism*, 85.

framework yields a seemingly paradox: Rabbi Yehudah includes *gerim* in the *qahal*, yet he prohibits the daughters of male converts from marrying priests;[55] whereas Rabbi Yose allows the daughters of converts to wed priests, but he does not include them in the *qahal*, and thereby permits them to marry *mamzerim*. However, this apparent contradiction only holds if these stances are analyzed in terms of stringency and leniency. Rabbi Yehudah's ruling, which has been deemed more stringent, as it requires an Israelite father to claim an Israelite pedigree, stems from a position that elevates the status of *gerim* and includes them in "the congregation of the Lord." In contrast, Rabbi Yose's stance, which has been perceived as more lenient since the daughter of two converts may marry a priest, actually assigns a lower rank to proselytes, for they are analogous to freed slaves, who are not members of the *qahal* and may marry *mamzerim*. Yet, this model of granting citizenship to manumitted slaves offers a path to full integration in Israel after a single generation (at least in regard to permission for the daughter of converts to marry a priest).

While the Mishnah locates both converts and freed persons between members of the *qahal* and those who cannot marry into it, in the case of the daughter of *gerim*, m.Qiddushin 4:6–7 does not show a preference for any of these three opinions. However, m.Bikkurim 1:4–5 (not discussed here), which addresses the recitation of liturgical passages that mention Israelite ancestry, seems to endorse Rabbi Eliezer ben Ya'aqov's view.[56] Thus, at that halakhic stage, the Roman freedman model had limited influence, since neither the Mishnah nor the Tosefta implement it in regard to the second generation, namely by granting equal status to the children of freed slaves, as provided by Roman legislation. This element of the law is applied to second-generation converts only in a minority opinion of Rabbi Yose. That changes in amoraic literature, where the Jerusalem Talmud (Bikkurim 1:5, 64a and Qiddushin 4:7, 66a) explicitly states on this subject: "*Halakhah* is according to Rabbi Yose."

---

55 Due to this apparent contradiction in Rabbi Yehudah's view, Porton, *The Stranger*, 35–36 writes: "The major question is whether or not consistent views are attributed to Judah," and he concludes: "It appears that Tosefta contains contradictory opinions attributed to Judah."
56 On m.Bikkurim 1:4–5, see Wilfand, "Roman Concepts of Citizenship."

Conclusion

Most tannaitic debates over the status of converts within the Jewish people—typically Rabbi Yehudah versus the sages, or Rabbi Yose—are recorded in the Tosefta. At their core, these disagreements hinge on whether converts belong to the *qahal*. This status dictates their possibilities or prohibitions in marriage (t.Qiddushin 5:1–3). Arguments over the place of converts in the congregation, and particularly the number of congregations, are absent from Mishnah Yevamot 8:2. Rather, this source unanimously rules that converts and freed-slaves are not part of the *qahal*. Similarly, m.Qiddushin 4:1, which presents an elaborate schema for determining the marital options for its list of ten genealogical categories, does not mention this difference in opinion between Rabbi Yehudah and the sages. This source places converts in a liminal position together with freed slaves. In both of these passages from the Mishnah, converts and freed persons share the same status. The sole mishnaic account of a dispute between Rabbi Yehudah and Rabbi Yose on the standing of proselytes addresses converts' daughters and their eligibility to wed priests (m.Qiddushin 4:6–7). A close analysis of these sources suggests that two major legal models—the *ḥalal* and the freedman/freedwoman—informed the sages' perspectives on the status of converts in marriage. The latter model suggests yet another example of the impact of Roman law on *halakhah*, especially on matters of civil status.

An analysis of rulings by prominent second-century sages on the position of converts in Israel on two subjects—the permissibility of marriage between proselytes and *mamzerim*, and the eligibility of proselytes' daughters to marry priests—yields an apparent inconsistency. However, when examined through the prism of legal models, their distinct stances and the logic beyond their seemingly contradictory rulings are clarified: Rabbi Yehudah raises the status of converts by placing the *ger* on a par with the *ḥalal*. He therefore distinguishes between converts and freed slaves, as freed men and women are not included in the *qahal*.[57] In contrast, the sages link these two categories of people and, consequently, reduce the status of *gerim*. Yet, following the opinion by Rabbi Yose, which was later endorsed by the Jerusalem Talmud, the freedman/freedwomen model provides a path for marriage between daughters of converts and priests. This diminution of status facilitated integration in the next generation. More generally, the eventual progression of *halakhah* to Rabbi Yose's stance reflects a transition from a legal model that defines status by genealogy to one that relies

---

57 This division between *gerim* and freed persons reflects the differentiation of freed and freeborn that was prevalent in the Roman world.

on statutory determination. The dynamic revealed in this study may serve as a caution to two scholarly conventions that are often applied to these texts: the stringency-leniency paradigm is insufficient for analyzing them and, the common assertion that freed persons were legally equated to converts may be overly simplistic since, in the cases discussed here, the reverse tendency seems to be at work.

Acknowledgements

I extend thanks to Clifford Ando, Katell Berthelot, Yair Furstenberg, and Menachem Katz for reading an earlier draft of this paper and for their helpful suggestions, and to Thomas McGinn and Matthew Perry for their advice. Quotations and references from rabbinic literature follow MA'AGARIM The Hebrew Language Historical Dictionary Project of the Academy of the Hebrew Language, Jerusalem. All translations of rabbinic texts are my own.

Bibliography

Bamberger, Bernard J. *Proselytism in the Talmudic Period.* Cincinnati: Hebrew Union College Press, 1939.

Baumgarten, Joseph M. "The Exclusion of 'Netinim' and Proselytes in 4Q Florilegium." *Revue de Qumrân* 8 (1972) 87–96.

Berthelot, Katell. "La notion de גר dans les textes de Qumran." *Revue de Qumrân* 19 (1999) 171–216.

Besson, Arnaud. "Fifty Years before the Antonine Constitution: Access to Roman Citizenship and Exclusive Rights." In *Citizens in the Graeco-Roman World: Aspects of Citizenship from the Archaic Period to AD 212*, edited by Lucia Cecchet and Anna Busetto, 199–220. Leiden: Brill, 2017.

Cohen, Boaz. *Jewish and Roman Law: A Comparative Study.* New York: The Jewish Theological Seminary of America, 1966.

Cohen, Shaye J.D. *The Beginnings of Jewishness: Boundaries, Varieties, Uncertainties.* Berkeley, CA: University of California Press, 1999.

Cohen, Shaye J.D. "The Judaean legal tradition and the 'Halakhah' of the Mishnah." In *The Cambridge Companion to the Talmud and Rabbinic Literature*, edited by Charlotte E. Fonrobert and Martin Jaffee, 277–286. Cambridge: Cambridge University Press, 2007.

Dohrmann, Natalie B. "Manumission and Transformation in Jewish and Roman Law." In *Jewish and Biblical Interpretation and Cultural Exchange: Comparative Exegesis in*

Context, edited by Natalie B. Dohrmann and David Stern, 51–65. Philadelphia: University of Pennsylvania Press, 2008.

Falk, Ze'ev W. "Those Excluded from the Congregation." *Beit Mikra: Journal for the Study of the Bible and Its World* 19 (1975) 342–351. (Hebrew)

Friedman, Shamma. *Tosefta Atiqta: Pesah Rishon: Synoptic Parallels of Mishna and Tosefta Analyzed with a Methodological Introduction*. Ramat-Gan: Bar-Ilan University Press, 2002.

Furstenberg, Yair. "The Rabbis and the Roman Citizenship Model: The Case of the Samaritans." In *In the Crucible of Empire: The Impact of Roman Citizenship upon Greeks, Jews and Christians*, edited by Katell Berthelot and Jonathan Price, 181–211. Leuven: Peeters, 2018.

Gardner, Jane F. *Being a Roman Citizen*. London and New York: Routledge, 1993.

Gardner, Jane F. *Women in Roman Law & Society* (Bloomington: Indiana University Press, 1986).

Harrington, Hannah K. "Keeping Outsiders Out: Impurity at Qumran." In *Defining Identities: We, You, and the Other in the Dead Sea Scrolls*, edited by Florentino García Martínez and Mladen Popović, 187–203. Leiden: Brill, 2008.

Hayes, Christine. "Genealogy, Illegitimacy, and Personal Status: The Yerushalmi in Comparative Perspective." In *The Talmud Yerushalmi and Graeco-Roman Culture III*, edited by Peter Schäfer, 73–89. Tübingen: Mohr Siebeck, 2002.

Hayes, Christine. *Gentile Impurities and Jewish Identities: Intermarriage and Conversion from the Bible to the* Talmud. Oxford: Oxford University Press, 2002.

Hayes, Christine. "The 'other' in Rabbinic Literature." In *The Cambridge Companion to the Talmud and Rabbinic literature*, edited by Charlotte Elisheva Fonrobert and Martin S. Jaffee, 243–269. Cambridge: Cambridge University Press, 2007.

Hayes, Christine. *What's Divine about Divine Law?: Early Perspectives*. Princeton and Oxford: Princeton University Press, 2015.

Hempel, Charlotte. *The Laws of the Damascus Documents: Sources, Tradition, and Redaction*. STDJ 29; Leiden: Brill, 1998.

Hezser, Catherine. *Jewish Slavery in Antiquity*. Oxford: Oxford University Press, 2005.

Hezser, Catherine. "Slaves and Slavery in Rabbinic and Roman Law." In *Rabbinic Law in its Roman and Near Eastern Context*, edited by Catherine Hezser, 133–176. Tübingen: Mohr Siebeck, 2003.

Jackson, Bernard S. "On the Problem of Roman Influence on the Halakha and Normative Self-Definition in Judaism." In *Jewish and Christian Self-Definition II*, edited by E.P. Sanders, A.I. Baumgarten and Alan Mendelson, 157–203. Philadelphia: SCM, 1981.

Kahana, Menahem I. *Sifre on Numbers: An Annotated Edition*. 5 vols. Jerusalem: Magnes Press, 2011–2015.

Katz, Menachem. Jerusalem Talmud: *Tractate Qiddushin—Critical Edition and a Short Explanation*. Jerusalem: Yad Izhak Ben Zvi and Schechter Institute of Jewish Studies, 2015. (Hebrew)

Katzoff, Ranon. "Children of Intermarriage: Roman and Jewish Conceptions." In *Rabbinic Law in its Roman and Near Eastern Context*, edited by Catherine Hezser, 277–286. Tübingn: Mohr Siebeck, 2003.

Koehler, Ludwig, and Walter Baumgartner, The Hebrew and Aramaic Lexicon of the Old *Testament*. Translated by M.E.J. Richardson. Leiden: Brill, 1994.

Koren, Yedidah. "'Look through Your Book and Make Me a Perfect Match': Talking about Genealogy in Amoraic Palestine and Babylonia." *Journal for the Study of Judaism* 49 (2018) 417–448.

Lavan, Myles. "The Spread of Roman Citizenship, 14–212 CE: Quantification in the Face of High Uncertainty." *Past and Present* 230 (2016) 3–46.

Lavee, Moshe. "'A Convert is Like a Newborn Child'—The Concept and its Implications in Rabbinic Literature." PhD diss., Ben-Gurion University of the Negev, 2003.

Lavee, Moshe. "No Boundaries for the Construction of Boundaries: The Babylonian Talmud's Emphasis on Demarcation of Identity." In *Rabbinic Traditions between Palestine and Babylonia*, edited by Ronit Nikolsky and Tal Ilan, 84–116. Leiden: Brill, 2014.

Lieberman, Saul. *The Tosefta: According to Codex Vienna, with Variants from Codex Erfurt, Genizah MSS. and Editio Princeps (Venice 1521): Together with References to Parallel Passages in Talmudic Literature and a Brief Commentary*. New York: Jewish Theological Seminary of America, 1955. (Hebrew)

Lieberman, Saul. *Tosefta Ki-Feshutah: A Comprehensive Commentary on the Tosefta*. New York: Jewish Theological Seminary of America, 1955. (Hebrew)

Malka, Orit, and Yakir Paz. "*Ab hostibus captus et a latronibus captus*: The Impact of the Roman Model of Citizenship on Rabbinic Law" *The Jewish Quarterly Review* 109 (2019) 141–172.

McGinn, Thomas A.J. *Prostitution, Sexuality, and the Law in Ancient Rome*. New York: Oxford University Press, 1998.

Mélèze Modrzejewski, Joseph. "'Filios Suos Tantum' Roman Law and Jewish Identity." In *Jews and Gentiles in the Holy Land in the Days of the Second Temple, the Mishnah and the Talmud*, edited by Menachem Mor, at al., 108–136. Jerusalem: Yad Ben-Zvi, 2003.

Monnickendam, Yifat. "The Exposed Child: Transplanting Roman Law into Late Antique Jewish and Christian Legal Discourse." *American Journal of Legal History* 59 (2019) 1–30.

Moreau, Philippe. "Loi Iulia de maritandis ordinibus." In *Lepor. Leges Populi Romani*, dir. By Jean-Louis Ferrary and Philippe Moreau. [On line]. Paris: IRHT-TELMA, 2007. URL: http://www.cn-telma.fr/lepor/notice449/. Last update: 18/09/17.

Mouritsen, Henrik. *The Freedman in the Roman* World. Cambridge: Cambridge University Press, 2011.

Mouritsen, Henrik. "Manumission." In *The Oxford Handbook of Roman Law and Society*, edited by Paul J. du Plessis, Clifford Ando, and Kaius Tuori, 402–416. Oxford: Oxford University Press, 2016.

Na'aman, Nadav. "Sojourners and Levites in the Kingdom of Judah in the Seventh Century BCE." *Tarbiz* 77 (2007–2008) 162–186. (Hebrew)

Novak, David. "Gentiles in Rabbinic Thought." In *The Cambridge History of Judaism: Volume IV: The Late Roman-Rabbinic Period*, edited by Steven T. Katz, 647–662. Cambridge: Cambridge University Press 2006.

Ophir, Adi and Ishay Rosen-Zvi. *Goy: Israel's Multiple Others and the Birth of the Gentile*. Oxford: Oxford University Press, 2018.

Palmer, Carmen. *Converts in the Dead Sea Scrolls: The Gēr and Mutable Ethnicity*. STDJ 126. Leiden: Brill, 2018.

Perry, Matthew J. *Gender, Manumission and the Roman Freedwoman*. Cambridge: Cambridge University Press, 2014.

Porton, Gary G. *The Stranger within Your Gate: Converts and Conversions in Rabbinic Literature*. Chicago: The University of Chicago Press, 1994.

Rosen-Zvi, Ishay. "Is the Mishnah a Roman Composition?" In *The Faces of Torah. Studies in the Texts and Contexts of Ancient Judaism in Honor of Steven Fraade*, edited by Michal Bar-Asher Siegal, Tzvi Novick and Christine Hayes, 487–508. Göttingen: Vandenhoeck & Ruprecht 2017.

Satlow, Michael L. *Jewish Marriage in Antiquity*. Princeton, NJ: Princeton University Press, 2001.

Simon-Shoshan, Moshe. *Stories of the Law: Narrative Discourse and the Construction of Authority in the Mishnah*. New York: Oxford University Press, 2013.

Schwartz, Daniel R. "Doing like Jews or Becoming a Jew? Josephus on Women Converts to Judaism." In *Jewish Identity in the Greco-Roman World*, edited by Jörg Frey, Daniel R. Schwartz and Stephnie Gripentrog, 93–109. Leiden: Brill, 2007.

Tigay, Jeffrey H. *Deuteronomy: Introduction and Commentary: Volume Two*. Tel Aviv and Jerusalem: Am Oved and Magness, 2016. (Hebrew)

Urbach, Ephraim E. "*Halakhot* regarding Slavery as a Source for the Social History of the Second Temple and the Talmudic Period." *Zion* 26 (1960) 141–189. (Hebrew)

Wilfand, Yael. "Did Roman Treatment of Freedwomen Influence Rabbinic halakhah on the Status of Female Converts in Marriage?" *The Journal of Legal History* 40 (2019) 182–202.

Wilfand, Yael. "'A Proselyte whose Sons Converted with Him': Roman Laws on New Citizens' Authority over Their Children and Tannaitic Rulings on Converts to Judaism and Their Offspring" *Zion* 84 (2019): 445–461. (Hebrew)

Wilfand, Yael. "Roman Concepts of Citizenship and Rabbinic Approaches to the Lineage of Converts and the Integration of their Descendants into Israel" (forthcoming in the *Journal of Ancient Judaism*).

CHAPTER 5

Shimon b. Shatah, the Donkey, and the Diamond: The Treasure and the Blessing, Law and Artistry

Nachman Levine

Introduction

The Midrashic story of R. Shimon b. Shatah and his 'transaction' with the Arab idolator whose donkey he purchases (*Midrash Deuteronomy Rabbah* 3:3) is worth examining, both for its virtuosic literary properties, and for the way it employs them to relate to Halakhic legal and meta-legal ethical issues. This is valuable and important in the area of the literary reading of Talmudic stories and Midrashim (and the biblical texts they explicate) and in the much-discussed relation of *halakhah* and *aggadah*. It is also relevant to a new rich scholarly field interested in the relationship of law and literature in Talmudic legal texts, in the *literary* properties of Mishnah and Tosefta[1] and talmudic *halakhah*,[2] and even in the editorial contextualization of stories or *aggadah* within legal *sugyot*.[3]

My primary interest here, however, will be in a literary analysis of the R. Shimon b. Shatah story. In its lapidary terse brevity of perhaps three lines of direct speech, it subtly and artistically uses a broad range of literary techniques. These include allusion, wordplay, intertextuality, implied syntactic multivalence, structural reversal, and more, to consider and adjudicate Halakhic legal, meta-legal, and meta-ethical issues in succinct and condensed narrative form.

---

1   Walfish, "The Mishnah in the Intertextual Perspective," 233; מרבדי משנה וכח הערוכה היוצרת וכח היוצר"; "Approaching the Text and Approaching God;" Simon-Shoshan, *Stories of the Law*.
2   Rubenstein, *Talmudic Stories*, 10–15. Wimpfheimer, *Narrating the Law*.
3   See: Segal, "Law As Allegory," 245–246; Rubenstein, *Talmudic Stories*; "Bavli Gittin 55b–56b," 21–48; Feintuch, *Maasei Hachamim*; ,פנים אל פנים; Meir, *HaSipur Teluy–HaHeksher*, 103–119; Lavee, "Welfare and Education vs. Leadership and Redemption;" Valler, *Women and Womenhood in the Talmudic Stories*, 17–19; *Women in Jewish Society in the Period of* the *Mishnah and Talmud*, 30–51; Brandes, *Aggadah Le-Ma'aseh*; The Izbitser Rebbe is reported as saying that every Talmudic statement, though appearing randomly included in a *Sugya*, has a deep connection to the Halachic discussion there (*Mei HaShiloah*, 223; R. Tzadok HaKohen of Lublin, *Yisrael Qedoshim*, p. 24).

Though a Midrashic text, it alludes to and presumes the awareness of legal Halakhic issues, and pointedly does not spell them out directly. That artistry and silence and the way it is used to weigh in on the issues it engages deserves careful study. Because while the short story about the commercial and ethical transaction between R. Shimon and the *Yishmaeli* is charming and instructive even at face value, a closer reading of its brevity and structure reveals its own hidden treasure, a gem with a density of meaning in subtle artistry and meta-legal complexity.

Midrash Deuteronomy Rabbah 3:3[4]

מעשה ברבי שמעון בן שטח שלקח חמור אחד מישמעאלי אחד
הלכו תלמידיו ומצאו בו אבן אחת טובה תלויה לו בצוארו
אמרו לו: "רבי, 'בִּרְכַּת ה' הִיא תַעֲשִׁיר'" (משלי י,כב)
אמר להם רבי שמעון בן שטח: "חמור לקחתי, אבן טובה לא לקחתי"
הלך והחזירה לאותו ישמעאלי
קרא עליו אותו ישמעאל: "ברוך ה' אלהי שמעון בן שטח"
הוי מאמונתו של בשר ודם
את יכול לידע אמונתו של הקדוש ברוך הוא
שנאמן לשלם שכר טוב לישראל
... אבל מתן שכרן "וְהָיָה עֵקֶב תִּשְׁמְעוּן": בעקב אני פורע לכם

A story about R. Shimon (שמעון) b. Shatah, who acquired a donkey from an Ishmaelite (ישמעאלי).
His students went and found a precious stone hanging from its neck.
They said to him, "Master: *'It is the blessing of God that enriches,'*" (Prov. 10:22).
R. Shimon b. Shatah said to them, "A donkey I purchased; a precious stone I did not purchase."
He went and returned it to that Ishmaelite.
That Ishmaelite called upon him, *"Blessed is the Lord*, the God of Shimon b. Shatah."
Thus from the trustworthiness of flesh and blood
you may know the trustworthiness of the Holy One Blessed be He
that He is trustworthy to pay good reward to Israel
... but the giving of reward, "And if you will heed" (תִּשְׁמְעוּן), will be in the end

---

[4] Leiberman Edition, Jerusalem 1940, from Oxford mss. 147. The parallel y.Bava Metsia 2:5 story, discussed below, is helpful in clarifying some details, but has a different focus.

Wordplay and the Transaction

The story opens with a *triple*-play wordplay in a *Midrash* on the reward for good deeds in Deuteronomy 7:12: "וְהָיָה עֵקֶב תִּשְׁמְעוּן", "And if you *will heed*": "*Tishmeun*,"[5] connecting R. *Shimon* ("שמעון") and the *Yishmaeli* ("ישמעאלי") in it. The parallel version of this account recorded in the Yerushalmi (*y.Bava Metsia* 2:5) makes the wordplay on R. Shimon's name[6] more explicit: "He said: '*Shimon* ("שמעון") b. Shatah wishes to *hear* ("משמע") 'Blessed is the God of the Jews,' more than all the reward in this world,'" (but does not connect it with "*Tishmeu*" or the "*Yishmaeli*" which raises the question of which is the original version.)[7]

Furthermore, the description of R. *Shimon's* protagonist as a "*Yishmaeli*" is the only such description of an individual Arab in all of the Babylonian or Palestinian Talmuds, or any Halakhic or Aggadic Midrashim, when not describing a Biblical personage called that way in the Bible.[8] More than mere ornamental

---

5   Deuteronomy Rabbah generally comments only on a *Parashah's* opening verse. (See Lieberman, *Devarim Rabah* Introduction; Mirkin, *Midrash Rabah*, Introduction to *Deuteronomy Rabah*.)

6   Wordplays on this sage's name appear in y.Nazir 5:3 (and *Kohelet Rabbah* 7; Genesis Rabbah 91:3): "Yanai *heard* ("שמע") and was angry, *Shimon* b. Shatah *heard* this ("שמע שמעון בן שטח") and escaped … Yanai told him, 'I have never heard ("לא שמעית") 'Yanai' in the Blessing';" the Genesis Rabbah 91:3 version continues: "R. Yohanan said, 'They dispute the *traditions* of *Shimon* b. Shatah ("על שמועת שמעון בן שטח")'." (Similarly, b.Menahot 18a: כשהלכתי למצות מדותי). אצל ר' אלעזר בן שמוע … אמר לו: יוסף, כמדומה אני שלא כיוונו שמועתינו עד עתה B.Makkot 5b cites t.Sanhedrin 6:6 that *Shimon* b. Shatah showed Yehudah b. Tabai that his ruling wrongly executed someone, and then continues, reversing the name of "שמעון בן שטח": "All his days Yehudah b. Tabai would *prostrate* ("משתטח") on the executed one's grave and his voice was *heard*" ("נשמע"). Levine, "על מדרשי שמות תלמודיים".

7   On wordplay on sages' names: מהר"ץ חיות, מבוא התלמוד, פרק יז, הגהות לתלמוד בבלי בבא מציעא כה, א; ר' ראובן מרגליות, "הפסידונים בתלמוד", לחקר שמות וכנויים בתלמוד; ש"י פרידמן, תלמוד ערוך, ב"מ פ"ו, ירושלים תשנ"ז; הנ"ל, "השם גורם: דברי החכם נופלים על שמו", ואלה שמות: מחקרים באוצר השמות היהודיים, רמת גן, תשנ"ט; צ"ה ליעווין, "העלם דבר", השחר, יב (תרמ"ד); מנחת יהודה לבראשית רבה, ע' 776; צ' מלטער, מסכת תענית, ניו יורק, תר"ץ, תש"ב; י' קאפח, "על שמות בעלי שמועה הזהים עם שמועתם", סיני נז (תשכ"ה); י"א זליגמן, מחקרים; ש' ליברמן, יוונית ויונות בארץ ישראל, ירושלים תשכ"ג; ש"מ רובנשטיין, "שמות מלאכותיים", קובנה, תרצ"ב.

Horowitz "Ueber einege Namen der Rabbinen im Talmud und Midrasch"; Wynkoop, "A Peculiar Kind of Paranomasia in the Talmud and Midrash"; Jacobs, "How Much of the Babylonian Talmud is Psuedoepigraphic?".

8   In the Mishnah (m.Kelim, 5:10; 24:1; 26:4; 29:1; m.'Ohalot 18:10; m.Shabbat 6:6) the term is "ערביין" or "הערביים" or "ערביות"; in Sifre Deuteronomy 343: "ערב". Throughout the *Bavli* (and *not* the *Yerushalmi*) an Arab is a "טייעא", referring to the Arabic *Tayyi'* (طيّ) tribe of Syria and Mesopotamia, and sometimes "ערביי". The *Tayyi* were so widespread and influential throughout the Syrian Desert that Syriac authors from Mesopotamia used their name, *Taienos, Tayenoi, Taiyaya* or *Tayyaye* (ܛܝܝܐ), to describe Arab tribesmen in general in much

style (though charmingly, that too), the wordplay on their names and its connection to the verse it expounds demarcates their relationship in a transaction of values constructed in three lines of direct speech: the students to R. Shimon b. Shatah, his response, and the *Yishmaeli*'s response in blessing R. Shimon's God.

Reversal as Structure

The direct speech triad creates a chiastic structure, or *inclusio* envelope, beginning and ending in subtle symmetry with *blessing*. It *begins* with: "It is *the blessing of the Lord* that enriches," and *ends* with: "*Blessed is the Lord*, the God of Shimon b. Shatah."

"ברכת ה׳ היא תעשיר"	"It is ***the blessing of the Lord*** that enriches," (Prov. 10:22).
"חמור לקחתי, אבן טובה לא לקחתי"	"I purchased a donkey; I did not purchase a precious stone."
"ברוך ה׳ אלהי שמעון בן שטח."	"***Blessed is the Lord***, the God of Shimon b. Shatah."

And well it should, since this is a Midrash about the verses in Deuteronomy 7:12–13 which describes the rewarded *blessing* for *heeding* God:

(יב) וְהָיָה עֵקֶב **תִּשְׁמְעוּן** אֵת הַמִּשְׁפָּטִים הָאֵלֶּה וּשְׁמַרְתֶּם וַעֲשִׂיתֶם אֹתָם וְשָׁמַר ה׳ אֱלֹהֶיךָ לְךָ אֶת הַבְּרִית וְאֶת הַחֶסֶד אֲשֶׁר נִשְׁבַּע לַאֲבֹתֶיךָ: (יג) וַאֲהֵבְךָ **וּבֵרַכְךָ** וְהִרְבֶּךָ וּבֵרַךְ פְּרִי בִטְנְךָ וּפְרִי אַדְמָתֶךָ דְּגָנְךָ וְתִירֹשְׁךָ וְיִצְהָרֶךָ שְׁגַר אֲלָפֶיךָ וְעַשְׁתְּרֹת צֹאנֶךָ עַל הָאֲדָמָה אֲשֶׁר נִשְׁבַּע לַאֲבֹתֶיךָ לָתֶת לָךְ: (יד) **בָּרוּךְ תִּהְיֶה מִכָּל הָעַמִּים** לֹא יִהְיֶה בְךָ עָקָר וַעֲקָרָה וּבִבְהֶמְתֶּךָ:

---

the same way "*Saracenos*" was often used by authors from Byzantine Syria and Egypt as a generic term for Arabs (see Retsö, *The Arabs in Antiquity*, Shahid, *Byzantium and the Arabs in the Fifth Century*). Many of the references in the Bavli to *Tayyi* are about their interactions with amoraim in Bavel (see: Carmeli, "*Jahiliyyah*: The Figure of the Arab," 77–109). In the Yerushalmi in general, as in *this* story's version, an Arab is a "סרקי" ("*Saracen*") or "ערבייא" or "ערבי" (y.Shevi'it 6:1; y.Megillah 1:9). In b.Sukkah 52b; b.Mo'ed Qatan 44a, the designation "ישמעאלים" is generic. There is, to be sure, wordplay on the *Tayyi* in the Bavli, in b.Shabbat 155a: "לדידי חזי לי ההוא **טייעא** דאכלא כורא **ואטעינא** כורא": "I saw an *Arab* (**טייעא**) who fed his camel a *kor* of food and *loaded* (**ואטעינא**) it with another *kor* on its back".

At first, the students poetically declare a biblical verse, Proverbs 10:22: "It is *the blessing of the Lord* that enriches"–its unspoken end, "ולא יוסיף עצב עמה": "and toil *will add nothing* to it," is as if artfully reversed to: "*no toil is needed to add* to it." Indeed, this is how the verse is read in *Tanhuma Ki Tisa* 29 and *Midrash Tehilim* 78,[9] and implied in the *Yerushalmi* story: "They told him, 'From now you *no longer need to toil hard*.'" ("אמרין ליה 'מן כדון לית את צריך לעי תובן'"). R. Shimon's brusquely factual response, "I purchased a donkey; I did not purchase a precious stone," which is not at all poetic (and as such becomes completely poetic) generates the closing actual blessing, *"Blessed is the Lord*, the God of Shimon b. Shatah".

In a maneuver *hidden in plain sight*, the verse's inherent syntactic (genitive, possessive) ambiguity reverses subtly to be the story's framework. In the *opening* students' declaration, the verse, *"It is the blessing of God* ("ברכת ה'") *that enriches,"* (Proverbs 10:22), means "a blessing *from* God." By contrast, at the story's closing, where the *Yishmaeli* blesses R. Shimon's God, with *"Blessed is the Lord*, the God of Shimon b. Shatah", "the blessing *of God*" ("ברכת ה'") now reverses unspoken as if to mean: "It is the *blessing*—"*to God*"—that enriches." The closing narrative blessing is *not* a biblical verse or interpretation, but the *Yishmaeli*'s real-life statement which becomes a reinterpretation of the verse as well as its *enactment*.

Moreover, "That *Yishmaeli called upon him, 'Blessed is* the God of ...,'" sounds *as if* it were the classic Talmudic narrative formula, "He *called/read* upon him *this verse* ..." ("... קרא עליו המקרא הזה") that appears often in Talmudic stories,[10] in which sages cite biblical verses that acquire new meaning when applied to a new reality to interpret an event it reflects.[11] It is simply, however, the Ishmaelite's stated reaction, *not* a biblical verse or interpretation. We would have in fact expected such a locution to appear at the story's *beginning* to describe *the students* in this way: "His students found a precious stone hanging on its neck *and they called/read upon him this verse*: "It is the blessing of God that enriches" (Proverbs 10:22)."

But it does not. Nor is it appropriate that it should, since according to R. Shimon their statement is mistaken and misrepresents the verse's meaning in this context. The *proper meaning* in this context of *"It is the blessing of* God that

---

9   Or in a Halachic re-reading prohibiting mourning on the Sabbath: y.Berakhot 2:7; y.Mo'ed Qatan 3:5; Genesis Rabbah 1:1; 100:7: "ויברך": "ברכת ה' היא תעשיר" ... "ומנין שאין אבל בשבת אלהים את יום השביעי" (בר' ב, ג), "ולא יוסיף עצב עמה": זה האבל".
10 For the phenomenon, see Frankel, *Sipur HaAgadah*, 198–219; *Darkei HaAgadah VeHaMidrash*, 247–253 at length.
11 Variously in many sources: "He/she/they/ *called/read* upon [him/her/them/himself]."

enriches," emerges reinterpreted by the *Yishmaeli* as if in the classic Talmudic locution. The biblical verse declared by *the students* (and *not* their teacher) is reversed in real life to be an *actual* blessing *not* made in erudite *scholarship* about benefit for the Torah's *study*, but by the *Yishmaeli*, because of its *observance*.

What's more, the Midrash's syntactically reversed blessing in effect semantically reverses the blessing in the *next verse*, Deuteronomy 7:14, concerning the reward for good deeds: "ברוך תהיה מכל העמים", "You shall be blessed *more than*[12] all peoples," to read as: "You shall be blessed *by* all peoples." Indeed, the reversal is made clear three passages later in Deuteronomy Rabbah 3:6: "R. Hiyya bar Abba said, 'You shall be blessed *from all peoples*': It is not the queen's praise when she is praised by her relatives, but when *she is praised by her rivals*.'" In several places the *Yerushalmi* contains similar readings in a *Halakhic* context:[13] "If a non-Jew blesses you, *you must answer 'Amen'*, as it says: "ברוך תהיה מכל העמים" (Deuteronomy 7:14), 'You shall be blessed *from all peoples*'."

In this way, the Deuteronomy Rabbah story is revealed to be a commentary on the pericope's first three verses, the reward for heeding God ("וְהָיָה עֵקֶב תִּשְׁמְעוּן אֵת הַמִּשְׁפָּטִים הָאֵלֶּה וּשְׁמַרְתֶּם וַעֲשִׂיתֶם אֹתָם" (7:12)), which becomes the reward of being blessed *for such heeding* by others of the non-Jewish nations ("בָּרוּךְ תִּהְיֶה מִכָּל הָעַמִּים" (7:14)).

The Blessing That Enriches

The blessing of God enriches everyone in the story, including its readers. R. Shimon is enriched in the blessing of his God, as well as in the sanctification of His Name, although *he never intended* nor mentioned that (this silence will be significant). The students are enriched by the new blessing that validates their teacher's position and teaches them (and us) a new level of ethical behavior and a new interpretation of the verse. The *Yishmaeli* is enriched not only in the return of the precious stone or even in recognizing R. Shimon's God and His ethical commandment, but in its rationale which has validated him. The non-articulated rationale is conveyed in this silence. For in the students' citation of "It is *the blessing of the Lord* that enriches," which expresses concern for their teacher, there is hidden however indirectly, a clear Halakhic argument, unspo-

---

12 R. Bahyei Al HaTorah, ad. loc.
13 Y.Berakhot 8:8; Sukkah 3:10; Megillah 1:9. The lexically creative but grammatically correct reading is codified in Jewish law in *Rema, Shulhan Aruch* 1:215.

ken as if obvious: while theft from an idol-worshipper is forbidden,[14] his lost object is permitted.[15]

Indeed, this *Yishmaeli*, a *first-century* contemporary of R. Shimon b. Shatah,[16] *is* a full-fledged polytheistic *idol worshipper, not* a Moslem monotheist. Until the fourth century and perhaps much after, the pre-Islamic world embraced a broad panoply of worshipped gods, goddesses, and idols. Throughout the Talmudim and Midrashim the pre-Islamic Arabs of the contemporaneous Mishnaic-Talmudic periods were presumed to be active polytheistic idolaters,[17] and in fact were also described as such in *Islamic* writings afterwards as pagans.[18] Deuteronomy Rabbah is generally dated to the time of the *Tanhuma*, roughly the sixth century[19] and the Yerushalmi to around the fifth century, both predating Islam significantly. Consequently, this *Yishmaeli* would be outside the purview of even the Meiri's extreme position (*Beit HaBehirah, Bava Qamma* 113b) that return of a lost object ("of *your brother*," Deuteronomy 22:3) would extend even to a non-Jew *if he believed in God in some manner and was not an idolater.*

The legal argument in regard to this *Yishmaeli* is more explicitly articulated in the Yerushalmi version, y.Bava Metsia 2:5 (though the moral idea there is different). R. Shimon b. Shatah would sell flax; his students told him, "Master, leave it and we will buy you a donkey and you will not need to work so hard." They went and bought him a donkey from an Arab ("*Sirkai*", "סרקיי": *Saracen*) merchant and it had a pearl hanging from its neck. They came to him and said, "Now you do not need to work hard anymore." When he asked them if the seller knew about it, and they said he did not, he told them, "Go return it."

The question is then raised[20] (in its *own* wordplay), "Didn't Rav Huna Baybei bar *Gozlon* ("גוזלון") say in Rav's name that they asked this before R. Yehudah HaNasi, who said even according to the opinion that **theft from an idol worshipper** ("גזילו של עכו״ם") is forbidden, *his lost object is permitted?*" The response

---

14   Sifra, Behar 6; b.Bava Qamma 113b.
15   Midrash Tanaim, Deuteronomy 22; b.Bava Qamma 113b.
16   Josephus, *Antiquities*, Vol. 13:12,1 320.
17   See for instance, b.Avodah Zarah 11b; b.Avodah Zarah 33a; b.Hullin 39b; b. Sukkah 52b and y.Ta'anit 3:4.
18   Retsö, *The Arabs in Antiquity*; Shahid, *Byzantium and the Arabs*.
19   See Lieberman Edition, Introduction; Bergman, *The Tanhuma-Yelammedenu Literature*.
20   Apparently in an *editorial* discussion in the Yerushalmi '*stama*', as it could not be a debate between R. Shimon and his students about the positions of Rav and R. Yehudah HaNasi who lived much later. Lieberman in his notes to the Yerushalmi Escorial Manuscript, Lieberman-Rosenthal 1983 Edition, feels it is extracted from the Yerushalmi's later discussion.

comes in further *opposed* wordplay: "[R. Shimon b. Shatah said] 'What do you think, that Shimon b. Shatah is a barbarian? Shimon ("שמעון") b. Shatah wishes to *hear* ("משמוע") 'Blessed is the God of the Jews,' more than all of the reward in this world'."

In the Deuteronomy Rabbah version, R. Shimon does not relate to the celebratory verse's imbedded argument, but simply declares *of himself*: "I purchased a donkey; I did not purchase a precious stone." This effectively undoes the story's opening triad of opposed value of "*ones*" in the transaction:

[מעשה ברבי שמעון בן שטח]
שלקח חמור **אחד**
מישמעאלי **אחד**
הלכו תלמידיו ומצאו בו אבן טובה **אחת** תלויה לו בצוארו

A story about R. Shimon b. Shatah
who bought *one* donkey ["חמור **אחד**"]
from *one* Ishmaelite ["ישמעאלי **אחד**"]
[His students went and found] *one* precious stone ["אבן טובה **אחת**"]
    hanging on its neck

In the students' estimation, the prime value in the "אחד"\"אחד"\"אחת" hierarchy is the "*one precious stone*" ["אבן טובה אחת"], *not* for its material worth but because of its transcendent significance as "blessing of God" so that their teacher may live an easier life and perhaps be fully involved in teaching them Torah. This effectively lowers the triad's other elements, the "*one donkey*" ["חמור **אחד**"] and "*one Yishmaeli*" ["ישמעאלי **אחד**"], and thus possibly equates them.

The relation in the Deuteronomy Rabbah version of the donkey and the Arab named as a "*Yishmaeli*" might subtly reinforce such an equation's biblical or Midrashic associations. In Genesis 16:12: "[Yishmael] will be a wild *donkey* of a man"; in Leviticus Rabbah 20:2, Abraham at the *Akeidah* tells Yishmael [and Eliezer] who don't see the mountaintop cloud that he and Isaac do: Therefore, "Stay here with *the donkey*" (שבו לכם פה עם החמור) [*im he-chamor*] (ibid 22:5), is read as '*am he-chamor*': "*nation like* the donkey" ("עם הדומה לחמור")).

But R. Shimon's negating (or ignoring) the ethnic factor with, "I purchased a donkey; I did *not* purchase a precious stone," breaks the triad and its assumptions. Undoing the "*one Yishmaeli*" and "*one donkey*" equation raises the "*one Yishmaeli*" to equal the "*one* precious stone" which thus returns in ownership and status to him. The "blessing *from* God", according to the students—the stone, and *the blessing itself*—is reversed and transferred back to the *Yishmaeli* to become the blessing he gives *to* God.

The Ideological Dialogue

The beauty in the ideological dialogue between R. Shimon and the *Yishmaeli* is that there *is no* dialogue between them. R. Shimon's words are to his students and the *Yishmaeli*'s are said about, or to, R. Shimon's God, while the moral principle and its results stand on their own. In R. Shimon's formulation there is no difference between them from the legal and ethical perspective. His uprightness is expressed in blunt explanation about an action beyond the letter of the law (*Lefnim MiShurat HaDin*) as if it were *the letter of the law*. It is a declaration about himself; it does not relate to the *Yishmaeli* as the recipient of his action, nor to a final Halakhic ruling, or one that opposes an existing *halakhah*.

Nor, significantly, does he mention *any objective* of a *Qiddush HaShem*, a Sanctification of God's Name, but simply defines his action *as if it were the law*. While some read R. Shimon's intent as for a *Qiddush HaShem*,[21] I see no indication of that, particularly since the Midrash ends with: "Thus from the *trustworthiness*, i.e., the *integrity*, of flesh and blood [R. Shimon], you may know the Holy One Blessed be He's trustworthiness." It is a story about integrity. A *great* sanctification of God's Name *is* in fact created, precisely because *he did not* intend one. If he had, the story might not have ended as it does with the *deeply* impressed *Yishmaeli* blessing R. Shimon's God for His ethical laws, legal imperatives beyond *any* contingent considerations, *even* that of a *Qiddush HaShem*.

Maimonides's ruling (*Gezeilah VeAveidah* 11:3) to return a non-Jew's object in a case that could involve Sanctification or desecration of God's Name is not based on the Deuteronomy Rabbah story but, as *Kesef Mishneh* ad loc. notes, on the y.Bava Metsia 2:5 version. The discussion in the Yerushalmi there is explicitly about sanctifying God's Name and the story appears in a series of necessarily inter-ethnic ones about lost articles returned to non-Jews. In the triple-ethnic triad there, the pearl is returned to the "*Sirkai*" ["סרקאי", "Saracen", Arab[22]] since R. Shimon says of himself that he is not a "*Barabaron*" ("ברברון",

---

21 Ranging from the commentary *Etz Yosef* (Zundel) on Devarim Rabbah, to Levine, Introduction, *The Oxford Handbook of Judaism and Economics*.

22 The Latin term "*Saraceni*", used here in the Yerushalmi in Roman Palestine, is of unknown original meaning, perhaps derived from the Semitic triliteral root *šrq* "east" and *šrkt* "tribe" (*Toral-Niehoff*, "*Saraca*"). Both Hippolytus of Rome and Uranius mention three distinct peoples in Arabia during the first half of the third century: the *Taeni*, the *Saraceni*, and the *Arabes*. (Retsö, *The Arabs in Antiquity*, 505). Sokoloff, *Dictionary of Jewish Palestinian Aramaic*, "סרקיי", notes its usage in Christian Palestinian Aramaic, and cites, besides its appearances in the *Talmud Yerushalmi*, its translation in fragments of the *Targum Yerushalmi/Pseudo-Jonathan* and *Neofiti* of Biblical "יִשְׁמְעֵאלִים" (Genesis 37:25, 27, 28; 39:1) as "סרקאין", "סרקאי", and "סרקעיך".

"Barbarian"²³) but desires only to hear the blessing of "the God of *the Jews* ("דיהודאי")." (There may be an irony in the Yerushalmi (in Roman Palestine) as the Romans in fact classified the *Saraceni* as *Barbarians*.²⁴)

Since the *Yishmaeli* is an idol-worshipper, R. Shimon b. Shatah's God that he blesses is not one they share. Nevertheless the *Yishmaeli* is joined with R. Shimon as he blesses his God for teaching such ethicality as the law. Despite *and because of* the distance between them, R. *Shimon* and the *Yishmaeli* are connected in sound (שמעון\ישמעאלי) and in blessing in a way the students are not. In reversal, the 'blessing' precipitated by "His students went ("הלכו תלמידיו") and found a precious stone", excludes the *Yishmaeli*, after which, "[R. Shimon] went ("הלך והחזירה") and returned it," connects R. Shimon and the *Yishmaeli* in a blessing that now excludes the students.

Since the *Qiddush HaShem* was unintended, the resultant blessing comes as a surprise, so that *both* hidden "*blessings*", i.e. the stone, and the *Yishmaeli*'s blessing God for its return, are opposed unanticipated treasures. As it turns out, the hidden stone is *not* the "blessing of the Lord", possessing no lasting worth in R. Shimon's estimation and certainly when as a result he does not accept it. It is rather the *blessing of the Lord* that becomes the treasure whose value is as in the *Yerushalmi* story, "*more than all of the reward in this world.*" As a result, the story itself turns out to be for us the hidden gem, 'the blessing of God that enriches', enriching us as its artistry and aesthetic is used to richly enhance our moral consciousness.

Conclusion

We have seen how in the concise Midrash Deuteronomy Rabbah version of the story, a variety of literary and stylistic techniques are used to succinctly convey a meta-Halakhic stance on ethical or meta-ethical behavior beyond the law. As it re-reads and reverses *Prov.* 10:22, it expounds on the verses it interprets, Deuteronomy 7:12–13, the reward for heeding and obeying God's laws. It also subtly reinterprets Deuteronomy 7:14 to mean the reward of being blessed,

---

23 From Ancient Greek: βάρβαρος (*barbaros*) to describe those who did not speak Greek or follow classical Greek customs; the Romans used the term *Barbarus* for uncivilized people, as it is used here in the *Yerushalmi* story. Ptolemy's 2nd-century *Geography*, describes *Sarakēnḗ* (Σαρακηνή) as a region in the northern Sinai Peninsula, and also mentions Saracen a people called the *Sarakēnoí* (οἱ Σαρακηνοί) living in the northwestern Arabian Peninsula (Retsö, *The Arabs in Antiquity*, ibid).

24 Retsö, ibid. Midrash Deuteronomy Rabbah was of course also created in *Roman Palestine*.

not only *more than* all the nations, but even *by them* for heeding those laws, or beyond them, in dealing with the nations, to set a new meta-Halakhic ethical standard.

However, the Halakhic issue with which the Midrash deals is complicated and its relationship to it is more complex than appears. From the legal perspective, the Midrashic story's concluded message is *not* the law and perhaps even in conflict with it.[25] Unlike the Yerushalmi version, there is no *direct* discussion in the story about the legal issue of an idolater's lost object,[26] although it is implied and assumed in it. There is only a description of R. Shimon's action beyond the law, which he appears to present as if it was the strict letter of the law. The legal permission to acquire an idolater's lost object is derived in the Talmud from Deuteronomy 22:3: "[And so you shall do the same with his *donkey* ...] and so shall you do with any lost article of *your brother* that you find,"[27] and the *Yishmaeli* is not R. Shimon's brother. While there is extensive discussion within Talmudic law about the legal status and obligation of *"Lefnim MiShurat HaDin,"* to go beyond the letter of the law,[28] this story goes beyond *even that* by portraying an action beyond the obligation of the law—*as if that were* the law.

Moreover, the story cannot be a source of law since the Talmudic rule is, "We do not derive *halakhah* from *aggadah*,"[29] a vast topic in rabbinic literature in itself. Yet it has been argued that this does not reflect a difference in authority between the two categories, but parallels the rule within *halakhah* that "We do not derive *monetary laws* from laws of *prohibitions*,"[30] or "We do not derive laws of *prohibitions* from *monetary* laws,"[31] because the rules and values in the two categories of law, or the two genres, are dissimilar and cannot be derived reciprocally.[32] It is even proposed that an Aggadic story or statement may be *purposely* included *within* a Halakhic Talmudic *Sugya* discussion as a *counter-*value in order to oppose the *Sugya's* legal conclusion.[33] Clearly, within legal Halakhic *Sugyot*, inherent tensions and conflicts between values and principles operate persistently in the discussion by their very nature.[34]

---

25 Baraita, b.Bava Qamma 113; b.Sanhedrin 76b.
26 B.Bava Qamma 113b; Midrash Tannaim 22.
27 Ibid.
28 Mekhilta de'Rabbi Yishmael, Yitro, Mesekhta de'Amaleq 2; Mekhilta de'Rabbi Shimon 18:20., etc.
29 Y.Peah 2:4 and y.Hagigah 1:8.
30 B.Ketubbot 40b, 46b; b.Qiddushin 32.
31 B.Berakhot 19b, Bava Metsia 20b.
32 Schneerson, *Likutei Sihot*, 399.
33 Brandes, *Agadah LeMaaseh*, extensively.
34 Ibid.

In that same way, the R. Shimon b. Shatah story's dynamic opposition of legal and meta-legal values greatly enriches our awareness and moral consciousness. With its dialectic tension—and its subtle artistry—the story itself turns out to be for us the hidden gem, 'the blessing of God that enriches.'

Bibliography

Bergman, Marc, The Tanhuma-Yelammedenu Literature: Studies in the Evolution of the Versions (Hebrew) Piscataway: Gorgias Press, 2003

Brandes, Yehuda, *Aggadah Le-Ma'aseh*, (Hebrew), Jerusalem: Beit Morasha, 2005

Carmeli, Yehonatan, "*Jahiliyyah*: The Figure of the Arab, Taya'ei and Ishmaelite in the Talmudic Literature" (Hebrew), *Pe'amim: Studies in Oriental Jewry*, 158, 2019, 77–109

Chajes, Rabbi Zvi Hirsch, מבוא התלמוד, פרק יז, Lvov: Margulies Press, 1845

Chajes, Rabbi Zvi Hirsch, הגהות לתלמוד בבלי בבא מציעא כה, ע"א, Vienna, 1869

Feintuch, Yonatan, *Maasei Hachamim VeHaSeguyot Hamechilot otan biMasechet Nezikin* (Bavli), doctoral dissertation, Bar-Ilan University 2019

Feintuch, Yonatan, *Agadot HaTalmud*, Yeshivat Har Etzion Virtual Beit Midrash, 2010

Feintuch, Yonatan, פנים אל פנים, שזירת ההלכה והאגדה בתלמוד הבבלי, Jerusalem: Maggid, 2019

Frankel, Yonah, Darkei HaAgadah VeHaMidrash, Givatayim: Kibbutz HaMeuchad, 1991, 247–253

Sipur HaAgadah, Ahdut Tochen VeTzurah Chapter 6: "The Literary Function of Biblical Verses Cited by Sages" (Hebrew), Tel-Aviv: Kibbutz HaMeuchad, 2001, 198–219

Friedman, Shamma Yehudah, תלמוד ערוך, ב"מ פ"ו, ירושלים תשנ"ז

Friedman, Shamma Yehudah, "השם גורם: דברי החכם נופלים על שמו", ואלה שמות: מחקרים באוצר השמות היהודיים, רמת גן, תשנ"ט

Horowitz, J., "Ueber einege Namen der Rabbinen im Talmud und Midrasch", *Monatsschrift für Geschite und Wissenschaft des Judenthums*, 32 (1883)

Jacobs, Louis, "How Much of the Babylonian Talmud is Psuedoepigraphic?", *JJS* 28 (1997)

Josephus, *Antiquities*, Vol. 13:12,1 320, Cambridge: Loeb Classical Library, Harvard University Press, 1943

Lavee, Moshe, "Welfare and Education vs. Leadership and Redemption: The Stories about Rabbi and Rabbi Hiyya as an Example of the Image of the Tannaitic Past in the Babylonian Talmud" (Hebrew); *JSIJ* 6, 2009

Levine, Aron, *The Oxford Handbook of Judaism and Economics* Oxford University Press, New York, 2010

Levine, Nachman, "על מדרשי שמות תלמודיים: עיצוב ספרותי ומשמעותו", *JSIJ* 11, 2013

Lieberman, Saul, יוונית ויוונות בארץ ישראל Jerusalem: Bialik Press, 1962

Kafih, Rabbi Yosef, (תשכ"ה) "על שמות בעלי שמועה הזהים עם שמועתם", סיני נז

Malter, Tzvi, מסכת תענית, ניו יורק, תר"ץ, תש"ב

Margoliot, Rabbi Reuven, "הפסידונים בתלמוד", לחקר שמות וכנויים בתלמוד, Jerusalem: Mossad HaRav Kook, 1989

Meir, Ofra, *HaSipur Teluy–HaHeksher BaTalmud, Bikoret UParshanut* 20 (1985), 103–119

Mirkin, Moshe Aryeh, *Midrash Rabah* 1957, Introduction, Jerusalem, 1980

Retsö, Jan, *The Arabs in Antiquity: Their History from the Assyrians to the Umayyads*, London & New York 2003

Rubenstein, Jeffrey, *Talmudic Stories: Narrative Art, Composition, and Culture*, Baltimore: Johns Hopkins University Press, 2010

Rubenstein, Jeffrey, "Bavli Gittin 55b–56b: An Aggadic Narrative in its Halakhic Context", *Hebrew Studies* 38 (1997) 21–48

Rubenstein, S.M., "שמות מלאכותיים", קובנה, תרצ"ב

Schneerson, Rabbi Menachem Mendel, *Likutei Sihot, Parshat Vayishlah*, Vol. 8, Brooklyn: Kehot Publishing, 1972

Segal, Eliezer, "Law As Allegory: An Unnoticed Device In Talmudic Narratives", *Prooftexts* 8 (1988), 245–246

Shahid, Irfan, *Byzantium and the Arabs in the Fifth Century*, Washington DC: Dumbarton Oaks Research Library and Collection, 1989

Simon-Shoshan, Moshe, *Stories of the Law: Narrative Discourse and the Construction of Authority in the Mishnah*, Oxford University Press, 2012

Sokoloff, Michael, *Dictionary of Jewish Palestinian Aramaic of the Byzantine Period*, Bar-Ilan University Press, Ramat-Gan, 1990

Toral-Niehoff, Isabel, "Saraca" in *Brill's New Pauly: Encyclopaedia of the Ancient World*, Leiden, Boston: Brill, 2006

Valler, Shulamit, *Women and Womenhood in the Talmudic Stories* (Hebrew), Tel Aviv: Hakibbutz Hameuhad, 1993, 17–19

Valler, Shulamit, *Women in Jewish Society in the Period of the Mishnah and Talmud*, Tel Aviv: Kibbutz HaMeuchad, 2000, 30–51

Walfish, Avraham, "The Mishnah in the Intertextual Perspective: a Study of Three Mishnahs in Light of Agadic Sugyot in Tannaitic and Amoraitic Literature", [Hebrew], *Al Derech HaAvot*, Tevunot: Alon Shvut, 2001

Valler, Shulamit, "מרבדי משנה—פרקי ברכת: עיון ספרותי ורעיוני במשנת ברכות", אלון שבות תשע"ח

Valler, Shulamit, "העריכה היוצרת וכח היוצר: עיון בעריכת מסכת קידושין במשנה בתוספתא ובבבלי", *JSIJ* 7

"Approaching the Text and Approaching God: The Redaction of *Mishnah* and *Tosefta Berakhot*", *Jewish Studies* 43 (2006)

Wimpfheimer, Barry, *Narrating the Law: A Poetics of Talmudic Legal Stories*, PA: University of Pennsylvania Press, 2011

Wynkoop, J.D., "A Peculiar Kind of Paranomasia in the Talmud and Midrash", *JQR* 2 (1911).

Zeligman, Yitzhak Aryeh, מאמרים במקרא ובעולם העתיק, ג, Jerusalem: Rubinstein Press, 1982

Zundel, R. Chanoch, *Etz Yosef on Devarim Rabah*, Warsaw, 1867

CHAPTER 6

Whence Leprosy? An Inquiry into the Theodicies of the Tannaim

Shlomo Zuckier

Discussions[1] of possible causes of the biblical malady known as *tsara'at* appear throughout rabbinic literature. However one precisely defines *tsara'at*,[2] its onset represents a break from the norm, yielding questions as to its purpose and source. Drawing upon mixed biblical evidence as to whether or not *tsara'at* is to be seen as a response to sin, the ancient rabbis developed fairly complex accounts of the sin(s) that cause(s) *tsara'at*, and even consider the possibility that *tsara'at* is not a punishment, but rather a reward. In a study on this topic, Jonathan Klawans argues that tannaitic literature minimizes the phenomenon of *tsara'at* as a punishment.[3] This paper will diverge from that approach in contending that the rabbis clearly and strongly associated *tsara'at* with a divine cause, generally seeing it as a punishment in retribution for sin.

---

1 The title of this essay, which explores how and why God imposes the affliction of *tsara'at*, includes a nod to Prof. Elman's "Righteousness as Its Own Reward: An Inquiry into the Theologies of the Stam," one of several important essays he wrote on issues of theodicy. It is also worth noting that one of Prof. Elman's first published articles was "An Akkadian Cognate of Hebrew *šeḥîn*" in the *Journal of the Ancient Near Eastern Society*, volume 8, pp. 33–34.

   I am deeply grateful for the years that I was lucky enough to study with Prof. Elman. The material and methods that I studied with him, both inside and outside the classroom, have had an indelible impact on me. I particularly appreciate the opportunity to be introduced to academic methods in Talmud by someone who was not only a leading Talmudist but also a *ben Torah* and *talmid hakham*. Studying with Prof. Elman at a time when *nega'im* were a part of his life only served to further demonstrate his commitment to his students. *Yehi zikhro barukh.*

   A portion of this paper was originally submitted as a term paper to Prof. Elman in 2013. He expressed interest in seeing my further research on the topic, and I hope this publication succeeds in some way in fulfilling his request.

2 This is not the place to litigate the proper definition and diagnosis of *tsara'at*, which is apparently not "leprosy" or "Hansen's disease," despite the common association. For an account of that issue, see Jacob Milgrom, *Leviticus 1–16*, 816–818; and J.G. Andersen, "Leprosy in Translations," 207–212. This essay will generally use the Hebrew term *tsara'at*, although on rare occasions (including in the title!) the word "leprosy" will be used as a stand-in for the Hebrew term (following the Septuagint's use of the term λεπρα).

3 Jonathan Klawans, *Impurity and Sin*, 98–104. His treatment will be analyzed and critiqued towards the end of this paper.

The Biblical *Nega* (and) *Tsara'at*

Leviticus 13–14 applies the term *nega tsara'at* ("*tsara'at* affliction"), at times shortened simply to *(ha-)nega*, to refer to the specific skin affliction of *tsara'at*, as well as the similar phenomenon that can occur in clothing (Leviticus 13:47–59) and buildings (Leviticus 14:33–57). Priests and judges are to evaluate these *nega'im* in order to determine their impurity status (Deuteronomy 17:18, 21:5, 24:8[4]). The term *nega* has a general meaning (hypernym) of "malady" or "affliction," making it parallel to *mahalah* (see, e.g., 1 Kings 8:37 = 2 Chronicles 6:28, Exodus 15:26); it can refer to affliction born of punishment, which is why it appears in parallel to "the rod" (*shevet*) at Ps. 89:33 and 2 Samuel 7:14. At the same time, there is also a specific (and particularly common) meaning (hyponym) of *nega* that denotes the *tsara'at* that appears very prominently within the Bible.[5]

The primary ritual treatment of the *nega tsara'at* appears at Leviticus 13–14, where a priest diagnoses *tsara'at* blotches appearing on human skin and hair, clothing, or buildings and directs various courses of treatment or quarantine. (The blotch is called *tsara'at* or *nega tsara'at*, and the person it afflicts is called a *tsaru'a* or *metsora*.) In extreme cases, one who is found to have contracted *tsara'at* is expelled from the camp, clothing containing *tsara'at* is burned, and houses afflicted with *tsara'at* are knocked down.

These chapters in Leviticus describe *tsara'at* as a technical, antiseptic (so to speak) law of impurity that reflects physiological dysfunction, similar to the genital fluxes of a *zav* or *zavah* (see Leviticus 15). The text avoids associating a sense of punishment with the impurity, and instead focuses on the technicalities of diagnosing and resolving this sort of impurity, which can affect both human and non-human entities.

In contrast to the ritual laws of impurity at Leviticus 13–14 relating to *tsara'at*, which avoid judgment, the Bible's literary passages describing figures who contract *tsara'at* offer a different, albeit mixed, perspective.[6] The Bible features sev-

---

4   While Deuteronomy 17:18 and 21:5 refer to *nega*, Deuteronomy 24:8 refers to *nega ha-tsara'at*.
5   It is helpful to delineate the various terms used to refer to *tsara'at*, and particularly to distinguish between *nega*, *tsara'at*, and *nega tsara'at*. (As noted in T. Seidl, "צרעת," 471: "Because *nega'* refers to an 'onset of illness in a general sense,' and can appear with other substantives as well [e.g., *neteq* {13:31}], one cannot rashly equate *sara'at* and *nega'* as synonyms.") In biblical literature, the term *nega* is used to refer to an unspecified malady. One Pharaoh is afflicted with *nega'im* at Genesis 12:17, and another Pharaoh (more famously) at Exodus 12:1, where each of the ten plagues is referred to as a *nega*. Maladies in general are referred to as *nega* in Solomon's prayer (1 Kings 8:37≈2 Chronicles 6:28); *nega'im* can also serve as a punishment for wrongdoing, as is established at Isaiah 53:8, Proverbs 6:33, Psalms 89:33.
6   See Baden and Moss, "The Origin and Interpretation of ṣāra'at," 643–662, which also notes the

eral accounts of people contracting *tsara'at*, some more explicitly blameworthy than others. The Lord afflicts Moses' hand with *tsara'at*, "[white] as snow," at Exodus 4:6, as a sign that he was chosen for the task of leading the Israelite people. Miriam is apparently punished for her words in opposition to Moses, as she contracts *tsara'at* at Numbers 12:10, whereupon Aaron pleads for her well-being, Moses prays for her, and she leaves the camp for seven days, then returns, healed. As punishment for Yoav killing Avner, David curses Yoav's family that it will "never cease to have [cases of] *zav* and *metsora*," along with other maladies (2 Samuels 3:29). In 2 Kings 5, the warrior Na'aman, facing *tsara'at*, approaches the prophet Elisha seeking a cure, and is advised to wash in the Jordan River. After that successful treatment, his offer of a reward to Elisha is declined; Elisha's student Gehazi then requests and receives a gift, and when Elisha finds this out he curses Gehazi that "Na'aman's *tsara'at* shall stick to you and your seed" (2 Kings 5:27). Four lepers sitting outside the city, starving, discover the abandoned Aramean camp (2 Kings 7:3–9). Among the few things known about King Azariah ben Amatsiah of Judah are that he did not remove the *bamot* and that God afflicted him with *tsara'at* (2 Kings 15:4–5). Similarly, Uzziahu rebelled against God, attempting to bring an offering himself instead of sending it with a priest, and was smitten with *tsara'at* for the rest of his life (2 Chronicles 26:19).

There is thus mixed evidence on this point, with some cases of *tsara'at* clearly serving as punishments (Miriam, Yoav, Gehazi, Amatsiah, Uzziahu), some cases at least neutral if not positive (Moses), on the issue, and some ambiguous cases (Na'aman, the four lepers).[7] Still, outside Leviticus 13–14 there is extensive biblical evidence that *tsara'at* can be, and often is, caused by sin.

Ritual vs. Moral Discourses on *Tsara'at*

It would thus seem that we have two distinct discourses regarding *tsara'at* in the Hebrew Bible: (1) Leviticus 13–14, which presents *tsara'at* as a neutral, possi-

---

distinction between Leviticus and other biblical materials on whether the Lord is presented as the source of a (punitive) *tsara'at* ailment or not (pp. 644–645):

> If the narrative portions of the Hebrew Bible are united in the claim that *sâra'at* is the result of sin, the Priestly regulations concerning the disease in Leviticus 13–14 are equally clear that this is not the case: *sàra'at*, in the Priestly presentation, carries no religious or moral guilt, is not associated with any kind of sin, but is rather a simple fact of human existence, one that, like many others, has cultic and ritual implications.

7 Nearly all of these characters appear in rabbinic literature in the context of *tsara'at* as a punishment. See Leviticus Rabbah 16:1, 17:3, b.Arakhin 15b–16a, and Tanhuma 14:2.

bly medical phenomenon, that has various ritual ramifications; (2) narratives throughout the Hebrew Bible that depict the contracting of *tsara'at* as a reflecting moral failing of sorts.

This dichotomization of biblical discussions of *tsara'at* into two distinct discourses, one focused on ritual matters and the other moral ones, has some close parallels. Within biblical scholarship on impurity, it is now commonplace to distinguish between "ritual impurity" and "moral impurity."[8] This distinction in terminology suggests that the Bible offers two divergent discourses on impurity—one based on coming into contact with impure sources and the other based on immoral action. The Bible refers to both of these as "impurity" (ט.מ.א); but they actually point to divergent phenomena that must be understood and treated separately to some degree. Additionally, I have elsewhere proposed that it is possible to understand the Hebrew Bible as presenting two discourses on atonement—a moral atonement and a ritual atonement discourse. While both utilize the term כ.פ.ר, one discourse (especially concentrated within Leviticus 1–16) uses the term to refer to a technical, ritualistic act of purging the altar of impurity (and thereby indirectly resolving sin) while the other uses the term to refer to interpersonal reconciliation, including reconciliation between a sinner and God. Various differences exist between these discourses, as well.[9]

With *tsara'at*, as in the case of atonement and impurity, the cause of the phenomenon is divergent—does the *tsara'at* stem from one's character and actions or from various technical, ritualistic, or accidental causes? In each of these three cases, the ritual discourse appears primarily in Leviticus and associated literature, while the moral discourse appears across other genres, including narrative ones.

Tsara'at also differs in other ways between its ritual and moral discourses, specifically as pertaining to its resolution. *Tsara'at* in Leviticus cannot be resolved other than by waiting, while multiple therapies are proposed for dealing with *tsara'at* in other biblical scenarios: at Exodus 4:6–7, Moses' hand can be miraculously cured; at 2 Kgs 5, Na'aman can bathe in the Jordan to cure his malady. This paper, however, will focus on the primary distinction among the discourses, namely the question of *tsara'at*'s cause. In particular, it considers the ways in which tannaitic literature understands the malady to originate as a punishment for sin.

---

8   These terms at times are also referred to in some places as "permitted impurity" and "prohibited impurity." For treatments of this issue, see Buechler, *Studies in Sin and Atonement*; Wright, "The Spectrum of Priestly Impurity,"; idem., "Unclean and Clean (OT)"; Klawans, *Impurity and Sin*; Klawans, *Purity, Sacrifice, and the Temple*, 53–59; and Hayes, *Gentile Impurities*.

9   See Zuckier, *Flesh and Blood*, chapter 2, and Zuckier, *Theologies of Sacrifice*, forthcoming.

Second Temple Literature

Texts of the Second Temple period discuss *tsara'at* and its ritual applications,[10] but generally do not see it as resulting particularly from sin. The two possible exceptions appear at the fragmentary 4Q270 and 4Q274.

The 4Q270 passage is a version of the Damascus Document. At frag. 2 ii 11–14 appears:

... בשמותם לטמא את רוח קודשו [...] 12 או ינוגע בנגע צרעת או זוב טמ[אה ... וכל]
13 אשר יגלה את רז עמו לגואים או יקלל א[ת עמו או ידבר] 14 סרה על משיחי רוח הקדש ותועה ב[...]

> ... *11* by their names, defiling his holy spirit [...] *12* or infected by the disease of leprosy or one with an impu[re] discharge. [... And whoever] *13* divulges the secret of his people to the pagans, or curses [his people or preaches] *14* rebellion against those anointed with the spirit of holiness and error [...]

Within what appears to be a list of transgressions we find the contraction of an affliction of *tsara'at* or *zav* impurity. Most likely, these outcomes should be read as punishment for sin.

Consider also the passage at 4Q274 (4QPurification Rules A) frag. 1 I 1–2, regarding an individual with *tsar'at*:

1 יחל להפיל את תיכונו משכב יגון ישכב ומושב אנחה ישב בדד לכול הטמאים ישב ורחוק מן 2 הטהרה שתים עשרה באמה בדברו אליו ומערב צפון לכול בית מושב ישב רחוק כמדה הזות

> *1* he shall begin to lay down his rank; he shall lie down in a bed of sorrows, and in a residence of lamentation he shall reside; he shall reside apart from all the impure, at a distance of *2* twelve cubits from the pure food; in the quarter reserved for him, to the North-east of every dwelling he shall dwell, at the distance of this measure.

This version of the text associates the *metsora* only with suffering (and reasonably so!), not sin. However, Jacob Milgrom offers the reading יחל להפיל את

---

10   See, e.g., Temple Scroll at columns XLVIII–XLIX and various materials among the D fragments. See also the parallel accounts of Jesus cleansing a leper at Matthew 8:1–4, Mark 1:40–45, and Luke 5:12–16.

תח[נונ]נו at the outset of the passage, translated as "he shall begin to lay down his pl[ea]." Milgrom's reading has broad implications:

> These few opening words suffice to indicate—in conformance with biblical, Mesopotamian, and later rabbinic tradition—that צרעת ("scale-disease") was regarded as a divine punishment for various egregious sins. Qumran adds a new element, that the afflicted person should be penitent ... presumably admit his wrongdoing ...[11]

The reconstruction is somewhat debatable (the García Martínez-Tigchelaar edition restores תיכונו instead),[12] which would retain the *tsara'at* context but remove the prayer aspect. Even if one retains that text, the fact that pleaful prayer is offered in response to crisis does not necessitate that its cause was sin.[13] (For example, many chapters in Psalms feature תחנון with no appearance of sin.) If so, these are the only two Qumran texts to associate *tsara'at* with sin, neither of which are fully clear.[14] Although several Second Temple texts treat leprosy and/or other ailments as a symbol of sin,[15] they do not draw the causal connection implied by other biblical texts.[16] Some sources also note treatments for *tsara'at* outside the ritual realm.[17] Thus, while there may be some degree of connection between *tsara'at* and sin in Second Temple literature, it seems somewhat less pronounced than in the biblical context.

---

11 See Milgrom, "4QTohora*a*," esp. 59–61.
12 The Leon Levy Dead Sea Scrolls Digital Library represents the line as follows (יחל להפיל את תיוונו??):

13 See, e.g., Feder, "Was Prayer Prohibited?," esp. 141–143, which summarizes the different views on the subject of the passage (*zav* or *metsora*); see Birenboim, "Expelling the Unclean," esp. pp. 21–23, which raises several possibilities as to why the *metsora* in the passage may be praying.
14 Most appearances of *tsara'at* within the Dead Sea Scrolls are focused on the technical (ritual *tsara'at*) aspects; see 4Q267 9:1–14 and 11QT*a* 48:15–49:4; Tigchelaar, "Early Christian Concept of the Holy Spirit," pp. 199–200. More generally, see Harrington, "Purity," 726.
15 Philo (*Alleg. Interp.* 1.49; *Worse* 16; *Posterity* 47; *Unchangeable* 123–131; *Planting* 111; *Sobriety* 49; *Dreams* 1.202; *QG* 2.29) and the Syriac version of Apocryphal Psalm 155 (5 Apoc. Syr. Ps. 3:12–13 [trans. Charlesworth and Sanders, OTP 2:624]).
16 See Gould, "The Social Condition of Lepers," pp. 921–925.
17 See the synoptic passages at Mathew, Mark, and Luke (Mt. 8:1–4; Mk. 1:40–45; Lk. 5:12–16) with the story about Jesus healing the Galilean leprosy patient, and Luke's (Lk. 17:11–19) story about Jesus healing ten leprosy sufferers.

Tannaitic Literature on *Tsara'at* as Punishment

As laid out above, Qumran features two possible cases connecting *tsara'at* to sin, while multiple biblical narratives—but not biblical ritual texts—draw this connection. As will be demonstrated, rabbinic literature more clearly and consistently presents the idea that those with *tsara'at* can attribute their malady to some sin.[18] The remainder of this paper examines the various presentations of the blameworthiness of the *metsora* throughout rabbinic literature and especially tannaitic material.

Some tannaitic passages indicate that *tsara'at* is connected to sin but do not go into detail regarding the nature of that sin.[19] For example, Sifre Numbers Naso 1 states:[20]

> ר' יוסי הגלילי אומר בוא וראה מה כח עבירה קשה שעד שלא פשטו ידיהם בעבירה
> לא היה בהם זבים ומצורעים ומשפשטו ידיהם בעבירה היו בהם זבים ומצורעים

> Rabbi Yose ha-Gelili says: Come and see the harsh power of sin. As long as [Israel] did not participate in sin, they had no *zavim* (those with a genital flux) or *metsoraim*. Once they participated in sin, they had *zavim* and *metsoraim*.

While such passages strengthen the connection seen in some biblical texts between sin and *tsara'at*, that association is general, in multiple ways: The grouping of *zav* along with *metsora*, when the *zav* has no strong biblical tradition associating sin with malady, indicates a looser *tsara'at*-sin connection. Interestingly, this passage's combination of *zav* and *metsora* as diseases associated with sin appears to closely parallel the passage at 4Q270 discussed above,

---

18   This paper largely agrees with Hannah Harrington's critique of Jacob Neusner that, while LR is emphasizing ethical and homiletical concerns, it cannot be said to be totally detached from the Book of Leviticus, but instead is building upon the bases of moral teaching already present in the biblical text (although in this case that includes primarily materials outside of Leviticus). Still, Neusner is correct that the rabbinic view diverges from that of Leviticus. This is a case where invoking the dual biblical discourses serves to clarify the significance of the reception history. See Neusner, *The Later Midrash Compilations*, 91; Harrington, "Rabbinic Reception of Leviticus," esp. pp. 392–393 (although the argument from sacrifice is not without problems). See also Harrington, *Holiness*, 174–175; Levine, *Leviticus*: ויקרא, 75; and Milgrom, *Leviticus 1–16* 820–824.
19   See Mishnah Nega'im 12:6.
20   Sifre Numbers is cited from the Horowitz edition, Sifra from the Vatican 66 manuscript, Sifre Deuteronomy from Finkelstein's edition, Tosefta Nega'im from Vienna manuscript, Leviticus Rabbah and Bavli texts from the Vilna edition.

although the latter's fragmentary nature makes it impossible to draw a stronger connection. Specifically, the fact that sin is presented here not as the proximate cause of *tsara'at* but as responsible for the onset or "unlocking" of the disease to the Israelite population overall, means that this passage may be read as consistent with *tsara'at* as a natural cause, once the fallen state of Israel has created a medical condition including those *zav* and *metsora* individuals who are ill.[21]

However, other passages offering particular sins as causes for the onset of *tsara'at* make the *tsara'at*-sin nexus substantially clearer. The Sifra's commentary on Leviticus 14:35 (at *Metsora* 5[3]:7–9) introduces two reasons to explain why one contracts *tsara'at*:

אשר לו [הבית] שלא [ישלח] ביד שליח יכול אפילו זקן אפילו חולה תל' לו' ובא והגיד לכהן ידקדק הכהן כיצד בא הנגע לביתו לאמר יאמר לו הכהן דיברי כיבושין בני אין הנגעין באין אילא על לשון הרע שכן מצינו במרים שלא ניענשה אילא על לשון הרע שני' השמר בנגע הצ' וג' זכור את אשר עשה יי אל"ך למרים וכי מה עינין זה לזה אילא מלמד שלא נענשה אילא על לשון הרע

והרי דברים קול וחומר מה אם מרים שדיבירה שלא בפניו שלמשה כך נענשה על אחת כמה וכמה המדבר (גניתו) [גנותו] שלחבירו בפניו

ר' שמעון בן אלעזר או' אף על גסות הרוח הנגעים באים שכן מצינו בעוזיה שני' וכחזקתו גבה לבו עד להשחית וימעל ביי אלהיו ויבא אל היכל ייי להקטיר על מזבח הקטרת ויבא אחריו עזריהו הכהן ועמו כהנים לי שמונים בני חיל ויעמדו על עוזיהו המלך ויאמרו לו לא לך עזיהו להקטיר לי כי לכהנים בני אהרן המקדשים להקטיר צא מן המקדש כי מעלת ולא לך לכבוד מיי אלהים ויזעף עוזיהו ובידו מקטורת להקטיר ובזעפו עם הכהנים והצרעת זרחה במצחו לפני הכהנים בבית יי מעל למזבח הקטרת

"[The Person] Who Owns the House [Should Go and Tell the Priest]" (Leviticus 14:35)—[teaching] that he should not send [this message] with a messenger. Maybe [he cannot send a messenger] even if [the homeowner is] elderly, even if [he is] sick? The verse teaches, "and he shall go and tell the priest" (Leviticus 14:35) [implying others may do so]. The priest should clarify how the *nega* entered the house. "Saying" (Leviticus 14:35)—The priest should say to him words of rebuke: 'My son, *nega'im* only come on account of evil speech, as we found regarding Miriam that she was punished only for evil speech, as it is said: "Be careful with the *nega* of tsa[ra'at, to be very careful in acting] ... Remember what the Lord your God did to Miriam" (Deuteronomy 24:8–9). What does this have to do with that? Rather, it teaches that she was punished only for evil speech.'

---

21 This passage contains some suggestive parallels to the corruption of the original sin, certainly on its biblical account; see Genesis 3:16.

And this is an a fortiori argument: If Miriam, who spoke not in front of Moses, received this punishment, then all the more so for one who speaks ill about their fellow in front of them!

R. Shimon ben Eleazar says: *Nega'im* also come on account of haughtiness, as we find with Uzziah,[22] as it is said: "But when he was strong, his heart was lifted up so that he acted corruptly, and he trespassed against the Lord his God; for he went into the temple of the Lord to burn incense upon the altar of incense. And Azariah the priest went in after him, and with him eighty priests of the Lord, that were valiant men; and they stood by Uzziah the king, and said unto him: 'It pertains not to you, Uzziah, to burn incense to the Lord, but to the priests the sons of Aaron that are consecrated it pertains to burn incense; go out of the sanctuary, for you have trespassed; neither shall it be for your honor from the Lord God.' Then Uzziah was angered; and in his hand he had a censer to burn incense; and while he was wroth with the priests, the leprosy broke forth in his forehead before the priests in the house of the Lord, beside the altar of incense" (2 Chronicles 24:16–19).

The starting assumption of this passage is the apparent requirement that the owner of the house be the one to tell the priest that it has contracted *tsara'at*, even if the owner is elderly or sick. The Sifra rejects this, possibly for the reason that the owner's participation is required in order for the priest to have the opportunity to hold a discussion with the homeowner: the priest whispers to the owner that the cause of *tsara'at* is improper speech, or *lashon ha-ra*.[23] This is derived from the juxtaposition of the charge to be careful regarding *tsara'at* and the exhortation to remember what God did to Miriam (Deuteronomy 24:8–9):

(ח) הִשָּׁמֶר בְּנֶגַע־הַצָּרַעַת לִשְׁמֹר מְאֹד וְלַעֲשׂוֹת כְּכֹל אֲשֶׁר־יוֹרוּ אֶתְכֶם הַכֹּהֲנִים הַלְוִיִּם כַּאֲשֶׁר צִוִּיתִם תִּשְׁמְרוּ לַעֲשׂוֹת:
(ט) זָכוֹר אֵת אֲשֶׁר־עָשָׂה יְקֹוָק אֱלֹהֶיךָ לְמִרְיָם בַּדֶּרֶךְ בְּצֵאתְכֶם מִמִּצְרָיִם:

Take heed regarding the plague of leprosy, to observe diligently, and do according to all that the priests the Levites shall teach you, as I com-

---

22 This biblical character's name is inconsistently spelled Uzziah (עזיה) and Uzziahu (עזיהו) across different biblical and rabbinic texts. This paper will generally follow the Hebrew spelling in the immediate text being translated or analyzed.

23 This transliteration is based on the absolute rather than construct form of the phrase. See Bargagarin, "*Lashon Hara*," 177–180.

manded them, so you shall observe to do. Remember what the Lord your God did to Miriam, on the way as you came forth out of Egypt.

Of course, the juxtaposition of these verses may indicate that the biblical text itself is drawing a connection between Miriam's improper speech and her punishment in receiving *tsara'at*, a cause and effect that is manifestly clear in Numbers 12.

The Sifra's advice continues: speaking ill of a person in front of them is even worse than Miriam's sin of speaking behind Moses' back and certainly is deserving of *tsara'at*. The priest's role, then, is to exhort the person whose house is afflicted with *tsara'at* to help them refrain from the sins that caused it, and especially the sin of *lashon ha-ra*.

The same teaching just analyzed from the beginning of the Sifra passage also appears in Sifre Deuteronomy 275, at the very location of these verses, and it may well have been the original locus of the teaching. Consider the text as it appears in Sifre Deuteronomy 275:9:

(ט) זכור אשר עשה ה׳ אלהיך למרים, וכי מה ענין זה לזה נתנו הענין לו ללמדך שאין נגעים באים אלא על לשון הרע, והלא דברים קל וחומר ומה מרים שלא דברה אלא שלא בפניו של משה ולהניתו של משה ולשבחו של מקום ולבנינו של עולם כך נענשה המדבר בגנותו של חבירו ברבים על אחת כמה וכמה שיענש.

"Remember what the Lord your God did to Miriam" (Deuteronomy 24:9) —but what does this have to do with that [the passage on being careful regarding *tsara'at* appearing in the verse immediately prior] that they gave this matter to him [to teach here]? To teach you that afflictions come only for evil speech. And are these matters not an a fortiori argument? Miriam, who only spoke [negatively] not in front of Moses and for his benefit and praise of the Omnipresent and for the building of the world,[24] and she was so punished; one who speaks ill of their fellow publicly, all the more so that they will be punished!

Returning to the second half of the Sifra passage, Rabbi Shimon ben Eleazar offers another possible reason why *tsara'at* might come about (although this teaching is not necessarily placed in the priest's mouth in this scenario). Referring to the Uzziah story, Rabbi Shimon ben Eleazar asserts that haughtiness

---

24 This interpolation, "and for his benefit ... the world," does not appear in the Sifra passage and may be a gloss on the passage that was inserted later.

(גסות הרוח) can be a cause of *tsara'at*. It is clear from the presentation of this passage that Rabbi Shimon ben Eleazar saw the "evil speech cause of *tsara'at*" view as presented as an authentic rabbinic view.[25] He agrees that this is a sufficient cause of *tsara'at*, but thinks it is not the sole cause; drawing upon another biblical precedent, he argues that haughtiness suffices as well. While the first, unattributed position in the Sifra passage and the position of Rabbi Shimon ben Eleazar may be in disagreement as to whether haughtiness also qualifies as a cause of *tsara'at*, they both agree that *tsara'at* comes about *only* because of sin. That, of course, is why the priest is drawn to speak to the homeowner and investigate the case of *tsara'at*—"the priest should clarify how the *nega* entered the house"—in the first place. The only question is *which* sin causes *tsara'at*—only evil speech or also haughtiness? Thus, in pointing to two distinct sins that might cause *tsara'at*, and two corresponding paradigmatic biblical characters who suffered for that sin, this Midrash is fully assertive and clear that *tsara'at* occurs only as a form of punishment.

This view fully associating *tsara'at* with sin is consistent with another passage (Metsora 5[3]:12) where the Sifra refers to *tsara'at* in passing.

וצוה הכהן ופינו הציווי בכהן והפינוי בכל אדם ופינו את הבית אפילו חב[י]לי עצים אפילו חבלי קנים דברי ר׳ יהודה ר׳ שמעון אומר ע'סק הוא לפינוי, א' ר' מאיר וכי מה מיטמא לו אם תאמר כלי עצו ובגדיו ומתכתו מטב[י]ל(י)ן והן טהורין ועל מה חסה התורה על כלי חרסו ועל פיכו ועל תיפיו וכי מ(י) מיטמא בנגעין הרש(י)עין או הצדיקין הוי או' הרשעים אם כך חסה התורה על ממונו הבזוי קול וחומר על ממונו הח[ב]יב אם כך על ממונו קול וחומר על נפש בניו ובנותיו אם כך על שלרשע קול וחומר על שלצדיק.

"And the priest commands, and they empty out [the house]" (Leviticus 14:36)—the command [must be done] by the priest, but the emptying out can be done by anyone. "And they empty out the house" (Leviticus 14:36)—even bundles of wood or bundles of reeds, the words of Rabbi Yehudah. Rabbi Shimon says: It is a matter to empty [the house and it should be done only for a purpose].[26] Rabbi Meir says: What does it defile?

---

25 This runs against Klawans' reading that this explanation of the cause of *tsara'at* is somehow less authoritative because it is placed in the mouth of the priest. See further analysis in the final section below.

26 The line might be read as a statement—"it is a matter of emptying out [for purpose]" and therefore only items that would be destroyed if remaining inside should be removed. Alternatively, it can be read as a rhetorical question: "Is it a matter of emptying out?" with the clear implication that the goal is to save items, not to empty them for the sake of emptying them. See the commentary *Qorban Aharon* (R. Aharon ibn Hayyim, first edition 1609–1611) to this passage.

If you say [it defiles] his wooden utensils, clothing, and metal, he can dip them [in a ritual bath] and they are pure! What does the Torah have mercy on? On his earthen vessels and jugs and ovens [which cannot be purified in a ritual bath but must be destroyed]. Who is defiled by *nega'im*? Evildoers or righteous people? I would say evildoers. If the Torah so has concern for his disgraced possessions [his mere earthen jugs], all the more so for his beloved [i.e., more expensive] possessions; If this is true about his possessions, all the more so about the life of his sons and daughters; if so for an evildoer, all the more so for a righteous person!

The query "who is defiled through *nega'im*—evildoers or righteous people? I would say evildoers!" is used to demonstrate that even the sinners are afforded the privilege of removing their belongings from the house, thus saving them before the house is condemned as impure. That only sinners are afflicted by *tsara'at* is presented as on par with the rule that only certain items become impure and must be destroyed, i.e. it is treated as a basic ritual fact.[27] And, notably, this factor has legal ramifications in Rabbi Meir's interpretation.

Tosefta Nega'im (6:7) presents a parallel version to the Sifra passage at Metsora 5(3):7–9, with some points fleshed out further and others concatenated:

כיצד ראיית הנגע ספק יש בו כשני גריסין ספק אין בו ספק ירקרק שברוקין אדמדם שבאדומין היה בא אצל הכהן והכהן אומ' ואמר לו בני צא ופשפש בעצמך וחזור בך שאין הנגעים באין אלא על לשון הרע ואין הצרעת באה אלא על גסי הרוח ואין המקום דן את האדם אלא ברתיון הרי הן באין על ביתו חזר בו טען חל[י]צה ואם לאו טען נתיצה הרי הן באין על בגדיו חזר בו טען קריעה ואם לאו טען שריפה הרי הן באין על גופו חזר בו חוזר ואם לאו בדד ישב מחוץ למחנה מושבו ר' שמעון בן לעזר או' משום ר' מאיר אף על גסות הרוח נגעים באין שכן מצינו בעזיהו:

How does one view the *nega*? If there is a doubt whether it is [a size of] two *gris* or not, or a doubt whether it qualifies as "[most] yellow of the yellows" or "[most] red of the reds," he would go to the priest and the priest would tell [him] and [also] say to him: 'My son: Exit [the building] and examine yourself and return [i.e. repent], because *nega'im* only come on account of evil speech, and *tsara'at* only comes on haughty peo-

---

27 While this text doesn't associate a specific sin with *tsara'at*, it is the clearest association between the malady and sin. In contrast to Sifre Numbers *Naso* 1, it presents sin as a direct cause of *tsara'at* rather than a prerequisite overall, and it does not group *zav* with *metsora*, which that passage does. Note also the parallel text at m.Negaim 12:6, wherein the reference to sinners is significantly obscured.

ple, and [yet] the Omnipresent only judges people with leniency.'[28] Thus they come on his house [rather than immediately onto him]. If he retracts [i.e. repents], it [the house] requires that [its stones] be pulled out and if [he does] not [repent], it must be torn down. [If he still does not repent,] behold they come upon his clothes. If he retracts [i.e. repents], it requires ripping; if not, it requires burning. [If he still does not repent,] behold they [*nega'im*] come upon his body. If he retracts [i.e. repents], he goes back [to his home]. If not, "he must sit alone; outside the camp is his dwelling place" (Leviticus 13:46). R. Shimon ben Eleazar says in the name of R. Meir: *Nega'im* also come on account of haughtiness, as we find with Uzziyahu.

The Tosefta features the same scenario of the priest informing the owner of the house afflicted with *tsara'at* of the perils of improper speech (and haughtiness), although he does so in a more exhortative way, asking the homeowner to introspect and change his ways (פשפש בעצמך וחזור בך). Additionally, the priest fills in the logic of how a person's actions would affect their house: the affliction on the house is a first step, a warning of sorts. The homeowner has the chance to repent and save the house, albeit with some stones removed (*hallets*); continuing in his ways leads to the house being destroyed (*netitsah*). If the subject still doesn't relent, his clothing will contract this affliction and either be ripped or be burnt. Finally, if all those warnings do not work, the person himself is afflicted, whereupon he can repent and merely suffer temporary quarantine, or continue in his ways and be exiled from the camp.

Whereas the Sifra featured two opinions (an unattributed statement and one attributed to Rabbi Shimon ben Eleazar), each equipped with its own source text pointing to either improper speech or haughtiness as the cause of these afflictions (*nega'im*), the formulation earlier in this Tosefta passage accepts both causes without prooftext but applies each to a slightly different disease: improper speech causes afflictions (*nega'im*) while haughtiness causes *tsara'at*—אין הנגעים באין אלא על לשון הרע ואין הצרעת באה אלא על גסי הרוח.[29] At the

---

28   The word רתיון is a hapax legomenon in Rabbinic literature; context dictates this translation.
29   This parallelism might be understood as presenting two terms either synonymous or somewhat divergent in meaning. As noted in the opening section, the biblical term *nega* refers to afflictions in general, while *tsara'at* refers specifically to a subset of that, namely the skin ailment. For the rabbis, although *nega* is often used to gloss the biblical *tsara'at* (see, e.g., b.Gittin 82a below and Leviticus Rabbah 16:1's interpretation of Genesis 12:17), the biblical term *nega* is also correlated to *yissurin*, or suffering in general (see, e.g., b.Shabbat 55a and b.Yoma 86a). It is not clear whether this teaching assumes that evil speech leads to all *nega'im* or only the *nega* of *tsara'at* in particular.

end of the piece, however, R. Shimon ben Eleazar's teaching is cited just as in the Sifra (although here he is citing R. Meir) asserting that haughtiness can also be a cause for afflictions (*nega'im*).[30] This passage features the clearest statement of sin-to-*tsara'at* correlation within tannaitic literature. Not only does the priest make clear the process of steady escalation of *tsara'at* in response to continued sin, but the person whose house (and possibly clothing and skin) is afflicted with *tsara'at* has full control over the extent of the disease. Repentance is presented as a failsafe treatment that can remove the *tsara'at* directly and completely.

Amoraic Literature on *Tsara'at* as Punishment

The cause of *tsara'at* is the subject of much writing in amoraic literature and other later Midrashim, although reasons of space dictate that a frontal treatment of most of these materials will have to await another opportunity.

---

30 Notably, Leviticus Rabbah 18:4, in a parallel formulation, seems to take this tradition to mean the former, as it presents *nega'im* in the more general sense: ללמדך שאין הנגעין באין אלא על לשון הרע, לפיכך נתחייבו ישראל בזיבות ובצרעת, "... teaching that *nega'im* come only on account of evil speech; therefore Israel was liable for genital fluxes (*zivut*) and *tsara'at*." Note that *nega'im* here is a hypernym, including both *tsara'at* and fluxes. It is not immediately clear how best to reconstruct the relationship between these sources. It is possible that the Tosefta draws upon the Sifra, integrating the two opinions together while differentiating *tsara'at* from *nega'im*, and the stray final line is a representation of Rabbi Shimon ben Eleazar's opinion as originally formulated (whether added later or, more likely, part of the original core of the Tosefta). Alternatively, although less likely, the somewhat messier Tosefta came first and the Sifra simplified the first opinion by only asserting its teaching about improper speech causing *nega'im* and leaving out the assertion that haughtiness causes *tsara'at*, only to then cite an alternate opinion about haughtiness causing *nega'im*. It is also possible that there is some additional earlier source and/or that the interaction between these two sources is more complicated than the possibilities presented here. Among these possibilities, it seems that the first reconstruction, with Sifra primary and drawn upon by Tosefta, is to be preferred, but this is by no means proven. In terms of the relation between these two traditions and the relevant Sifre passage, it is difficult to draw clear conclusions, but educated guesses are possible, Klawans writes (*Impurity and Sin*, p. 199 n. 57), regarding the Sifre Deuteronomy 275 and Sifra Metsora 5:7–9 texts:

> It is not perfectly clear to me in what way these two traditions relate to one another chronologically, though I would tentatively suggest that Sifre § 275 is an abbreviation of the Sifra.

Additionally, one reader suggested the possibility that Sifre passage is prior to the Tosefta Nega'im 6:7 text as the former contains prooftexts that the latter then presumed.

Multiple amoraic texts, several of which cite tannaitic materials, argue for the cause of *tsara'at* being based in sin.[31] Some texts build upon the word play of *metsora* = *motsi* (*shem*) *ra* (one who expresses bad [speech]) or upon other such biblical interpretations and assert that evil speech is the cause. Others draw upon the litany of biblical characters who received *tsara'at* and discern what their sin might have been. The resulting lists yield anywhere from seven to thirteen sins that cause *tsara'at*. Thus, in these cases it is clear that sin is the cause of *tsara'at*; The only question is *which* sins qualify as potential causes. A recurring formulation in these texts is על א דברים נגעים באים, "afflictions [of *tsara'at*] occur for X reasons,"[32] with the ensuing list consisting fully of sins, leaving no room for any non-sin causes.

To give a sense of the manner in which amoraic and other midrashic texts further the idea that sin is the cause of *tsara'at*, we will consider one extended treatment of an amoraic text here. The fifth century text Leviticus Rabbah, in its characteristic homiletical midrash style,[33] offers a lengthy treatment of broader concerns of *tsara'at* beyond the technical rules expounded in Leviticus. Both *parashah* 16 and 17 devote much attention to the question of *tsara'at*'s cause. That section's discussion of *tsara'at* opens with an interesting teaching that sets the stage for this amoraic trend of multiplying the sins that cause *tsara'at*.

[א] זאת תהיה תורת המצורע (ויקרא יד, ב) הה"ד שש הנה שנא ה' ושבע תועבת נפשו (משלי ו, טז). ר' מאיר ורבנן ר' מאיר אומר שש ושבע הרי י"ג ורבנן אמרי שבע. מקיימין ושבע דכתיב זו שביעית שקשה כנגד כולם, ואיזה זה משלח מדנים בין אחים.

> "This shall be the law of a leper ..." (Leviticus 14:2) That which it says: "Six things the Lord hates; seven are an abomination to Him" (Proverbs 6:16). R. Meir and the rabbis [interpreted the verse]: R. Meir said: Six and seven make thirteen things [that God hates]. The rabbis said: [only] seven things [are meant]. [The rabbis] understand "And seven" that is written refers to the seventh, which is the worst of them all. And which is it? This is "One who incites brothers to quarrel."

The rabbis and R. Meir debate whether God hates seven or thirteen things in the context of *tsara'at*, as these abominations to God are presumably causes of

---

31 See y.Sotah 2:1; Leviticus Rabbah Metsora 16:1–6, 17:3; Arakhin 15b–16b; Tanhuma Metsora 1,5,6,10 (Buber).
32 See Leviticus Rabbah 17:3, a teaching attributed to Rabbi Yohanan at Arakhin 16a, and Tanhuma 14:2. and parallels at b.Sotah 15a, b.Shevu'ot 8a, and b.Keritot 26a.
33 See Heinemann, "The Art of Composition in Leviticus Rabba," 141–150.

that malady. Indeed, a variety of amoraic texts will propose lists with anywhere between seven and thirteen sins that can cause *tsaraʿat*.

The immediately following passage at Leviticus Rabbah 16:1, explicating the view of the rabbis,[34] goes through a virtual tour of Jewish history, providing a list of seven sins that cause *tsaraʿat*, with each cause correlating to a biblical case that serves as a proof.[35] The causes include: (1) a haughty eye, learned from daughters of Zion (Isaiah 3:16); (2) a lying tongue, learned from Miriam (Numbers 12:1); (3) hands shedding innocent blood, learned from Yoav (1 Kings 2:32); (4) a mind hatching evil plots, learned from Uzziahu (2 Chronicles 26[36]); (5) feet quickly running to evil, learned from Gehazi (2 Kings 5:20); (6) a false witness testifying lies, learned from Israel (Exodus 32:4); and (7) one who incites brothers to quarrel, learned from Pharaoh (Genesis 12:13).[37]

It is noteworthy that all prooftexts are from biblical stories, several of which appeared in tannaitic sources. As Tamar Jacobowitz argues,[38] this passage has a particular interpretive agenda: tying the seven sins listed at Proverbs 6:16–19 (many of which are tied to body parts) to *tsaraʿat* through biblical characters, some of whom have clearer cases of *tsaraʿat* than others.[39] It also shows how the starting point for these interpretations is the biblical characters who suffered from *tsaraʿat*; understanding their precise sin is then a more malleable endeavor, which can be shifted to best fit one's interpretive agenda.

The text at 17:3 expounds further on the matter, laying out a total of ten causes for *tsaraʿat*, and following the familiar formula "Afflictions [of *tsaraʿat*] occur for X reasons" (על א דברים נגעים באים):

---

[34] Leviticus Rabbah never returns to explicate Rabbi Meir's list of thirteen abominations to God. It is possible that Rabbi Meir's position was originally stated outside the context of *tsaraʿat*, although LR seems to be applying it to the context of *tsaraʿat*. Although we possess no list of Rabbi Meir's thirteen sins, other lists of sin-causes of *tsaraʿat* noted throughout amoraic literature might be reconstructed for that view.

[35] This passage does not employ the formula "For X causes *tsaraʿat* comes" (על א דברים נגעים באים), but it clearly is functioning within the same orbit.

[36] Compare with 2 Kings 15, where the King seizing the priesthood is called Azariah rather than Uzziah. See further Visotsky, *Golden Bells and Pomegranates*, 61.

[37] These cases are treated at some length by Jacobowitz, "Leviticus Rabbah," pp. 169–183.

[38] Jacobowitz, "Leviticus Rabbah," pp. 164–165. It is also worth noting the fascinating study of Galit Hasan-Rokem on an earlier piece of this passage, which does not bear on the interpretation of the cause of *tsaraʿat*: Hasan-Rokem, "'Odysseus and the Sirens,'" 159–189.

[39] As Jacobowitz notes (Jacobowitz, "Leviticus Rabbah," 160–183), the cases of the daughters of Zion, the Israelites, and Pharaoh are less than fully clear. Her literary analysis of this passage overall offers an insightful treatment of some of the relevant factors relevant to LR's interpretation.

על עשרה דברים נגעים באים על ע״ז ועל גילוי עריות ועל שפיכות דמים ועל חילול השם ועל ברכת השם ועל הגוזל את הרבים ועל גוזל את שאינו שלו ועל גסי הרוח ועל לשון הרע ועל עין רע,

על ע״ז מישראל שהעידו עדות שקר בהקב״ה ואמרו לעגל (שמות לב) אלה אלהיך ישראל ומנין שלקו בצרעת שנא׳ (שם /שמות ל״ב/) וירא משה את העם כי פרוע הוא שפרחה בהן צרעת,

ועל גילוי עריות מבנות ציון שנאמר (ישעיה ג) יען כי גבהו בנות ציון ומנין שלקו בצרעת שנאמר (שם /ישעיהו ג׳/) ושפח ה׳ קדקד בנות ציון,

ועל שפיכות דמים מיואב שנאמר (שמואל ב ג) יחולו על ראש יואב

ועל חילול השם מגיחזי (מ״ב =מלכים ב׳= ה) ויאמר גחזי נער איש האלהים מהו מאומה מן מומא דאית ביה ומנין שלקה בצרעת שנאמר (שם /מלכים ב׳ ה׳/) וצרעת נעמן תדבק בך,

ועל ברכת השם מגלית שנאמר (שמואל א יז) ויקלל הפלשתי את דוד באלהיו ומנין שלקה בצרעת שנאמר (שם /שמואל א׳ י״ז/) היום הזה יסגרך ה׳ בידי ואין הסגרה האמור כאן אלא לשון צרעת שנאמר והסגירו הכהן,

ועל גוזל את הרבים משבנא שהיה נהנא מן ההקדשות ומנין שלקה בצרעת שנאמר (ישעיה כב) הנה ה׳ מטלטלך טלטלה גבר ועוטך עטה ואין ועוטך עטה אלא צרעת שנאמר (ויקרא יג) ועל שפם יעטה,

ועל הגוזל את שאינו שלו מעוזיהו דכתיב (ד״ה =דברי הימים= ב כו) ויהי המלך עוזיהו מצורע עד יום מותו,

ועל גסות הרוח דכתיב (שם /דברי הימים ב׳ כ״ו/) וכחזקתו גבה לבו עד להשחית וימעל בה׳ אלהיו,

ועל לשון הרע ממרים דכתיב (במדבר יב) ותדבר מרים ואהרן במשה ומנין שלקתה בצרעת שנאמר (שם /במדבר י״ב/) והענן סר מעל האהל,

ועל עין הרע שנאמר (ויקרא יד) ובא אשר לו הבית מי שייחד ביתו לו ואינו רוצה ליהנות לאחרים, כי הא דאמר ר״א שקערורות שקיע ביתו באלין לווטייא לפיכך משה מזהיר את ישראל כי תבאו אל ארץ כנען.

Afflictions [of *tsara'at*] occur for ten reasons: for (1) idolatry; (2) sexual impropriety; (3) murder; (4) desecration of God's name; (5) cursing God's name; (6) stealing from the community; (7) stealing what is not one's own; (8) haughtiness; (9) improper speech; and (10) the evil eye.

For (1) idolatry: [This is learned] from Israel, who falsely testified about the Holy One, blessed be He, and said about the [golden] calf "these are your gods, Israel" (Exodus 32:4). And how do we know that they were stricken with *tsara'at*? As it says, "And Moses saw that the nation was scattered" (Exodus 32:25), i.e., that they had *tsara'at* spread out among them.[40]

---

40   Other passages (see LR 16:1 and 18:4) making this connection apply a wordplay between

For (2) sexual impropriety: from the daughters of Zion, as it says, "because the daughters of Zion were haughty" (Is. 3:16). And how do we know they were stricken with *tsara'at*? As it says, "and the Lord will strike with a scab the daughters of Zion" (Isaiah 3:17).

For (3) murder: from Yoav, as it says, "May it whirl over the head of Yoav [… and may the house of Yoav never be without someone suffering from flux or *tsara'at*]" (2 Samuel 3:29).

For (4) desecration of God's name: from Gehazi, "And Gehazi the youth of the man of God said [to himself, 'My master was too easy on Naaman the Aramean by not accepting what he brought. As the Lord lives, I will run after him and take from him something'"] (2 Kings 5:20). What is "something" (*me'umah*)? A sort of blemish (*muma*) that he had. And how do we know that he was stricken with *tsara'at*? As it says, "And the *tsara'at* of Na'aman will stick to you" (2 Kings 5:27).

For (5) cursing God's name: from Goliath, as it says, "And the Philistine cursed David's God" (1 Samuel 17:43). And how do we know he was stricken with *tsara'at*? As it says, "Today the Lord will deliver you (*yesag-gerkha*, lit. 'close you') in my hand" (1 Samuel 17:46). And "closing" here is nothing other than *tsara'at*, as it says, "And the priest should close him [in quarantine]" (Leviticus 13:5).

For (6) stealing from the community, from Shevna, who was benefitting from the holy accounts. How do we know he was stricken with *tsara'at*? As it says, "Behold the Lord will take hold of you and hurl you away and roll you up tightly like a ball (*otekha ato*)" (Is. 22:17–18). And *otekha ato* is nothing other than *tsara'at*, as it says, and "on their lips they will cover (*ya'teh*)" (Leviticus 13:45).

For (7) stealing that which is not one's own: from Uzziahu [who sought to seize the high priesthood], as it says, "And King Uzziahu had *tsara'at* until the day of his death" (2 Chronicles 26:21).

For (8) haughtiness, as it says, "And when he was powerful, he became proud, leading to his destruction; he rebelled against the Lord his God" (2 Chronicles 26:16).

For (9) evil speech: from Miriam, as it says, "And Miriam and Aaron spoke against Moses" (Numbers 12:1). And how do we know that she was stricken with *tsara'at*? As it says, "And the cloud left the tent [and Miriam was white as snow with *tsara'at*]" (Numbers 12:10).

"scattered" (*parua*, Exodus 32:25) and the requirement that a *metsora*'s head be exposed (*parua*; Leviticus 13:45). This text may presume that interpretation, or it may simply indicate that the people were scattered on account of their *tsara'at*.

And (10) for the evil eye [i.e. miserliness], as it says, "And the one who has the house [comes to the priest]" (Leviticus 14:35)—one for whom the house is exclusively his and he does not wish to benefit others. As R. Eleazar said, *sheka'arurot* ("cavities") (Leviticus 14:37)—his house sinks with these curses.[41] Therefore Moses warns Israel "when you enter the Land of Canaan … I will place afflictions of *tsara'at* on the houses of the land of your inheritance" (Leviticus 14:34).

The prooftexts in this list are exclusively biblical, based on narratives involving various characters who were stricken with *tsara'at* (or at least can be midrashically interpreted to have been so stricken). This list draws upon the list appearing at Leviticus Rabbah 16:1, which drew upon biblical cases as well, and also introduces a number of categories, including idolatry, desecrating God's name, and cursing God's name.

This extended midrashic passage is representative of several more Aggadic midrashim that are extant. This trend to find multiple sins tied to *tsara'at* continues and expands the tannaitic trend of attributing the contraction of *tsara'at* to sins of the diseased party.

Tsara'at as a Reward

Until this point, all causes of *tsara'at* discussed—whether general sinfulness or some number of specific factors—fall within the category of sins. However, rabbinic literature also includes a thread of interpretation that sees *tsara'at* not as a *punishment* for sinful acts of the diseased person, but rather a *reward*. Significantly, this possibility only appears with regard to house *tsara'at*, not skin *tsara'at*. Some of the seeds of this interpretation exist in the Sifra, but this interpretation only truly emerges at a later point in time, as will be demonstrated.

Sifra on *Tsara'at* Tidings

The original source from which the conception of *tsara'at* as a blessing emerged is the Sifra Metsora 5:4, which asserts that the Lord announces that there will be houses with *tsara'at* when Israel enters the Land:

---

41 As is clear from the parallel in Tanhuma 14:2, this reads *sheka'arurot* as *sheka arurot*, "sinking cursed." The passage here translates and explicates those Hebrew words in Aramaic, partially obscuring the word play of the original interpretation.

ונתתי נגע צר' א' ד' ר' יהודה וכי⁴² בסורה להם שהן באים עליהם נגעים ר' שמעון או'
ונתתי נגע צר' פרט לניגעי אנסים בבית ארץ פרט לבית הבנוי בספינה או באכסדיה⁴³
על ארבע קורות להביא את הבנוי על העצים ועל העמודים

"[When you come into the land of Canaan, which I give to you as a possession,] I shall place *nega tsara'at* [in the house of the land of your inheritance]" (Leviticus 14:34). R. Yehudah said: Is it a tiding (בסורה) for them that *nega'im* are coming upon them? R. Shimon says: "And I shall place *nega tsara'at*" (Leviticus 14:34)—this excludes *nega'im* that are beyond one's control.⁴⁴ "In the house of the land [of your inheritance]" (Leviticus 14:34)—this excludes a house built on a board or in a hall [standing] on four poles, and includes that which is built on wood and on beams.

Rabbi Yehudah asks why the specter of *tsara'at* on houses awaiting the Israelites when they enter the land is presented as some sort of good tiding or promise—why the Lord announces "I will place afflictions of *tsara'at* on the houses of the land of your inheritance" (Leviticus 14:34). Following the manuscripts rather than the editions (which delete the word וכי), this is a question rather than a statement. R. Yehudah can see no explanation as to why *tsara'at* could be a good tiding.⁴⁵ R. Shimon thus responds to his question by reading the text dif-

---

42 All extant manuscripts have the word וכי, although some editions have taken it out or placed it in parentheses (apparently without justification). This reading is confirmed by Lieberman, *"Hazanut Yannai,"* 230:

תני ר' חייא (הכוונה לתו"כ מצורה פרשה ה' ה"ד, ע"ג ע"א: ונתתי נגע צרעת. א"ר יהודה וכי בשורה היא להם שבאים עליהם נגעים. והמפרשים מחקו שם את המלה "וכי", אבל ברור מהמדרש שאין למוחקה, ור' יהודה תמה ולא נתן תשובה) ותני ר' שמעון בן יוחאי, כלומר מתרץ את התמיה של התני ר' חייא בתני ר' שמעון בן יוחאי.

See the analysis of the two possible readings in the main text below.

43 This term appears in three different forms in the manuscripts: אכסדרה, appearing in the Vatican 31 and JTS Rab. 2171 manuscripts, meaning "hall" or "parlor"; אסכריא/אסכרייא, appearing in the Oxford and JTS Rab. (marginal) manuscripts, and meaning either "spying place/mast" or "raft/float"; and אכסדיה/אכסדיא in the Venice edition and Vatican 66 and Parma manuscripts, which is a *hapax legomenon* and presumably means one of the other two meanings noted above. See also m.Nega'im 12:1, a teaching that is parallel (and nearly identical) to this Sifra passage, which reads בית הבנוי בספינה או באסקריא, and some versions read ובאכסדיא in place of the final word.

44 See a discussion of this teaching at b.Horayot 10a.

45 Although at times the word בשורה can be used with either a positive or a negative valence—see, e.g., Mekhilta de'Rabbi Yishmael Bo 12, which discusses whether Exodus 12:26 refers to a positive or a negative בשורה—in context R. Yehudah seems to read this term as denoting a good tiding, and to object to that prospect.

ferently, as excluding cases that are beyond one's control rather than reflecting a promise of good tidings.⁴⁶

Mere lines later, at Sifra Metsora 5(3):7–9, appears the passage analyzed above, which delineates the various sins that cause *tsara'at*, as well as the progression of *tsara'at* from the house to the clothing to the person himself. While one could imagine a dichotomy between two types of leprous houses, no such indication of dual causality exists in the text. Thus, R. Yehudah is raising the prospect of *tsara'at* of the house as good tidings but rejects it out of hand—how could the destruction of one's house be good news? It must be caused by sin.

Horayot 10a on *Tsara'at* Tidings

R. Yehudah's proposed interpretation of ונתתי נגע צרעת as meaning that house *tsara'at* was being announced, which he is unable to sustain, remains a live option for amoraic interpreters, in different ways.⁴⁷ In particular, b.Horayot 10a and Leviticus Rabbah 17:6 have differing interpretations of R. Yehudah's "tidings" reading that yield divergent understandings of the biblical text. B.Horayot 10a reads as follows:

> ת״ר אשר נשיא יחטא יכול גזרה ת״ל אם הכהן המשיח יחטא מה להלן לכשיחטא אף כאן לכשיחטא אמר מר יכול גזרה מהיכא תיתי אמרי אין אשכחן דכתיב ונתתי נגע צרעת בבית ארץ אחוזתכם בשורה היא להם שנגעים באים עליהם דברי רבי יהודה רבי שמעון אומר פרט לנגעי אונסין לאו אמר רבי יהודה הכא נמי אימא גזרה היא הלכך כתיב אם

> It was taught: "When a prince sins" (Leviticus 4:22)—I might think it is a decree [that he will certainly sin]. The verse teaches: "If the anointed priest sins" (Leviticus 4:3)—just like here it is if he [the anointed priest] sins, so too there it is if he [the prince] sins. Master said [above]: 'I might

---

46 R. Shimon's reading may be that the alternative formulation, כי יהיה, "if there shall be," lends itself to cases of accident or necessity more than the more intentional ונתתי, "and I shall place."

47 Both amoraic approaches see this "tiding" as a prediction, one positive and the other negative. Whatever the valence, accepting the verse as predictive would presumably be at odds with the tradition, recorded at t.Nega'im 6:1 and later at b.Sanhedrin 71a, that בית המנוגע לא היה ולא עתיד להיות, that "the leprous house did not occur and will not occur" and that its function is דרוש וקבל שכר, "study and receive reward."

think it is a decree.' A decree—from where would one bring that [assumption]? They said: Yes, we find [a precedent for that], as it is written, "and I shall place a *nega tsara'at* in the house of the land of your inheritance" (Leviticus 14:34)—it is a tiding (בשורה) for them that *nega'im* are coming upon them, the words of Rabbi Yehudah. Rabbi Shimon says: This excludes *nega'im* that are beyond one's control. Didn't Rabbi Yehudah say "it is a tiding"? So too, here, I can say it is a decree! Therefore it is said, "if" (Leviticus 4:3).

The unattributed voice in this passage is bothered by the Bible's presentation of the *nasi*'s *hattat* offering, which is said to be offered "when a *nasi* sins" (אשר נשיא יחטא). Is it truly predetermined and decreed, a *gezeirah*, that the *nasi* will sin? The Talmud's anonymous voice responds in the affirmative and draws upon the Sifra passage immediately above as a prooftext. Just as it is predetermined that the *nasi* will sin, there is a predetermined decree (*gezeirah*) as well that the houses in the Land will be afflicted by *tsara'at*.[48] This passage gives every indication that what R. Yehudah calls a tiding (בשורה) is in fact a decree (גזרה) predicting *tsara'at* on houses in Israel, one that presumes that Israel will sin and be punished.

Rabbi Yehudah's teaching that Leviticus 14:34 reflects a divine commitment to cause *tsara'at* is accepted, but his understanding that this will yield a good tiding is inverted. Here *besorah* is taken simply to mean that there will cer-

---

48 The clear reading of this passage is that this decree of *tsara'at* on the house is a bad thing. While Tosafot Rosh to this passage asserts that this *tsara'at* is ultimately for the best, basing his reading on the Midrash (Leviticus Rabbah 17:6, discussed below) that the Israelites would receive the treasures hidden in those houses, that is not presumed by the Talmudic passage itself. In fact, the entire force of the parallel between the *nasi* and the *tsara'at* is the surprising prospect that God would predict something negative, as Rashi spells out (and Tosafot Rosh acknowledges).

Rashi to Horayot 10a

דכתיב ונתתי נגע צרעת בבית ארץ אחוזתכם בשורה היא להם—שהכתוב מבשרן שעתיד להיות אף על פי שדבר רע הוא הכא נמי אימא גזרה הלכך כתב אם הכהן המשיח יחטא לכשיחטא וה"נ אשר נשיא יחטא לכשיחטא.

Tosafot haRosh to b.Horayot 10a

ומי כתיב קרא הכי. לבשר על הרעה. אין והתניא ונתתי נגע צרעת בבית ארץ אחוזתכם בשורה היא להם. אלמא אורחיה דקרא לרמוז העתידות אפי' הרעות, ואף על גב דלא דמי כולי האי דאותה בשורה טובה היתה דאמרינן במדרש שהאמוריים הטמינו אוצרותיהם בכותלי בתיהם ובמקום המטמון הביא הקדוש ברוך הוא צרעת כדי שיסתרו הכותלים וימצאו המטמון.

Compare Rashi's negative evaluation of this situation with Tosafot Rosh's acknowledgement of Rashi's use of the term *ra* ("bad") along with his attempt to emphasize that it also contains a positive element.

tainly be house *tsara'at* in the future, but it will occur only when people sin and deserve to be punished! (The parallel to the case of *nasi* is instructive here.) Thus, *Horayot* 10a is yet another text that sees *tsara'at* as inextricable from sin, and it even turns Rabbi Yehudah's use of the term *besorah* upside down in order to do so.

Leviticus Rabbah 17:6

On the other hand, the midrash at Leviticus Rabbah 17:6 takes a different perspective,[49] retaining the meaning of בשורה as a good tiding:

וכתיב נגע צרעת, תני ר' חייא וכי בשורה היא להם שנגעים באים עליהם, תני רבי שמעון בן יוחאי כיון ששמעו כנענים שישראל באים עליהם עמדו והטמינו ממונם בבתים ובשדות אמר הקדוש ב"ה אני הבטחתי לאבותיהם שאני מכניס את בניהם לארץ מלאה כל טוב שנאמר (דברים ו) ובתים מלאים כל טוב מה הקדוש ברוך הוא עושה מגרה נגעים בביתו והוא סותרו ומצא בו סימא

And it is said, "[When you come into the land of Canaan, which I give to you as a possession, I shall place] *nega tsara'at* [in the house of the land of your inheritance]" (Leviticus 14:34). R. Hiyya taught: Is it a tiding (בשורה) for them that *nega'im* are coming upon them? R. Shimon bar Yohai taught, once the Canaanites heard that Israel was coming upon them, they arose and hid their money in houses and fields. The Holy One, blessed be He, said: 'I promised their forefathers that I will bring them into a land filled with all good, as it is said, "[When the Lord your God brings you into the land He promised to your forefathers, Abraham, Isaac, and Jacob to give you ...] and houses filled with all good"' (Deuteronomy 6:11). What does the Holy One, blessed be He, do? He sends *nega'im* at their house, and he [the owner] breaks it and finds hidden things.

The expanded Midrash as presented in Leviticus Rabbah is very clear as to what is in store. Rabbi Hiyya presents the apparent announcement in the verse as a

---

49 This teaching was later popularized by Rashi's commentary on the Torah. See Rashi to Leviticus 14:34:

ונתתי נגע צרעת—בשורה היא להם שהנגעים באים עליהם, לפי שהטמינו אמוריים מטמוניות של זהב בקירות בתיהם כל ארבעים שנה שהיו ישראל במדבר, ועל ידי הנגע נותץ הבית ומוצאן:

problem—how could *tsara'at* be good?—and Rabbi Shimon ben Yohai answers that the goal of the *tsara'at* was to cause buildings to be knocked down, such that the treasure that the Canaanites left inside the walls could be discovered, thus fulfilling God's promise to Israel that they would inherit "houses filled with all good" (Deuteronomy 6:11) when they entered the land. This understanding of the *tsara'at* of the house portends an entirely different direction and understanding of the cause of *tsara'at*—not as a punishment but actually as a *reward* or entitlement.[50]

This passage in Leviticus Rabbah is the only one of these texts interpreting God's *besorah* to sustain an interpretation in which house *tsara'at* is good news. Indeed, it is apparently the only passage in classical rabbinic literature that attributes the cause of *tsara'at* to anything other than sin. It is worth considering why this might be. Jacobowitz has argued that Leviticus Rabbah has a unique project regarding the leprous house. In contrast to the predominant understanding of *tsara'at* as caused by sin throughout biblical passages and rabbinic literature, several passages in Leviticus Rabbah 17 show a redemptive or positive side to the affliction, as a way of demonstrating God's everlasting love to Israel.[51] If Jacobowitz's analysis is accurate, this amoraic source has a particular interpretive agenda that drives it to understand *tsara'at* as something other than a punishment, against all other rabbinic texts.

It emerges that, alongside the dominant view throughout rabbinic literature that *tsara'at* is caused by sin, there is a single, post-tannaitic source indicating that house *tsara'at* is caused in *some* cases by the impetus of rewarding the owners of the homes. What does not appear in any source is an explicit assertion that *tsara'at* is random or a standard biological function—any explanation of the phenomenon in rabbinic literature has it divinely caused.[52] Moreover, never is skin *tsara'at* presented as a reward.

---

50   Lieberman, "*Hazanut Yannai*," asserts that this interpretation is present for the Sifra as well, that the R. Shimon who argues with R. Yehudah is actually R. Shimon bar Yohai seen at Leviticus Rabbah 17:6, and that although he doesn't mention his view about the money hidden in the houses, this is somehow implied. Given the tenuousness of his reading, it seems far more likely that (whether or not we identify R. Shimon with R. Shimon bar Yohai) this approach should be seen as a product of Leviticus Rabbah rather than of the Sifra.

51   Jacobowitz, "Leviticus Rabbah," 187–188. See further the entirety of chapter 3, "Treasure within the House: LR 17 and the Hermeneutic of Inversion," pp. 185–221.

52   Of course, there are some texts, including many across the Mishnah, that do not express any view on this issue, on which see below.

Jonathan Klawans' Position

Jonathan Klawans has argued for a radically diminished account of the extent to which *tsara'at* is triggered by sin in rabbinic and especially tannaitic literature. He asserts that the Mishnah never clearly states that *tsara'at* is caused by sin, that other tannaitic materials are somewhat cagey about the proposition, and all should be seen as "*aggadot*: passages of moral/theological concern that do not, strictly speaking, have any legal force (p. 102)." Some don't state that sin is the only cause of *tsara'at*, he notes, and the sources that do assert that one-to-one correlation place the assertion in the mouth of the priest rather than a rabbi. One is diagnosed with impurity based on physical symptoms of affliction alone and not based on an investigation as to whether one sinned or not, and the impurity ends after undergoing a ritual process, not a repentance protocol. While there are some tannaitic ideas that sin can cause *tsara'at* and more amoraic teachings in this vein, asserts Klawans, this is to be expected, given the biblical pedigree of the concept of *tsara'at* as punishment for sin.[53] This argument is presented as part of Klawans' larger thesis that the rabbis generally did not associate sin with impurity in the way that texts from Qumran do. *Tsara'at* is arguably the case with the clearest association between sin and malady, and Klawans presents this argument with the goal of minimizing and disarming this apparent counterpoint to this thesis.

This article diverges from Klawans' approach. Several of Klawans' points to minimize the role of *tsara'at* as a punishment are problematic. The attribution of *tsara'at*'s being caused only by sin to the priest indicates not that the rabbis were less convinced of this point but that they wished to insert it into the mouth of the ritual expert for whom the Bible prescribes a role in this situation. It would be a misrepresentation of the tannaitic view to downplay its commitment to the idea that *tsara'at* can be a punishment for sin by saying it appears in merely "a few tannaitic traditions" (p. 100). All tannaitic works include connections between *tsara'at* and sin, as demonstrated above. Furthermore, every account of what causes *tsara'at* invokes sin, usually as the exclusive cause. Similarly, in amoraic sources this view is not just "reiterated and even expanded somewhat" (p. 102). Those sources present a detailed elucidation of this concept, yielding a whole economy of sins that *tsara'at* can result from, to the point that we find boundary skirmishes between *tsara'at* and other procedures associated with multiple sins (the priestly garments and the beheaded heifer; see b.Arakhin 16a).

---

53   See Klawans, *Impurity and Sin*, pp. 98–104.

It remains necessary to address Klawans' argument that, for the most part, the Mishnah avoids these conversations. As he puts it, rightly, "The Mishnah … does not directly associate defiling afflictions with sin and does not even clearly allude to the biblical traditions that make such associations." (p. 100) It is first worth noting that, while this is true, there are some sources in the Mishnah that, more obliquely, do indicate that *tsara'at* occurs as a result of sin (see m.Keritot 2:3 and m.Nega'im 12:6). But still, why is the Mishnah the outlier in not having a clear statement connecting *tsara'at* and sin amidst a consistent tannaitic view making that association?

The answer to this question draws, ironically, from Klawans' work itself. He has been one of the clearest proponents of the distinction between two discourses on impurity—moral and ritual—in the Hebrew Bible.[54] A very similar discursive distinction, applied specifically to *tsara'at*, and noted above, can help explain this point. In the Hebrew Bible, Leviticus and other materials discussing *tsara'at* present it in a fully technical, ritual fashion—'if X occurs, the ritual result is Y, and one undergoes procedure Z.' By contrast, the depiction of *tsara'at* elsewhere in the Hebrew Bible clearly presumes that sin is the cause of the malady.[55] These texts do not *contradict* one another; they simply have distinct purposes. One is a manual for how to treat the disease ritually, while the other explains how it originates. An identical distinction can be identified within tannaitic literature—the Mishnah continues the "ritual *tsara'at*" presentation of Leviticus 13–14, going through the technical rules regarding the malady. By contrast, the other tannaitic sources that discuss *tsara'at* make the point that it is caused by evil speech and/or haughtiness (Sifre Deuteronomy 275:9, Sifra Metsora 5(3):7, t.Nega'im 6:7). Those texts draw upon the biblical "moral *tsara'at*" discourse in presenting the etiology of the malady.

This point can be strengthened by considering how the rabbis deploy the ritual details and moral explanations for another phenomenon—sacrifice and atonement. As discussed above, one might similarly see alternate discourses of moral and ritual atonement in the context of sacrifice, both throughout the Hebrew Bible and rabbinic literature. Here, as well, Leviticus and the Mishnah are focused on presenting the ritual details clearly, while allowing other texts to offer broader explanations for why the rituals are called for and what reconciliatory outcomes they lead to.[56]

---

54 See the discussion above.
55 See the examples noted at the outset of this essay.
56 While this assertion holds in a general sense, there are certainly many cases throughout the Mishnah where ethical and so-called aggadic matters are considered. (See Simon-Shoshan, "Nomos and Mishnah," for an analysis of the trend of studies on narrative mat-

Despite his protestations that the rabbis are not partial to a sin-based explanation of *tsara'at*, Klawans may actually agree with this depiction of two discourses within both biblical and tannaitic literature that are largely continuous. As he puts it, "The theme of these [tannaitic] passages—that defiling afflictions can come about as punishments for sins—is articulated clearly in Scripture and is simply reiterated by the tannaim" (p. 101).

Still, while Klawans wishes to minimize the strength of the sin-*tsara'at* connection in rabbinic literature, seeing it as at most a continuation of the biblical account, the presentation of the rabbinic materials in this chapter, including the prevailing rabbinic view that *only* sins can cause *tsara'at*, make it clear that the rabbis extend this theme well beyond a straightforward reading of the biblical text.

The strong association between sin and *tsara'at* for the tannaim can be taken a step further. Klawans notes several times in his treatment of the issue that "there is no assumption that the afflicted individual may have sinned" (p. 102) or that "there is no one-to-one correspondence between sin and defilement [by *tsara'at*]" (p. 100), indicating that there may be other causes of the malady. Relatedly, he notes that "the purification of the afflicted individual depends not on atonement… but on the disappearance of the affliction and the performance of the requisite rituals" (p. 99). These points, and what they entail, become increasingly difficult to accept in light of the broader context of the tannaitic treatment of the topic.

Most significantly, as noted above, the *only* cause skin lesions of *tsara'at* noted in rabbinic literature is sin. And this is reiterated multiple times, consistently across cases where the cause of *tsara'at* is discussed, and often said to be the exclusive cause. Is it indeed so clear that the afflicted individual has sinned? Certainly, the rabbinic presentation of the priest at Sifra Metsora 5(3):7 seems to assume that the person sinned, as he exhorts the person to examine his ways and repent. Furthermore, the idea that the reassumption of ritual purity results directly from the healing and ensuing purification is only relevant if the healing process *itself* is not predicated on repentance. The mere fact that the direct cause of the change in ritual purity status is physical does not mean that the cause of *tsara'at* is not sin; it would seem reasonable to assume, as is implied at t.Nega'im 6:7, that the rabbis understood that one only heals through repentance, and/or that continued sinning

ters, including framing narratives, in the study of Mishnah.) Still, as compared to other areas of classical rabbinic literature, the Mishnah is particularly focused on the legal and ritual details.

would only cause the malady to recur.[57] As the priest's actions in Sifra Metsora 5(3):7 indicate, the way to find out why the *tsara'at* was inflicted is to figure out what the person's sin is and the best method of curing it is to get them to stop.

The strength of the rabbinic view that *tsara'at* is associated with sin, and only with sin, can be further determined from a consideration of amoraic literature. The explosion of causes for *tsara'at*, from two in tannaitic literature to lists involving seven, ten, or more causes in amoraic literature, is telling. It seems clear that these amoraim received and extended a tannaitic tradition that fundamentally sees the cause of *tsara'at* in sin. While some tannaitic traditions are specific to particular sins and others are of a more general sin-*tsara'at* associative nature, it is clear that the robust tannaitic sin-*tsara'at* nexus was built onto and extended by their amoraic inheritors.

The unique association between *tsara'at* and sin can be further strengthened through consideration of *tsara'at* of the house, discussed above. Klawans notes the rabbinic discussions regarding the impurity of the house. As he puts it, "There are... traditions that view the afflictions that strike houses as a blessing... The clear implication is that defiling afflictions were not viewed as categorically bad." (p. 103) While this point is technically accurate, examining it in broader context only further clarifies the association between skin *tsara'at* and sin. If we are to consider the full panoply of causes for the different forms of *tsara'at*, we find that house *tsara'at* occurs either as a reward (Sifra Metsora 5:4, at least on the interpretations of it at LR 17:6) or as a punishment (Sifra Metsora 5[3]:7–9), while the only noted cause for skin *tsara'at* is that of sin. No sources indicate that any form of *tsara'at* is neutral or a natural sickness; in all cases the affliction is imposed actively by God, a view the rabbis are remarkably consistent about. Why, then, does LR 17:6 present the possibility that house *tsara'at* can serve as a reward? I would suggest, in addition to Jacobowitz's arguments noted above, that this is largely due to exegetical considerations. Some rabbis assume that the divine announcement that "I will place the affliction *tsara'at* in the home of the land of your inheritance (Leviticus 14:34)" clearly indicates that this is a reward; otherwise, why would God announce it to all of Israel? Thus

---

57   Klawans himself seems to concede this point, although he does not extend it to its next logical step, namely its support for a strong sin-*tsara'at* connection:
> Even though repentance in this tradition will impact upon the severity of the defilement, repentance is not tantamount to purification. Nor, for that matter, is it even necessary. Purification is not denied to the guilty and unrepentant, it is just prolonged. (*Impurity and Sin*, p. 100)

emerges the view that *tsara'at* of houses and particularly of houses, can be a reward. Even so, there is significant pushback. This view is rejected in Sifra and reinterpreted as based on punishment in b.Horayot 10a. The singular source of LR 17:6 is therefore best understood as an outlier rather than pointing to any broad-based weakness in the sin-*tsara'at* connection.

Conclusion

All rabbinic approaches to the cause of *tsara'at* discussed here take the view that *tsara'at* happens for some concrete reason. With the exception of one amoraic source, that reason is always sin. While the rabbis drew upon Leviticus' more mechanical laws at great length in determining the proper *procedures* and treatments to respond to *tsara'at*, when determining the *cause* of the malady the rabbis consistently drew upon the Bible's narratives that feature *tsara'at* as a punishment, such as the stories of Miriam, Naaman, and Uzziah.

The tannaitic rabbis were fully committed to the idea that *tsara'at* is always caused by sin. The biblical materials on *tsara'at* that the rabbis have to work with are fairly mixed and complicated, including the puzzling tension between the many stories with clear etiologies of *tsara'at* and the discussion in Leviticus of the regulations pertaining to *tsara'at* that offer no reason for its onset. The rabbis clearly move to assert that sin is the cause for contracting *tsara'at*. This accounts for the multiple formulations that "*tsara'at* only comes about as a result of evil speech" (Sifra Metsora 5[3]:7) and similar. The Mishnah avoids explicitly asserting this for generic reasons, as noted above, but never offers any view to the contrary. This account diverges from Klawans' approach, which minimizes the sin-*tsara'at* association in early rabbinic literature.[58] By contrast, this paper has demonstrated from tannaitic sources that the rabbis were consistent in seeing a fundamental connection between the sin and *tsara'at* throughout. For the rabbis and their extensive literature on *tsara'at*'s cause, the question is less about *whether tsara'at* is caused by sin; the more salient question is *which* and *how many* sins cause *tsara'at*.

---

58 Of course, this entire argument does not undermine Klawans' larger point about the separation between sin and impurity in Tannaitic literature. As he puts it, "even when there is a causal relationship between ritual impurity and sin, the real connection is not between sin and defilement, but with sin and punishment." (p. 104)

Bibliography

Andersen, J.G. "Leprosy in Translations of the Bible," *BT* 31 (1980): 207–212.
Baden, Joel S. & Moss, Candida R. "The Origin and Interpretation of *ṣāra'at* in Leviticus 13–14." *JBL* 130 (2011): 643–662.
Bargagarin, N. "Lashon Hara, Ayin Hara" (Hebrew), in *Studies in the Hebrew Language— Sources and Studies* 3 (1995): 177–180.
Birenboim, Hanan. "Expelling the Unclean from the 'Camp' according to 4Q274 1 i, 11QTa and the Writings of Josephus" (Hebrew). *Meghillot* 10 (2013): 15–23.
Buechler, Adolf. *Studies in Sin and Atonement*. Edited by I. Brodie and J. Rabbinowitz. London: Oxford University Press, 1956.
Elman, Yaakov. "Righteousness as Its Own Reward: An Inquiry into the Theologies of the Stam." *Proceedings of the American Academy for Jewish Research* 57 (1991): 35–67.
Elman, Yaakov. "An Akkadian Cognate of Hebrew *šeḥîn*." *Journal of the Ancient Near Eastern Society*, 8:1 (1976): 33–34.
Feder, Yitzhaq. "Was Prayer Prohibited to the Impure at Qumran?" (Hebrew). *Meghillot* 7 (2009): 145–155.
Gould, Ezra P. "The Social Condition of Lepers in the Gospels." *Journal of Biblical Literature* 137:4 (2018): 915–934.
Hayes, Christine. *Gentile Impurities and Jewish Identities*. New York: Oxford University Press, 2002.
Harrington, Hannah K. *Holiness: Rabbinic Judaism in the Graeco-Roman World*. Routledge, 2002.
Harrington, Hannah K. "Purity." *The Encyclopedia of the Dead Sea Scrolls* 2:724–728. Edited by L.H. Schiffman and J. VanderKam. New York: Oxford University Press, 2000.
Harrington, Hannah K. "The Rabbinic Reception of Leviticus." Pages 383–402 in *The Book of Leviticus: Composition and Reception*. Edited by Rolf Rendtorff and Robert A. Kugler. VTSup 93; Leiden: Brill, 2003.
Hasan-Rokem, Galit. "Leviticus Rabbah 16, 1—'Odysseus and the Sirens' in the Beit Leontis Mosaic from Beit She'an." Pages 159–189 in *Talmuda de-Erets Israel: Archaeology and the Rabbis in Late Antique Palestine*. Edited by Steven Fine and Aaron Koller. Berlin: De Gruyter, 2014.
Heinemann, Joseph. "Profile of a Midrash: The Art of Composition in Leviticus Rabba." *Journal of the American Academy of Religion* 39:2 (1971): 141–150.
Jacobowitz, Tamar. "Leviticus Rabbah and the Spiritualization of the Laws of Impurity." PhD diss. University of Pennsylvania, 2010.
Klawans, Jonathan. *Impurity and Sin in Ancient Judaism*. Oxford: Oxford University Press, 2000.

Klawans, Jonathan. *Purity, Sacrifice, and the Temple*. Oxford: Oxford University Press, 2005.

Lieberman, Saul. *"Hazanut Yannai," Sinai* 4 (1939): 221–250.

Levine, Baruch A. *Leviticus:* ויקרא. *The Traditional Hebrew Text with the New JPS Translation*. JPS Torah Commentary; Philadelphia: Jewish Publication Society, 1989.

Milgrom, Jacob. "4QTohora^a: An Unpublished Qumran Text on Purities." Pages 59–68 in *Time to Prepare the Way in the Wilderness. Papers on the Qumran Scrolls*. Edited by D. Dimant and L.H. Schiffman. STDJ 16; Leiden: Brill, 1995.

Milgrom, Jacob. *Leviticus 1–16: A New Translation with Introduction and Commentary*. New York: Doubleday, 1991.

Neusner, Jacob. *The Later Midrash Compilations: Genesis Rabbah, Leviticus Rabbah and Pesiqta deRab Kahana*. Vol. 3 of The Judaism behind the Texts: The Generative Premises of Rabbinic Literature. Atlanta: Scholars Press, 1994.

Seidl, T. "צרעת," *TDOT* 12 (2003): 468–475.

Simon-Shoshan, Moshe. "Nomos and Mishnah: The Turn to Narrative in Recent Mishnah Scholarship," forthcoming.

Tigchelaar, Eibert J.C. "Historical Origins of the Early Christian Concept of the Holy Spirit." Pages 167–240 in *The Holy Spirit, Inspiration, and the Cultures of Antiquity*. Edited by Jorg Frey, John Levison. Berlin/Boston: Walter De Gruyter, 2014.

Visotsky, Burt L. *Golden Bells and Pomegranates: Studies in Midrash Leviticus Rabbah*. Tubingen: Mohr Siebeck, 2003.

Wright, David P. "The Spectrum of Priestly Impurity." in *Priesthood and Cult in Ancient Israel*. Edited by Gary Anderson and Saul Olyan. Sheffield: England: JSOT Press, 1991.

Wright, David P. "Unclean and Clean (OT)." *ABD* 6:729–741.

Zuckier, Shlomo. "Flesh and Blood: The Reception of Biblical Sacrifice in Selected Talmudic Sources in Comparative Context." PhD diss. Yale University, 2020.

Zuckier, Shlomo. *Theologies of Sacrifice and Atonement in Ancient Judaism*, forthcoming.

CHAPTER 7

Feasting, Fasting, and the Bounty of the Land: Rituals of Sukkot in Samaritan and Rabbinic Antiquity

Laura S. Lieber

Few ritual items are as striking to and unexpected by outsiders as Samaritan sukkahs. These structures differ dramatically from the sukkahs of rabbinic Jews, both in terms of location and construction. Rabbinic sukkahs are built outside, open to the elements in a way that allows the stars to be seen through the roof; and while they are customarily decorated with fruits and vegetables as symbols of the harvest, the essential element is the סכך (*s'khakh*) which covers the roof with intentional inadequacy. In contemporary Samaritan practice, by contrast, sukkahs are built inside the home, and the historical record suggests that either interior or exterior locations were acceptable.[1] The roof is the only element of the sukkah with which the Samaritans are concerned; walls, an important element of rabbinic sukkahs and a subject of much rabbinic halakhic discussion, are not a factor at all. Locating the sukkah within the house is explained as having served a protective function, in that it concealed the festival observance from anti-Samaritan antagonists; it is maintained in the present day out of custom.[2] Building these structures in the home also protects Samaritan sukkahs from pilfering—a possible temptation given that Samaritan sukkahs consist of ornate roofs carefully constructed out of hundreds of pounds of luscious fruit

---

1   Thus, while an interior sukkah is invalid according to rabbinic law, in Samaritan law a sukkah could be built inside or outside; either would be equally valid. For a thorough analysis of Samaritan sukkot customs, and a precise summary of how those practices seem to have developed from antiquity to the present, see Pummer, "Synagogues—Samaritan and Jewish," 51–74.
2   In addition to Pummer's reconsideration of elements of the observance of Sukkot in his essay "Synagogues—Samaritan and Jewish," see also his detailed overview of the festival in his richly illustrated volume, *The Samaritans*, 23–25; and his recent monograph, *The Samaritans: A Profile* (Grand Rapids, MI; Cambridge, UK: Eerdmans, 2016), 264–266. It remains an open question whether the custom of building sukkahs inside the home is a recent custom or, as is accepted within the community, one dating back to the medieval period or earlier. Ultimately, the issue of location is something of a red herring, in that the possibility of building them inside distinguishes them from rabbinic law, which requires a sukkah not be under a roof.

(פרי עץ הדר).[3] The fruit are not hung randomly, but in carefully planned patterns that make visible both abundance and beauty. Above the fruits, on the top of the frame, open palm branches (כפת התמרים), alternately spread out right side up and upside down, are placed, and above those, boughs of thick-leafed trees (ענפי עץ עבות) are arranged such that they form a kind of thatched roof (making the gorgeous fruit a "ceiling" within the structure). Alongside those boughs are the branches of another species of tree (ערבי נחל; lilac chaste trees, in modern custom), brought from the banks of streams and rivers. In this way, the four species mentioned in Leviticus 23:40 are brought together not *under* but *in* one roof, not in the form of a bouquet of items that is ritually waved, as in the Jewish synagogue, but as a remarkable display of craftsmanship within the Samaritan home.[4]

Rabbinic sukkahs are public and visible, and in the diaspora often a source of questions from non-Jews who witness their neighbors' rituals. Modern Samaritan sukkahs, by contrast, are like carefully concealed gems, stunningly brilliant but not commonly seen.[5] Each reflects different understandings of a shared biblical text, and offers distinctive traditions for understanding a gapped yet insistent set of ritual instructions. The physical structures of sukkahs, so dramatically different between rabbinic Jews and contemporary Samaritan Israelites, remind us how wrong it is to assume that Samaritan practices are simply minor variations of the more commonly known rabbinic ways of understanding the Torah. In this essay, the holiday of Sukkot—the feast of booths—provides a lens into a much wider realm of Samaritan history, thought, and practice, particularly in Late Antiquity but also beyond. It will, in turn, help us contextualize elements of Sukkot observance in rabbinic Judaism, as well.

---

3 Binyamim Tsedakah offers an estimate of ca. 350 kg (750–800 lbs) of fruit for a sukkah; see https://www.israelite-samaritans.com/religion/sukkah/#addendum.
4 See Jacoby, "The Four Species in Jewish and Samaritan Tradition," 225–230; also note Levine, *Visual Judaism in Late Antiquity*, 360–362. Pummer, in "Synagogues—Samaritan and Jewish," cites evidence from Late Antiquity that Samaritans may also have used bouquets of the four species at that time (57–58).
5 Samaritans do visit each other, to admire and compare sukkahs, as hospitality is an important element of the holiday among their community as it is among rabbinic Jews.

Part One: "How Does Your Garden Grow?"

The festival of Sukkot is one of the three biblical pilgrimage festivals in the Torah, along with Passover and Shavuot ("the feast of weeks"). As with the other two pilgrimage festivals, Sukkot possesses agricultural significance—it is connected with the fall harvest—as well as associations with Israel's sacred history. The prominence of agricultural themes alongside the ritual requirements for the use of produce in the observance of Sukkot raises the question of farming more generally in Late Antiquity, and the Samaritan role in the agrarian economy in the Levant at the time. Such contextual evidence will provide a sense of the larger societal environment in which Samaritans celebrated Sukkot in Late Antiquity: understanding the harvest will help us understand the harvest festival.

A common impression of Late Antiquity is that it was a period of political turbulence and religious conflict, based on the cumulative picture of law codes, historical chronicles, and later recollections of the period. The archaeological and material record, however, paints a far more positive picture of the period from roughly the third through sixth centuries CE, as a time of thriving and expanding communities in the eastern Mediterranean. The number of civic structures (theaters, amphitheaters, etc.), religious structures (Jewish and Samaritan synagogues as well as churches), and domiciles all indicate a robust economy and thriving society, one built largely on agriculture. Settled areas apparently experienced robust growth, while "frontier" areas throughout the Land of Israel were increasingly developed and settled, thanks to both general peacefulness and improved technologies. As Doron Bar writes, "Not only did the number of settlements increase dramatically during [Late Antiquity], but many experienced expansion, with many farms extending into villages, and villages into small towns … [P]rosperity in the rural parts of Palestine was independent of ethnic or religious affiliation; it was part of a broad reality that involved all the inhabitants of the land, Samaritans, Jews, pagans, and Christians alike."[6] And elsewhere, he notes, "the land's natural landscape was dramatically altered, as the region experienced population and cultivation increase not seen in any previous period of its history."[7]

---

6 Bar, "Geographical Implications of Population and Settlement Growth in Late Antique Palestine," 5.
7 Bar, "Frontier and Periphery in Late Antique Palestine," 78. Note also Bar's earlier monograph, with historical commentary by Applebaum, *Landscape and Pattern*.

The Samaritan community participated in and benefitted from this social and agricultural renewal. Indeed, Joseph Patrich, writing about Caesarea, notes, "The Samaritans were another vital component in Caesarean society, representing the lucrative peasantry of the fertile agricultural hinterland of the city—the Sharon plain and the hilly country of Samaria."[8] Samaritan village-dwellers, like their non-Samaritan compatriots, thrived within a richly agrarian society; as Yizhar Hirschfeld writes, "The majority of village dwellers earned their living as farmers, cultivating grains, vegetables, grapes, and olives, herding sheep, and raising cattle. Numerous presses for wine and oil attest to large-scale production of these commodities."[9] The produce of the land was abundant, and increasingly so. Bar offers the region of Samaria as an exemplar of robust Late Antique agricultural innovation:

> The Samaria region, to give an example, was a 'stable settlement area,' populated almost continuously before Late Antiquity. Nevertheless, the survey in this area reveals an impressive spread of advanced devices for processing agricultural produce and a doubling of the number of settled sites in Late Antiquity.[10]

The construction of Samaritan settlements, furthermore, provides concrete evidence of a healthy society, a society grounded in thriving agriculture; as Shimon Dar writes, "The Samaritan rural settlements from Late Antiquity are well built, with a high architectural standard and excellent technical execution ... The houses have large courtyards with agricultural installations, mostly olive oil presses nearby, as well as ritual baths ... The high quality of Samaritan hill-country agriculture has been observed in surveys and excavations in Samaria, and it enabled the Samaritans to achieve their high standard of material culture, as seen in archaeological excavations."[11] Far from being a precarious "dark age," Late Antiquity was a period of expansion and growth, of population, settlements, and arable land. It was an age of abundance.

In sum, the fourth through seventh centuries in the Land of Israel were, as Bar notes, not a grim era of scarcity but rather "a long period of relief, lived in relative security, and benefited from the fruits of the *pax Romana*."[12] This was not, to be sure, a completely tranquil period, but the disturbances of these centuries—wars, plagues, and earthquakes, and the resultant societal disruption and economic distress—were comparatively less in the Land of Israel,

---

8   Patrich, "Urban Space in Caesarea Maritima, Israel," i 78.
9   Hirschfeld, "Farms and Villages in Byzantine Palestine," 60.
10 Bar, "Frontier and Periphery," 78.
11 Dar, "Archaeological Aspects of Samaritan Research in Israel," 195–196.
12 Bar, "Frontier and Periphery," 91.

and the events that rocked the Roman Empire overall were felt somewhat less intensely in Palestine.[13]

This picture of agricultural abundance helps us to understand and envision the Samaritan community in Late Antiquity—a community that was evidently robustly agrarian and economically prosperous, as were their non-Samaritan neighbors. This is not to ignore the turbulence of the period, and particularly the Samaritan unrest, even uprisings, recorded in 484 CE, 529 CE, and 572 CE.[14] Religiously motivated political unrest does not depend on economic scarcity or food insecurity, and indeed, prosperity may well have fueled ambitions for independence. Rather, awareness of material prosperity helps us understand the *realia* underlying the joyful abundance of the Samaritan celebration of Sukkot in antiquity, even as the political and religious tensions help explain other elements of this festival's observance.

Part Two: "Shabbat Gan Eden"

Samaritan sukkahs, with their hundreds of pounds of produce and their weaving together of the four species, give ritualized, concrete shape to the abundance of the land. We lack evidence from antiquity for the construction of Samaritan sukkahs, but building booths out of the four species reflects an old, and perhaps surprisingly common (if non-rabbinic) understanding of Leviticus 23:40. First, let us examine the Leviticus verse, which is the same in the Samaritan Pentateuch and the Masoretic text:

---

13 Bar notes, "[A] comparison of the survey maps permits us to observe and ascertain with a reliable measure of confidence that the early parts of the Late Antique period were one of the most prominent periods of prosperity in the history of Palestine. Archaeological findings indicate that the four century dramatic turn to Christianity cannot be regarded as a turning point in the settlement of Palestine. In fact, as early as in the second century and even during the economic crisis that befell the Roman Empire during the third century, Palestine saw one of its finest periods of prosperity, both in the urban centers as well as in the rural areas ... Many scholars label the time from the second century up to the days of the Emperor Constantine in the fourth century as one of the darkest periods in the history of Palestine. Contrary to that view, in this article I have demonstrated how after the dust of the two Jewish rebellions had settled and the Jewish population accepted Roman rule, a period of prosperity followed. It seems that the main reason for this unique phenomenon is related to the fact that from the second century to the sixth century, during Late Antiquity, Palestine witnessed a period of calm, in which wars, plagues, and earthquakes were scarce" (Bar, "Geographical Implications," 4, 7).

14 See Sivan, *Palestine in Late Antiquity* especially Chapter 3; "Recalcitrance, Riots, and Rebellion," 107–142.

ולקחתם לכם ביום הראשון פרי עץ הדר כפת תמרים וענף עץ עבת וערבי נחל ושמחתם
לפני יהוה אלהיכם שבעת ימים

> On the first day [of Sukkot], you shall take the fruit of *hadar* trees, branches of palm trees, boughs of leafy trees, and *aravah* of the brook, and you shall rejoice before the Eternal your God for seven days.

Samaritan identification of these species differs from the understandings codified in rabbinic writings. The "fruit of *hadar*-trees" is taken by Samaritans as any beautiful fruit, rather than specifically a citron; and the *aravah* is understood not specifically as a willow but as any deciduous tree growing in *wadi* Shechem, although there is a preference for the lilac chaste tree (*Vitex agnus-castus*), indigenous to the Land of Israel.[15] Pliny the Elder (*Natural History* 24.38) describes the lilac chaste tree as "not so different from the willow (*non multum a salice vitilium*)," and goes on to note that Athenian matrons would sprinkle their beds with it during the festival of Thesmophoria, when women left their husbands to celebrate Demeter and Persephone.[16] This holiday, it bears noting, possessed agricultural significance (celebrating the harvest or the sowing of seeds, depending on location), and it was celebrated in the late summer or autumn (September or October) for a period of three to ten days.[17]

The verse's injunction to "take" these four species provides little in the way of concrete ritual instruction—what is to be done with them, precisely? In rabbinic Judaism (as in m. Sukkah 3.1), the four species are taken into a bundle and bound together as the lulav and etrog (myrtle, palm and willow bound together and held along with the citron).[18] In Samaritan practice, by contrast, they are

---

15   The Lilac Chaste Tree is also known as "Abraham's Balm" and "monk's pepper." Pummer says that red peppers may be substituted; see Pummer, "Samaritan Rituals and Customs," 688.

16   Pliny also credits this plant (among other benefits) with inhibiting sexual desire (*ad venerem impetus inhibent*) and goes on to note that it neutralizes the poison of serpents (*adversantur venenis serpentium*). These elements of sexual suppression and the healing of serpent bites mentioned by Pliny make the plant suggestive in the context of Eden, with its traditional associations with both sex and snakes.

17   See Chlup, "The Semantics of Fertility: Levels of Meaning in the Thesmophoria," 171. Also note *The Sacred and the Feminine in Ancient Greece*, edited by Blundell and Williamson.

18   In m.Sukkah 3:1, it is written: "A *lulav* [a palm branch, one of the four species which it is a mitsvah to take on Sukkot] which was stolen or dried out is invalid. One which comes from an *ashera* [a tree dedicated to idolatry], or from a condemned city [an idolatrous city which must be destroyed] is invalid. If its tip was snapped off, or its leaves missing, it is invalid; if its leaves were [merely] separated, it is valid. Rabbi Yehudah says: One must bind it together from the top [in order for it to be valid]. The palms of Iron Mount are valid

taken and transformed into the materials from which the booths themselves are made. As different as Samaritan practice may be from rabbinic practice, however, it recalls the celebration of Sukkot as it is recorded in Nehemiah 8:14–16. In this passage, part of the Jewish Bible but not the Samaritan canon, we are told:

> They found written in the Teaching that the Eternal had commanded Moses that the Israelites must dwell in booths during the festival of the seventh month; and that they must announce and proclaim throughout all their towns and Jerusalem as follows, 'Go out to the mountains and bring leafy branches of olive trees, pine trees, myrtles, palms and [other] leafy trees to make booths, as it is written.' So the people went out and brought them, and made themselves booths on their roofs, in their courtyards, in the courtyards of the House of God, in the square of the Water Gate and in the square of the Ephraim Gate.

The community of the returnees, often depicted in Ezra-Nehemiah as being in conflict with the Samaritan community, here builds their sukkahs from the leafy boughs of trees, in a style strongly reminiscent of eventually-attested Samaritan custom. It seems plausible that the Nehemiah passage records a once-familiar, unsurprising alternative means of constructing sukkahs that, while eventually discarded by rabbinic Jews, was once a normative practice—and one practiced by Karaite Jews down to the present, as well.[19]

It is not only through ritual items and practices that Samaritan observance of Sukkot differs from rabbinic celebration of the same. Rather than linking the holiday of Sukkot to the fragility of life and the formative period of wandering in the wilderness, as the rabbis do, Samaritan tradition views the festival through the lens of the creation story in Genesis, and the Sabbath that falls dur-

---

[for use as a *lulav*]. A *lulav* that has three hand-breadths [in length] by which to shake it, is valid." The lulav and etrog constitute important elements in early Jewish synagogue art, and the absence of depictions of these items can help determine to which community a synagogue may have belonged; see the discussion in Pummer, "Samaritan Synagogues and Jewish Synagogues,"105–142; on the basis of more recent excavations, however, he reconsiders this position in his more recent essay, "Synagogues—Samaritan and Jewish", 51–74. Jacoby also discusses the use of the imagery of the four species in Judean coins ("The Four Species," 226–227).

19   On Karaite practices, see Yaron and Qanaï, *An Introduction to Karaite Judaism: History, Theology, Practice, and Custom*; and also https://www.karaites.org/uploads/7/4/1/3/7413835/mikdash_meat_section_9_chag_hasukkot.pdf. As the website https://www.karaites.org/sukkot.html states, "The majority of the Karaite Sages, in accordance with the practice recorded in the book of Nehemiah, determined that we are to build our *sukkot* out of the materials listed in Leviticus."

ing Sukkot is, at least in modern custom, called *Shabbat Gan Eden*, the Sabbath of the Garden of Eden.[20] The sukkah in some sense reflects the abundance of the pristine past and the hoped-for future. For this reason, Samaritans begin construction of their sukkahs immediately after the conclusion of Yom Kippur, as they are, at that moment in a state of purity—restored, as it were, to their own Edenic state.[21] The abundance of the natural world is transformed, through the purest human craft, piety, and skill, into a symbol of the world restored. When one fulfills the Torah's commandment (Leviticus 23:42) to sit in the sukkah, one dwells, however transiently, in Paradise.

Part Three: "Exegetical Eden"

The association of Sukkot with the Garden of Eden may have occurred relatively recently, as the term "Shabbat Gan Eden" is not attested in premodern sources (of which we have precious few in Samaritan tradition). But even if the coinage is recent, it reflects an astute weaving together of far older motifs and practices. We have already seen how the physical structure of the sukkah makes the ripe abundance of the land visible to all beholders (and the fragrance, too, offers sensual appeal, particularly during the course of the week, as hung fruits ripen). The symbolism of the sukkah extends beyond the Edenic plethora of produce, however.

An evocative tradition is recorded in the Samaritan exegetical work, *Tibat Marqe* ("the ark—that is, anthology—of Marqe"); this passage likely dates to its earliest stratum of that work, ca. third or fourth century CE, and it suggests additional layers of meaningfulness to the practice of sitting in a booth (a sukkah). After a brief prose introduction, the work offers a poetic paean to the Israelites, likening them to both produce and farmers:

> "*And the people of Israel journeyed from Rameses to Sukkot*" (Exodus 12:37[22]); the cloud[23] was above them, and the fire was before them—six hundred thousand appareled in humility, goodness and grace supporting

---

20   For a brief overview of the Garden of Eden in Samaritan thought, see Dexinger, "Samaritan Eschatology," 289–290.
21   In rabbinic Jewish custom, too, one begins construction of the Sukkah immediately after Yom Kippur, in order to demonstrate eagerness to fulfill commandments, having now atoned for the previous year's transgressions and failures. The action is similar, but the motivations are distinctive.
22   The biblical text here is in Aramaic translation; the language is close to but not identical with the Samaritan Targum, which dates to roughly the same period as this stratum of TM.
23   The connection of Sukkot to "the cloud" recalls a tradition preserved in an early rabbinic

them there. Sukkot was situated on a great pathway, a place to which all travelers went.

Abraham's stars were graceful
    And Sarah's chicks[24] were shining bright
Crowned were Isaac's multitudes,
    Garlanded were Rachel's young
Beautiful were Jacob's cypresses,
    Arrayed were Leah's ranks
Sukkot resembled the Garden of Eden,
And the Israelites were the trees in it.
The House of the Oath[25] resembled the Ark,
and Sarah's chicks were in its baskets.

---

midrash on Leviticus, Sifra (*Emor* 17:11), which also draws the passage from Nehemiah 8 into its exegesis:

> And thus does Ezra say (in Nehemiah 8:15): "And that they must announce and proclaim throughout all their cities and Jerusalem, saying: Go out to the mountains and bring olive leaves, and olive-tree leaves and hadas leaves, and date-palm leaves, and plaited-tree leaves to make succoth, as it is written: 'So that your generations know that I caused the children of Israel to dwell in booths when I took them out of the land of Egypt' (Leviticus 23:43)." Rabbi Eliezer says that **they were booths, literally** (סוכות ממש היו). Rabbi Aqiva says that they were **clouds of glory**. "When I took them out of the land of Egypt" (Leviticus 23:43): We are hereby taught that even the sukkah is a reminder of the Exodus from Egypt.

The cloud-sukkah is the minority opinion here—rabbinic tradition accepts both the literal booth and the idea that it commemorates the Exodus—but the alternative is nonetheless known, and may indeed be the stronger case (see Rubenstein's essay http://thetorah.com/sukkah-and-its-symbolism/). The prose opening of the passage, in which the divine cloud shelters all travelers, can be read as a metaphorical description for God extending protection to all who journey through life.

A similar tradition, lacking the Nehemiah 8 reference but explicating Exod. 12:37 specifically, occurs in Mekhilta Bo 14 [Horowitz-Rabin, 48]. This parallel states:

> "To Sukkot" (Exodus 12:37): **"Sukkot," ("booths") literally**, as in (Genesis 33:17) "And Jacob traveled to Succoth, and for his cattle he made sukkot (booths), for which reason the place was named Sukkot." These are the words of R. Eliezer. R. Aqiva says: **"Sukkot" refers to the clouds of glory**, as in (Isaiah 4:5) "And the Lord will create on the entire base of Mount Zion and on all of its branchings a cloud by day and smoke with a glow of flaming fire by night, on all the glory, a canopy."

The Mekhilta of Rabbi Shimon bar Yochai reverses the positions of Aqiva and Eliezer: סכתה. ר׳ עקיבה אומר סכות ממש עשו להן בסכות: ר׳ אליעזר אומר סכות ענני כבוד כאו וחנו על נבי רעמסס.

24 That is, her descendants.
25 "The House of the Oath" refers to Bethel ("the House of God") where God promised Jacob the land and Jacob made a vow to God (see Genesis 28:11–22). In Samaritan tradition, Gerizim and Beth El (as the House of God) are often conflated.

> The ram of Isaac[26] paced with it,
> Goring with his horns any who would smite him.
> A crop in the House of the Oath,
> Sprouting up and gathered in,
> And heaped up by the arm of the Good One
> And gathered by three glorious ministers,[27]
> Hedged in by three great fences—
> By cloud, fire, and holy spirit
> One leading, one illuminating, one protecting
> A good crop, with no end to its greatness,
> Sown among the Philistines
> And sprouting in the Land of Egypt
> And it was tended after being sown,
> (For) four hundred and thirty years earlier[28]
> The years are weighed in truthful scales:
> Half of them in the Land of Egypt
> And half of them in the Land of Canaan.
> At the end of these years they were gathered together[29]
> And became a repository in the plain of Sukkot.
> Excellent were these favored farmers,
> Whose beauty was outstanding among His creatures![30]

This passage expands on a verse from Exodus 12 that mentions not the festival of Sukkot but rather the geographic region known as "Sukkot," presumably a place of booths.[31] But despite the fact that the focus is not on the holiday, this passage evokes a number of compelling themes with affinities for the holiday. It seems plausible that the place-name Sukkot at least hinted at the ritual practice that bears the same name; dwelling in a booth is significant.

---

26 Isaac here seems to be identified with the sheep of the burned offering from Genesis 22.
27 That is, Eleazar, Pinchas, and Itamar.
28 See Exodus 12:40.
29 See Exodus 12:41.
30 *Tibat Marqe* Book 1 (§ 71); text from *Tibat Marqe: A Collection of Samaritan Midrashim*, 98. The translation is the present author's.
31 Most likely an area within the eastern Nile delta region, in the territory of Goshen. A tradition in ExodR 18:6 notes that God honored Egypt by calling it "the Garden of Eden." Genesis Rabbah 78:16 connects the place-name *Sukkot* to the place where Jacob offered the water libation associated with the festival of Sukkot.

What is most striking about this passage—beyond its richly poetic structure in what is conventionally regarded as a prose text[32]—is the density of agrarian and agricultural imagery. The place, Sukkot, is compared to the Garden of Eden, and the children of Israel are the trees within it. They are the "crop" of God's House (Beth El), planted, tended, and harvested by God and God's designated priestly leaders, fenced in protectively by the divine elemental manifestations of cloud (water), fire, and spirit (wind). The Israelites are a uniquely migratory crop (protected by their mobile hedge), thriving in exile as well as in the land. Like produce at the market, their years are weighed in accurate scales, and their assembly on the plains of Sukkot is likened to a storehouse or granary. As the poem concludes, the Israelites are praised as "favored farmers" (אריסי רחותה).

Figurative language rooted in agriculture is hardly innovative; children are often called "seed" or, as here, "chicks," to the point where such terms may not even be translated in strictly literal terms. What stands out here is the density of the imagery and the consistency with which the theme is developed. It seems at least plausible that the mention of a place named "Sukkot" called to mind the abundance of the harvest season—particularly as it would have been experienced by a Samaritan in the expansive agrarian world of Late Antiquity—whether it was the agricultural plenty of the Nile Delta or the richness of the Land of Israel that was envisioned—or the lushness of the Garden of Eden, to which this poem explicitly compares the place called "Sukkot."

In this passage, Marqe blurs the boundary between the place named "Sukkot" and the agricultural richness celebrated by the festival of the same name. Elsewhere, Marqe makes the reverse move: he transforms sacred time (the Sabbath) into sacred space: In Book 2 of *Tibat Marqe* (§ 16), the Sabbath is described as "a city entirely of blessing (מדינה כהלה ברכה)" and "a place entirely holy (אתר כהלה קדיש)."[33] We find a similar translation of time into space in the liturgical poetry of Amram Dare, who writes: "Woe to the one who departs from it (the Sabbath) /—The garden that tends its owner: / Every tree within it is Life!"[34] And likewise in the three poems attributed to "al-Dustan," in which we find stated: "The Sabbath resembles a city / built at the end of creation;" "a beautiful garden is the Sabbath day;" "a garden which will never close is the Sabbath;"

---

32   One of the few recent treatments of poetry, or near-poetry, embedded in *Tibat Marqe* can be found in Novick, *Piyyut and Midrash*, 68–75. He treats the specific rhetorical structure of the "iterative verse header," but gestures toward the larger body of embedded poetry more generally.

33   *Tibat Marqe*, 123–125.

34   Amram Dare #18, lines 14–16; Ben-Hayyim, *The Literary and Oral Tradition of Hebrew and Aramaic Amongst the Samaritans*, III:2, 80 [hereafter abbreviated *LOT*].

"the seventh day is a beautiful city;" and "the seventh day is likened to the city of a king."[35] In his poetry, Marqe makes a similar move, translating a concept into a spatial image, transforming the Torah into the Garden of Eden. In one poem, he writes: "(Torah is) an Eden, extending life / To those who drink from it; / An Eden—that it is rooted / In eternal life."[36] And in another poem, a somewhat softer formulation, according to which the Torah is a tendril that grows forth from the primordial garden: "A sliver of life, unlike any other / (Torah) transmits wisdom into the world / A sliver of life eternal / and this is from Eden, / when it is opened by God / it sustains all its generations / and all are prolonged by its light."[37] Eden, it seems, represents both the Sabbath and Torah; thus while the designation of the Shabbat that falls during Sukkot as "Shabbat Gan Eden" may be relatively late, it is woven out of threads that emerge from classical sources. For Sukkot to be a place in space as well as a place in time, and for it to be both a city and a garden, reflects an extension of extant exegetical motifs as well as the experience (or memory) of the agricultural abundance of Samaria in Late Antiquity.

Part Four: "Edenic Politics"

If the sukkah brings a bit of Eden into the home, Samaritan observance of sukkot also entails a pilgrimage to Paradise—or, rather, Mount Gerizim, which represents (at least in medieval Samaritan writings) the gateway to the Garden of Eden, or the location of Eden itself.[38] The eschatological promise of Eden (and Gerizim) restored had the potential to transform Sukkot into a kind of political flashpoint among the Samaritans, conceptually and perhaps even in practice; in this, Sukkot is akin to Passover, a festival so often associated with

---

35 See *LOT*, 280–287; and the discussion in Miller, "Sabbath-Temple-Eden," 46–74. The identity of the poet known as "al-Dustan" ("the Dosithean") is unknown, but the language of the poems suggests they are from Late Antiquity, as indicated by their inclusion among the JPA poems in the *Comprehensive Aramaic Lexicon* (cal.huc.edu (accessed on 11/15/21)). See the discussion in *LOT*, 17–18.
36 Marqe #9, lines 61–64 (*LOT*, 191–192).
37 Marqe #21, lines (not in LOT, but in Cowley, *The Samaritan Liturgy* 1:57).
38 Gerizim is known in Samaritan tradition as הר הקדם, "the eastern (or ancient) mountain," which Marqe explains is because it was a twin of the Garden of Eden (דו וגן עדן תאמים); Adam was made from the earth of the mountain (TM 2 [§ 44], 143). Samaritan associations of Eden with the holy mountain resonate with biblical and rabbinic ideas about Jerusalem/Zion and Paradise; see Ezek. 28:13, 16 which equates the garden with "the mountain of God."

political unrest among Jews. For Samaritans and Jews alike, the contemplation of an ideal past and the promise of future restoration can make the imperfection of the present tense frustrating, even unbearable.

One of the more striking customs practiced among Samaritans today is the tradition of burning the dried palm fronds and dry leafy matter of the booths at the conclusion of the festival.[39] A medieval chronicle offers what became, in the modern period, the source of this custom. This account rehearses a stunning Samaritan victory over the Byzantine Christians under the leadership of the great Samaritan reformer, Baba Rabba (ca. third or fourth century?):

> One night all the people were mustered and ascended Mount Gerizim and Baba Rabba was in the van of the troops. Levi [his nephew] then arose with the might and power of God and smote the guards of the king, the monks and the priests, crying out in a loud voice: 'The Lord is a man of war. The Lord is His name!' And when Baba Rabba heard the voice of Levi his nephew, they all raised their voices saying as he had said. They unsheathed their swords and killed many of the Romans, not ceasing until they had wiped out everyone who was on Mount Gerizim.
>
> Then they kindled the fire on the top of the dome and all the Samaritans arose and killed all the overseers who had been put over them. Not one of them remained. And they continued throughout the whole night to burn the churches of the Romans, destroying them until they effaced the name from Mount Gerizim and round-about.
>
> The memory of this [that is, the Samaritan triumph] has lasted up to our day: on the first day of the seventh month, the Samaritan children gather wood and burn it in the evening at the end of the first day of the seventh month.[40]

This account does not itself align with Sukkot, as it describes events on the first day of the seventh month, where the festival of Sukkot begins on the fifteenth of the month, and it refers to gathering and burning wood, not taking

---

39   While the sukkah's dried greenery is burned, the abundant fruit from which the interior of the sukkah roof is constructed is consumed or carefully preserved and then enjoyed throughout the year; see https://www.israelite-samaritans.com/religion/sukkah/#after-holiday.

40   Stenhouse, *Kitāb al-Tarīkh of Abū 'l-Fatḥ: The Chronicle of Abū 'l-Fatḥ*, 199. This work is the oldest complete Samaritan historical chronicle, composed in 1355 at the behest of the High Priest, Pinchas. Eclectic texts, such as that offered by Sivan (p. 111) often include the reference to Sukkot from the modern Chronicle, which attempts to align the medieval source with developed practice.

material from the festival booth. But at some point, over the centuries, it seems that this memory of a triumph from Late Antiquity merges into the conclusion of Sukkot—a festival which provided an abundance of desiccated foliage that could be burned. By the early 20th century, the Samaritan Chronicle II, an expansion of the medieval chronicle, records that the burning occurs at the end of the festival, on Shemini Atseret, and it is the sukkahs that are burned, reflecting contemporary practice.[41] Over the period of centuries, foundational stories from Late Antiquity, filtered through medieval historiography and developing practices, transformed flames of destruction into an enduring tradition of bonfires of celebration.[42]

This custom of burning components of the sukkah reminds us that while Samaritans build their sukkahs within their homes, key elements of the festival—including the pilgrimage to Mount Gerizim on the first day and the bonfires of Shemini Atseret—are manifestly external, public, communal events. Indeed, the Samaritan sukkah consists of elements from the outside, natural world, symbolizing paradise, that are brought into the home and constructed, by human hands, into something new; then, after eight days of festivities, components are returned to the outside world and returned unto the earth. Ritual transforms an event from Samaritan sacred history into a communal memory, extending a triumph from the Late Antique past into a present moment, even as it enacts a cycle of nature-civilization-nature. Past and future epochs— the Garden of Eden, the time of Baba Rabba, the awaited restoration that will accompany the Time of Favor—are not collapsed into flat, ahistorical observance of ritual but are instead tellingly juxtaposed and interwoven, showing that the distances among the periods is meaningful, but also ultimately small.

---

41   The modern chronicle (Chronicle II) concludes the same episode as follows: "From the day the Samaritan Israelite community did this to the Romans, Samaritan children have set fire to the wood of their Sukkahs on the night of the conclusion of the festival of the Eight Day of Solemn Assembly, which concludes the festivals of the Lord. This episode has thus remained a memorial among them to this day," *Chronicle II* § 19.65, from Cohen, *A Samaritan Chronicle*, 96. See also the discussion in Pummer, "Synagogues—Samaritan and Jewish," 60–61. See Pummer, *The Samaritans* (1987), 23 and Plate XLIC; for an "insider" perspective, see the discussion by Benyamim Tsedaka online, at https://www.israelite-samaritans.com/religion/sukkah/#retaking-gerizim.

42   This episode is, in some ways, reminiscent of the Jewish festival of Chanukah (a holiday not observed by Samaritans, as it is not a holiday found in the Torah). It commemorates a military triumph over hostile forces and is remembered by means of flame. It is worth noting that the celebration of Chanukah was itself modeled on the festival of Sukkot; see the discussion in Regev, *The Hasmoneans*, especially pages 38–46 ("Hanukkah as the 'Festival of Tabernacles' in 2 Maccabees").

This nexus connecting structure, theology, history, and exegesis into a harmonious whole reflects the power of ritual, and a key component of ritual is liturgy: words that shape experiences, build community, and constitute the essential human component of the ongoing dialogue with the deity. Thus in the final section of this paper, we turn our attention to the Samaritan liturgy of Sukkot.

FEASTING AND FASTING: The Liturgy of Sukkot

The published version of the Samaritan liturgy for Sukkot is modern, although not recent; the two-volume edition by Cowley in 1909 draws on manuscripts from the 18th and 19th centuries, and while this work is, at the very least, a product of its time and place, it has not yet been replaced by a more modern scholarly edition.[43] The earliest stratum of the prayer service for Sukkot, as for other occasions, likely consisted of the recitation of verses from scripture; these readings were later embellished by hymns. The Sukkot liturgy as published by Cowley opens with a poem by the 19th century High Priest Amram ben Solomon, modeled on the poetry of the Late Antique payyetan and exegete Marqe. Other hymns are scattered through the service, most from the 18th century but a few earlier, from the 14th century.[44] None of the hymns in the service belong to the "classical" period of Samaritan poetry—the period of Amram Dare, his son Marqe, and Marqe's son, Ninna, in the third or fourth century CE—and where the classical poems are written in Samaritan Aramaic, the medieval and modern poems were composed in the hybrid Aramaic-Hebrew commonly called "Samaritan."[45]

In terms of the liturgy in Late Antiquity, we have little idea of what it might specifically have included. We do, however, have two hymns from that period which came to be associated with Sukkot, although we cannot know if that

---

43 Cowley, *The Samaritan Liturgy in Two Volumes*; the liturgy for Sukkot can be found in 2:716–817.

44 The hymns in the service are as follows, with page numbers indicating location in Cowley: one (p. 731) by Murjan b. Abraham [18th c.], another (p. 738) by Seth Aaron b. Isaac [15th c.], another (p. 742) by Solomon b. Tabiah [18th c.], another (p. 746) by Abdallah b. Solomon [14th c.], another two (p. 770 and p. 815) by Tabiah b. Isaac [18th c.], another (p. 779) by Pinchas b. Eleazar [date uncertain], another (p. 796) by Abraham b. Jacob Danfi [18th c.], another (p. 801—very long!) by Eleazar b. Pinchas [date uncertain]. A fine resource for dating these works is A.D. Crown's *Samaritan Scribes and Manuscripts* (Tübingen: Mohr Siebeck, 2001).

45 On the language called "Samaritan," see Florentin, *Late Samaritan Hebrew*.

was their original setting or if they simply broadened out from general "seventh month" orientations; the Marqan hymn is explicitly focused on the Day of Atonement. I close this essay with a brief discussion of these two poems, one by Amram Dare and another by his son, the great Samaritan sage, Marqe.

The first poem, by Amram Dare, is (according to modern practice) said daily for most of the seventh month, from its first day until the conclusion of the festival of Sukkot on Shemini Atseret.[46] It states:

> Great is God, who thus commanded
> Concerning the beginning of the seventh month,
> Premier among all the new moons,[47]
> That it should be called, by the authority of God,
> By four exalted titles:
> *Shabbaton*,[48] Remembrance, Trumpet Blast, and Sacred Convocation[49]
> In order that it should be a Sabbath-among-Months,
> And a Sabbath[50]-of-Sabbaths among the Festivals,
> And the crown of the Festival of the Time of Favor
> Within it[51] are the Day of Repentance—
> Holy, expelling sin—
> And the pilgrimage of booths and the pilgrimage of the harvest,
> And the Eighth Day of Assembly,[52]
> Seventh of the Festivals and the holy of holies.
> And all Israel is nourished (מהר) by them[53]
> And they are all destined, one with another,
> Threefold[54] within it.
> May God be praised!
> There is no God but the one!

---

46 Amram Dare #21 (*LOT*, 84–86).
47 The word ארשי means, literally, "foundation, origin;" see Avraham Tal, *Dictionary of Samaritan Aramaic*, 2 vols. (Leiden: Brill, 2000), 67.
48 The seventh month is the "Sabbath" of months.
49 These four names appear in Leviticus 23:24.
50 For שב as "Sabbath," see Tal, *Dictionary of Samaritan Aramaic*, 870.
51 That is, within the seventh month.
52 That is, Shemini Atseret.
53 Israel is nourished—fed learning, as it were—by the holiday and its many names. The root of מהר is מור, lit., "to procure food"—as befits the harvest festival.
54 This may refer to the three holidays—Rosh Hashanah, Yom Kippur, and Sukkot—that fall within the seventh month, but the Samaritan calendar considers Shemini Atseret a separate holiday, meaning that there are four festivals in the seventh month. Alterna-

FEASTING, FASTING, AND THE BOUNTY OF THE LAND   153

This poem tells us little about the observance of Sukkot beyond its place in the calendar. It is simply one of many holidays that falls during the seventh month. The repetition of the poem throughout the seventh month ensures that the poem adorns the celebration of the many holidays it mentions: the first day of the month, the Day of Repentance, the seven days of Sukkot, and the Eighth Day of Assembly (Shemini Atseret) that concludes the season of joy. But elements of the poem, particularly the linking of the Day of Atonement ("holy, expelling sin") to the festival of both booths and harvest suggests the practice of beginning construction of the sukkah while in a state of purity, and its association with agrarian riches. The poem weaves together all the festivals of the seventh month, but it links the Day of Atonement and Sukkot in this specific way. Furthermore, later in the hymn, Amram describes Israel as being "nourished" (מהר) by these festivals, underscoring the connection between the autumnal agricultural festivals and the idea of physical as well as spiritual sustenance.

The connection of Sukkot to spiritual as well as physical nourishment is made even more explicit in the second classical Samaritan hymn associated with Sukkot, by Marqe.[55] This poem is longer, and includes a partial alphabetical acrostic; it is recited on the preparatory feast (ṣimmūt) of Sukkot, observed on the Sabbath seven weeks prior to the Festival,[56] and from the first day of the seventh month ("the festival of the seventh month") until the Day of Atonement.[57] Its text is as follows:

א   Come in peace, O day of fasting
     On which two goats for sin-offerings
     Are offered on the heights:
     One for Azazel and one for YHWH

ב   On the tenth of the month—it is said—
     "You shall afflict your souls" (Leviticus 16:31)
     A Hebrew, abstaining from food,
     Denies himself on account of his sin

---

     tively, it may be a reference to the three pilgrimage festivals. The language is clear, but the significance—and its implications for Amram Dare's calendrical conception—is not.
55 Marqe #17 (*LOT*, 238–241).
56 Both Passover and Sukkot are preceded by feast-days (which always fall on Shabbat), known as צמות (lit., "meeting, conjunction"). The special Sabbath falls seven weeks prior to the Festival itself. See Pummer, "Samaritan Rituals and Customs," 689.
57 See Zsengellér, "The Day of Atonement Among the Samaritans," 139–161.

| ג | Praises (accrue) to the one who fasts on it,
And great disgrace upon the one who violates it
They will depart, empty, from all goodness,
These (Hebrews) who abstain from fasting

| ד | A remembrance that shall never be nullified,
A remembrance of a day of fasting, for (all) generations
O choicest[58] of the nations, O Israel:
(You) fast upon it, and He grants forgiveness

| ה | Indeed, any soul that does not fast
Shall be cut off from the midst of its people
A word that God uttered—
Who is able to deny it?

| ו | Woe to them!—To these who are not fasting;
Or fasting, but not praying—
For they are like a blind man in the dark
Hurting themselves, day and night

| ז | The moon and the sun bear witness
To the nature of this day of forgiveness
A holy convocation in the name of the Holy One
For the holy congregation—there is none like it!

| ח | Lo, a jubilee comes at this very moment:
Once a year for (all) Israel
If one fasts upon it and repents
Then he merits redemption

| ט | Who has seen a day better than the day of fasting?
Happy is the congregation that is worthy of it
The dew of forgiveness
Glistens over all who fast upon it.[59]

---

58 The term דמע can mean both "offering" (תרומה) and "choicest, best," which creates a resonant double-meaning here: Israel is the best of the nations but, through fasting, it also makes an offering of itself.

59 This line evokes a metaphor rooted in the world of agriculture.

| | The day upon which praise is rendered
ז | The day of forgiveness for Israel
| | Let them fast upon it in repentance
| | These who are petitioning their Master

ב | All nations observe fast-days[60]
| | But none resemble this one
| | All those of the nations are like nighttime
| | But this one, of Israel, is sunshine![61]
| | ...[62]

ת | Reciting today, O fasters,[63]
| | Lift your faces to the Abode
| | And say: Forgive Your people Israel
| | Whom You redeemed, O YHWH!

Nothing in this hymn explicitly evokes the festival of Sukkot at all; it speaks clearly, rather, to the Day of Atonement, particularly through its emphasis on the importance of fasting. This poem is not, in fact, said on Sukkot, but rather in anticipation of the Festival: it appears in the liturgy of the preparatory feast day (ṣimmūt), on the Sabbath seven weeks prior to the Festival itself; on the first day of the seventh month, inaugurating the period of holy days that culminate in the Festival; and on the tenth day of the seventh month, when the community is cleansed of its sins and, in that state of purity, begins to build the sukkahs that epitomize the Festival. And so, despite its emphasis on fasting, it attends closely to issues of nourishing abundance and makes use of imagery which is clearly agrarian: the dew which enables seeds to sprout, the sun which coaxes them to grow.

∴

Classical Samaritan poetry—both the hymns and the "exegetical" poems embedded in *Tibat Marqe*—do not resolve our questions concerning Samaritan observance of Sukkot in antiquity. They do not reveal where Samaritans built

---

60 This line offers an unusual acknowledgement of non-Samaritan Israelite religious practice.
61 Lit., "daylight."
62 Presumably there is a gap of ten stanzas, based on the acrostic.
63 Language of a liturgical formula; see Cowley 435.

FIGURE 7.1 General view of succa of the Samaritan Community on Mount Grizim, Mark Neyman
NATIONAL PHOTO COLLECTION OF ISRAEL

their sukkahs, or of what they made them; they do not describe the four species or how they were used; they do not describe customs, such as the burning of palm fronds, which stand out so clearly in modern practice. And yet, we can find within these classical and medieval Samaritan sources the traces of motifs which suggest, anticipate, or allude to modern practices: connections between the idea of "sukkot" and the Garden of Eden, a linking of the purity of the Day of Atonement to the subsequent festival of booths, the paradoxical linkage of fasting to sustenance. Particularly when we read these writings in light of what we know about the rich agricultural milieu of Late Antiquity and the diversity of other Jewish practices (ancient, rabbinic, and Karaite), it becomes ever more feasible to understand why Sukkot became for the Samaritans not a festival of fragility, but one of abundance.

Acknowledgements

I would like to express my gratitude to Dr. Claudia Bergmann and the Max-Weber Kolleg in Erfurt, Germany, for their support of this project, and to Yeshiva University and especially Prof. Steven Fine, for including me in this volume. I dedicate this piece to the memory of Professor Yaakov Elman (z"l), whose scholarship served as a constant reminder of how large the world of Jewish antiquity was.

Bibliography

Bar, Doron. "Geographical Implications of Population and Settlement Growth in Late Antique Palestine," Journal of Historical Geography 30 (2004): 1–10.

Bar, Doron. "Frontier and Periphery in Late Antique Palestine," Greek, Roman and Byzantine Studies 44 (2004): 69–92.

Bar, Doron and Shimon Applebaum, Landscape and Pattern: An Archaeological Survey of Samaria, 800 BCE–636 CE, BAR International Series 308, 2 vols (Oxford: BAR, 1986).

Ben-Hayyim, Ze'ev. The Literary and Oral Tradition of Hebrew and Aramaic Amongst the Samaritans, III:2 (Jerusalem: The Academy of the Hebrew Language, 1967).

Chlup, Radek. "The Semantics of Fertility: Levels of Meaning in the Thesmophoria," Kernos 20 (2007); http://journals.openedition.org/kernos/171; DOI: 10.4000/kernos.171.

Cohen, Jeffrey M. A Samaritan Chronicle: A Source-critical Analysis of the Life and Times of the Great Samaritan Reformer, Baba Rabbah (Leiden: Brill, 1981)

Cowley, A.E. The Samaritan Liturgy: The Common Prayers, 2 vols. (Oxford: Clarendon, 1909).

Crown, Alan D. Samaritan Scribes and Manuscripts (Tübingen: Mohr Siebeck, 2001).

Dar, Shimon. "Archaeological Aspects of Samaritan Research in Israel," in Religious Diversity in Late Antiquity, edited by David Gwynn and Susan Bangert (Leiden: Brill, 2010), 189–198.

Dexinger, Ferdinand. "Samaritan Eschatology," in The Samaritans, ed. Alan D. Crown (Tübingen: JCB Mohr [Paul Siebeck], 1989), 289–290.

Florentin, Moshe. Late Samaritan Hebrew: A Linguistic Analysis of Its Different Types (Leiden: Brill, 2005).

Hirschfeld, Yizhar. "Farms and Villages in Byzantine Palestine," Dumbarton Oaks Papers 51 (1997): 33–71.

Jacoby, Ruth. "The Four Species in Jewish and Samaritan Tradition," in From Dura to Sepphoris: Studies in Jewish Art and Society in Late Antiquity, ed. by Lee I. Levine and Zeev Weiss (Portsmouth, RI: Journal of Roman Archaeology, 2000), 404–409.

Levine, Lee I. Visual Judaism in Late Antiquity: Historical Contexts of Jewish Art (New Haven: Yale University Press, 2012).

Novick, Tzvi. Piyyut and Midrash: Form, Genre, and History (Göttingen: Vandenhoek and Ruprecht, 2019).

Patrich, Joseph. "Urban Space in Caesarea Maritima, Israel" in Urban Centers and Rural Contexts in Late Antiquity, edited by Thomas S. Burns and John W. Eadie (Grand Rapids, MI: Michigan State University Press, 2001), 77–110.

Pummer, Reinhard. "Synagogues—Samaritan and Jewish: A New Look at their Differentiating Characteristics," in The Samaritans in Historical, Cultural and Linguistic Perspectives, ed. Jan Dušek (Berlin: DeGruyter, 2018), 51–74.

Pummer, Reinhard. The Samaritans (Leiden: Brill, 1987).

Pummer, Reinhard. The Samaritans: A Profile (Grand Rapids, MI; Cambridge, UK: Eerdmans, 2016).

Pummer, Reinhard. "Samaritan Rituals and Customs," in The Samaritans, ed. Alan D. Crown (Tübingen: JCB Mohr [Paul Siebeck], 1989), 650–690.

Qanaï, Avraham An Introduction to Karaite Judaism: History, Theology, Practice, and Custom (Albany, NY: Qirqisani Center, 2004).

Regev, Eyal. The Hasmoneans: Ideology, Archaeology, Identity (Göttingen: Vanhoek & Ruprecht, 2013).

Sivan, Hagith. Palestine in Late Antiquity (Oxford: Oxford University Press, 2008).

Stenhouse, Paul. Kitāb al-Tarīkh of Abū 'l-Fath: The Chronicle of Abū 'l-Fath. Mandelbaum Studies in Judaica 1 (Sydney: Mandelbaum Trust, 1985).

Tal, Avraham. Dictionary of Samaritan Aramaic, 2 vols. (Leiden: Brill, 2000)

The Sacred and the Feminine in Ancient Greece, edited by Sue Blundell and Margaret Williamson (London/New York: Routledge, 1998).

Tibat Marqe: A Collection of Samaritan Midrashim, ed. by Z. Ben-Hayyim (Jerusalem: Israel Academy of Sciences and Humanities, 1988).

Yaron, Yoseif and Avraham Qanaï, An Introduction to Karaite Judaism: History, Theology, Practice, and Custom (Albany, NY: Qirqisani Center, 2004).

Zsengellér, József. "The Day of Atonement Among the Samaritans," in The Day of Atonement: Its Interpretations in Early Jewish and Christian Traditions, edited by Thomas Heike and Tobias Nicklas (Leiden: Brill, 2012), 139–161.

CHAPTER 8

Two Parallel Consolatory Poems for Tisha be'Av in Aramaic and Hebrew

Moshe J. Bernstein

לע״נ ר׳ יעקב אלמן ז״ל
שכן טוב וחבר טובי[1]

∴

Six of the ten Aramaic poems associated with the fast of the Ninth of Av published by Joseph Yahalom and Michael Sokoloff in 1999 derive from a single quire in CUL T-S 14.64.[2] In a seminal article on the relationship between classical Hebrew *piyyut* and the poetry written during roughly the same era in Jewish Palestinian Aramaic, Michael Rand suggested that this group of lament poems might have been "intended (*if only by the copyist of TS H14/64*) [emphasis MJB] as a liturgical series." One of his arguments is that "the series of dirges concludes with a poem of consolation. In this regard, the Aramaic poems show a typological similarity to the Qillirian tradition, in which the *qinot* are followed by *piyyutim* of consolation (פיוטי נחמה)."[3] Rand takes a further step in propos-

---

1 Yaakov, z"l, was my שכן, my "neighbor," quite literally, for more than 30 years at Yeshiva University, due to the proximity of our offices, and he was a חבר, a "colleague," in the fullest sense of that word. His loss is felt, and will continue to be felt, by his family, his colleagues at Yeshiva, and all of us in the academic world who benefited from his creative contributions to the broad range of disciplines in which he worked. I, for one, deeply miss him and the three decades of interaction with him that I was fortunate to have. יהי זכרו ברוך.
2 Sokoloff and Yahalom, *Jewish Palestinian Aramaic Poetry from Late Antiquity* (*JPAPLA*), 152–165 and 344–349; our focus in this paper is on the poem on 164–165. Almost all the poems in this collection have recently been translated into English by Lieber, *Jewish Aramaic Poetry*, with these Tisha be'Av poems found on 68–78, and the one on which we shall focus on 76–78.
3 Rand, "JPA Poetry and the Hebrew Piyyut Tradition," 136–137. Rand's suggestion that these poems, taken together, may be a "liturgical series," is quite important, but discussion of that point must be postponed until a further occasion. This is because the manuscript contains, in addition to the texts of the poems published by Sokoloff and Yahalom, a variety of marginal liturgical instructions that were apparently not of interest to the editors in their primary, and

ing a specific liturgical location for the group, "Furthermore, on the basis of the analogy to the Ashkenazic rite, it appears that the series was intended to be recited after the reading of Lamentations on the eve of the Ninth of Av." In this way, these Jewish Palistinian Aramaic (JPA) lament poems can be seen as filling a different liturgical "slot" from the Qillirian ones that are attached to a *qerova* for the morning *'Amidah* on Tisha b'Av. In the absence of very much evidence for the liturgical *Sitz im Leben* of most JPA poetry, his proposal is a valuable suggestion for further consideration.⁴

One of the pieces of evidence that Rand adduces for his suggestion that these poems belong to the evening service is the fact that Poem #23 in Sokoloff and Yahalom "whose main theme is consolation, is the last of the series, and is followed by two of the same scriptural verses that appear at the end of the series of *qinot* recited after the reading of Lamentations on the eve of the Ninth of Av according to the Ashkenazic rite: Zechariah 1:16 (corresponding to Zechariah 1:16, 17 in Ashkenaz) and Isaiah 51:3."⁵ Several years ago, when I first read through the Yahalom-Sokoloff collection, I was also struck by the analogous usage of the verses in the poem to those in the Ashkenazic evening service and thought along lines similar to Rand's. I now believe, however, that there is other evidence of a similar nature that might point in a somewhat different direction in terms of when on Tisha b'Av this Aramaic poem might have been recited.

Poem #23 in the Sokoloff-Yahalom edition, אדיק בבעו על ציון, as Rand points out, is composed of two-line strophes, with the first concluding with ציון and

---

virtually sole, goal of presenting the Aramaic text. Those comments need to be analyzed carefully and taken into consideration before Rand's point can be evaluated properly. We probably must distinguish between the intentions of the composers of the individual poems and of the copyist of the manuscript. Toward the end of this paper, I shall actually suggest a liturgical context for one of the poems in the quire that is predicated on its *not* being part of a liturgical series.

4 Rand's student, Pesach Eliav Braverman Grossman, in "A Critical Edition" and more recently in "Three Aramaic Piyyutim for Purim," 198–255, building on Rand's argumentation, argued that the JPA poems and classical piyyut do not stand as far apart as is often presumed, but share a variety of structural and conventional themes and motifs. My argument in this essay can be said to support Grossman's extension of Rand's reasoning at the same time as it undermines Rand's specific conclusion about the liturgical location of at least one of the poems.
5 Rand, "JPA Poetry and the Hebrew Piyyut Tradition," 136. The finality of that poem is underlined sharply by the fact that nothing appears after it in the manuscript, with the half-page following its conclusion being left blank. I am not fully content with the generally accepted description of these two poems as "poems of consolation" (or "consolatory poems"). They are perhaps better characterized as prayers for restoration, since restoration, and not consolation, appears to be their primary theme. I shall, nevertheless, maintain the current terminology through the rest of this article.

the second with ירושלם. There is a Hebrew poem that has a virtually identical structure, one which, I believe, is not found often in classical *piyyut*.[6] That poem, first published by Menahem Zulay, and then contextualized more fully by Shulamit Elizur, is תאסוף נפוצות ציון, the third of the expansion poems (פיוטי הרחבה) for the doxology of בונה ירושלים in an *'Amidah* for *minḥa* of Tisha b'Av.[7] This is the liturgical location in which, as Elizur has demonstrated, consolatory poems were introduced on Tisha b'Av.[8] I believe that despite the fact that we usually do not think of Hebrew and Aramaic poetry as functioning in the same way liturgically, these two poems are so much alike that comparison with the Hebrew text can lead us to speculate further about how the Aramaic one might have been employed.

Let us begin by considering the similarities and differences between the two poems. We shall see that the most striking similarities are primarily formal and

---

[6] Dr. Shmidman informs me that there are only two other poems that show the fixed pair (*millot qeva*) ציון\ירושלים. אוהלך אהל בציון and נחם ציון ואבליה both appear at the end of a qedushta for נחמו in Oxford MS d.31/13. If that is the case, then the pairing ציון\ירושלים is clearly (and perhaps unsurprisingly) established as a fixed pair for poetry around the 9th of Av. (A *yotser* for Passover is a third poem with similar, but not identical, employment of these words: אתה אדון לציון אתה בחור לישראל אתה גדול לירושלים [CUL T-S NS 235.164 and T-S 8H5]).

[7] Zulay, without title, in לוח הארץ תשי"א; reprinted in his מפי פייטנים ושופכי שיח, 74 and 234; and Elizur, "מאבל לנחמה," 137. It is found in Oxford Bodleian a.3/32 (2873), on which the text printed at the end of this article is based, and Paris, Alliance Israelite Universelle, IV C, 191v (copied, according to Elizur, "מאבל לנחמה," 130 n. 25, by the 11th century Jerusalem figure Eli b. Yeḥezqel haKohen). In the latter manuscript, it is secondarily attached to the Qillirian *silluq* in the *qedushta* for *Naḥamu*. Regarding its date, Zulay, מפי פייטנים, 74, suggests it is מתקופת קליר, "from the era of Qillir," whereas the more recent Ma'agarim database of the Academy of the Hebrew Language (https://maagarim.hebrew-academy.org.il consulted 5/24/20), dates it loosely as "before the year 1000." Depending on how much before the year 1000 is meant, this could make it somewhat later than the Aramaic poem that is claimed to belong to the Byzantine era. At any rate, there is no a priori reason to claim that the Hebrew antedates the Aramaic.

[8] Elizur, "מאבל לנחמה," 126–128 and esp. nn. 6 and 7, points out that there was a tradition to introduce consolatory material even into *qinot* for the morning of Tisha b'Av (cf. Goldschmidt, סדר הקינות לתשעה באב, 9, and the group of optimistic texts that follow תוקד בקרבי אש, the final *qina* in the Italian *maḥzor* [ed. S.D. Luzzatto; Leghorn, 1856], 183b–186a [discussed by Elizur, "מאבל לנחמה," 128 n. 14]). On 128–129 she introduces her edition of a poeticized *Qerovat* יח לנחמו (which she demonstrates convincingly must refer to Tisha b'Av and not the following Shabbat), with a discussion of the custom of using *minḥa* on Tisha b'Av as a locus for consolatory material. (Cf. the oft-cited *Shibbolei haLeqeṭ* § 269, referred to by Fleischer, "לעניין המשמרות בפיוטים," 32 n. 6 and Goldschmidt, סדר הקינות, 9 n. 18.) Following the doxology of בונה ירושלים in this *'Amidah* are three expansion poems, the third of which is the subject of this discussion. (Dr. Shmidman suggests, based on the location of expansion poems for 9 Av in many other Geniza manuscripts, that the placement of the poems following the doxology is likely to have been a scribal error.)

structural, while the divergences belong to the realms of focus and emphasis. The most conspicuous and overarching similarity, of course, is that both are acrostics, with the first of each pair of lines ending with ציון and the second with ירושלים. As pointed out above, the same verses from Zechariah and Isaiah are appended at the end of each poem. The contents of both poems consist of very analogous prayers for the restoration of Zion and Jerusalem as well.

Elizur has noted that the Hebrew poem consists of three-stress lines with a second-person verb addressed to God, and with the entire poem expressing faith in the ingathering of the exiles and the building of Jerusalem.[9] The Hebrew poem is actually a virtual double acrostic, except for lines 1, 2, and 6, with both the first and second words sharing the acrostic letter.[10] This doubling of the acrostic in each line effectively precludes any repetitive use of language in the course of the poem, and the independence of short lines disconnected from one another produces a sort of staccato effect. The diction of the poem is relatively uncomplicated, and it appears to me that it could be followed without too much difficulty by an audience which might have had difficulties with Qillirian sophistications and complexities.[11]

The Aramaic poem handles the acrostic aspect in a manner that differs from the Hebrew. Each line begins with the acrostic letter, but only in lines 1 (אדיק), 6 (ותנחם), and 22 (תתוב) is a verb the first word of the line. The alliteration of the acrostic is doubled only in lines 2 ברחמין תבני, 4 דרתא דדויד, 5 הודא והדרא, 14 נהורא תנהר, 15 ששון ושמחה,[12] and 18 צמח יצמח. This Aramaic poem does not

---

9   Elizur, "מאבל לנחמה," 130. If we render the Hebrew imperfects as precative, "May You," rather than indicative, "You will," then they might be taken to indicate hope rather than confidence and faith. In the translation of the poems appended to the end of this article, however, I have rendered those precatives as imperatives, at the suggestion of Professor Novick, in order to echo the vigorous and concise idiom of the original.

10 Line 16 actually alliterates triply תעטר בעוז עיר ירושלים (as does 10, of course, perforce). I wonder whether, in light of the doubling of the acrostic, we should acknowledge in line 6 the assonance of the vowels of בהוד and תופיע as a sort of doubling.

11 Elizur, "מאבל לנחמה," 130, refers to it as having an אופי 'רהיטי', "the character of a *rahit*." The Aramaic poem under discussion can probably be described similarly. The "*rahit*," is a rapidly paced poem that occupies the seventh position in the "standard" *qedushta*. Rehitim are often characterized by tightly constructed alphabetical acrostics and fixed words at line endings (cf. Elizur, *Sod Meshalshei Qodesh*, 13–14). The two poems under consideration might be described from a formal standpoint as "very minimalist *rehitim*."

12 A Hebraism, of course, as is רגלי מבשר in 20. Might the presence of ששון ושמחה be due to its occurrence in the second of the following prooftexts? It is not clear why Sokoloff and Yahalom, *JPAPLA*, 165, choose to furnish a reference for this word pair to Ps 51:10 instead of to the prooftext (despite Elizur's observation, below n. 16). In 15, תשמיע is a Hebrew hiphil, not an Aramaic aphel; might the preceding Hebraism ששון ושמחה be the reason for its presence (although it appears in the fully Aramaic line 19 as well)?

contain any of the Greek terms that often characterize JPA poetry, and its diction, like that of the Hebrew poem, is fairly simple, without any features that could complicate its meaning for a non-sophisticated listener.[13] From a performative perspective, the short lines with regular alternating endings in both poems could also engender active congregational participation, as the audience would very quickly take up chanting the final word of each line along with the poet.[14]

Unsurprisingly, the two alphabetical acrostics share some vocabulary: Heb (= Hebrew poem) 5–6 תהדר ... תופיע בהוד; Ar (= Aramaic poem) 5 הודא והדרא; Heb/Ar 10 כלילין /כלילת תכונן ; Heb/Ar 19 תקרא קול/קל; and Heb/Ar 22 תשיב/תתוב. The second lines of each poem are similar, but not because of the acrostic: Heb תבנה חומות ירושלם and Ar תבני ירושלים ברחמין.[15] It is also likely that, in light of the synonymity of the key words, the Aramaic גנונין תת{כ}⟨ק⟩ן בציון (3) is the equivalent of Hebrew תחופף חופת ירוש⟨לים⟩ (8), whether they refer to the Temple, as the editors of both the Hebrew and Aramaic poems suggest, or to bridal canopies, as the Aramaic plural might imply, based on the verses in Jeremiah 33:10–11 עוד ישמע במקום הזה ... קול ששון וקול שמחה קול חתן וקול כלה.[16]

---

13   Rand, "JPA Poetry and the Hebrew Piyyut Tradition," 138, collects the Greek and Latin loanwords in the *qinot* published by Sokoloff and Yahalom, and it is perhaps worth noting that only three are found in the six poems in T-S H14.64, one each in Poems 19, 21, and 22, while there are no fewer than fourteen in the other four Tisha be'Av poems in the collection.

14   Lieber, "Rhetoric of Participation," 124, writes of the *rahit*, to which these poems have been compared (above n. 12), "Refrains are not a defining feature of the rahit, but they are particularly common in this unit, and the terseness of the rahit refrain—typically a single word—is strongly suggestive of congregational participation." She furnishes, 125, a *rahit* by Yannai (for the lectionary section beginning Deuteronomy 6:4) with a refrain using forms of אחד, noting, "The community at this point has the opportunity to join the poet in the performance of the *piyyut*." Another example of this type is the second *rahit* to the first *qerova* for Numbers 1:1 with the refrain ראש (Rabinowitz, יני, 2.15–16).

15   Elizur, "מאבל לנחמה," 137, commenting on line 103 (= line 2) תבנה חומות ירושלים, points to Ps 51:20b and suggests that "the entire poem is based on this verse." That observation, if intended to include the whole of 51:20 היטיבה ברצונך את ציון תבנה חומות ירושלים, and not just 51:20b, is quite to the point. The reading in line 2 of the Paris MS of the Hebrew poem ותבנה חרבות ירוש⟨לים⟩, for תבנה חומות ירושלים of the Oxford manuscript, combines language from both prooftexts that follow.

16   Elizur, "מאבל לנחמה," 137, note on line 106 (= line 8), citing Isa 4:5–6; Sokoloff and Yahalom, *JPAPLA*, 165, translate גנונין as מקדשים = "sanctuaries." Kister, in his review of *SYAP*, "שירת בני מערבא," 163 n. 308, cites the same verse about Aramaic line 3, as does Elizur regarding Hebrew 8, but suggests only translating literally as חפות, rather than מקדשים. Lieber, *Jewish Aramaic Poetry*, 77, renders "garden-bowers may you repair in Zion." Dr. Shmidman suggested, quite plausibly, that the language may be intentionally multivalent.

Despite these commonalities, there are, of course, features that differentiate the two poems. We might speak of the Aramaic poem as being less formal and mechanical than the Hebrew one, since it does not adhere to as rigid a pattern as does the Hebrew. The flexibility in the Aramaic is manifest in two ways: first, it does not demand a verb for each line of the acrostic, and, when a verb is required, it need not be a precative second person verb. Second, unlike the Hebrew poem, where the lines are unconnected to one another, in four of the surviving ten Aramaic couplets, the pairs of brief lines must be read as linked with one another: 3–4 where the verb of 3 תתכן (to be emended to תתקן) must be supplied to govern the object in 4; 11–12 and 15–16 where the second line, in each instance, is a temporal modifier of the verb in the first line; and 19–20 where the verb of 19 governs line 20 as an object. This actually slows down the staccato pace, and works a bit against the rapidity of the *rahit* style. The Aramaic poet chooses to repeat roots in several places: שמע in 8, 15, 19, and 21; לבש in 5 and 11; זיו in 7 and 13; נהר in 7 and 14 (*bis*); אתא impf. in 12 and 17; and ברחמין in 2 and 22. I do not believe that this is the sign of a limited vocabulary, but rather, like the enjambment that we pointed to above, serves as an integrating factor linking some of the lines of this *rahit*-like composition with each other and tightening it somewhat.

The two poems also stress different aspects of restoration, although they share the common (and commonplace) theme of the renewal of glory and splendor in Zion/Jerusalem (Heb 5, 6, 7 and perhaps 10; Ar 5, 7, 13, 14). The Hebrew poem might be said to be more "concrete," as it focuses on people, with references to נפוצות (1), גולי (3), דחויי (4), and שבות (21), and perhaps מלך (13) and נגיד (14); and the physical city, mentioning חומות (2), היכלי (5), חופת (8), טירות (9), סוכת (15), עיר (16), and פינת (17). The Aramaic poem is more "abstract," with no reference to the human former inhabitants of Jerusalem/Zion or their return, and a bare minimum of allusions to the physical city, גנונין (3) and דרתא דדויד (4). Because of the different way in which it handles the acrostic form, the Aramaic poem can employ repetitive language to point toward its emphases which the Hebrew cannot. Thus the recurrences of the roots שמע, נהר, and זיו, noted above, underline the audio-visual dimension of the poet's description, focusing on sound, light, and brightness.

Finally, there is an almost explicit messianic/redemptive/eschatological motif in the Aramaic poem that can only be discerned at all in the Hebrew if we insist on reading מלך and נגיד in 13–14 in that fashion. In the Aramaic, we read of God's coming to Jerusalem (12) and revealing himself in Jerusalem (16), followed by "great redemption" arriving in Zion and a sprout springing up in Jerusalem (17–18). The root צמח is a common messianic term, based on Zechariah 6:12 הנה איש צמח שמו, and appears idiomatically in this sense elsewhere in the corpus of JPA poetry.[17] And רגלי מבשר, deriving from Isaiah 52:7, is frequently employed in messianic contexts in rabbinic literature.[18] So, whatever else we may conclude, neither one of these poems is, in any way, a direct copy of the other.

Although both poems conclude with the same two prooftexts in their respective manuscripts, לכן כה אמר ה' שבתי לירושלים ברחמים ביתי יבנה בה נאם ה' צ-באות וקו ינטה על ירושלם. (עוד קרא לאמר כה אמר ה' צ-באות עוד תפוצינה ערי מטוב ונחם ה' עוד כי נחם ה' ציון נחם כל־חרבתיה (Zechariah 1:16[–17]) and את־ציון ובחר עוד בירושלם.) וישם מדברה כעדן וערבתה כגן־ה' ששון ושמחה ימצא בה תודה וקול זמרה (Isaiah 51:3), it seems that the Aramaic poem connects to them a bit more closely than the Hebrew one.[19] In the latter, the only lines that come close to picking up the language of those verses are תבנה חומת ירושלים and תשיב שבות ציון, echoing one word from each of the verses.[20] The Aramaic poet, on the other hand, frames his poem with תתוב ברחמין לירושלים and ברחמין תבני ירושלים, recalling the first prooftext with each and every one of those words, and also includes language that links smoothly to the second prooftext, such as ותנחם, ששון ושמחה, and שירין וזמרין.

Despite the literary and aesthetic/artistic divergences that we have noted, it should be quite clear that the two texts that we have examined are sufficiently alike formally and structurally that we can think about their having been employed in similar liturgical contexts. Because the whole of each poem is consolation and the Hebrew one does not merely end with consolation like the Hebrew evening poems that Rand cites as analogues, I believe that this Hebrew poem furnishes a better model for comparison to the Aramaic one than the evening *qinot* to which Rand referred. Especially in light of the facts that

---

17   Cf. Sokoloff and Yahalom, *JPAPLA*, #26:43 and #43:37–40 conjoined, unsurprisingly, with פורקנא in both texts.

18   It is likely, although not certain, that דרתא דדויד (4), "dwelling of David," with its possible echo of Amos 9:11 אקים את סכת דויד הנפלת, is probably to be taken eschatologically as well.

19   For any argument connecting the prooftexts to the poem to be valid, regardless of location, we have to presume that they were connected to the poems originally, and not only through the material remains of the manuscript which might very well attest to later liturgical practice. That later practice, however, ought not to be ignored completely in our thinking.

20   In the Paris MS there is an "extra" couplet (not noted by Elizur in the apparatus) תתמוך נפילת צ⟨יון⟩\תכונן נוה ירוש⟨לים⟩, which does not manifest even that minimal link to the prooftext which the penultimate line of the poem has (and the prooftext itself is omitted in that manuscript). I confess to not being able to explain the presence of the additional couplet, which does not even match the expected acrostic in the way that we would expect.

Elizur has shown that the Hebrew poem is part of a *minḥa* service, and that אדיק בבעו appears at the end of a series of Aramaic *qinot* in its manuscript, we might surmise that at the time the manuscript was written it was recited toward the end of the service or of the day.[21] So I suggest, as an alternative to Rand's theory, that this fully consolatory Aramaic poem was recited at a *minḥa* service or at some other point late in the day on Tisha b'Av. The possibility which has been raised that similar Hebrew and Aramaic poems might have been employed in synagogues with diverse sorts of populations, with the more learned hearing the Hebrew poem and the average layperson hearing the Aramaic, strikes me as plausible, and could support a claim for these poems occupying the same liturgical "slot" in different sorts of congregations.[22]

At this point, I should like to take my comparison of these two poems a step further, in each of two different directions, one literary and one liturgical. From a literary perspective, even though it is clear that neither of these poems is a copy of the other, should we consider the possibility that one of these poems has been modeled on the other one, perhaps even the Hebrew one on the Aramaic one? Even though the contents of the poems are quite commonplace, and despite the differences between them that we stressed above, the structural similarity of the two works can readily be claimed to point to some kind of connection between them. Since we cannot be sure of the date of either poem (although the date suggested for the Hebrew poem in Ma'agarim could point to a date a little later than the implied Byzantine-era one for the JPA poem), I would allow for the possibility that the influence might have gone in either

---

21   If I am correct in seeing a series of adumbrations of messianism and eschatology in the Aramaic poem, I believe that those references as well would also seem more appropriate for a service looking toward the future at the end of the day, similar to the poems at the end of the recitation of the laments in the morning service in the Italian rite (above n. 9).

22   I am not necessarily suggesting at this point that the Aramaic poem needed to function as a פיוט הרחבה in the *minḥa 'Amidah*, although Grossman has evidence that the three Aramaic Purim poems were actually employed in that fashion. He presents the theoretical possibilities well in writing, "Critical Edition," 12,

> We might imagine synagogues with learned congregants listening to the *piyyutim* of Yannai and Qillir, while synagogues populated by average laypeople heard JPA poetry. Or, in a less bifurcated manner, we might suggest that Classical *piyyutim* and JPA poetry were deployed at different points in the same synagogue service, to satisfy the tastes of a variegated congregation comprised of both erudite scholars and laypeople.

If my suggestion regarding the parallel, but separate, usage of these Hebrew and Aramaic poems is correct, the latter possibility becomes less likely. For discussion of elements of classical *piyyut* not aimed solely at learned audiences, see Fleischer, שירת הקודש, 273–275 and Elizur, "קהל המתפללים," 171 and 194.

direction. Regardless, if this possibility is entertained, then we have taken a different kind of step toward considering the connection or relationship between classical *piyyut* and JPA poetry.[23]

My liturgical question may strike us as a bit more radical, going beyond the argument that I made a couple of paragraphs above for the time of day that might have been suitable for the poem. Is it possible that the Aramaic poem functioned, as the Hebrew one did, as an expansion poem (פיוט הרחבה) in the *minḥa 'Amidah*? I do not think that we need to posit that the poem was composed for that purpose, but the presence of the same prooftexts at the end of the poem as are found at the end of the Hebrew one could certainly serve as a pointer to their being used in such a fashion.[24] The overall thrust of the poem, it could be claimed, would lead smoothly into the doxology of בונה ירושלים, in the same way that the Hebrew poem follows that doxology.[25] The fact that the three Purim poems published by Grossman were also employed in this fashion, inserted into either the doxology of המכניע or מבטח, may indicate that this suggestion should not be discounted out of hand. The proposal, on the other hand, should not be taken as an attempt to completely blur the lines that distinguish Aramaic poetry from classical Hebrew *piyyut* in so many ways. But it allows for the possibility that they were not as totally dichotomized from each other as is often postulated. We simply do not know enough about liturgical practices in *Erets Yisrael* to make broadly sweeping statements about it. The Aramaic poetry from late antiquity that has been published, and continues to be published, was not written only for the perusal of twenty-first century scholars, but for the liturgical employment of Jews in *Erets Yisrael* in some way. If it was not being used in some manner, why was it being written? I am suggesting, with all due hesitation, one such possible usage.

---

23 Whatever the difficulties may be raised by the notes appearing between the individual poems in TS H14.64 regarding the liturgical location of אדיק בבעו, they apply both to Rand's suggestion and to my own. I believe that neither of our two possibilities depends on whatever liturgical framework that the manuscript presents. They both stand or fall on their own internal reasoning.

24 This suggestion is further bolstered by Fleischer's oft-repeated view that the citation of verses in *piyyutim* must have had a liturgical function, leading into the doxologies that concluded them. Cf. Fleischer, שירת הקודש, 142; "עיונים במבנה הקדושתא הקלאסית," 294; "קדושת העמידה," 307. The presence of such texts at the end of this poem could point toward its having been employed in such a liturgical context.

25 Tzvi Novick suggested insightfully that the paired terms of the poem ציון and ירושלים would dovetail neatly into any doxology of נחם that concludes מנחם ציון ובונה ירושלים, although we do not have clear attestation of that language in that doxology according to the Palestinian rite.

The Poems

TABLE 8.1   Hebrew—Oxford Bodleian heb. a. 3 fol. 32 (2873) FGP No. C456489

Gather the scattered of Zion	תאסוף נפוצות ציון.	1
Build the walls of Jerusalem	תבנה חומות ירושלם.	2
Redeem the exiles of Zion	תגאול גולי ציון.	3
Seek out those driven from Jerusalem	תדרוש דחויי ירושלם.	4
Glorify the palaces of Zion	תהדר היכלי ציון.	5
Appear in splendor over Jerusalem	תופיע בהוד על ירוש⟨לם⟩	6
Burnish the brightness of Zion	תזריח זוהר ציון.	7
Cover the canopy of Jerusalem	תחופף חופת ירוש⟨לם⟩	8
Purify the towers of Zion	תטהר טירות ציון.	9
Honor the loveliness of Jerusalem	תיקר ידידות ירוש⟨לם⟩	10
Establish the crown of Zion	תכ(ו)נן כלילת ציון.	11
Array garments of salvation on Jerusalem	תלביש לבושי ישע לירוש⟨לם⟩	12
Enthrone a king in Zion	תמליך מלך בציון.	13
Elevate a prince in Jerusalem	תנשא נגיד בירוש⟨לם⟩	14
Support the tabernacle of Zion	תסמוך סוכת ציון.	15
Crown with power the city of Jerusalem	תעטר בעוז עיר ירוש⟨לם⟩	16
Beautify the battlements of Zion	תפאר פינת ציון.	17
Set righteousness in Jerusalem	תציב צדק ירוש⟨לם⟩	18
Proclaim a voice from Zion	תקרא קול מציון.	19
Multiply the choruses of Jerusalem	תרבה רננות ירוש⟨לם⟩	20
Restore the captivity of Zion	תשיב שבות ציון.	21
Grant praise to Jerusalem	תתן תהילה לירוש⟨לם⟩	22
As it is written, "So says the Lord, 'I have returned to Jerusalem etc.'" "for the Lord has comforted Zion etc."	כך "לכן כה אמר יי שבתי לירושלם וג' כי נחם יי ציון וג'"	

TABLE 8.2   Aramaic—CUL T-S H14.64 Fragment 2v–2r FGP No. C241196-C241195

Please gaze down upon Zion	אדיק בבעו על ציון	1
With mercy build Jerusalem	ברחמין תבני ירושלים	2
May you establish canopies in Zion	גנונין תת{כ}⟨ק⟩ן בציון	3
the dwelling of David in Jerusalem	דרתא דדויד ירוש⟨לים⟩	4
In splendor and glory bedeck Zion	הודא והדרא תלבש לציון	5
And comfort Jerusalem	ותנחם ירושלים	6
May you shine the splendor of your grandeur in Zion	זיו יקרך תנהר בציון	7
May joy be heard in Jerusalem	חדותא תשתמע בירוש⟨לים⟩	8
	[ט	9
	[י	10
With ten crowns bedeck Zion	כלילין עשרה תלבש לציון	11
for the day when You will come to Jerusalem	ליומא דתיתי לירושלים	12
With the splendor of your presence, restore Zion	מזיו שכינתך תשכלל לציון	13
May You shine light on Jerusalem	נהורא תנהר ירוש⟨לים⟩	14
May You proclaim happiness and joy to Zion	ששון ושמחה תשמיע לציון	15
at the time that You reveal yourself in Jerusalem	עידן דתתגלי בירוש⟨לים⟩	16
May the great redemption arrive at Zion	פרקנא רבא ייתי לציון	17
May a shoot sprout in Jerusalem	צמח יצמח בירושלים	18
Proclaim the sound of your power in Zion	קל גבורתך תשמיע בציון	19
the feet of the messenger in Jerusalem	רגלי מבשר בירושלים	20
Let songs and melodies be heard by Zion	שירין וזמרין ישתמעון לציון	21
May You return with mercy to Jerusalem	תתוב ברחמין לירושלים	22
As it is w[ritten], "And thus says the Lord, 'I have returned to Jerusalem in mercy etc.'"	ככ' ⟨לכ⟩ כה אמר יי שבתי לירושלים ברחמים וג'	23
"For the Lord has comforted Zion, comforted all etc."	כי נחם יי ציון נחם כל וגמ'	24

Acknowledgements

This is the second in what I hope will be a series of discussions of the sequence of Aramaic poems for Tisha be'Av that are found in CUL T-S H14.64. The first has appeared as Bernstein, "Reading an Aramaic *Qina*," 174–197. I have profited in working on this material from email conversations with Dr. Michael Rand of Cambridge University, Dr. Avi Shmidman of Bar-Ilan University, and Professor Tzvi Novick of the University of Notre Dame. Dr. A.J. Berkovitz of HUC, Mr. Binyamin Goldstein, Professor Laura Lieber of Duke University, and Dr. Shani Tzoref also contributed valuable critique of later drafts.

Bibliography

Bernstein, Moshe. "Reading an Aramaic *Qina* Framed by a Biblical One." *Aramaic Studies* 17:2 (2019) 174–197.

Elizur, Shulamit. "מאבל לנחמה: על מנהג קדום בתפילת מנחה של תשעה באב." *Tarbiz* 73 (2004) 125–138.

Elizur, Shulamit. *Sod Meshalshei Qodesh: The Qedushta from its Origins until the time of Rabbi El'azar Berabbi Qillir* [Hebrew]. Jerusalem: World Union of Jewish Studies, 2019.

Elizur, Shulamit. "קהל המתפללים והקדושתא הקדומה." In *Knesset Ezra: Literature and Life in the Synagogue: Studies Presented to Ezra Fleischer*. Edited by Shulamit Elizur, Moshe David Herr, Gershon Shaked, and Avigdor Shinan. 171–194. Jerusalem: Yad Izhak Ben-Zvi, 1995.

Fleischer, Ezra. "לעניין המשמרות בפיוטים." *Sinai* 62 (1968) 13–40.

Fleischer, Ezra. "עיונים במבנה הקדושתא הקלאסית." *Proceedings of the Fifth World Congress of Jewish Studies* (1969) 3.291–295.

Fleischer, Ezra. "קדושת העמידה (ושאר הקדושות): היבטים היסטוריים, ליטורגיים ואידאולוגיים." *Tarbiz* 67 (1998) 301–350.

Fleischer, Ezra. שירת הקודש העברית בימי הבינים. 2nd ed.; Jerusalem: Magnes, 2007.

Goldschmidt, Daniel. סדר הקינות לתשעה באב: כמנהג פולין וקהילות האשכנזים בארץ ישראל. Jerusalem: Mosad haRav Kook, 1968.

Grossman, Pesach Eliav Braverman. "A Critical Edition of Three Expansion Piyyutim for Purim from the Cairo Genizah With Introduction and Commentary." M.Phil. thesis, Jesus College, Cambridge University. July 2017.

Grossman, Pesach Eliav Braverman [Eliav]. "Three Aramaic Piyyutim for Purim: Text, Context, and Interpretation." *Aramaic Studies* 17:2 (2019) 198–255.

Kister, Menahem. "שירת בני מערבא: היבטים בעולמה של שירה עלומה." *Tarbiz* 76:1–2 (2006) 105–184. (review of *SYAP*)

Lieber, Laura S. *Jewish Aramaic Poetry from Late Antiquity: Translations and Commentaries*. Études sur le Judaïsme Médiéval LXX; Cambridge Genizah Studies Series 8. Leiden: Brill, 2018.

Lieber, Laura S. "The Rhetoric of Participation: Experiential Elements of Early Hebrew Liturgical Poetry." *Journal of Religion* 90 (2010) 119–147.

Rabinowitz, Zvi Meir. מחזור פיוטי רבי יניי. 2 volumes. Jerusalem: Mosad Bialik, 1985.

Rand, Michael. "Observations on the Relationship between JPA Poetry and the Hebrew Piyyut Tradition—the Case of the Kinot." In *Jewish and Christian Liturgy and Worship: New Insights into Its History and Interaction*, Edited by Albert Gerhards and Clemens Leonhard. 127–144. Jewish and Christian Perspectives 45. Brill: Leiden, 2007.

Sokoloff, Michael, and Joseph Yahalom. *Jewish Palestinian Aramaic Poetry from Late Antiquity* [Hebrew]. Jerusalem: Israel Academy of Sciences and Humanities, 1999.

Zulay, Menahem. מפי פייטנים ושופכי שיח. Edited by Shulamit Elizur. Jerusalem: Yad Ben Zvi, 2005.

PART 2

Torat Erets Yisrael in Babylonia

∴

CHAPTER 9

The Motif of the Forgetting and Restoration of Law: An Inter-Talmudic Difference about the Divine Role in Rabbinic Law

Alyssa M. Gray

1   Introduction

The myriad differences between the late antique *Erets* Israel and Babylonian rabbinic communities and their literatures have been and will likely continue for some time to be a major concern of contemporary academic Talmud scholarship. This essay's goal is to revisit and train a high-powered lens on one such difference: the Jerusalem and Babylonian Talmuds' ("Yerushalmi" and "Bavli," respectively) distinct approaches to the motif of the forgetting and restoration of law ("the forgetting and restoration motif") and the related topic of the Bavli's portrayal of both similarity and difference in the forgetting of law by Babylonian and *Erets* Israel sages in other ways and contexts.[1]

Christine Hayes' pioneering work on this subject is foundational to this essay. In a short, yet remarkably rich survey of sources set within her larger study of the category of laws known as *halakhah le-Moshe mi-Sinai*, "a law to Moses from Sinai," Hayes tackles what she terms the Yerushalmi's "forgotten/reestablished strategy" and the Bavli's near elimination of it.[2] Hayes describes the "forgotten/reestablished strategy" as the forgetting and subsequent independent reestablishment of "a law to Moses from Sinai" through the argumentation of later rabbis, who may be entirely unaware of the law's ancient origin. She observes toward the end of her survey that "the Yerushalmi adopts the forgotten/reestablished strategy and transforms it into a metaphor" while "the Bavli all but ignores and rejects it." She aptly notes that the Bavli's rejection of the "forgotten/reestablished strategy" is perplexing ("remarkable," as she puts it) in light of the ubiquity in the Babylonian Talmud of the motif

---

1   [Editor's note: See also Michal Bar-Asher Siegal's article in this volume, "Tosefta Eduyot 1:1 On the Fear of Losing Torah and the Redaction of Tannaitic Materials," which likewise discusses the concern that Torah may be forgotten as being, in the view of tannaitic texts she examines, a primary impetus for the rabbinic movement.]
2   Hayes, *"Halakhah le-Moshe mi-Sinai* in Rabbinic Sources," 102–108.

of forgetting law.³ She observes that although the Bavli rejects the strategy in halakhic contexts (the very contexts in which the Yerushalmi applies it), the Bavli curiously employs the "forgotten/reestablished strategy" in aggadic or "hyperbolic" contexts.⁴ Hayes closes her survey with the suggestion that the Bavli employs the "forgotten/reestablished strategy" for "rhetorical purposes"; these include "grandiose claims on behalf of rabbinic authority or in praise of a particular sage or Babylonian sages generally."⁵ Hayes' conclusions are sound, and her observations suggest that a deeper study of this phenomenon is likely to be fruitful. This essay will expand the inquiry into the forgetting and restoration motif by examining a broader array of sources and searching out finer and deeper patterns (or at least tendencies) that characterize or distinguish various texts.⁶ The forgetting and restoration motif will be demonstrated to be emblematic of (and illuminated by) a larger pattern of inter-Talmudic legal and religious difference: distinct *Erets* Israel and Babylonian understandings about the role of the Divine in overseeing the rabbinic legal enterprise and ensuring the intact transmission of legal content.

The analytical journey being long and winding, a summary of the findings at the outset may be useful. The Bavli has a discernible pattern of minimizing the role of the Divine in human affairs and emphasizing the role of human agency, or even *mazal* (astrological destiny), instead. Yaakov Elman observed many years ago that the amora Rava "recurs over and over in *sugyot* which tend to limit the operation of Divine Providence."⁷ Elman also demonstrates that this tendency to place limits on Divine providence is also characteristic of the anonymous voice of the Bavli.⁸ In my recent book I also demonstrate a similar Bavli tendency to minimize the Divine role and accentuate the human role in two other areas: the charitable transaction between donor and recipient, and in aspects of the revelation and transmission of Torah.⁹ The two Talmuds'

---

3   Hayes, *"Halakhah le-Moshe mi-Sinai* in Rabbinic Sources," 107.
4   ibid.
5   Hayes, *"Halakhah le-Moshe mi-Sinai* in Rabbinic Sources," 108.
6   Although not relevant to this essay's inquiry, mention should be made of another, very recent study of a different aspect of rabbinic forgetting: Mira Balberg's thorough analysis of the agricultural law of the forgotten sheaf (*shich'chah*), entitled "Unforgettable Forgotten Things."
7   Elman, "Righteousness As Its Own Reward": 54.
8   Elman, "Righteousness As Its Own Reward": 53, 54–56, 58 and *passim*.
9   See Gray, *Charity in Rabbinic Judaism*, 157–173 and *passim*. Cf. Richard Kalmin's relevant observations about the Babylonian rabbis' tendency to emphasize the divine origins of the Torah to a lesser degree than *Erets* Israel sages, and their concomitant diminished concern with arguing against the view that the Torah is of human origin. See Kalmin, *The Sage in Jewish Society of Late Antiquity*, 94–98.

descriptions of the exchange between Esther and Second Temple-era sages over the establishment of a fixed commandment to read the Esther scroll pointedly exemplify this pattern. The Yerushalmi's gathering of "eighty-five elders" is explicitly described as including "a number of prophets." The elders' anguish over how to justify the addition of a new commandment to those decreed at Sinai is resolved when "God lit up their eyes and they found it written in the Torah, and in the Prophets, and in the Writings."[10] In the Bavli, by contrast, there is no mention of prophets' having been part of the gathering of "sages," and the Bavli's sages resolve their own puzzlement about how to justify the law by searching "until they found a verse ...." with no mention of God's having lit up their eyes.[11] The Bavli thus quietly removes—or at least occludes—the Divine role.

This inter-Talmudic legal and religious difference about the role of the Divine in human affairs (including, but not limited to, law and the legal process) is the genus of which the forgetting and restoration motif is a species. This essay argues that overall, the Yerushalmi envisions a more robust Divine oversight role over the rabbinic legal enterprise than does the Bavli. This oversight ensures that no laws or legal institutions will be permanently forgotten. A law or legal institution forgotten after its initial enactment is represented as restored to rabbinic awareness and practice by a later generation unaware that it is restoring, rather than newly enacting, the law. The Yerushalmi constructs a later generation's unknowing restoration of a forgotten law as a tacit sign of Divine oversight of the rabbinic legal enterprise. Bavli parallels to the Yerushalmi's examples of forgetting and restoration strikingly eliminate this motif. The Bavli transforms what in *Erets* Israel is a forgetting and later *unknowing* restoration of forgotten law into earlier and later *deliberate rabbinic acts* of similar, yet distinct legislation. But the Bavli deploys the forgetting and restoration motif in cases in which a later generation either was or reasonably *had to have been aware* that a law or legal institution had been forgotten. Significantly, in these latter cases neither the forgetting nor the restoration is done by Babylonian rabbis. However, such cases allow the Bavli to highlight the dialectical prowess of the human sage or the indispensable role of rabbinic oversight as the means through which the human error of forgetting law is later rectified by a distinctly human restorative effort.

Overall, the Bavli portrays the forgetting and restoration motif as an *Erets* Israel phenomenon. It also attributes to *Erets* Israel sages a related, darker

---

10   y.Megillah 1:4, 70d (ed. Academy, 745).
11   b.Megillah 7a. For a discussion of this example, see Gray, *Charity in Rabbinic Judaism*, 162–164.

view that Torah might have once been, or could be, forgotten *tout court*. Taken together, these are categories of forgetting Torah that we might term "systemic forgetting." While no Babylonian sage teaches that Torah might be (or once was) forgotten entirely, the Bavli does describe three historical episodes in which Babylonian sages restore Torah forgotten either in *Erets* Israel or on the watch of *Erets* Israel sages. The Bavli tacitly and intertextually suggests that these Babylonian restorations of Torah were accomplished through rabbinic dialectical prowess. Moreover, a Babylonian sage even trumpets his own method for prophylactically ensuring that no such systemic forgetting will ever occur: the deliberate and systematic dissemination of Torah knowledge to small groups of learners, each charged to propagate their learning more widely. The Bavli's point is clear: *Erets* Israel may be associated with the forgetting of Torah, but Babylonia is associated with its restoration and even the anticipatory prevention of systemic forgetting.

The Bavli also represents individual *Erets* Israel sages as forgetting laws. This type of forgetting may be termed "individual forgetting" (as opposed to "systemic forgetting"). The Bavli also presents cases of Babylonian rabbinic individual forgetting, but with a crucial caveat: the only sages so portrayed are amoraim of the first three generations. Amoraim of the fourth generation and later are not represented as forgetting laws as individuals.[12] Apropos, the forgotten learning of an individual *Erets* Israel sage is portrayed as having been restored through rabbis' prayers (that is, through a request for Divine intervention), while the forgotten learning of a third-generation Babylonian amora is restored through the patient and entirely human activity of a fourth-generation Babylonian amora, with no prayer or Divine involvement.[13]

The evidence that substantiates all these claims will be sorted into the following five sections. Section 2 presents the three cases in which the Bavli reworks and replaces the forgetting and restoration motif found in the earlier Yerushalmi parallels. Section 3 analyzes the Bavli's attributions to *Erets* Israel sages of the willingness to acknowledge that Torah was or could be forgotten *tout court*. Section 4 analyzes the cases in which the Bavli applies the forgetting and restoration motif. Sections 5 and 6 study examples of individual forgetting by *Erets* Israel and Babylonian sages, respectively. Finally, Section 7 draws together the essay's various analytic conclusions and presents a reading of a lengthy Bavli *sugya* that appears to, but does not quite, allow for a Divine role

---

12 We will explore the significance of this observation in Section 6.
13 For the restoration through prayer of the *Erets* Israel sage's forgotten learning, see b.Shabbat 147b. For the restoration without prayer of a Babylonian sage's forgotten learning, see b.Nedarim 41a. We will examine these two cases in greater detail in Section 6.

in the rabbinic legal process. Section 7 also offers suggestions about the historical context of the distinct approaches of *Erets* Israel and Babylonia to the forgetting and restoration motif as well as the larger difference regarding the Divine role in human affairs.

2 Bavli Parallels to Yerushalmi *Sugyot* Eliminate the Forgetting and Restoration Motif

There are five examples in the Yerushalmi of the forgetting and restoration motif, two of which are intra-Yerushalmi parallels. The Bavli eliminates the motif from its parallels to each of these three cases, putting in its place a portrayal of deliberate rabbinic legislative action at two points in time.

y.Pe'ah 1:1, 15b (ed. Academy, 78)

1. And this is like what R. Shimon ben Laqish said in the name of R. Yehudah ben Hanina: "They voted in Usha that a man should separate a fifth of his possessions for mitsvot."

•••

2. R. Gamliel ben Ininya asked R. Mana: "Is it one-fifth each year? Then in five years he will lose everything!"
3. [R. Mana] said to him: "In the first [year], it's one-fifth of the principal. From then on, one-fifth of the [annual] appreciation [in income]."

•••

4. It once happened that R. Yeshebab stood up and distributed all his possessions to the poor. Rabban Gamliel sent to him: "Didn't they say, 'one-fifth of his possessions for mitsvot'?"
5. And wasn't Rabban Gamliel prior to Usha?
6. R. Yose b. R. Bun said in the name of R. Levi: "Such was the law in their hands and they forgot it. And 'the two' stood up and agreed upon what the intention of the early ones had been. This is to teach you that every matter as to which the *bet din* gives their lives will in the end be upheld as if it was said to Moses at Sinai. And this is like what R. Mana said (Deuteronomy 32:47): *'For this is not a trifling thing for you: it is your very life.'* And if it is a trifling thing for you, why is that? Because you do not wear yourselves out over it. When is it your very life? At a time when you do wear yourselves out over it."[14]

---

14   See Gray, *Charity in Rabbinic Judaism*, 166. In this and all other cases, translations of the

R. Shimon ben Laqish quotes R. Yehudah ben Hanina as saying that the Ushan sages enacted an annual charitable maximum of one-fifth of a person's possessions. This poses a chronological difficulty: the pre-Ushan authority Rabban Gamliel (of Yavneh) was said to have rebuked R. Yeshebab for violating the 20% maximum by donating all his possessions to charity. But how could the 20% maximum have been the law in Rabban Gamliel's time if it was an enactment of the Ushan sages? The fifth-generation sage R. Yose b. R. Bun resolves the chronological conundrum: the 20% maximum was indeed the law in Rabban Gamliel's time, a law which "they forgot." Later "the two"—the plural apparently serving as a reference to the collectivity of Ushan sages—apparently unknowingly (re)enacted into law the very same 20% charitable maximum that had been in force in Rabban Gamliel's time.

R. Yose b. R. Bun makes an additional, crucial point. The Ushan restoration of the forgotten Yavnean law teaches that any law for which a *bet din* "gives their lives" will be established with the certainty of laws conveyed to Moses at Mount Sinai. Following this additional point, either R. Yose b. R. Bun or the anonymous Yerushalmi comments that R. Yose b. R. Bun's additional point is consistent with R. Mana's interpretation of Deuteronomy 32:47: the Torah is *a trifling thing* when its adherents do not wear themselves out over it, but it is *your very life* when they do. The Ushan court's diligence (their "wearing themselves out" over the Torah) thus did not only result in the restoration of the old 20% charitable maximum, but also in this law's now-metaphorical equivalence to a law stated to Moses at Sinai. In other words, due to the Ushan court's diligence, the 20% charitable maximum is now established with the same certainty as a law stated to Moses at Sinai.

The Yerushalmi goes on in this literary context to adduce the examples of the Biblical characters Bezalel (the architect of the wilderness tabernacle) and Joshua (Moses's successor), both of whom are said to have independently divined God's instructions to Moses at Sinai about their tasks, although they were not physically present on Sinai to receive those instructions personally. By juxtaposing these examples to the case of the Ushan restoration of the forgotten Yavnean law, the Yerushalmi is making a strong point: A *bet din*'s (in this case, the Ushan court's) willingness to give its life for a particular law (in this case, the 20% charitable maximum) will result in that law's being established with the certainty of a Sinaitic law, and this is equivalent to the certainty of Bezalel and Joshua, who did in fact intuit literal Sinaitic instructions to Moses

---

Hebrew Bible follow NJPS (unless otherwise noted). See also the pertinent discussion of this passage in Hayes, *"Halakhah le-Moshe mi-Sinai* in Rabbinic Sources," 102–103.

about their respective tasks. In sum, the same Divine providence that made for certainty in the cases of Bezalel and Joshua also operates in any future diligent *batei din* (courts) that unknowingly restore forgotten law. The Yerushalmi passage concludes on the following notes:

7. R. Yohanan in the name of Benaiah; Rav Huna in the name of Rabbi (Malachi 2:6): *"Proper rulings were in his mouth*—this refers to things he heard from his teacher; *and nothing perverse was on his lips*—[this refers] even to things that he did *not* hear from his teacher."
8. And the Rabbis say (Proverbs 3:26): "For the Lord will be your trust [of the root k-s-l]; He will keep your feet from being caught—even things as to which you were a fool (*kesil*), he will keep your feet from being caught."
9. R. Dosa said: "[God will protect you from making errors] in legal rulings."
10. And the Rabbis say: "[God will protect you] from sin."
11. R. Levi said: "[God will protect you] from demons."[15]

R. Yohanan's interpretation of Malachi 2:6 is of a piece with the Yerushalmi's earlier discussion of Bezalel and Joshua. If one is diligent so that *proper rulings were in his mouth* as to things heard from one's teacher, then *nothing perverse* will be on one's lips as to other matters. R. Dosa's reading of Proverbs 3:26 sharpens the point further: God will protect those who trust in him from errors in legal rulings; that is, rabbinic trust in God will result in God's exercising protective oversight over the rabbinic legal process. In sum, the Yerushalmi's juxtaposition of traditions about the Ushan restoration of the forgotten Yavnean law, R. Mana's interpretation of Deuteronomy 32:47, Bezalel's and Joshua's independent intuiting of revelations to Moses about their tasks, and R. Dosa's interpretation of Proverbs 3:26 all converge on a single point: God exercises continuing and protective oversight over the rabbinic legal process.

The Bavli Parallel: b.Ketubbot 50a

1. R. Il'a said: "In Usha they instituted that the one who scatters [his wealth] should not scatter more than one-fifth."
2. It was also taught thus [in a baraita]: "The one who scatters [his wealth] should not scatter more than one-fifth, lest he need the help of other created beings."

---

15 See Gray, *Charity in Rabbinic Judaism*, 167–168.

3. And it once happened that one sought to spend [more than one-fifth] and his companion did not allow him. And who was it? R. Yeshebab. And some say: It was R. Yeshebab [who wished to spend more than one-fifth] and his companion did not allow him. And who was that? R. Aqiva.[16]

The short Bavli parallel on b.Ketubbot 50a eliminates the forgetting and restoration motif, not to mention the earlier Talmud's broader literary context of Divine oversight of the integrity and completeness of transmitted rabbinic tradition. R. Il'a represents the 20% charitable maximum as a straightforward enactment of the Ushan sages. Paragraph 3's recollection that someone—whether it was R. Yeshebab or someone else—unsuccessfully tried to dispose of more than 20% of his assets as charity appears *after* paragraph 1's statement about the Ushan enactment; the passage as composed thus strongly suggests that this attempt occurred at some point after the Ushan sages instituted the law. What is more, the Bavli gives no indication of any Divine oversight of the law concerning the 20% charitable maximum—or even a need for such oversight.

y.Shabbat 1:4, 3d (ed. Academy, 372–373)[17] *and b.Shabbat 14b–15b*
M.Shabbat 1:4 mentions the "eighteen matters" decreed in Hananiah ben Hezeqiah ben Gurion's upper chamber, with the involvement of Bet Hillel and Bet Shammai. Y.Shabbat 1:4, 3c (ed. Academy, 371) indicates that among these "eighteen matters" were "the laws of the lands of the nations" (that is, the ritual impurity of the lands of the nations). Later, on y.Shabbat 1:4, 3d (ed. Academy, 372–373), the opinion is offered that "the laws of the lands of the nations" were actually instituted decades before Bet Hillel and Bet Shammai, by the scholarly pair Yose ben Yo'ezer Ish Tseredah and Yose ben Yohanan Ish Yerushalayim. The Yerushalmi resolves the chronological puzzlement just as it did in Pe'ah—by deploying the forgetting and restoration motif. As in Pe'ah, the Yerushalmi first quotes a contextually appropriate version of R. Yose b. R. Bun's tradition: the law was indeed instituted by the earlier pair but was forgotten, and "the two" (i.e., Bet Hillel and Bet Shammai) "stood up and agreed upon what the intention of the earlier ones had been." This resolution is followed here—as it is in Yerushalmi Pe'ah—by a reiteration of R. Mana's interpretation of Deuteronomy 32:47.

---

16 See Gray, *Charity in Rabbinic Judaism*, 168.
17 There is a parallel on y.Ketubbot 8:8, 32c (ed. Academy, 996).

On b.Shabbat 14b, the decree about the ritual impurity of the lands of the nations is straightforwardly attributed to the scholarly pair Yose ben Yo'ezer Ish Tseredah and Yose ben Yohanan Ish Yerushalayim. This attribution is called into question on b.Shabbat 15a because of another tradition that this decree was the work of sages who lived later than this scholarly pair, eighty years prior to the Temple's destruction. The Bavli calls these sages the "rabbis of the eighty years." A full study of the details of the Bavli's debate through 15b about these conflicting traditions need not detain us, but two aspects are most relevant. First, the Bavli eliminates the Yerushalmi's solution, the forgetting and restoration motif. Second, the Bavli's own resolution is that the (at least) two legislative enactments about the impurity of the lands of the nations were not repetitious enactments of the same law; there were *successive* rabbinic enactments about two differing, albeit related aspects of this impurity. Yose ben Yo'ezer Ish Tseredah and Yose ben Yohanan Ish Yerushalayim decreed as to one of these aspects and not the other; the "rabbis of the eighty years" decreed differently from the pair as to the one and newly enacted a decree as to the other; and finally, the Ushan sages decreed differently from both the pair and the "rabbis of the eighty years" as to the first aspect, but let stand the decree of "the rabbis of the eighty years" as to the second aspect. The Bavli thus eschews the Yerushalmi's path of using the forgetting and restoration motif; it chooses instead to posit successive, deliberate, and distinct rabbinic legislative interventions over the course of years.

y.Sukkah 4:1, 54b (ed. Academy, 649)[18] *and b.Sukkah 44a–b*

According to R. Ba and R. Hiyyah (in the name of R. Yohanan), the laws concerning the willow and water-libation are laws to Moses from Sinai. R. Ba bar Zavda in the name of R. Hunya of Barat-Havran holds instead that willow and water-libation (along with the law of the "ten plantings") were a subsequent "establishment of the prophets." The Yerushalmi resolves the discrepancy through resort to the forgetting and restoration motif. As in Pe'ah and Shabbat, it quotes both R. Yose b. R. Bun and R. Mana to make the point that the law was forgotten (after Moses) and subsequently restored (by the prophets).

On b.Sukkah 44a, the Bavli determines that R. Yohanan holds the law of the willow to be an "establishment of the prophets."[19] R. Zera questions R. Abbahu about a contrary tradition, in which R. Yohanan deems it to be a law to Moses at Sinai. The Bavli portrays R. Abbahu as being momentarily stunned by the

---

18 There is a parallel on y.Shevi'it 1:6, 33b (ed. Academy, 181).
19 See the discussion in Hayes, "*Halakhah le-Moshe mi-Sinai* in Rabbinic Sources," 104–106.

question. Upon recovering from his shock, he offers R. Zera the forgetting and restoration motif as the solution to the conflict of traditions: the law of the willow had been forgotten (after Sinai) and (re)established by the prophets.[20] This, however, is immediately rejected. Instead, the Bavli explains that the two traditions about the establishment of the law of the willow are distinct acts of legislation applicable to different circumstances: the Sinaitic revelation of the law of the willow was applicable to the Temple, while the prophetic enactment applied to areas outside the Temple (44b).

B.Sukkah 44a–b is noteworthy for three reasons. First, the Bavli initially allows the forgetting and restoration motif to surface as a (provisional) solution to the problem of conflicting traditions—but significantly, it is suggested by an *Erets* Israel amora (R. Abbahu). Second, the Bavli (nevertheless and characteristically) rejects the forgetting and restoration motif. Finally, consistent with Ketubbot and Shabbat, the Bavli describes the alleged two enactments of the law of the willow as successive, deliberate acts of legislation applying the law first to the Jerusalem Temple and then subsequently to the areas outside the Temple.

Appendix: The Case of y.Berakhot 5:2, 9b (ed. Academy, 46) and b.Berakhot 33a

In this case an *Erets* Israel amora invokes the forgetting of law to explain a puzzling (to him) tannaitic dispute about a common, frequently practiced law, while the Bavli characteristically eliminates the forgetting of law, putting deliberate rabbinic legislative intervention in its place. This example differs from the preceding three in that the Yerushalmi invokes the forgetting of law, but not its restoration motif.

M.Berakhot 5:2 records a three-way dispute between the first *tanna*, R. Aqiva, and R. Eliezer about the placement within the *Amidah* prayer of the *havdalah* passage which must be recited at the conclusion of the Sabbath. In the Yerushalmi, Shimon bar Vava asks R. Yohanan how these sages can disagree about what must have been a frequently recited passage. R. Yohanan's response is: "Since [*havdalah*'s] principal place is over 'the cup' (that is, the recitation of *havdalah* over a cup of wine is the primary one, not its recitation in the syna-

---

20   The Bavli attributes to R. Abbahu a linguistic formulation of the forgetting and restoration motif that we will later observe is characteristically Babylonian: *shach'chum v'hazru v'yasdum* ("they forgot it and went back and established it"). The significance of this formulation of the motif in this and other places will be explored in Section 4.

gogue prayer), they forgot [where] it [is] in the prayer." The Yerushalmi's only reaction to R. Yohanan is to observe that he holds the principal recitation of *havdalah* to be that done over a cup of wine, and not the one included in the evening prayer. The Yerushalmi notably displays no anxiety about this (relatively recent) forgetting of law, and simply moves on to present a tradition that appears to maintain, *contra* R. Yohanan, that the recitation of *havdalah* in the *Amidah* is in fact the principal one. In this case, the "forgetting" is not only concerned with where the *havdalah* passage is to be placed in the *Amidah* (as in m.Berakhot 5:2) but also about what this forgetting signifies: which *havdalah* recitation is the principal one?

Arguably, the forgetting and restoration motif is missing from the Yerushalmi because the "restoration" had not yet occurred at the time of R. Yohanan's response to Shimon bar Vava. The "restoration" is, in actuality, a *resolution* as to which *havdalah* recitation is the principal one. R. Yohanan is portrayed both as having an opinion about which *havdalah* recitation is the principal one, and as unaware that this matter is even in dispute. It is the anonymous Yerushalmi that orchestrates the various traditions so as to portray the matter as disputed. Thus unaware of the dispute, R. Yohanan is naturally also unaware of the resolution, which is offered at the end of the *sugya*: the anonymous Yerushalmi's quotation of a tradition of Shmuel that shows "[*havdalah*'s] principal place is [both] here (in the *Amidah*) and here (over wine)."

B.Berakhot 33a presents "Rav Shemen bar Abba's" (i.e., Shimon bar Vava) question to R. Yohanan as: "the Men of the Great Assembly instituted blessings, prayers, sanctifications, and *havdalot* for Israel. Let us consider: How did they institute them?" Rav Shemen bar Abba's query is not the Yerushalmi equivalent's question of how the *tannaim* can disagree about a common liturgical practice, and the Bavli's R. Yohanan likewise makes no mention of forgetting: "At the beginning, [the Men of the Great Assembly] instituted [*havdalah*] in the prayer. When [Israel] became wealthy, they established [the recitation of] it on a cup. When [Israel] became poor, they went back and established [the recitation] of it in the prayer. And they said: 'The one who makes *havdalah* in the prayer must make it over a cup.'" The Bavli replaces the Yerushalmi's reference to "forgetting" with deliberate legislative intervention, which eventuates in a legal resolution like that of Yerushalmi Berakhot: recitation of the *havdalah* passage is required both in the *Amidah* and over a cup of wine.

3 The Bavli Represents *Erets* Israel Sages as Acknowledging That Torah Was or Could Be Systemically Forgotten

Section 2 demonstrates the Bavli's awareness that the forgetting and restoration motif is characteristic of *Erets* Israel sages. This being so, it is hardly surprising that the Bavli also represents *Erets* Israel sages as acknowledging that Torah was, or could be, entirely forgotten. On b.Bava Batra 21a, Rav Yehudah in the name of Rav calls for R. Yehoshua ben Gamla to be remembered for good, for "were it not for him the Torah would have been forgotten from Israel." R. Yehoshua ben Gamla prevented that disaster by instituting local schools, thereby ensuring the education even of boys whose fathers could not teach them Torah. On b.Eruvin 54a, R. Eleazar teaches that had the first set of tablets received by Moses on Mount Sinai not been destroyed, the Torah would not ever have been forgotten from Israel. The destruction of those tablets thus introduced into the world the distinct possibility that Torah could be forgotten.

While the Bavli attributes to *Erets* Israel sages the idea that Torah can be forgotten entirely, it quite forthrightly presents Babylonian rabbis as its restorers, or as taking steps to guarantee it will not be forgotten. R. Hanina and R. Hiyya—both of whom ascended to *Erets* Israel from Babylonia—were locked in dispute (b.Ketubbot 103b). R. Hanina argued "if God forbid the Torah were to be forgotten from Israel, I could restore it through my dialectical ability."[21] R. Hiyya responds with a solution that will prevent Torah's being forgotten to begin with: he would go to towns with no teachers and write five scrolls of the Pentateuch for five boys and teach the six Orders of the Mishnah to six other boys. Those six would be instructed to teach the Order they learned to the others.

Apropos, on b.Sukkah 20a, the *Erets* Israel amora R. Shimon ben Laqish proclaims himself to be the "atonement" of R. Hiyya and his sons, for when "Torah was forgotten in Israel" Ezra came from Bavel to establish it; when it was again forgotten, "Hillel the Babylonian" came to establish it, and when it was again forgotten, "R. Hiyya and his sons" came to establish it.[22] R. Shimon ben Laqish thus admits that Torah can be forgotten "in Israel," not only among the peo-

---

21 R. Hanina's statement is a perfect blend of Babylonian and *Erets* Israel ideas: on the one hand, he expresses the *Erets* Israel perspective that Torah *could* be forgotten from Israel; on the other hand, he proposes what this essay will shortly demonstrate is the distinctly Babylonian notion that should this happen, his dialectical ability will be equal to the task of restoring the forgotten Torah.

22 The word I have rendered as "establish it" is *yasdah*. The significance of this point will be explained in Section 4.

ple Israel, but in the Land of Israel. Moreover, on the three historical occasions when Torah was indeed forgotten, Babylonian sages ascended to the Land of Israel to re-establish it. Although R. Shimon ben Laqish does not spell out precisely how Ezra, Hillel, and R. Hiyya and his sons did their restorative work, their methods may be discerned intertextually: dialectical ability (R. Hanina) or the wide dissemination of Torah knowledge (R. Hiyya). Indeed, the latter method appears to be the one the Hebrew Bible itself ascribes to Ezra (Nehemiah 8).

4 Bavli Applications of the Forgetting and Restoration Motif

We saw in Section 2 that the Bavli consistently eliminates the forgetting and restoration motif from its parallels to the Yerushalmi *sugyot*. In this section we will examine five cases where the Bavli invokes the motif yet, even in these instances, distances itself somewhat from it. All five Bavli applications of the motif take place in the Land of Israel and involve either Rabbis from the Land of Israel or Biblical characters. Nevertheless, these cases are an important vehicle for the Bavli's negotiation of its own ideas about the forgetting of law, the Divine and human roles in its restoration, and the rabbinic legal process more generally. The first step to discerning how this is so is to note the most significant commonality among the Bavli's five applications of the forgetting and restoration motif: in at least four of these five cases, the later rabbis who restore the forgotten law *knew or had to have known* that the law was forgotten. This presumed knowledge distinguishes these cases from the three Yerushalmi cases in Section 2, in which the later rabbis were apparently *unaware* that they were restoring a forgotten law. The restoring sages in the Bavli accounts are thus aware of the human error and frailty that resulted in the earlier forgetting of law and they knowingly apply their own human effort (notably dialectical ingenuity) to mend the broken consequences. In Section 2 the Yerushalmi describes the subtle intervention of Divine providence in solving a human problem (forgetting); in Section 4, by contrast, the Bavli describes a thoroughgoing human solution to this human problem.

We will survey these applications of the motif in the chronological order of the protagonists in the passages. The first (earliest) example is also the most complex. B.Temurah 16a is a lengthy *sugya* that collects different traditions about a major crisis of forgotten law that occurred in the wake of Moses's death.[23] Initially, Rav Yehudah in the name of Shmuel reports that

---

23 On this passage, see, e.g., Kolbrener, *The Last Rabbi*, 22–35; Gray, *Charity in Rabbinic Judaism*, 164–166.

3,000 laws were forgotten during the mourning period for Moses. A second tradition reported by Rav Yehudah in the name of Rav indicates that Joshua forgot 300 laws and became instantaneously doubtful about 700 more after spurning Moses's dying request that he take advantage of the time remaining to ask Moses any questions he might have. A third, unattributed tradition reports that 1,700 *qal v'homer* and *gezerah shavah* derivations and *diqduqei soferim* (fine points of the scribes) were forgotten during Moses's mourning period.

The people of Israel's response to the initial account of forgotten law is to consult Joshua and then later, the prophet Samuel to restore the lost laws. They both respond by pointing to scriptural prohibitions of their doing so: the Pentateuch declares that the Torah *"is not in the heavens"* (Deuteronomy 30:12), and that *"these are the commandments"* (Leviticus 27:34), which implies that "a prophet cannot innovate anything from this point." Israel then consults the priests Phinehas and Eleazar, who give the same responses. Both prophetic and priestly authority are thus unequal to the task of restoring the forgotten laws. Joshua's implied response to the second account of forgotten law is to ask God to restore the laws, but God refuses ("to tell you is impossible"); presumably God himself is bound by Deuteronomy 30:12. The third account of the crisis of forgotten law is happily resolved by the minor biblical character Othniel ben Qenaz, who "restored [the forgotten laws] through his dialectics." The attribution of this restoration to Othniel is based on a fanciful interpretation of Joshua 15:17, according to which Othniel conquered a town identified in the previous verse as *"Qiryat Sefer,"* literally, "the town of the book." The Bavli delightfully and unmistakably implies that Othniel's conquest of the "town of the book" stated in the verse is his use of his dialectical ability (*pilpulo*) to restore the forgotten laws. While the declared completeness and accuracy of Othniel's restoration may be an indication even in the Bavli of the Divine's hidden hand, there is a telling difference between this example and those of Section 2. In Section 2, the later, restoring sages were unaware that the law(s) had been lost; the Divine took the initiative of tacitly moving later rabbis to legislate back into existence that which they did not even know had been lost. In this case, the literary structure of b.Temurah 16a strongly implies that the restoring sage Othniel knew or at least had to have known that the laws were forgotten.

B.Temurah 16a identifies Othniel ben Qenaz as the Biblical character Jabez, who surfaces on b.Yoma 80a.[24] R. Yohanan states there that various standards of measurement were stated as "a law to Moses at Sinai." A baraita supports

---

24 For references to Jabez in the Hebrew Bible, see 1 Chronicles 4:9–10; cf. 1 Chronicles 2:55.

this view, but "others" claim that the *bet din* of Jabez instituted these standards of measurement. The Bavli resolves this contradiction (in the course of responding to another challenge)[25] through the forgetting and restoration motif: "*shach'chum v'hazru v'yasdum*"; "they (Israel after Sinai) forgot [the standards of measurement] and they (the *bet din* of Jabez) went back and established them." The Bavli's identification of Othniel ben Qenaz with Jabez on b.Temurah 16a means that these forgotten standards of measurement on b.Yoma 80a were presumably among the laws Othniel ben Qenaz restored through his dialectical ability after they had been forgotten during the period of mourning for Moses. Thus, once again, Othniel ben Qenaz (= Jabez) either knew or had to have known that these standards of measurement had been forgotten and that he was restoring forgotten law.

Indeed, a case can be made that the very linguistic formulation the Bavli employs on b.Yoma 80a implies that the later, restoring sages are aware that the law they are restoring had been forgotten. "*Shach'chum* ('they forgot them') *v'hazru* ('and they went back') *v'yasdum* ('and they established them')." "And they went back"—that is, later sages actively "went back" to restore laws they knew or had to have known had been forgotten. This formulation is subtly different from R. Yose b. R. Bun's equivalent statement in the Yerushalmi: "Such was the law in their hands and they forgot it. And 'the two' stood up and agreed upon what the intention of the early ones had been." The Yerushalmi's formulation—especially in Yerushalmi Pe'ah, which explicitly places this formulation in a larger literary context of Divine oversight of the rabbinic legal enterprise—implies that the later scholars' "agreement" with the "intention of the early ones" was serendipitously brought about by the Divine. The Bavli's "and they went back" implies a more conscious effort on the part of later rabbis to see to the restoration of something they knew or had to have known was forgotten. The common use of the Hebrew root *y-s-d* on b.Sukkah 20a and in the Babylonian formulation of the forgetting and restoration motif also lends support to the idea that "*shach'chum v'hazru v'yasdum*" means that later sages knew or had to have known of the forgetting of law. We saw on b.Sukkah 20a that Babylonian sages (re)established Torah on three occasions when it was forgotten in Israel: Ezra established it (*yasdah*), Hillel the Babylonian established it (*yasdah*), and R. Hiyya and his sons established it (*yasduha*). In each of these cases the Babylonian sages either knew or had to have known that they were ascending to the Land of Israel to establish Torah that had been forgotten. At

---

25 Namely, how measurements could have been an enactment made by the court of Jabez when there is a biblical prohibition against a prophet establishing something new.

the very least, b.Sukkah 20a equates the restorations of Hillel and R. Hiyya (and sons) with that of Ezra, whom the Hebrew Bible depicts as entirely aware that he was (re)establishing lost Torah.

But what about b.Sukkah 44a (one of the three cases discussed in Section 2)? There, it will be recalled, the Bavli attributes its formulation of the forgetting and restoration motif ("*shach'chum v'hazru v'yasdum*") to R. Abbahu in order to explain conflicting traditions of R. Yohanan, only to dismiss the use of the motif in favor of its characteristic resort to the portrayal of successive acts of rabbinic legislation. The motif as applied on b.Sukkah 44a appears to be the typical *Erets* Israel case of later sages' (unknowingly) re-establishing forgotten law. B.Sukkah 44a thus seems to imply that "*shach'chum v'hazru v'yasdum*" does *not* necessarily mean that later sages knew they were restoring forgotten law.

Nevertheless, b.Sukkah 44a need not be fatal to the claim that "*shach'chum v'hazru v'yasdum*" implies later sages' awareness they are restoring lost law. In the other two cases discussed in Section 2 the Bavli silently expunged the forgetting and restoration motif found in the Yerushalmi parallels, substituting deliberate rabbinic legislation in its place. In contrast, b.Sukkah 44a is a case in which the Bavli *follows* its Yerushalmi parallel's lead in presenting the motif explicitly, but it does so only to immediately reject it and (characteristically) substitute rabbinic legislative activity for it. B.Sukkah 44a explicitly invokes the *Erets* Israel forgetting and restoration motif in order to teach a lesson about it: the idea that later sages *unknowingly* restore forgotten law is unacceptable and must be dismissed. B.Sukkah 44a's "*shach'chum v'hazru v'yasdum*" is thus meant to be identical to the Yerushalmi's use of the motif and by highlighting it, the Bavli's point is to reject it. Naturally the Bavli expresses the *Erets* Israel forgetting and restoration motif in its own terms; the Bavli is well-known to have characteristic terms and ways of referring to concepts and other phenomena.[26] It is therefore unsurprising when it consistently employs its own characteristic formulation of an *Erets* Israel motif. But again, b.Sukkah 44a's point is explicitly to reject the *Erets* Israel idea that later sages can/will *unknowingly* restore lost law. B.Sukkah 44a thus does not foreclose the possibility that *shach'chum v'hazru v'yasdum* can refer to later sages' conscious restoration of law they knew or had to have known had been forgotten.

Moving on from Othniel ben Qenaz (= Jabez), R. Yirmiyah (or R. Hiyya bar Abba) taught that the alternative forms of the Hebrew letters *mem*, *nun*, *tsadi*, *pey*, and *khaf* were instituted by the "*tsofim*," literally, the "watchers," a ref-

---

26 See, e.g., Gray, *A Talmud in Exile*, 101–121; Friedman, "Ha-baraitot she-be-Talmud ha-Bavli ve-yahasan le-Tosefta."

erence to the prophets (b.Megillah 2b). The Bavli instantly objects that the "watchers" could not have instituted these alternative forms because of Leviticus 27:34, which, as noted above, prohibits prophets from instituting new laws after Sinai (3a). After some argumentation about this issue that need not detain us, the Bavli's solution (as on b.Yoma 80a) is to argue instead that "they [Israel] forgot [the alternative forms of these letters after Sinai], and [the 'watchers'] went back and established them" (*shach'hum v'hazru v'yasdum*) (3a). It strains credulity to posit that the "watchers" could have been entirely unaware that there had been alternative forms of the letters *mem, nun, tsadi, pey,* and *khaf* beginning with the Sinai revelation. But regardless of how much strain one's credulity can bear, the Bavli's formulation "they forgot them, *and they went back* and they established them" indicates that "they went back" to "establish" something "they" knew had been forgotten.

In the same literary context, R. Yirmiyah (or R. Hiyya bar Abba) also states that Onqelos the proselyte produced his Aramaic translation of the Pentateuch under the guidance of R. Eliezer and R. Yehoshua (b.Megillah 3a). A contrary tradition originating with Rav attributes the Aramaic translation to Ezra, which seems to be the clear view of the Hebrew Bible (Nehemiah 8:8).[27] Once again, the Bavli's response to this discrepancy is: "they forgot them, and went back and established them" (*shach'hum v'hazru v'yasdum*); that is, Ezra established the Aramaic *targum*, it was subsequently forgotten, and then Onqelos, under the guidance of R. Eliezer and R. Yehoshua, went back and (re)established it. Two points require emphasis. First, from the Bavli's perspective Onqelos (and his rabbinic guides R. Eliezer and R. Yehoshua) had to have known Nehemiah 8:8, or at least the historical context described there. Hence, Onqelos and his guides had to have known that the Aramaic *targum* had once existed and was forgotten. Thus, the restoration of the Aramaic *targum* was not due to Divine providence's contriving to use later rabbis to bring about the restoration of a legal institution those rabbis did not even know had been forgotten; rather, the rabbis (and Onqelos) were independently taking the initiative to restore a legal institution they *knew* or had to have known had been forgotten. Moreover, the Bavli explicitly describes Onqelos's efforts to restore the lost Aramaic *targum* as overseen by (the very human hands of) R. Eliezer and R. Yehoshua, not implicitly by the hidden hand of the Divine.

The last example is that of Shimon Ha-pequli, said to have arranged the "Eighteen Blessings" (i.e., the *Amidah* prayer), in the presence of Rabban Gamliel at Yavneh (b.Berakhot 28b). This tradition is repeated on b.Megillah 17b,

---

27 See also b.Nedarim 37b.

where a competing tradition is immediately juxtaposed to it: 120 elders, "among whom were a number of prophets," instituted the Eighteen Blessings in order. The Bavli turns to a resolution of the conflict between these traditions on b.Megillah 18a, where it asks: "Since 120 elders, among whom were a number of prophets, instituted the [*Amidah*] in order, what did Shimon Ha-pequli place in order?" The Bavli uses a linguistic formulation very similar to that on b.Yoma 80a and b.Megillah 3a in formulating its answer: "They forgot them and he went back and placed them in order" (*shach'hum v'hazar v'sidrum*). That is, the 120 elders put the *Amidah* in order, that order was forgotten, and then Shimon Ha-pequli restored it in the presence of Rabban Gamliel at Yavneh. Nevertheless, unlike the preceding four cases, the bare facts of this example of forgetting and restoration do not unequivocally support the idea that Shimon Ha-pequli (and Rabban Gamliel) knew or had to have known that the order of the "Eighteen Blessings" had been forgotten.

But the Bavli's employment of the forgetting and restoration motif on b.Megillah 18a, although not clearly an example of later sages' knowing restoration of lost law, does other relevant work. In this example (as on b.Temurah 16a and the case of the Hebrew letters on b.Megillah 2b–3a) the Bavli undermines prophetic authority and bolsters rabbinic authority. A legal institution (in this case, the order of the Eighteen Blessings) enacted by a legislative body that included prophets was forgotten; that legal institution is restored (one presumes, permanently) by Shimon Ha-pequli's actions at Yavneh, from which prophets were absent. And, as in b.Megillah 3a's case of Onqelos, Shimon Ha-pequli's restorative effort is explicitly declared to have been overseen by (the very human) Rabban Gamliel of Yavneh.

In sum, the Bavli employs the forgetting and restoration motif five times. All five cases of the Bavli's use of the motif take place in the Land of Israel, three in the Biblical period, and none involve Babylonian sages. In all five cases the Bavli uses what we can now identify as a distinctly Babylonian linguistic formulation of the motif ("*shach'chum v'hazru* [or *hazar*] *v'yasdum* [or *v'sidrum*])." Human dialectical prowess is specified as the means of restoration on b.Temurah 16a and implied to be such by its b.Yoma 80a intertext. An important commonality among at least four of the five cases is one that distinguishes them from the Yerushalmi examples in Section 2: the restoring sages likely either knew or had to have known that the legal institution they were restoring had been lost. Moreover, in all five cases the Bavli presents a distinctly Babylonian perspective about the centrality of human, rather than Divine, initiative in ensuring the integrity and intact transmission of law. This is accomplished either by describing later sages as restoring laws they either knew or had to have known had been forgotten (b.Temurah 16a; b.Yoma 80a;

b.Megillah 2b–3a; b.Megillah. 3a), and/or by undermining prophetic authority and concomitantly buttressing (non-prophetic) rabbinic authority (b.Temurah 16a; b.Megillah 2b–3a, 17b–18a). While one need not posit that Divine providence is entirely absent from these five (or four) cases, they evince the Bavli's pattern of minimizing the role of the Divine and centering the role of the human sage.

5 The Forgetting of Law by Individual *Erets* Israel Sages

We now move from systemic to individual forgetting of law. Given that the forgetting and restoration motif overall is essentially an *Erets* Israel one, the Bavli's representations of *Erets* Israel sages' individual forgetting hardly come as a surprise. R. Eliezer forgot something he had taught R. Aqiva (b.Pesahim 69a), there is a thrice-repeated tradition about R. Yannai's forgetting a law (b.Qiddushin 57a, b.Zevahim 70b, b.Hullin 82a), Rabbi forgot the scriptural verse key to the determination of whether vessels from the Onias Temple in Egypt could be used in the Jerusalem Temple (b. Avodah Zarah 52b), and R. Asi forgot a law he had learned in the name of R. Yohanan, although R. Eleazar reminded him of it (b.Hullin 103b). A charming homiletical exposition by R. Simlai of tangential relevance to our inquiry posits that the unborn fetus is taught the entire Torah, only to be made to forget it at birth (b.Niddah 30b).

R. Zera is associated with the forgetting of law in three places. He acknowledges that were it not for R. Abba of Akko, he would have forgotten a law concerning legal documents (b.Ketubbot 22a). He also reports from R. Yehudah ben Beteyra in Nisibis that one must be careful of an elder who has forgotten his learning (b.Sanhedrin 96a). This last tradition is an illuminating intertext to the report that R. Zera engaged in 100 fasts to forget the "Babylonian *gemara*" before he ascended to the Land of Israel (b.Bava Metsia 85a). These three traditions may be representative of a Babylonian perception that R. Zera had a penchant for forgetting and, (with due allowance for compounded speculation), that of Bava Metsia may be an effort to find some worthwhile purpose in what was otherwise likely viewed as a distressing personal failing.

Finally, R. Eleazar ben Arakh was said to have visited Perugita and Dayumeset (b.Shabbat 147b). The former's wine and the latter's (bathing) waters were allegedly so alluring that they brought about the ruin of the ten northern tribes of Israel by putting them on a path of hedonistic indulgence. R. Eleazar ben Arakh was likewise "pulled after them" (i.e., the wine and the bathing waters), and consequently forgot his learning. Indeed, he forgot his learning to such an extent that when he stood up to read the words "*ha-hodesh ha-zeh lakhem*" from the Torah scroll (*"This month shall mark for you"*; Exodus 12:2), he mispronounced *"ha-hodesh"* (*"this month"*) and *"lakhem"* (*"for you"*). The rabbis sought "mercy upon him" (that is, they prayed for him) and "his learning returned." The Bavli relates R. Eleazar ben Arakh's experience to m.Avot 4:14, in which R. Nehorai (i.e., R. Eleazar ben Arakh, according to one opinion) advises that one seek exile to a place of Torah, quoting Proverbs 3:5 (*do not rely on your own understanding*). One must not assume that the Torah will follow them to just any place; one needs colleagues to uphold one's learning. The clear implication that individual forgetting is somehow related to sin is reinforced by Resh Laqish's teaching that one who forgets (even) one word of his study violates the negative commandment *"But take utmost care ... so that you do not forget the things ...."* (Deuteronomy 4:9) (b.Menahot 99b).[28]

6   The Forgetting of Law by Individual Babylonian Sages

The Bavli also portrays individual Babylonian sages as forgetting their learning. Hillel is famously represented as forgetting (b.Pesahim 66a), Rav twice so (b.Sanhedrin 82a, b.Zevahim 59a), students of Rav forgot his teachings (b.Pesahim 106b), R. Ahadaboi bar Ami offended Rav Sheshet and (consequently) forgot his learning (b.Bava Batra 9b), Rav Yosef became ill and forgot his learning (b.Nedarim 41a), and Avimi forgot Mishnah tractate Menahot (b.Menahot 7a).

The case of the third-generation amora Rav Yosef and his interaction(s) with Abaye is instructive. Rav Yosef, like R. Zera, counsels respect for the scholar who has forgotten his learning (b.Menahot 99a), which has a poignant personal relevance in that he is said to have forgotten his own learning due to illness (b.Nedarim 41a). But Bavli Nedarim takes pains in the case of Rav Yosef to point out that his individual forgetting is more than a personal tragedy. The Bavli identifies Rav Yosef's illness and consequent forgetting as underlying the multiple instances in that Talmud in which Rav Yosef denies knowing a

---

28   Resh Laqish's stigmatizing of individual forgetting as sin is consistent with the Yerushalmi's portrayal of Divine oversight of the rabbinic process and reversal of the effects of systemic forgetting. Recall R. Mana's teaching that a *bet din* that "wears itself out" over a law will merit having that law established with the certainty of a law to Moses at Sinai (based on Deuteronomy 32:47). Presumably, then, the sin of failing to "wear oneself out" has the adverse consequence that the law not labored over will be forgotten for good. Resh Laqish similarly cites Deuteronomy 4:9's *take utmost care ... so that you do not forget*. "Forgetting" is presumably the consequence of failing to "take utmost care."

particular tradition, only to be reminded by Abaye that he had in fact taught it.[29] Rav Yosef's poignant exchanges with Abaye in Bavli Nedarim and elsewhere underscore how threatening a specter forgetting is in a predominantly oral intellectual culture; Rav Yosef's forgetting of his learning and even *denial of what he had previously taught* threatens to undermine the accuracy of orally transmitted records of which tradents transmitted what traditions. Moreover, while the Bavli is willing to portray the third-generation Rav Yosef as *forgetting*, it portrays the fourth-generation Abaye as *restoring* the elder sage's forgotten learning. A closer comparison of Rav Yosef's forgetting and restoration of learning to that of R. Eleazar ben Arakh (b.Shabbat 147b) underscores not only this point, but also the all-important religious difference between the foregrounding of Divine initiative in *Erets* Israel rabbinic culture and that of human initiative in Babylonian rabbinic culture. R. Eleazar ben Arakh's learning is restored (somehow) through the prayers of the rabbis; that is, through rabbinic pleas to the Divine to restore the learning. Rav Yosef's learning is restored in a more straightforwardly human way: "Abaye restored it to him" (*ahadrei Abaye kameih*). Abaye does not pray for Divine assistance; he actively works to restore to Rav Yosef what the latter forgot. Similarly, when Avimi forgets Mishnah Menahot, he seeks to restore his knowledge by going to Rav Hisda for assistance. Prayer goes unmentioned (b.Menahot 7a). The Babylonian solution to individual forgetting, then, much like its solution to systemic forgetting, is not the intercession of the Divine; rather it is the very human activity of the rabbinic sage—rabbinic mutual aid, as it were.

Returning to the list of Babylonian sages represented as forgetting, we see that aside from Hillel (who is not an amora), they are all Babylonian sages of the first three amoraic generations. Tellingly, neither Rava, nor Abaye, nor any other sages of the fourth through the seventh Babylonian amoraic generations are represented as forgetting learning.[30] This pattern correlates with two other characteristics of the fourth and fifth generations in particular. First, the fourth and fifth generations are characterized by greater receptiveness to and engagement with *Erets* Israel learning than earlier Babylonian amoraic generations.

---

29   Rav Yosef is so represented on b.Eruvin 10a, 41a, 66b, 73a, 89b; b.Makkot 4a; b. Niddah 39a, 63b.

30   That is not to say that amoraim of these generations are entirely unaware of the perils of forgetting. Rava teaches that a person should verbally repeat his learning, even if he will forget it, and even if he does not understand what he is saying (b.Avodah Zarah 19a). There are other traditions as well there in Bavli Avodah Zarah about how to ensure that one's Torah "will be upheld" (*mitqayyem*), that is, not forgotten. Rav Ashi observes how easy forgetting is in his generation (b.Eruvin 53a). A full examination of these and related traditions is beyond this essay's scope.

This point has been demonstrated repeatedly in prior research and need not be relitigated here, although a couple of examples may be helpful.[31] There is a small pattern in Babylonian amoraic use of the word *"tsedaqah"* (meaning "charity") in commenting upon tannaitic compilations. Babylonian amoraim of the second and third amoraic generations use *"tsedaqah"* to mean "charity" in commenting on t.Megillah 2:15. Fourth- through seventh-generation amoraim deploy *"tsedaqah"* to mean "charity" in commenting as well on Sifre Deuteronomy, Mishnah Pe'ah, and Tosefta Bava Qamma.[32] Arguably, these later amoraim have become aware of a broader array of tannaitic compilations. Fourth- and fifth-generation Babylonian amoraim are also demonstrably engaged to a greater extent than earlier generations with edited *Erets* Israel amoraic learning: Rav Papa ponders two versions of an *Erets* Israel *sugya*, one transmitted in the name of the *nahota* Rav Dimi and the other in the name of the *nahota* Rabin (b.Ketubbot 57a), while Rav Nahman bar Yitshaq is demonstrably aware of an edited *Erets* Israel story about amoraim (b.Qiddushin 44a).[33]

The correlation between the lack of individual forgetting in the fourth through seventh amoraic generations and the increasing Babylonian receptiveness to *Erets* Israel learning in the fourth and fifth generations is meaningful in light of the regnant scholarly consensus that Babylonian rabbis privileged orality as their primary mode of transmitting, preserving, and producing new learning. The privileging of orality comes freighted with the potential peril of forgetting. As Babylonian amoraim of the fourth and fifth generations in particular absorbed a vast amount of new (to them) *Erets* Israel learning, one may reasonably assume that their anxiety about forgetting would concomitantly be heightened. Indeed, one may do more than assume. Rava advises that one should verbally repeat his learning, even if he does not understand it, and even if he will forget it (b.Avodah Zarah 19a). On b.Eruvin 53a, Abaye proclaims his generation's difficulty in learning *gemara* (traditional learning), Rava proclaims the difficulty of learning *sevara* (logical reasoning), and Rav Ashi proclaims his generation's ease of forgetting. The fourth (Rava) and sixth (Rav Ashi) generation amoraim thus assume that individual forgetting can occur,

---

31 See, e.g., Dor, *Torat Eretz Israel be-Bavel*; Kalmin, *Sages, Stories, Authors, and Editors*, 11 n. 31, 91–94; idem, *The Sage in Jewish Society*, 31, 43, 55–56, and *passim*; Kalmin, *Jewish Babylonia between Persia and Roman Palestine*, 4, 173–186, 249–250 nn. 6–8 and *passim*; Schwartz, "As They Journeyed from the East"; idem, *Rewriting the Talmud*, *passim*.

32 See Gray, *Charity in Rabbinic Judaism*, 20.

33 See also another such example involving Rav Nahman bar Yitshaq, this one on b.Yevamot 11b–12a (discussed in Kraemer, *The Mind of the Talmud*, 67–68).

yet unlike the *Erets* Israel amora Resh Laqish (b.Menahot 99b) they do not stigmatize individual forgetting as sin. Individual forgetting for Babylonian rabbis is an anxiety-producing fact of rabbinic life. Yet although they acknowledge the possibility of forgetting, the amoraim of the fourth through seventh generations do not portray themselves as forgetting. The anxiety is real and the possibility exists—but amoraim do not forget.

But how is this orality anxiety to be managed and the danger of forgetting neutralized? One solution comes to us by way of a second correlation: the association of third- and fourth-generation amoraim with more complex argumentation.[34] David Kraemer has observed that almost half of the cases of "explicit amoraic preservation of argumentation" are portrayed as having been transmitted to Babylonia from *Erets* Israel by the *nahote*.[35] I would add that when the *nahote* are portrayed as interacting with Babylonian sages, those are mostly sages of the fourth and fifth generations.[36] By the fourth generation, then, the twofold revolution of an influx to Babylonia of new *Erets* Israel learning and a growing tendency to preserve (complex) argumentation may have yielded not only "orality anxiety" but also the germ of a strategy to manage it: a growing stress on argumentation, on dialectical prowess. Thus Othniel ben Qenaz restores forgotten laws through his dialectical prowess, and R. Hanina declares that were Torah to be forgotten, he could restore it through his own dialectical prowess (b.Temurah 16a; b.Ketubbot 103b).

Dialectical skill emerges in another, different way as well as the solution to a different form of "orality anxiety" in a lengthy and complex *sugya* on b.Yevamot 32b–33b. This *sugya* downgrades the reliability of oral transmission and upholds argumentation instead as the way to establish the law. B.Yevamot 32b–33b's message appears to be that oral transmission is or can be flawed and unreliable in comparison with argumentation. Three cases are presented: a non-priest who (illegally) performed Temple service, a blemished priest who performed Temple service while ritually impure, and a non-priest who ate the meat of a bird that was "pinched" as required by the laws of sacrifice. In each case R. Hiyya declares the offender to be guilty of two transgressions, and Bar Qappara of one; moreover, in each case R. Hiyya and Bar Qappara jump up (the verb used is indeed "*qafats*," literally, "jump") and swears an oath that he

---

34 See, e.g., Kraemer, *The Mind of the Talmud*, 50–78 and *passim*.
35 Kraemer, *The Mind of the Talmud*, 67.
36 See the pertinent discussion in Gray, *A Talmud in Exile*, 5–7 and nn. 17–19. Two illustrative examples include b.Avodah Zarah 14b (Abaye interacting with the *nahota* Rav Dimi) and b.Niddah 68a (Rav Papa and Rava discuss a letter sent by the *nahota* Rabin from the Land of Israel).

heard his stated opinion from Rabbi. R. Hiyya's and Bar Qappara's reports about what they heard from Rabbi are contradictory. These reports cannot be verified or dismissed solely on their own authority or on that of Rabbi. The Bavli embarks upon a lengthy and complex course of argumentation in the name of each sage; this argumentation includes an inquiry as to why each sage would have "jumped" to take an oath about the accuracy of the view he presented. Ultimately the Bavli sides with R. Hiyya, proclaiming Bar Qappara's view to be (decisively) refuted (*t'yuvta d'Bar Qappara t'yuvta*). That is: Bar Qappara is refuted by *argumentation*; correlatively, R. Hiyya is vindicated by argumentation. Oral reports of Rabbi's view are simply insufficient and inconclusive to establish the law.

7   Conclusions

This essay's inquiry into the forgetting and restoration motif yields the following conclusions: (1) the Bavli eliminates the Yerushalmi's forgetting and restoration motif in its parallels to the pertinent Yerushalmi *sugyot*, substituting instead a portrayal of successive, deliberate acts of rabbinic legislation (Section 2); (2) *Erets* Israel sages (not Babylonian sages) represent that Torah was or could be forgotten *tout court*, with Babylonian sages represented as restoring (or as able to restore) Torah when it is forgotten in *Erets* Israel or under the watch of *Erets* Israel sages (Section 3); (3) the Bavli itself employs its uniquely formulated version of the forgetting and restoration motif in five cases, four of which are demonstrably cases in which the restoring sages knew or had to have known that the law had been forgotten (Section 4); (4) the Bavli portrays individual *Erets* Israel sages as forgetting laws (Section 5); (5) the Bavli represents only individual Babylonian sages of the first three amoraic generations as forgetting laws, but not sages of the pivotal fourth through the seventh generations. This difference is arguably related to a growing "orality anxiety" triggered by the arrival in Babylonia of a greater quantity of *Erets* Israel learning beginning in the fourth amoraic generation, the tendency to preserve more complex argumentation beginning with the third and fourth generations, and the growing emergence of the notion that dialectical skill (and also rabbinic mutual assistance, as seen in the case of Abaye and Rav Yosef and Rav Hisda and Avimi) can be a solution to the problem of forgetting. The Bavli refuses to allow that sages of the generations in which *Erets* Israel learning spikes in Babylonia, and in which more complex argumentation is being preserved, can be portrayed as forgetting laws—dialectical skill emerges as the solution to the problem of forgetting law.

Toward the beginning of this essay, we described the inter-Talmudic difference about the nature of the Divine role in human affairs as the genus of which the difference concerning the forgetting and restoration motif is a species. We noted a documented tendency among *Erets* Israel sages to point to a robust Divine role in overseeing the legal process, and an equally documented broad tendency in the Bavli to push the Divine role in human affairs into the background and to put human initiative and effort at the forefront instead. This broad Bavli tendency is discernible in the limitations it puts on Divine providence, the role (or lack thereof) it assigns the Divine in the transaction between a charitable donor and recipient, aspects of its narrative descriptions of the revelation and transmission of Torah, and in the forgetting and restoration motif that is the subject of this essay. But the Bavli has more to say about the issue of the Divine role in the rabbinic legal enterprise outside of the context of the forgetting and restoration motif, and this essay's inquiry will be incomplete without attention to it. On b.Bava Batra 12a–b, the Bavli grapples with both *Erets* Israel and Babylonian perspectives on the issue of Divine oversight over the rabbinic legal process. The *sugya* reads as follows:

> R. Avdimi of Haifa said, "From the day the [First] Temple was destroyed prophecy was taken from the prophets and given to the sages."

> This sage—isn't he (i.e., can he not be) a prophet? Thus did [R. Avdimi of Haifa] say, "even though [prophecy] was taken from the prophets, it was not taken from the sages."[37]

> Amemar said, "And the sage is preferable to the prophet, as it is said, *that we may obtain* [*v'navi*, literally, "and a prophet"] *a wise* [*hokhmah*, like *hakham*, "sage"] *heart* (Psalms 90:12). Who is dependent on whom? Say that the small [in importance] is dependent upon the great [in importance]."[38]

> Abaye said, "Know [that prophecy was not taken from the sages] for a great man says something and the same [idea] is said in the name of another great man."

---

37 The printed edition reads "*nitlah*" for "taken," as do Mss. Firenze, Biblioteca Nationale Centrale II.1.8–9 and Paris, Bibliotheque Nationale Suppl. Heb. 1337. Ms. Vatican, Bibliotheca Apostolica, Ebr. 115 reads "*nistalqah*." Other differences between and among the manuscripts and printed edition need not detain us.

38 That is, the verse's *that we may obtain* [*v'navi*] is meant to result in *a heart of wisdom*

Rava said, "And what is the difficulty (i.e., the unusualness) [of that]? Perhaps the two of them are under the same constellation."

Rather, Rava said, "Know [that prophecy was not taken from the sages] for a great man says something and the same [idea] is said in the name of R. Aqiva ben Yosef."

Rav Ashi said, "And what is the difficulty (i.e., the unusualness) [of that]? Perhaps as to that matter [the great man] is under [R. Aqiva ben Yosef's] constellation."

Rather, Rav Ashi said, "Know [that prophecy was not taken from the sages] for a great man says something and the same is said [as] a law to Moses at Sinai."

And perhaps [the sage] is like a blind man in the opening on the roof[39] (i.e., the sage happened serendipitously to state a law that turned out to be a law to Moses as Sinai)?

But doesn't [the sage] give a reason [for his views]?[40]

We will examine the passage in two parts: paragraphs 1–3 and 4–10. The *Erets* Israel sage R. Avdimi of Haifa states a straightforwardly *Erets* Israel view familiar to anyone who has ever encountered y.Pe'ah 1:1, 15b (Section 2): once the Temple was destroyed, prophecy was handed over to the sages. Thus, the same Divine oversight that was at work in the prophets is (now) at work in the sages. But R. Avdimi of Haifa also tacitly makes another point that troubles the author of paragraph 2. He implicitly understands "prophets" and "sages" to be two entirely distinct, non-overlapping categories; sages are not inherently prophets and prophecy was given to them only after it was taken from

---

[*hokhmah*]; so *v'navi* is of lesser importance than the goal—*hokhmah*. Hence the "prophet" (*navi*) is less than the "sage" (*hakham*).

39　The point of the comparison is that the sage is like a blind man groping about on a roof to find the opening that will allow him to descend into the house. The blind man may find the opening by accident; similarly, the contemporary sage may recite a law that quite by accident turns out to be a law to Moses at Sinai.

40　Following Rashi (s.v. "*v'lav ta'am qa'amar*"), the point is that the sage is not like the blind man groping for the *aruba* and finding it by chance; his reasoning was divinely inspired (Rashi actually says that his reasoning "came to him as prophecy") and the sage thus merited stating a law that was in fact a law to Moses at Sinai.

the prophets.[41] Paragraph 2 is an anonymous interpolation that questions the assumption that "prophets" and "sages" were always entirely distinct categories. Paragraph 2 makes the point that sages *qua* sages *can* have prophecy; after the First Temple's destruction, prophecy was taken from those prophets who were not also sages, but it was not taken from sages (who always had the potential for prophecy). To the author of paragraph 2 (*contra* R. Avdimi of Haifa), the categories "prophets" and "sages" may have and perhaps even did overlap prior to the First Temple's destruction. At "present" there are no more "prophets" who are not "sages," but there have always been "sages" who have the potential for prophecy.

The statement of the sixth-generation Babylonian amora Amemar (paragraph 3) requires greater attention. From a source-critical perspective, paragraph 3 may have originally been placed immediately after paragraph 1 as Amemar's direct response to R. Avdimi of Haifa—one attributed tradition responding to another. On this reading, R. Avdimi of Haifa is saying that the sages (of today), having received prophecy, are the equals of yesteryear's prophets. Amemar's response would then be a rejection of this idea: to Amemar, the sages (of today), although they first received prophecy after the First Temple's destruction, are actually the superiors of the pre-Destruction prophets. By implication, then, Amemar acknowledges that First Temple-era sages were *not* superior to the prophets. But if we read Amemar as he appears now, as a response to paragraph 2, his point is even stronger: sages *always* had the potential for prophecy, both "today" and in the First Temple period; moreover, sages were *always* superior to (non-sage) prophets, even *during* the First Temple period. However we read Amemar, it is clear that by the end of paragraph 3, even (the Babylonian sage) Amemar sees some role for the Divine in the rabbinic legal process. But what is that role and how is it to be discerned?

Paragraphs 4–10 seek to answer this question. Abaye begins with a simple idea: when one "great man" says the same thing as another, this happy convergence of legal perspectives is a sign of tacit Divine involvement in the rabbinic process (paragraph 4). Rava dismisses this idea, attributing the convergence to astrological coincidence. He opts instead for the idea that the involvement of the Divine may be discerned when one "great man" says the same thing as

---

41   R. Avdimi of Haifa's implicit separation of the two categories "prophets" and "sages" is echoed on y.Megillah 1:4, 70d (ed. Academy, 745), which we mentioned earlier in this essay. The "eighty-five elders" included "prophets"; by implication, "prophets" and those elders in the group who were not prophets were a distinct group.

an even greater sage (e.g., R. Aqiva ben Yosef) (paragraphs 5–6). Rav Ashi dismisses Rava, attributing even this convergence to a related, albeit distinct form of astrological coincidence. Rav Ashi instead proposes that Divine involvement may be discerned when one "great man" says something that turns out to be a law to Moses at Sinai (paragraphs 7–8). Rav Ashi's view is not rejected by another amora, although it is interrogated by the Bavli (paragraphs 9–10). This break in the pattern suggests that Rav Ashi's view has greater merit than the first two, although the matter is hardly settled at this point. In paragraph 9 the Bavli suggests that even the convergence of the legal opinion of "a great man" and a "law to Moses at Sinai" may be pure coincidence. The metaphor the Bavli uses to make its point is remarkable: a blind man groping about and accidentally finding his way to the opening on the roof that will enable him to descend through it into the house. Mapping this metaphor onto the legal quest of the "contemporary" Babylonian sage yields curious results. The "blind man" is the (contemporary) sage; the finding of the "opening" that leads from the roof into the house is the sage's coincidental stumbling upon a law that turns out to be a law to Moses at Sinai. But what exactly is the contemporary analogy to the blind man's groping about on the roof for the opening? The logical answer is that the blind man's groping is the sage's groping about in metaphorical darkness to find a law to Moses at Sinai. But how often will a Babylonian sage do that? We cannot know the answer for certain, but that activity does not seem characteristic of Babylonian amoraic activity. Putting together paragraphs 8 and 9, then, we see that the oversight role in the rabbinic legal process the Bavli is willing to grant to the Divine is very limited: it applies only to a sage's saying a law that turns out to be a law to Moses at Sinai (Rav Ashi; paragraph 8), and even that convergence is provisionally described as utterly coincidental (paragraph 9). But another Bavli voice objects in paragraph 10 that a sage's independent statement of law that turns out to be a law to Moses at Sinai is *not* the result of blind chance; the fact that a sage gives reasons for his views suggests that his reasoning was somehow Divinely guided. Paragraph 10 rejects paragraph 9's metaphor of the blind man groping on the roof while upholding Rav Ashi's view in paragraph 8 that Divine guidance is made manifest through a sage's providing argumentation for his statement of a law that turns out to be a law to Moses at Sinai. But again: does this happen often? Will Divine guidance of the Babylonian rabbinic legal process therefore be manifested very often?

The answer is "no," or at the very least, "probably not that often." Availing ourselves of Christine Hayes's list of twenty-six Bavli *sugyot* that employ the phrase *"halakhah le-moshe mi-Sinai"* ("a law to Moses at Sinai"), we find that in all cases the alleged "law to Moses at Sinai" is straightforwardly presented as such.[42] In none of these cases does one sage state a law only to be told (or to have the Bavli declare or otherwise affirm) that the stated law is actually a law to Moses at Sinai. Indeed, the Bavli and Mishnah provide (only) two documented historical contexts in which (in Rav Ashi's terms) a "great man" said something that turned out to be a law to Moses at Sinai. The first is (again) Othniel ben Qenaz's (or Jabez's) use of his dialectical skill to restore laws forgotten during the period of mourning for Moses (b.Temurah 16a; b. Yoma 80a). The second is m.Yadayim 4:3, in which R. Yose ben Dormasqit reports to R. Eliezer that "they voted" that poor man's tithe must be given during the Sabbatical year from produce grown in the lands of Ammon and Moab.[43] Upon hearing about this vote, R. Eliezer bursts into tears and assures R. Yose ben Dormasqit that the latter need not be concerned that this decision might be in error. Quoting Psalms 25:14 (*The counsel of the Lord is for those who fear Him; to them He makes known His covenant*), R. Eliezer avers that this law is actually a law to Moses at Sinai. The verse's *He makes known His covenant to those who fear Him* makes the point that God oversees and ensures the accuracy of legal tradition for those who fear him. We see, then, that while Rav Ashi allows for some Divine oversight of the legal process—a type of oversight that the Bavli supports (paragraph 10)—this oversight is actually very limited. The unknowing convergence of a sage's statement of the law with "a law to Moses at Sinai" only happened twice in rabbinic history: once during the period of Israelite settlement in the Land of Israel after Moses's death, and later during the tannaitic period. While Rav Ashi seems to indicate that this sort of convergence can happen again, the "historical record" indicates that this possibility is quite slim indeed.[44]

Moreover, b.Bava Batra 12b undermines even this slim possibility immediately following paragraph 10. R. Yohanan states that after the destruction of the Temple, prophecy was taken from the prophets and given over to "fools and children." The contrast between how the Bavli presents R. Yohanan's and Rav Ashi's traditions is telling. The Bavli portrays Rav Ashi as acknowledging the (limited) possibility of Divine oversight of the Babylonian rabbinic legal enter-

---

42 As Hayes points out, there are actually twenty-seven *sugyot*, one of which has a parallel in another tractate. See Hayes, "*Halakhah le-Moshe mi-Sinai* in Rabbinic Sources," 77 n. 29.

43 On this passage, see Hayes, "*Halakhah le-Moshe mi-Sinai* in Rabbinic Sources," 69–70.

44 Mention should also be made of Moses's visit to R. Aqiva's study house on b.Menahot 29b. There, Moses is lost and confused by the learned discourse of R. Aqiva, and only relaxes when a student asks the sage the source for something he said and the response is: "It is a law to Moses at Sinai." In this case R. Aqiva is already quite well aware that what he is saying is a law to Moses at Sinai; this is not a case in which either he or one of his students stated a law that turned out—unbeknownst to them—to be such. This is therefore not another "historical example" illustrating Rav Ashi's model of Divine oversight in action.

prise, but the Bavli does not illustrate how Rav Ashi's tradition was ever made manifest. The Bavli reader must find and supply the illustrations herself; these illustrations are the two documented cases described above of a "great man" saying something that turns out to be a law to Moses at Sinai in (pre-Babylonian amoraic) rabbinic history. The Bavli's tacit leaving to the reader the effort to locate these two cases graphically illustrates the Bavli's overall point: these cases are few, far between, and (consequently) statistically extremely unlikely to recur. But the Bavli does takes pains to colorfully illustrate R. Yohanan's tradition with two stories, the first showing how prophecy is the province of "fools," and the second, of "children." The first story is about Mar bar Rav Ashi's (Rav Ashi's own son!) heeding the words of a fool who uttered a prophecy that Mar bar Rav Ashi interpreted to mean that he would be the next head of the Mata Mehasya academy. The second story is the prophecy of Rav Hisda's very young daughter about her future marriage first to Rami bar Hama and then Rava. While Rav Ashi's model of Divine oversight is very limited in scope and scarcely attested in rabbinic history, the Bavli's stories show that R. Yohanan's is a more accurate assessment of Babylonian amoraic reality in the here and now, a reality in which prophecy is indeed made manifest in the daily lives of sages—but only through the mouths of fools and children, *not* other sages.[45]

B.Bava Batra 12a–b thus leaves us with the idea that while Divine oversight of the rabbinic legal enterprise is indeed possible, the likelihood of such oversight is low, and, in any case, such Divine oversight will only be made manifest in one type of case: a case in which a sage is searching for a law that will turn

---

45   Another, related topic that requires more attention than can be provided here is the Bavli's threefold repetition of some variant of the phrase "these are only words of prophethood" ("*ein elu ela divrei nevi'ut*"). This statement is attributed to R. Yose (b.Bava Batra 12a), R. Idi (b.Eruvin 60b), and R. Yohanan (b.Bekhorot 45a; in the form "they made their words like words of prophethood," "*asu divreihem k'divrei nevi'ut*"). As to the first three sources, Tosafot incline to the view that the description of a legal view as "words of prophethood" is meant to be negative; see Tosafot to b.Bava Batra 12a, s.v. *amar R. Yose*; Tosafot to b.Bekhorot 45a, s.v. "*asu*." Tosafot to b.Eruvin 60b, s.v. "*ein*" observe that R. Isaac of Dampierre held that the references to "words of prophethood" in Eruvin and Bava Batra were meant to be positive, i.e., the reasoning behind the stated legal view is so sharp that the stated view can only be Divinely inspired. The plain language and context of the Bavli in these three places tilt the scale in favor of the Tosafot (not the Ri of Dampierre); at the very least, the intra-Tosafist dispute demonstrates that these expert readers of the Bavli could not agree that the phrase is meant as a compliment to the rabbinic tradent. Mention should also be made of b.Hullin 124a, on which R. Ami states that even if "Joshua bin Nun" had told him a certain tradition, he would not have accepted it; his point seems to be that the tradition is so unacceptable to him that even undisputed prophetic transmission would not cause him to accept it.

out to be a law to Moses at Sinai. A (contemporary) sage is much more likely to hear prophecy (and hence, get Divine guidance) from fools and children. B.Bava Batra 12a–b is thus not a significant challenge to the inter-Talmudic difference to which this essay has repeatedly pointed: the Yerushalmi's portrayal of a robust Divine oversight role and the Bavli's tendency to place limits on the Divine while emphasizing human agency. Rather, b.Bava Batra 12a–b is another illustration of how the Bavli works to limit the Divine role in the rabbinic enterprise, even while appearing to acknowledge it.

Richard Hidary's observations about the external historical context for the Yerushalmi's tendency toward "monism" and the Bavli's greater tendency toward "pluralism" illuminate this essay's findings.[46] The Yerushalmi's portrayal of the role of the hidden Divine hand in ensuring later sages' inadvertent restoration of lost law echoes Hidary's limning of a "monistic" Yerushalmi.[47] If the one, right way to fulfill the mandate of a particular law is lost because the law has been forgotten—and if even the forgetting has been forgotten—then only the Divine can intervene to ensure the restoration of the lost law. A resort to the Divine indicates a preference for monism, as only the Divine can ensure the restoration of Divine truth about what the law should be. Hidary links the Yerushalmi's monistic tendency to ambient historical factors, notably the late Roman turn to legal codification and the Christian drive for theological orthodoxy.[48] Additionally, I suggest that late antique Christianity may also have catalyzed the *Erets* Israel rabbinic preference for a robust Divine role in another way: Christian theological claims and a growing Christian material and architectural presence in the late antique Land of Israel may have exerted pressure on the rabbis to stress that the rabbinic way of Torah was indeed a Divinely approved path under God's watchful eye.

The Bavli's limitations on the Divine and emphasis on human agency and initiative, in turn, are consistent with Hidary's findings about the Bavli's greater tendency than the Yerushalmi toward pluralism.[49] Hidary suggests that the Bavli's pluralism may be related to the apparent tolerance for differences of opinion among Iranian jurists in the Bavli's ambient Sasanian Zoroastrian con-

---

46 Briefly, Hidary defines "monism" as "the view that there is only one correct way to practice halakha." He points out that there are sub-definitions to monism, which need not concern us here. "Pluralism" is similarly complex; one can accept the validity of other viewpoints for others, but not for one's own group ("particular pluralism") or as acceptable options for one's own group as well ("universal pluralism"). See Hidary, *Dispute for the Sake of Heaven*, 2–5 and *passim*. See also Hidary, "Right Answers Revisited."
47 Hidary, *Dispute for the Sake of Heaven*, 2, 5, 385–393 and *passim*.
48 Hidary, *Dispute for the Sake of Heaven*, 77–80, 373–377 and *passim*.
49 Hidary, *Dispute for the Sake of Heaven*, 14–15, 370–385 and *passim*.

text.[50] I would add that by placing human agency, intellect, and initiative at the center, the Bavli creates the conditions for the emergence of the inevitable differences of opinion that human minds will produce.

An exploration of this inter-Talmudic difference need not end with the Bavli (though this essay must). During the Gaonic period, Pirqoi ben Baboi (early 9th c.) weaponizes the association of *Erets* Israel with forgetting by claiming that the people of *Erets* Israel forgot the Orders *Qodashim* and *Tohorot* entirely (*"nishtakach mehem"*).[51] A post-Bavli pro-Babylonian polemic found in the Warsaw edition of Midrash Tanhuma opens with the promise that God established a covenant with Israel that "the Oral Torah would not be forgotten from them and from the mouths of their children until the end of the generations."[52] Moreover, the two (Babylonian) *yeshivot* are described as immersing themselves uninterruptedly in constant Torah study and engaging "in the give-and-take of the 'war of Torah' until they establish a matter with certainty, and the law according to its truth, and they bring proofs from Scripture, from Mishnah, and from the Talmud, in order that Israel not stumble in words of Torah ...." Midrash Tanhuma's assertion that God covenanted that the Oral Torah would never be forgotten is consistent with the Bavli's refusal to represent the idea that Torah was or might be forgotten *tout court* as a Babylonian idea. Moreover, the passage's stress on the human effort to "establish a matter with certainty and the law according to its truth" through a diligent search of literary sources echoes the Bavli's repeated emphasis on the human efforts of sages to do the same (cf. b.Megillah 7a) as well as to establish the law by dialectical skill (cf. b.Yevamot 32b–33b). This pivotal legal and theological inter-Talmudic difference thus sets the stage for the study of what Abraham Joshua Heschel would later term "prophetic inspiration after the prophets."[53]

Bibliography

Balberg, Mira. "Unforgettable Forgotten Things: Transformations in the Laws of Forgotten Produce (*shikhehah*) in Early Rabbinic Literature." *Oqimta* 5 (2019) 1–33.

Dor, Zvi Moshe. *Torat Eretz Israel be-Bavel*. Tel Aviv: Devir, 1971.

Elman, Yaakov. "Righteousness As Its Own Reward: An Inquiry into the Theologies of the Stam." *Proceedings of the American Academy for Jewish Research* 57 (1990/1991) 35–67.

---

50 Hidary, *Dispute for the Sake of Heaven*, 374–375.
51 Letter of Pirqoi ben Baboi in Ginzberg, *Genizah Studies*, 559–560.
52 *Midrash Tanhuma* Noah 3 (ed. Warsaw).
53 See Heschel, *Prophetic Inspiration after the Prophets*.

Friedman, Shamma. "Ha-baraitot she-be-Talmud ha-Bavli ve-yahasan le-Tosefta." In *Atara L'Haim: Studies in the Talmud and Medieval Rabbinic Literature in Honor of Professor Haim Zalman Dimitrovsky*, edited by Daniel Boyarin, Marc Hirshman, Shamma Friedman, Menahem Schmelzer, and Israel M. Tashma, 103–201. Jerusalem: Magnes Press, 2000.

Ginzberg, Louis, ed. *Genizah Studies in Memory of Doctor Solomon Schechter, II: Geonic and Early Karaitic Halakah*. New York: The Jewish Theological Seminary of America, 1929.

Gray, Alyssa M. *A Talmud in Exile: The Influence of Yerushalmi Avodah Zarah on the Formation of Bavli Avodah Zarah*. Providence: Brown Judaic Studies, 2005.

Gray, Alyssa M. *Charity in Rabbinic Judaism: Atonement, Rewards, and Righteousness*. London and New York: Routledge, 2019.

Hayes, Christine. "*Halakhah le-Moshe mi-Sinai* in Rabbinic Sources: A Methodological Case Study." In *The Synoptic Problem in Rabbinic Literature*, edited by Shaye J.D. Cohen, 61–117. Providence: Brown Judaic Studies, 2000.

Heschel, Abraham. J. *Prophetic Inspiration after the Prophets: Maimonides and Other Medieval Authorities*. Hoboken: Ktav, 1996.

Hidary, Richard. "Right Answers Revisited: Monism and Pluralism in the Talmud." *Diné Israel* 26–27 (2009–2010) 229–255.

Hidary, Richard. *Dispute for the Sake of Heaven: Legal Pluralism in the Talmud*. Providence: Brown Judaic Studies, 2010.

Kalmin, Richard. *Sages, Stories, Authors, and Editors in Rabbinic Babylonia*. Atlanta: Scholars Press, 1994.

Kalmin, Richard. *The Sage in Jewish Society of Late Antiquity*. London and New York: Routledge, 1999.

Kalmin, Richard. *Jewish Babylonia between Persia and Roman Palestine*. New York: Oxford University Press, 2006.

Kolbrener, William. *The Last Rabbi: Joseph Soloveitchik and Talmudic Tradition*. Bloomington and Indianapolis: Indiana University Press, 2016.

Kraemer, David. *The Mind of the Talmud: An Intellectual History of the Bavli*. New York and Oxford: Oxford University Press, 1990.

Midrash Tanhuma. Warsaw, 1875; repr. Jerusalem, 1958.

Schwartz, Marcus Mordecai. "As They Journeyed from the East: The Nahotei of the Fourth Century and the Construction of the Rabbinic Diaspora." *Hebrew Union College Annual* 86 (2015): 63–99.

Schwartz, Marcus Mordecai. *Rewriting the Talmud: The Fourth Century Origins of Bavli Rosh Hashanah*. Tübingen: Mohr Siebeck, 2019.

Talmud Yerushalmi according to Ms. Or. 4720 (Scal. 3) of the Leiden University Library with Restorations and Corrections, introduction by Yaacov Sussmann. Jerusalem: The Academy of the Hebrew Language, 2001.

CHAPTER 10

The Use of Literary Considerations as a Key for Assessing the Reliability of Memrot in the Babylonian Talmud: The Case of the *Lo Shanu Ela* Traditions

Barak Cohen

Introduction

Modern scholars of talmudic history agree that a halakhic statement attributed to an amoraic sage in the Babylonian Talmud does not necessarily reflect the precise words uttered by him. Throughout the stages of their transmission and preservation, statements were frequently rephrased and formulated through the use of fixed linguistic structures. Many were removed from their original contexts and placed into others. At other times interpretations and expansions were added to the earlier core.[1] Original formulations were shed, and new ones were introduced, at times leaving the latter version entirely unidentifiable with the original. In some cases, statements ascribed to a particular amora ("R. X said") were not even uttered in any form by this sage, but rather originated in deductions from another of this same sage's statements, his general legal principles, or in concrete rulings he issued in cases brought before him.[2] Similar literary phenomena occur with statements ascribed to Palestinian sages in the Bavli. The Bavli transmits these statements that originated in Palestine as they were understood in Babylonia, or as the editors of the Bavli thought they should

---

1 The literature on this issue is vast, and this is not the place for a full bibliographical reference. For outstanding examples see the following works and the bibliographical references contained therein: Weiss, *The Talmud*, 64 [Hebrew]; Feldblum, *Talmudic Law and Literature*, 23–27 [Hebrew]; Kalmin, "Rabbinic Literature," 187; Schremer, "Stammaitic Historiography," 220; Halivni, *Introduction*, 198–203 [Hebrew]; Friedman, *Talmudic Studies*, 28, 42–43 [Hebrew]. See below (n. 70) for more radical claims that doubt whether any historical information whatsoever can be gleaned from amoraic statements and instead view the Bavli, or at least large portions thereof, as a pseudepigraphic creation.
2 See mainly, Weiss, *The Talmud*, p. 131; Albeck, *Introduction*, 452–459 [Hebrew]; Sacha Stern, "Attribution and Authorship," 45 (1995) 28–51.

be understood.³ These phenomena include patterns of language and dialectics that characterize the Bavli, partial phrasing of the statement in Aramaic, and changes in the content of the statement that reflect the *halakhah* as it developed in Babylonia during the amoraic period.⁴

These literary phenomena led scholars to doubt the historical authenticity of amoraic statements in the Bavli.⁵ In their opinion, such editorial trends prevent us from being able to draw reliable historical information from the Bavli. Not only are we unable to determine what the amoraim originally said, we also cannot date talmudic information based on the sages to whom these statements are ascribed. In light of the creative freedom of the late editors of the Bavli, everything should be dated to the time of these editors, and viewed as reflective of their world and culture, and not that of the earlier amoraim to whom the statements are ascribed.

However, such an extreme and comprehensive view of this thorny and complex phenomenon encounters one significant problem. It is based on general literary phenomena widespread throughout the ancient world, or on sporadic passages or phenomena from which a general assessment of all amoraic statements in the Bavli was drawn. As of yet, however, there has been no comprehensive and systematic analysis of the broad corpuses of amoraic statements in the Bavli through which the validity of these claims could be verified.⁶

This study examines the question of the historical authenticity of the corpus of Babylonian amoraic statements that use the term "they taught [this] only" (לא שנו אלא). There are parallels in the Yerushalmi for about 50 of the

---

3   Rosenthal, "Mekorot Eretz Yisraelim," 8.
4   The literature on this subject is vast. The following are a few notable examples: De-Vries, *Studies*, 187, 235–236, 258; Henshke, *The Original Mishna*, 222, 227, 267–268, 365 [Hebrew]; Hayes, *Between the Babylonian and Palestinian Talmuds*, 15; Kahana, "Shalosh Maḥlokot," 302–333; Hyman, "From Tiberias to Mehoza," 117–148; Steinfeld, *A People Alone*, 77–78 [Hebrew]; Friedman, *Talmudic Studies*, 40–44, 450–451; Sabato, *Talmud Bavli*, 560, 708–709, 711 [Hebrew].
5   This basic critique can already be found in the writing of nineteenth century scholars. An outstanding example is the critique of Wilhelm Bacher's work (The Aggadot of the Palestinian and Bablyonian amoraim), mainly by critical editors of rabbinic works. See for example, Theodor, "W. Bacher, Die Agada der Babylonischen Amoräer," 43–47, 84–87; Brill, "Die Agada der babylonischen Amoräer," 163–164; Ś. Horovitz, "Bacher, Prof. Dr. Wilhem.," 134. Talmudic and historical research has developed tremendously since this period, and this is reflected in the nature of the claims made by scholars related to this issue. See the references below in footnote 70.
6   See, Levine, "Talmudic Biography," 51 who wrote:
    החוקרים הספקניים ביותר חייבים להודות שהם מניחים הנחות היסטוריות וביוגרפיות על ספרות חז"ל ועל האנשים שיצרו אותה, לכן טוב יעשו אם יהיו מודעים להנחות שהם מניחים—אף במובלע שלא במודע—וייתנו דין וחשבון על הנחות אלו
    This problem characterizes all of the studies cited below, n. 70.

300 statements in which this term is used in the Bavli, which likewise contain attributions to the same sages who all belong to the first three generations of amoraim.[7] These fifty parallels are the focus of this study, with the goal of evaluating the content of these interpretive statements in the Bavli and comparing them with their parallels in the Yerushalmi, in order to determine the nature of their origin.[8] The choice of this corpus of interpretive statements as a test case is a result of the centrality of this term in earlier research into amoraic literature and the development of *halakhah* and Jewish civil law in talmudic Babylonia.[9]

In this article I will claim that despite the fact that many "*lo shanu ela*" statements underwent obvious Babylonian emendations, they still maintain the "original" halakhic content that can be found in the Yerushalmi. In light of these findings I argue that scholars ought to separate the language and style of the amoraic statements in the Bavli, which may well have undergone late emendations, from their halakhic content which remains faithful to the original statements transmitted by the amora to whom they are ascribed. This finding indicates that we should refrain from broadly denying the historical reliability of all amoraic statements in the Bavli based on formal-literary criteria, such as those described above.[10] My claim is that an amoraic statement found in the Bavli, even if it originated in Palestine and exhibits signs of late emendation, should not be presumed to be a late creation. The issue is far more complex than a simple determination that a statement is "reliable" or "unreliable," certainly without a systematic analysis of each statement on its own terms.

---

[7] Meaning, in this study I have examined only those instances of "*lo shanu ela*" which are attributed to the same sages in both Talmuds; these total fifty.

[8] On the use of the Yerushalmi to evaluate the source of statements in the Babylonian Talmud (Palestinian or Babylonian) see text near n. 20.

[9] These trends began already in the "general rules" literature ("כללי התלמוד") composed in the medieval period. For a summary of these methods see, Malakhi Ha-Cohen, *Sefer Yad Malakhi*, 329–330; Medini, *Sde Ḥemed*, vol. 2, 702–704. For some of the scholarly research on this subject see the literature cited below, nn. 20, 22 and throughout this entire article. See also: Zuri, *Toldot Hamishpat*, 170; Silberg, *The Writings of Moshe Silberg*, 19–22 [Hebrew]; Albeck, *The Law of Property and Contract*, 33–36 [Hebrew]; ibid, *Introduction*, 33–34 [Hebrew].

[10] For a demonstration of this claim with regard to "amoraic baraitot" in the Bavli, see, Cohen, *The Quest*, 1–27.

From Legal Rhetoric to Interpretive Rhetoric

The term, "they taught [this] only" (לא שנו אלא) (below, "*lo shanu ela*") appears over 300 times in the Bavli[11] and is used to limit the scope of a tannaitic or early amoraic statement.[12] This contextualization is presented in a fixed literary form containing two parts, both in Hebrew: "R. Peloni said: they taught [this] only in [case X] but in [case Y] (the rule is different)." The first part of the statement limits the *halakhah* to a particular case or condition, and the second part negates its applicability in other cases. The contextualizing interpretation is performed in one of the two following ways: (1) By limiting the *halakhah* taught in the original tannaitic or amoraic source to a particular case or condition not mentioned in the original source. (2) By limiting the source's rule to the case mentioned explicitly therein (by citing a few words or a sentence from the source), and then negating its applicability in other cases or conditions.[13] In contrast with other interpretive formulae in the Bavli, *lo shanu ela* statements follow directly after tannaitic sources (and at times were even taught together with them[14]) and are not presented as the resolution to a difficulty.[15] Moreover, *Lo shanu ela* statements are always attributed to named sages,[16] whose dating spans from the end of the tannaitic period (Rabbi, R. Yishmael b. R. Yose, Bar Qappara and others[17]) through the seventh generation of Babylonian amoraim

---

11   See, Kosowsky, *Otzar Leshon Hatalmud*, vol. 1, 131–140. The term appears about fifty times in the Yerushalmi (Assis, *A Concordance*, vol. 2, 835–836 [Hebrew]) some of which have full parallels in the Bavli. See below in the appendix.

12   For cases in which the formula is used in reference to amoraic statements see, Medini, *Sde Ḥemed*, vol. 2, 704; Epstein, *Introduction*, vol. 2, 810 [Hebrew]; De-Vries, *Studies*, 130 [Hebrew]; Breuer, "On the Hebrew Dialect," 145 n. 36 [Hebrew]. Cf. Efrati and Itzhaki, *Masekhet Yom Tov*, 123 n. 3 [Hebrew].

13   For a similar use of the term in the Yerushalmi, see Moscovitz, *Terminology*, 338–339 [Hebrew].

14   See, Bacher, *Tradition und Tradenten*, 263 n. 8; Albeck, *Meḥkarim*, 25 n. 2, 33–35; ibid, *Introduction*, 35 [Hebrew]; Efrati and Itzaḥki, *Masekhet Yom Tov*, 123 n. 3; Halivni, *Introduction*, 99.

15   This distinction is crucial for understanding the goal and nature of contextualizations in the Bavli. See, Kelman, "The Amoraic Oqimta," 272–274 [Hebrew].

16   See, Albeck, "Sof Ha-Hora'a," 75; Efrati and Itzḥki, *Masekhet Yom Tov*, 123 n. 3; Halivni, *Introduction*, 99; Kelman, "The Amoraic Oqimta," 251–252. Compare this formula with the "what are we dealing with here (הכא במאי עסיקינן)" formula used commonly by late Babylonian amoraim and also in anonymous, "stammaitic," passages (Kelman, ibid, 251–252).

17   Epstein, *Introduction*, vol. 2, 810 and De-Vries, *Studies*, 130 used this as evidence that the term was already in widespread use by the late tannaitic period. However, these terms appear in Babylonian *baraitot* and not in the tannaitic compositions themselves. It is possible that the term was inserted into these sources under the influence of the terminology

(Rafram, R. Ḥaviva, Mar b. R. Ashi[18]). The term is most common among the first four generations of amoraim (hundreds of cases) and is less frequently used by fourth- through seventh-generation Babylonian amoraim (only fifteen cases[19]). *Lo shanu ela* contextualizations exhibit a strong tendency to be based on reason as a source of interpretation, and not on tannaitic or early amoraic tradition.[20]

Analysis of Sugyot

The Yerushalmi is a crucial source for understanding the teachings of the amoraim, both Palestinian and Babylonian, and how they were later modified and adapted into the Babylonian discursive *sugya*. In his foundational article on the comparison between the Yerushalmi and the Bavli Jacob Sussman writes:

> It turns out that more than [the Yerushalmi] teaches us about its own traditions, it provides information for us about the state of the Babylonian traditions, for it provides a perspective offered at some distance… In truth, without the Yerushalmi, we would frequently lack an Archimedean point through which to view the original teachings of the amoraim, which have been obscured by the complicated Babylonian discursive passages.[21]

Sussman's broad assessment is supported by the existence of literary phenomena in parallels in the Bavli that reveal the typical processes of reworking, rephrasing, and elaboration that these statements underwent. These phenomena include: patterns of language and dialectics that characterize the Bavli, partial phrasing of the statement in Aramaic, and changes in the content of

---

used in the amoraic period, as Bokser correctly notes. See: Bokser, *Shmuel's Commentary*, 43 n. 107.

18 See below n. 18. For a discussion of these passages see, Kalmin, *Redaction*, 17, 169 n. 6.

19 Below is the full list: b.Shabbat 54a (R. Ashi); b.Eruvin 50b (R. Huna. b. R. Joshua); b.Pesaḥim 81b (Mar b. R. Ashi); b.Mo'ed Qatan 27b–28a ("The Nehardeans say"); b.Ketubbot 70a (Rafram); b.Gittin 30a (R. Papa); b.Bava Qamma 105a (R. Papa); b.Bava Batra 46a (R. Papa); b.Bava Batra 86a ("The Pumbedithans say"); b.Bava Batra 143b (R. Ḥaviva); b.Sanhedrin 42a = b.Pesaḥim 12b (R. Shimi b. Ashi); b. Avodah Zarah 60b (R. Papa); b.Menaḥot 33b (R. Aḥa b. D'Rava); b. Ḥullin 55a = ibid 42b (R. Avira); b.Bekhorot (R. Papa).

20 See mainly, Flursheim, "Rav Ḥisda," 33–35 [Hebrew]; Gordis, "Rav and Samuel," 334 [Hebrew]; De-Vries, *Studies*, 130–131; Albeck, *The Law of Property and Contract*, 32–34.

21 Jacob Sussman, "Veshuv Lirushalmi Nezikin," *Meḥqerei Talmud* 1 (1990): 114 and n. 213. See also, Schremer, "Stammaitic historiography," 222 n. 16.

the statement that reflect the *halakhah* as it developed in Babylonia during the amoraic period.[22] These same transformations occurred in a substantial number of *lo shanu ela* units, as I will demonstrate. Halakhic rulings phrased in the Yerushalmi in an apodictic manner and attributed mainly to Palestinian amoraim of the first generations, appear in parallels in the Bavli as interpretive units utilizing the *lo shanu ela* formula. The rulings in the Yerushalmi offer decisions in halakhic topics related to, and at times in disagreement with, a tannaitic source. In such cases, the Bavli harmonizes the amoraic ruling with the tannaitic sources. This accord is created through use of the term *lo shanu ela* which links the two sources: the *halakhah* taught in the tannaitic source is limited to case X, but the law is different in case Y, in which the amoraic sage ruled. This phenomenon seems to be part of the general trend in the Bavli to harmonize disparate tannaitic sources with each other or with conflicting amoraic teachings.[23]

The secondary editing of these statements in the Bavli, in comparison with the primary form in which they appear in the Yerushalmi, is recognizable through clear signs that reveal the hand of the Bavli's editors. These include the developed literary units that appear in the Bavli in comparison with the short apodictic statements in the parallel Yerushalmi;[24] Aramaic phrases included in the Bavli's version of the amoraic statement itself as opposed to the Hebrew used in the short statement in the Yerushalmi; the lack of correlation between the deduction made in the Bavli's contextualization and the tannaitic statement upon which it is based; and the general phrasing in the Bavli which at times makes it difficult to determine which source it is referring to.[25]

---

[22] See the literature cited above, in n. 4. Similarly, the Yerushalmi is an important tool for dating the anonymous portions of the Bavli to the amoraic period. See: Kretzmer-Raziel, "The Stam," 59–109 [Hebrew]; ibid, "Talmudic 'Stam'," 611–661 [Hebrew].

[23] For several notable examples see, Frankel, *Darkhei Hamishnah*, 336; Hoffmann, *Mar Samuel*, 31 n. 1; ibid, *Hamishna Harishona*, 4–5; Rappaport, *Erekh Milin*, vol. 1, 208; Weiss, *Dor Dor Vedorshav*, vol. 3, 4, 5–6; Halevi, "Matter of Fact Pshitta Arguments," 129–140 [Hebrew]; Cohen, "Hitpalgut," 107–129 and n. 114; Halivni, *Introduction*, 155; Rosenthal, "The Transformation," 36–44 [Hebrew]; Goldberg, *Literary Form and Composition*, 4, 149–150 and n. 18 [Hebrew].

[24] I use the word "apodictic" to refer to short, summarizing phrases, which include the rule but lack any explanation. See: Halivni, "Apodictic," 302, n. 3; Kalmin, "The Post—Rav Ashi Amoraim," 169; Halivni, *Introduction*, 95.

[25] These findings diminish the possibility that the origin of these variants lies in a source earlier than the "proto-talmud" from which both talmudim drew. For a negation of this possibility see, Gray, *A Talmud in Exile*, 18–19; Friedman, *Talmudic Studies*, 94–95 n. 119. This is also true with regard to parallels between Palestinian compositions, both tannaitic and amoraic. See for instance, Milikowsky, "On Parallels and Primacy," 221 n. 3 [Hebrew]; Atzmon, "Haggadah Dimegillat Esther," 280 [Hebrew].

The phenomena to which I refer, to be discussed in depth below, appear in about twenty of the instances in which there is a parallel between a *lo shanu ela* statement issued by an amora of one of the first three generations of Babylonian amoraim and a source in the Yerushalmi (over thirty per cent of the overall number of cases). These traditions are the focus of this study and will aid in determining the nature of the changes that occurred in this corpus of amoraic statements, and to what extent they preserve the original "kernel" as it was ascribed to that particular amora. In the other cases, the statements are attributed to the same amora in both talmudim as interpretations to tannaitic sources, but with differences in phrasing and literary style, which is typical in parallels between the two talmuds.[26] The parallel terms in the Yerushalmi are: "they taught [this] only" ... (לא שנו אלא), "the tannaitic Statement refers to X ... but in Y ..." (מתניתא ב ... אבל ...), "That which you say pertains only to ... but in ...," (הדא דאת אמר ב .... אבל ב), "We are dealing with X [in the tannaitic teaching] ... but in ..." (אנן קיימין ... ב .... אבל), and others.[27] I will demonstrate these phenomena by citing several representative examples.

B.Shabbat 113a

Mishnah (Shabbat 15:3): One may fold clothing, even four or five times.

Gemara: Those of the Academy of R. Yannai[28] said: 'They taught [this] only about one person, but for two people [to do so] is forbidden'. And for one person it was also only said about new clothing, but with old clothing it is forbidden.[29] And with new clothing it was only said about white clothing, but with colored clothing it is forbidden. And it was only said in a case where he has no change of clothing, but if he has a change of cloth-

---

I should also emphasize that the opposite phenomenon has not been located—a short halakhic ruling in the Bavli which appears in the Yerushalmi in the form of a *lo shanu ela* statement (see in the appendix). Moreover, the phenomenon is not found in the roughly fifty *lo shanu ela* statements in the Yerushalmi when compared with their parallels in the Bavli (based on the list compiled by Assis, above, n. 10). These facts reveal a unified trend in terms of the development of these statements, from their earlier form in the Yerushalmi to their later form in the Bavli and not in the reverse direction.

26 Concerning these phenomena, see: Friedman, *Talmudic Studies*, pp. 42–44, and the literature cited there in n. 41.
27 For a detailed list of these parallels see the appendix.
28 Ms. Cambridge T-S F2 (1) 162 reads, "R. Yannai said."
29 This sentence is missing in Ms. Cambridge T-S F2 (1) 162 and Munich 95.

ing it is forbidden. It was taught: Those of the house of Rabban Gamaliel would not fold their white clothing for they had a change of clothing.[30]

The term "Those of the Academy of R. Yannai" in the Bavli refers to a group of sages identified with the amora R. Yannai, founder of an academy in Akhbara and a member of the first generation of Palestinian amoraim.[31] This group was active mainly in the Galilee, and is dated from the second through the fourth generations of Palestinian amoraim.[32] The Bavli ascribes to this group an halakhic interpretation that limits the scope of the Mishnah. The Mishnah allows one to "fold"[33] clothing on the Sabbath, even a number of times, while "those of the Academy of R. Yannai" limit the Mishnah's lenient ruling to cases where the clothes are folded by one person alone. In this view, "folding" performed by two people is a more professional activity, deemed sufficiently similar to "fixing" a piece of clothing or removing its wrinkles,[34] such that it is prohibited on the Sabbath. The series of contextualizations that appears immediately after the amoraic statement and is introduced with the term "it was said only in ..." (placed in a smaller font) is not part of the statement of "those of the Academy of R. Yannai;" it seems to have originated in the post-amoraic period.[35]

Comparison of the statement with its parallel in y.Shabbat 15:3 (15a) highlights the differences in both language and style:

Mishnah: One may fold clothing, even four or five times.

Gemara: Those of the Academy of R. Yannai say: "Folding performed by two is forbidden." R. Ḥaggai [says] in the name of R. Shmuel b. Naḥman: "Two may not fold on the Sabbath, and one who folds on a bench, it is as if he is two."

---

30 The baraita appears in t.Shabbat 12:17 (ed. Lieberman, p. 56).
31 See mainly, Oppenheimer, "'Those of the School of Rabbi Yannai,'" 137–138, 142 [Hebrew]; Miller, *Sages and Commoners*, 349–350; Rosenfeld, *Torah Centers*, 150. For a comparison of this image and their literary contribution in the Yerushalmi see, Miller, *Sages and Commoners*, 250–393.
32 See above, n. 30.
33 Concerning the meaning of the root קפ״ל in the *pi'el* conjugation in tannaitic literature see: Kohut, ed., *Arukh Hashalem*, vol. 7, 162; Krauss, *Talmudische Archäologie*, vol. 1, 523–524 n. 281; Ben-Yehuda, *Milon Halashon Ha-Ivrit Hayeshana Ve-Haḥadasha*, vol. 12 6068; Levy, *Wörterbuch*, vol. 4, 354; Goldberg, *Commentary to the Mishna Shabbat*, 281 [Hebrew].
34 See Metzger, ed., *Perushe'i Rabbenu Ḥanan'el*, 225, s.v. *bishnei*. The same interpretation is found in the parallel in the Yerushalmi, see below.
35 See Stollman, *BT Eruvin Chapter X*, 306 n. 27 [Hebrew].

The statements issued by "those of the Academy of R. Yannai," and R. Shmuel b. Nahman (third generation[36]) are identical in content, and are both phrased as independent halakhic statements, "folding performed by two, is forbidden" and "two may not fold on the Sabbath." Both appear in close proximity to the mishnah and prohibit folding on the Sabbath when the act is performed by two people. In addition, R. Shmuel b. Nahman prohibits using a bench to fold, out of fear of stretching and straightening the article of clothing, an act similar to ironing.[37] Ze'ev Safrai noted the differences between the statements of "those of the Academy of R. Yannai" found in the Yerushalmi and Bavli and posited that the Babylonian version is an expansion of the original Yerushalmi one.[38] According to Safrai, the Bavli received "the Academy of R. Yannai's" prohibition of two people folding clothing together on the Sabbath, and phrased it in a Babylonian form regularly used for interpreting the Mishnah, "They taught [this] only about one person, but for two people [to do so] is forbidden." In this way the "Academy of R. Yannai's" ruling was harmonized with the *halakhah* in the Mishnah, which seems to allow folding without any limitations.[39] The reworking of this statement matches the general tendency of the Bavli to harmonize the sources it works with, as I described above. Importantly, despite the differences in form and language between the two versions, the halakhic core of the "Academy of R. Yannai" statements is identical in both corpuses.

B.Berakhot 16a

R. Ami and R. Asi were once tying a wedding canopy for R. Elazar. He said to them: "In the meantime, I will go and hear something in the study hall, and I will come and tell it to you." He went and found the *tanna* who was reciting in the presence of R. Yoḥanan: "One who recited [the Shema] and erred, and does not know where exactly he erred; if he was in the middle of a paragraph, he must return to the beginning of the paragraph; if he was between one paragraph and another, he must return to the first break between paragraphs. [If one erred] between 'writing' and

---

36   Albeck, *Introduction*, 266–267.
37   See Ratner, *Ahavat Tzion Virushalayim: Mesekhet Shabbat*, 142; Lieberman, *Hayerushalmi Kifshuto*, 190 [Hebrew].
38   Safrai, *Mishnat Eretz Israel: Tractate Shabbat*, vol. 2, 400 [Hebrew].
39   Goldberg, *Commentary to the Mishna Shabbat*, 281 n. 13.

'writing', he must return to the first 'writing.'"⁴⁰ R. Yoḥanan said to him: "They taught this only⁴¹ in a case where one did not yet begin to recite, 'In order to lengthen your days' (Deuteronomy 11:21). However, if he already began to recite, 'In order to lengthen your days', he can assume that he began his routine and continued." [R. Elazar] came and told them what he heard. They said to him: Had we come only to hear this, it would have been sufficient.

The Bavli describes an academic/analytic discussion occurring in the "study hall." R. Elazar witnesses a tanna reciting a baraita in the presence of R. Yoḥanan,⁴² who replies by using a *lo shanu ela* statement to limit its applicability. According to the baraita, one who mistakenly skips a word or verse while reciting the Shema, either in the middle of a paragraph or between paragraphs, or skips from the first appearance of the word "and you shall write" to the word's second appearance (Deuteronomy 6:9; 11:20), must return to the beginning of the previous unit. If in the middle of the paragraph, he must return to the beginning of the paragraph; if in between paragraphs, he must return to the previous paragraph; and if he errs from one appearance of the word "and you shall write," to the other, he must return to its first appearance. R. Yoḥanan limits this baraita to a case where he had not yet begun to say, "in order to lengthen your days." The explanation for this limitation is phrased in Aramaic, and is an integral part of R. Yoḥanan's statement, "They taught this only ... However, if he already began to recite: 'In order to lengthen your days,' he can assume that he began his routine and continued." (אמר ליה ר' יוחנן: לא שנו אלא שלא פתח ב'למען ירבו ימיכם', אבל פתח ב'למען ירבו ימיכם'—סרכיה נקט ואתי).⁴³ Scholars have

---

40   The baraita is found with some variants in t.Berakhot 2:5 (ed. Lieberman, p. 7), and in an abbreviated form in y.Berakhot 2:3 (5a).

41   This is the reading found in the commentary of R. Hananel, Metzger, ed., *Perushe'i Rabbenu Hanan'el Lemasekhet Berakhot*, 28; Friedman, ed., *Halakhot Rabbati*, 1; *Sefer Or Zaru'a Lerabbenu Hagadol Rabbi Itsḥaq Mivina*, 81, vol. 1, 84, s.v. *kara*; Wetheimer and Liss, eds., *Piskei Harid*, Vol. 37–38 [Hebrew]; Goldsmith, ed., *Maḥzor Vitri*, Vol. 1, 22, s.v. *Tannei Tanna*; Hilman, ed., *Perush Harashbats*, 79, s.v. *amar rabbi yoḥanan* and printed editions of BT. However, MSS. Munich 95, Paris 671, Oxford Opp. Add. Fol. 23, Florence, Oxford Heb. e. 74/105–112, and St. Petersburg Yevr. III B 871 read, "It was only stated (לא אמרן אלא)" (Oxford reads אמרו; Florence, אמרנא). *Halakhot Gedolot* vol. 1, ed. Hildesheimer, reads, "והוא דלא אמר."

42   Goodblatt, *Rabbinic Instruction*, 211; Rubenstein, *The Culture of the Babylonian Talmud*, 25–26.

43   Melamed, *Milon Arami-Ivri*, 326. Concerning this usage of the Babylonian Aramaic root סר"ך see, Kohut, ed., *Arukh Hashalem*, vol. 6, 138; Levy, *Wörterbuch*, vol. 3, 593; Sokoloff, *Dictionary*, 832.

long observed that switches from Hebrew to Aramaic within an amoraic statement are often a sign of a late Babylonian interpolation, and in this case, that assumption is bolstered by the parallel in the Yerushalmi.[44] Thus according to this late Babylonian explanation of R. Yohanan's statement, if the reader had already reached the end of the second paragraph and then feared that he may have skipped something, he need not return, for he may assume that he read all of the passages in the proper order.[45]

A parallel statement made by R. Yohanan in y.Berakhot 2:3 (5a) contains nearly identical content but in a different form:

> It was taught: If he erred between writing the first [paragraph] and the second [paragraph], he must go back to writing the first paragraph. If he erred but he does not know where he erred, he should go back as at the outset to the first place that is clear to him. It once happened: R. Hiyya, R. Yasa and R. Ami[46] went to make a canopy for R. Elazar. They heard the voice of R. Yohanan [and they said], "If he makes an innovation, who is going to go hear it from him?" They said: "Let R. Elazar go, for he is very sharp." He went down and came back. He said to them: "Thus R. Yohanan said, 'If he was reading and found himself at 'in order ...' he can assume that he read with proper intent'."

Here, R. Yohanan's statement is phrased as an apodictic *halakhah* related to a baraita, "If he was reading and found himself at 'in order ...' he can assume that he read with proper intent." As with the previous example, here too the halakhic "core" of the statement is identical in both talmudim: one who fears that he may have erred in reading the Shema after he has already reached, "In order to lengthen your days" need not return to the previous paragraph, as was dictated by the baraita. Rather, he can assume that he read with proper intent and recited the verses in their proper order.[47] Z. Frankel noted the difference in style between R. Yohanan's statement in the Bavli and the parallel in the Yerushalmi and suggested that the Bavli "expanded" the original Tiberian state-

---

44 Friedman, *Talmudic Studies*, 22; Rubenstein, "Talmudic Expression," 113 [Hebrew]; Amit, "Yemenite Manuscripts," 49 [Hebrew]. On the use of Babylonian Aramaic in the context of stories of the sages in Babylonia as evidence of Babylonian interpolation see mainly, Herman, "Persian Culture," 125 [Hebrew].

45 See *Beit Habeḥira*, 61; *Ḥidushei Harashba*, 107–108. See also: Ginzberg, *A Commentary*, 345 [Hebrew]. Cf. Rashi, s.v. *sarkhe nakat*.

46 R. Ami's name is missing in the geniza fragment T-S F 17.6. Ms. London and Paris 1389 do not read R. Ḥiyya.

47 Ginzberg, *A Commentary*, vol. 1, 345.

ment of R. Yohanan.⁴⁸ This claim seems correct. Evidence for the secondary editing of R. Yohanan's statement can be found in the Aramaic words inserted into the statement, and in the academic setting into which the statement was embedded in the Babylonian version. It is possible that the Babylonian editor wished to harmonize the sources, and therefore phrased the statement as an interpretation to the Mishnah through use of the term, "*lo shanu ela.*" The change in external form did not, however, impact the statement's content, which remains stable in both sources.

B. Nazir 7b

Mishnah: Behold I will be a nazirite for thirty days and one hour,⁴⁹ he is a nazirite for thirty-one days, for one does not become a nazirite for hours.

Gemara: Rav said: They taught [this] only when he said thirty-one days, but he if said thirty days and one day,⁵⁰ he must serve two [terms of naziriteship].

Rav holds like R. Aqiva, who derives meaning from extra words, as it was taught: Nor [has he sold] the cistern or the cellar, even though he had written in the deed of sale, "the depth and height." And he [the seller] must buy himself a path [from the new owner to reach the cellar or cistern], according to Rabbi Aqiva. But the Sages say: "He need not buy himself a path" [m.Bava Batra 4:2]. And R. Aqiva agrees when he says "besides these," that he need not purchase a path.

According to tannaitic *halakhah*, the term of a naziriteship is measured in full days and not hours,⁵¹ and thus one who vows to be a nazirite for thirty days and one hour must serve a naziriteship of thirty-one days.⁵² Rav limits the mishnah's rule through a deduction, "He is a nazirite for only thirty-one days, but if

---

48 Frankel, *Mavo HaYerushalmi*, 43b.
49 According to the original reading of the mishnah. See: Epstein, *Introduction*, vol. 2, 1107–1108.
50 The statement cited here is based on the reading of the geonim (*Otzar Hageonim: Tractates Nedarim* ed. Levine, vol. 11, 162), Ms. Munich 95, Moscow-Ginzburg 1134 and the printed editions. Vatican 110 reads, "when he said thirty [days] and one hour, but if he said thirty and one day."
51 See Sifre Numbers, Naso, 6 (ed. Kahana, p. 57) and Epstein, *Introduction*, vol. 2, 1107.
52 See, Albeck, *Shisha Sidrei Mishnah*, vol. 3, 196.

he said 'thirty days and one day,' he has made two nazirite vows, for he uttered an extraneous word by saying 'day' twice."[53] The extra "day" in the nazirite's vow is interpreted by Rav as an additional term of naziriteship of thirty days (the minimum number of days for a term of naziriteship).[54] However, Rav's deduction from the mishnah is not simple, and medieval commentators struggled to understand it: "The phrase 'thirty-one days' is not taught in the mishnah. Rather, it teaches 'thirty [days][55] and one hour.'"[56] How then could Rav deduce that the law in the mishnah applies only to one who vows "thirty one days" when the mishnah itself states, "thirty days and one hour"? The Tosafot explain that he made a "deduction from a deduction,"—meaning, the deduction is based on an earlier deduction made from the last clause of the mishnah: "Behold I am a nazirite for thirty days and one hour, **he is a nazir for thirty-one days**." However, this suggested interpretation (and others like it[57]) would mean that the term *"lo shanu ela"* is used in an unusual way in terms of making a deduction from a tannaitic source.

The difficulty in interpreting Rav's statement lies in the fact that the Bavli contains a secondary reading of his statement, as can be shown from the parallel in y.Nazir 1:3 (53a) [= Epstein, *Introduction*, vol. 2, 1107]

> Rav said: [If he said], "Behold I am a nazirite for thirty days and one day," he has made two nazirite vows, for he could have said, "thirty-one days."

David Gordis noted that Rav's statement in the Yerushalmi is phrased as an apodictic halakhic ruling, and not as an interpretation of the mishnah. In his opinion, "It seems that this framework [i.e. *'lo shanu ela'* in the Bavli] is a later addition by the editor, and that originally Rav stated an independent *halakhah* as is found in the Yerushalmi."[58] The statement in the Yerushalmi contrasts the rule for one who vows to be a nazirite for "thirty-one days" (who intends to make one nazirite vow) with one who vows "thirty days and one day" (who intends to make two nazirite vows). According to this opinion, had he intended to make only one vow of naziriteship of thirty-one days he should have said "thirty one days." Instead, he added an extra word and said, "Thirty **days and**

---

53 Tosafot, s.v. *lo shanu ela*. See also R. Asher's interpretation as cited in the *Shitah Mequbetset*, Nazir, s.v. *lo shanu*.
54 See Shemesh, *Punishments and Sins*, 34–38 [Hebrew].
55 The word in brackets is based on the mishnah. See Epstein, *Introduction*, vol. 2, 1107.
56 Tosafot, s.v. *lo shanu ela*.
57 See above, n. 52.
58 Gordis, "The Exegesis," 83.

one day," which means that according to Rav his intention was to vow a double term of naziriteship. The Babylonian editor, however, reworked Rav's statement by using the two halves of his statement from the Yerushalmi, "**They taught [this] only** when he said thirty one days (= that he serves one term), **but** he if said thirty days and one day, he must serve two [terms of naziriteship]," and framed it as a comment on the mishnah. The Babylonian version thus contains both elements of the Yerushalmi's version (thirty-one days/thirty days and one day), but applies it to the mishnah, thereby creating a textual gap between the statement and the mishnah. In summary, both versions of Rav's statement contain the same halakhic content and in both his innovation is with regard to one who says, "thirty days and one day." However, the original version in the Yerushalmi is a simple apodictic statement while the secondary version in the Bavli, a deduction from the mishnah, is more difficult to comprehend.

B.Eruvin 27a

Mishnah: With all [kinds of food] one may make an *eruv* or a *shittuf*, except water and salt. And all [kinds of food] may be purchased with second tithe money, except water and salt.

Gemara: R. El'azar[59] and R. Yose bar Hanina: One would teach it about the *eruv* and one would teach it about tithes. One would teach it about the *eruv*: they taught only that one may not make an *eruv* with water alone and salt alone. But with water and salt (mixed together) one may make an eruv. And one would teach it about tithes: They taught only that water alone and salt alone may not be purchased [with second tithe money]. But water and salt (mixed together) may be purchased with [second] tithe money. The one who teaches it about tithes would all the more so teach it about the *eruv*, and the one who teaches it about the *eruv*, would not teach it about tithes. Why? [The food bought with second tithe money] must be produce.

When R. Yitshaq came he taught it about tithes.

---

59   Following MSS Oxford 366, Vatican 109.

R. El'azar and R. Yose bar Hanina are second-third generation amoraim from Tiberias,[60] and both of them taught the same interpretive statement limiting the context of m.Eruvin 3:1. Their dispute is only whether the statement should be taught in reference to the first part of the mishnah (concerning the *eruv*) or about the end of the mishnah (concerning redeeming second tithe money in Jerusalem[61]). The statement is phrased as a deduction from the mishnah and posits that the mishnah's ruling is correct only with regard to the precise case mentioned, "They taught (the Mishnah) only that water alone and salt alone … But with water and salt (mixed together) one may make an *eruv*/may be purchased with [second] tithe money." The end of the sugya reports that when R. Yitshaq, a Tiberian amora from the same generation as R. El'azar and R. Yose bar Hanina,[62] arrived in Babylonia he related that the statement should be taught in reference to second tithes ("When R. Yitshaq came he taught it about tithes"). Indeed, this is how R. Eliezer's statement reads in the parallel in y.Eruvin 3:1 (20d). However, there it is phrased differently:

> R. El'azar said: "If he made saltwater with them, they can be purchased with [second] tithe money." R. Aha [said] in the name of R. Meysha: "This is true only if they mixed oil in with them." [R. Yose bar Hanina said: "If he made saltwater with them, one may tithe with them." R. Aha said: "This is true only if they mixed oil in with them."][63] R. Yose asked: "From here [we could conclude] that he can only make an *eruv* according to their reckoning."

Recently, N. Aminoah pointed out that in the Yerushalmi the statements of R. El'azar and R. Yose bar Hanina are phrased as apodictic halakhic rulings unconnected to the mishnah. Both statements allow the use of saltwater either for an *eruv* or to redeem second tithe money. R. Aha relates in the name of R. Meysha that oil must be added to the mixture for it to be considered food. R. Yose disagrees, claiming that were this true they would have to add enough oil equal to the amount of food necessary for a meal. According to Aminoah, both statements were originally taught as halakhic rulings as they are found in the Yerushalmi. However, there were doubts over the context in which the

---

60 Albeck, *Introduction*, 185–186, 224–227.
61 See: Albeck, *Shisha Sidrei Mishnah*, vol. 2, 428; Goldberg, *Commentary to the Mishna Shabbat*, 59–61; Safrai, *Mishnat Eretz Israel: Tractate Shabbat*, vol. 1, 79–81.
62 Albeck, *Introduction*, 252–253.
63 The text in brackets is Lieberman's reconstruction, Lieberman, *Hayerushalmi Kifshuto*, 257; Halivni, *Sources and Traditions: Erubin and Pesaḥim*, 67 n. 1 [Hebrew].

statements were recited already in Palestinian tradition. As a result of this uncertainty, the statements were rephrased in Babylonia as interpretive statements related to the two parts of the mishnah.[64] Whatever the reason for the secondary editing in the Bavli, the halakhic content remained the same as it was in the Yerushalmi; both traditions viewing salt water as a type of food which may be used to make an *eruv*.

B.Hullin 7a–b

What does "the beast of the righteous" refer to? R. Pinḥas b. Yair was going to redeem captives ... He went to a certain inn. They placed barley in front of his donkey and it did not eat. They beat [the barley] and it did not eat. They sifted it and it did not eat. He said to them: "Perhaps it is not tithed". They tithed it and the donkey ate. He said: "This poor thing is going to do the will of its maker and you are feeding it untithed produce?" But does [such produce] need to be tithed? Did we not teach: One who purchases [grain to use] for seed or for an animal [consumption], or flour for [use in processing] hides, or oil for a lamp or oil for greasing utensils, is exempt from *demai* (m.Demai 1:3).

There it has been stated about this: R. Yohanan said: They taught [this] only if he bought the grain from the outset for animal consumption, but if he bought it for human consumption and later decided to give it to animals, it must be tithed.

And so it has been taught:[65] One who buys produce in the market for eating and decides later to use it for animals, behold he may not give it either to his own animal or to his neighbor's animal without first tithing it.[66]

The "stam" cites a mishnah from Tractate Demai as a difficulty on R. Pinhas b. Yair, who refused to feed his donkey produce acquired from an *am ha'arets*.[67] Why did R. Pinhas b. Yair refuse to feed his animal such produce, when Mishnah Demai exempts such produce from being tithed if it was intended for animal consumption? As an answer, the stam presents R. Yohanan's contextualization of the mishnah, according to which the mishnah's exemption does not apply

---

64 Aminoah, *Redaction*, 808–809 [Hebrew].
65 Hamburg 169 and Vatican 122 read, "as it has been taught."
66 The baraita can be found with some variations in t.Demai 1:15 (ed. Lieberman, p. 65), and in the Yerushalmi cited below.
67 Rashi, s.v. *umi miḥayva*.

if the produce was originally intended for human consumption. According to the baraita which supports R. Yohanan's contextualization, produce purchased from an *am ha'arets* which was at first intended for human consumption and only subsequently given to an animal, must be tithed.[68] The introductory term, "Was it not taught on this" (הא איתמר עלה) in the Bavli indicates the existence of an earlier source which the editor of the passage wishes to use in the context of his discussion.[69] Indeed, y.Demai 1:3 (21d) reads:

> R. Yohanan said: And it was also taught (אמר ר׳ יוחנן: ותני כן):[70] If he purchased it for seed, and then decided to eat it, they enter by thought [they enter into the obligation of *demai* by his thought]. The thought [makes it liable for tithes]. If he purchased it for food, and then decided to use it for seed, he does not have the ability [to change its status, and he is liable to tithe it].

In the Yerushalmi, the term "R. X said, and it was also taught (אמר ר׳ יוחנן: ותני כן)" introduces amoraic statements that were also transmitted as baraitot, which is similar to "R. X said and it was also taught (אמר ר׳ פלוני וכן תנא/תני)" in the Bavli.[71] Thus, R. Yohanan and the baraita both added a halakhic statement to the mishnah: produce purchased from an *am ha'arets* which is intended to be human food must be tithed, even if afterwards he changes his mind and decides to use the food for seed (or animal consumption). While the mishnah in Demai exempts produce bought for seed or animal consumption from the obligation to be tithed, R. Yohanan's statement and the baraita delineate that produce given to an animal or used for seed must be tithed if at the outset it was designated for human consumption. This statement which was originally phrased as an independent halakhic ruling was transformed in the Bavli into a limitation on the mishnah through use of the "*lo shanu ela*" formula.

---

68   See: Saul Lieberman, *Tosefta Kifshuta: Zeraim*, vol. 1, 201.
69   Concerning the meaning of this term see, Weiss, *The Talmud*, 73–74; Albeck, *Introduction*, 562. This contextualization is not found elsewhere in the Bavli or in the parallel to the story in y.Demai 1:3 (21d) or Genesis Rabbah 60:8 (ed. Theodor-Albeck, p. 649). This was already noted by the Tosafot, ibid, s.v. *ha itmar ala*. See also Albeck's comment in Genesis Rabbah. Concerning these differences see, Moscovitz, "Development," 139–140.
70   This ("ותני כן") is the reading in all textual witnesses of the Yerushalmi. Ms. London Or. 2822–2824 reads, "ונתני כן."
71   Moscovitz, *Terminology*, 77; Assis, *Concordance*, vol. 1, 129 n. 1184 [Hebrew].

Summary and Conclusions

This study has reevaluated the connection between the literary editing of an amoraic source and its historical reliability. This was accomplished through the analysis of a broad corpus of statements employing the term "*lo shanu ela*" in regard to a tannaitic source found in the Bavli. A close examination of the original versions of these statements (mainly of Palestinian amoraim) in the Yerushalmi demonstrates that they were not originally interpretations of the Mishnah, but rather originated as short halakhic statements, independent of any tannaitic source. When first formed, these sources did not fully accord with Palestinian tannaitic tradition, and the Bavli, as it so frequently does, refashioned them to be interpretive statements. In such a way Babylonian editors harmonized them with tannaitic traditions. Evidence for the "Babylonian" nature of these statements is found in their style: they are partially phrased in Babylonian Aramaic, they do not always accord with the tannaitic source they interpret, and other such literary phenomena. However, such editorial ammedations should not be mistaken for a Babylonian origin **of the content** of these halakhot, for the halakhic innovation transmitted in the name of the same sage appears in both the Palestinian and Babylonian versions of the statement. The specific and original content of these statements can be uncovered through a careful analysis of the parallels.

With regard to the historic reliability of amoraic statements and the origins of the Bavli's technical terminology, many "*lo shanu ela*" statements have parallels in the Yerushalmi, which are attributed to the same sage as in the Bavli and often use similar language. This makes it difficult to view these statements as the late pseudepigraphic literary inventions of a sixth-seventh century editor.[72] What's more, for statements that did undergo late editing, there is often a halakhic core shared with the parallel in the Yerushalmi. Thus even the Babylonian versions should not be viewed as late, completely unreliable sources.[73] The research I have presented here demonstrates that scholars should be cautious when making broad historical assertions based on narrow literary-formalistic criteria denying the historical reliability of amoraic statements (Palestinian or

---

72 See, Green, "'Biography,'", 77–96; Neusner, "Attributions," 93–111; Kraemer, *Responses to Suffering*, 12–16; Lavee, "Rabbinic Literature," 325–326.

73 For a critique of those who view amoraic statements in the Bavli as a pseudepigraphic creation, see: Elman, "Talmudic Intellectual History," 361–386; Gafni, "A Generation of Scholarship," 219 [Hebrew]; Kalmin, "Babylonian Talmud", 840–876; Stern, "Attribution and Authorship," 38–51; Cohen, "Shmuel said: Hilkheta," 25–26 [Hebrew]. The matter is far more complex than can be described by the simple binary of reliable/unreliable attribution, and each instance requires its own systematic analysis.

Babylonian) found in the Bavli.[74] I intend to continue to research this assumption on the basis of other corpuses of amoraic statements.

The same seems to be true even with regard to the origin of the "*lo shanu ela*" terminology in the Bavli. It is difficult to view this terminology as the result of late, post-amoraic editing. The term "*lo shanu ela*" is found frequently in the Yerushalmi,[75] and some of these cases have full parallels in the Bavli (see in the appendix). It therefore seems clear that the term was already in use in early amoraic literature (at least in parts of it), and should not be viewed as a late literary creation. This finding accords with the conclusions of other scholars, who view the Bavli's technical terminology as an early part of the literary creation of the amoraim.[76]

Acknowledgements

This article is dedicated to a great scholar and *talmid hakham*, Professor Yaakov Elman of blessed memory, from whom I learned the true nature of magnanimity. His death has been difficult for us all, and his absence is continuously felt.

---

74 This conclusion is supported by studies that demonstrate consistent halakhic rulings of Babylonian amoraim whose statements are quoted in the Yerushalmi, even in cases where the statements have no parallels in the Bavli.
75 See above, n. 10.
76 See: Cohen, "Citation Formulae," 26–27 and the literature cited in n. 5.

Appendix: "Lo Shanu Ela" Statements in the Bavli and Their Parallels in the Yerushalmi[77]

Section One: Interpretive Statements

TABLE 10.1 Palestinian sages

The Babylonian sugya	The parallel in the Yerushalmi[78]
Hizkiyah (and R. Yohanan)	
Bava Qamma 9b (through Resh Laqish): referring to Mishnah Bava Qamma 6:4	Bava Qamma 6:4 (5c, p. 1203) = Lieberman, Yerushalmi Nezikin, p. 22, Hizkiyah said: "In … but …" R. Yohanan said: "Both …. and"
R. Yehoshua b. Levi	
Ketubbot 104b (in the name of Bar Kappara): referring to Mishnah Ketubbot 12:4	Ketubbot 12:4 (35c, p. 1012): R. Simeon said in the name of R. Yehoshua b. Levi: "It was taught only in … but …."
Yehudah son of R. Hiyya (beRabbi)	
Eruvin 103b (and parallels): referring to Mishnah Eruvin 10:14	Eruvin 10:14 (26d, p. 496): Yehudah beRabbi said: "It was taught only in … but …"
R. Yonatan	
Megillah 26a (through R. Shmuel b. Nahmani[79]): referring to Mishnah Megillah 3a	Megillah 3a (73d, p. 763): R. Shmuel b. Nahman said in the name of R. Yonatan: "That which you say refers to ….but in …"
R. Yohanan	
[A] Pesahim 91a (through Rabbah bar bar Hannah): referring to Mishnah Pesahim 8:6	[A] Pesahim 8:6 (36a, p. 548): R. Yose beRabbi Abun bar bar Hannah said in the name of R. Yohanan: "The mishnah refers to ….but …"

---

77 This list is limited to statements made by Babylonian amoraim of the first three generations that have parallels in both talmudim.

78 All references to the Yerushalmi are based on the Leiden manuscript as transcribed in the Academy of Hebrew Language edition (*Talmud Yerushalmi According to Ms. Or. 4720 [Scal. 3] of the Leiden University Library with Restorations and Corrections* [Jerusalem: The Academy of the Hebrew Language, 2005]).

79 For variants see above in the body of the article.

TABLE 10.1 Palestinian sages (*cont.*)

The Babylonian sugya	The parallel in the Yerushalmi
[B] Hagigah 24a (and Resh Laqish): referring to Mishnah Hagigah 3:2	[B] Hagigah 3:2 (79b, p. 796): R. Shimon b. Laqish said: "It was taught only in … but …" R. Yohanan said: "Even …"
[C] Gittin 7b (through R. Ami): referring to Mishnah Gittin 2:1	[C] Pesahim 2:1 (44a, p. 1059): R. Yassa said in the name of R. Yohanah: "And in …"
[D] Bava Qamma 20a (and Resh Laqish): referring to Mishnah Bava Qamma 2:2	[D] Bava Qamma 2:3 (3a, p. 1191)= Lieberman, Yerushalmi Nezikin, p. 1: R. Yohanan said: "On …" Resh Laqish said: "On …"[80]
[E] Bava Qamma 30a (through R. Ya'aqov[81]): referring to Mishnah Bava Qamma 3:2	[E] Bava Qamma 3:2 (3c, p. 1193) = Lieberman, Yerushalmi Nezikin, p. 5: R. Yohanan said: "Solve it, all refer to …"
[F] Bava Batra 173b (through Rabbah bar bar Hannah): referring to Mishnah Bava Batra 10:7	[F] Bava Batra 10:7 (17d, p. 1262): R. Abbahu said in the name of R. Yohanan: "In … but …"
[G] Sanhedrin 74b (through R. Dimmi): referring to a statement by R. Shimon b. Yehotsadaq	[G] Sanhedrin 3:3 (21b, p. 1281): R. Yohanan said in the name of R. Shimon b. Yehotsadaq … "That which you say refers to … but …"
[H] Sanhedrin 67a (through Rabbah bar bar Hannah): referring to Mishnah Avodah Zarah 5:2	[H] Avodah Zarah 5:2 (44d, p. 1407): R. Yohanan said: "That which you say refers to … but …"
[I] Avodah Zarah 12b–13a (and Resh Laqish): referring to Mishnah Avodah Zarah 1:4	[I] Avodah Zarah 1:4 (39d, p. 1379): R. Yohanan said: "In …" R. Shimon b. Laqish said: "In …"
R. Asi[82]	
Shabbat 54a: referring to Mishnah Shabbat 5:3	Shabbat 5:3 (7b, p. 392): Asi says: "It was necessary in the case of …"

---

80 Lieberman, *Yerushalmi Nezikin*, p. 113, line 1 and medieval commentaries.
81 Based on Ms. Munich 95, Ascorial G-I-3, Hamburg 165 and Vatican 116.
82 Based on geniza fragment T-S F2 (1) 205, Ms. Oxford Opp. Add. Fol. 23, and R. Alfasi. Ms. Munich 95 reads: Rabbah.

TABLE 10.1 Palestinian sages (*cont.*)

The Babylonian sugya	The parallel in the Yerushalmi
R. Yose bar Hanina	
Pesahim 46a:[83] referring to a statement by Resh Laqish[84]	Berakhot 8:2 (12a, p. 61): R. Abbahu said in the name of R. Yose b. R. Hanina: "That which it said … but …"
"The Elders of the South"[85]	
Zevahim 22b: referring to Mishnah Zevahim 2:1	Pesahim 7:7 (34d, p. 540): The Southerners say: "In … we refer to, but …."

TABLE 10.2 Babylonian Sages

Rav	
[1] Shabbat 37a (through R. Helbo in the name of R. Hama bar Guria): referring to Mishnah Shabbat 3:1	[1] Shabbat 3:1 (5c, p. 382): R. Helbo said in the name of R. Anan in the name of Rav: "It was taught only about … but … no."
[2] Shabbat 142a (through R. Huna): referring to Mishnah Shabbat 21:2	[2] Shabbat 3:6 (6c, p. 387): R. Ba in the name of R. Hiyya b. Ashi: "Rav solved it as referring to …."
[3] Ketubbot 71a (and Shmuel):[86] referring to Mishnah Ketubbot 7:1	[3] Ketubbot 7:1 (31b, p. 989): Shmuel said: "In …" R. Ze'ira R. Avina said in the name of Rav: "And even in …"
[4] Sotah 49b:[87] referring to Mishnah Sotah 9:14	[4] Sotah 9:14 (24c, p. 950): R. Ba said in the name of Rav: "Of … and of …"
[5] Bava Qamma 30a: referring to Mishnah Bava Qamma 3:2	[5] Bava Qamma 3:2 (3a, p. 1193) = Lieberman, Yerushalmi Nezikin, p. 5: Rav said: "Even …"

---

83 Ms. Munich 95 reads: "R. Hanina."
84 See: Epstein, *Introduction*, vol. 2, 810; Halivni, *Sources and Traditions: Erubin and Pesaḥim*, 106–107 [Hebrew].
85 On the identification of this group with the "Southerners" in the Yerushalmi and a discussion of the group and its literary contribution see, Miller, *Sages and Commoners*, 140; Rosenfeld, *Torah Centers*, 50.
86 Ms. Vatican 130 reads: "Rava" and there is a mark directing the letter א to be erased.
87 Mss. Oxford Bodl. Heb. D. 20 (2675) and Vatican 110 read: "Rava."

TABLE 10.2 Babylonian Sages *(cont.)*

Rav

[6] Bava Qamma 61a: referring to Mishnah Bava Qamma 6:4	[6] Bava Qamma 6:4 (5c, p. 1203) = Lieberman, Yerushalmi Nezikin, p. 22: Rabbah (= R. Abba)[88] said: "The mishnah refers to … but in …"
[7] Sanhedrin 34a: referring to Mishnah Sanhedrin 4:1	[7] Sanhedrin 4:1 (22b, p. 1286): Rav said: "As long as … but if …"

Shmuel

[1] Betsah 28a (through R. Yehudah): referring to Mishnah Betsah 3:7	[1] Betsah 3:7 (62b, p. 694): R. Yehudah said in the name of Shmuel: "This is agreed to by everyone …"
[2] Ketubbot 101a: referring to Mishnah Ketubbot 11:6	[2] Ketubbot 7:6 (31c, p. 990): R. Hanin taught in the name of R. Shmuel … "It was taught only …"[89]
[3] Bava Metsia 93a: referring to Mishnah Bava Metsia 7:8	[3] Bava Metsia 7:8 (11c, p. 1233) = Lieberman, Yerushalmi Nezikin, p. 71: Shmuel said: "The mishnah refers to … but …"
[4] Niddah 10b (and R. Yohanan): referring to Mishnah Niddah 1:3	[4] Niddah 1:6 (49c, p. 1437): Shmuel said: "It was taught only … but … Rav and R. Yohanan both say: It is the same in … and in …"

R. Huna

[1] Bava Qamma 19b:[90] referring to Mishnah Bava Qamma 2:1	[1] Bava Qamma 2:1 (2d, p. 1190): R. Huna said: "In … but …"
[2] Bava Metsia 29b: referring to Mishnah Bava Metsia 2:7	[2] Bava Metsia 2:7 (8d, p. 1219) = Lieberman, Yerushalmi Nezikin, pp. 49–50: R. Huna said: "All agree that if …"

---

88   Ms. Ascorial reads: Rav said (Lieberman, *Yerushalmi Nezkin*, 22). Concerning this reading see, Levy, *Mavo*, 176.
89   For the reading of this passage in medieval commentaries see, Lieberman, *Tosefta Kifshuta*, vol. 6, 292–293.
90   Ms. Vatican 116 reads, "Rava."

THE USE OF LITERARY CONSIDERATIONS AS A KEY 231

Section Two: Halakhic Rulings in the Yerushalmi

TABLE 10.3   Palestinian sages

R. Yohanan

[1] Berakhot 16a:[91] referring to a baraita (= Tosefta Berakhot 2:5, ed. Lieberman, p. 7 and parallels) | [1] Berakhot 2:3 (5a, p. 19): R. Yohanan said: "If he was reading and he found himself at 'In order to' he can assume he had proper intent."

[2] Shabbat 11a:[92] referring to Mishnah Shabbat 1:2 | [2] Shabbat 1:2 (3a, p. 368): R. Yohanan said in the name of R. Shimon b. Yohai: "For those like us, who are occupied with the study of Torah—even for the reading of the Shema we do not interrupt."

[3] Pesahim 27a (through R. Hiyya b. Ashi): referring to a baraita (= Tosefta Orlah 1:7, ed. Lieberman, p. 284). | [3] Orlah 3:4 (63a, p. 345): R. Ba said in the name of R. Hiyya who said in the name of R. Yohanan: Embers of orlah wood are permitted for use.

[4] Hullin 7b: referring to Mishnah Demai 1:3 | [4] Demai 1:3 (21d, p. 117): R. Yohanan said, and it was also taught [in a baraita]: If he purchased them for seed, and thought to use them for food the thought makes them liable; if he bought them for food and thought to use them for seed, he does not have the power [to exempt them from tithes].

[5] Niddah 29a (and R. Elazar): referring to Mishnah Niddah 3:5 | [5] Niddah 3:5 (51a, p. 1446): They disagreed ... R. Yohanan said: "His head counts as the majority [of his body]," R. Elazar said: "His head counts as one of his limbs."

R. Elazar and R. Yose bar Hanina[93]

Eruvin 27b: referring to Mishnah Eruvin 3:1 | Eruvin 3:1 (20d, p. 464): R. Elazar said: "If he made them into saltwater, they may be purchased with tithe money." R. Yose bar Hanina said: "If he made them into saltwater, they may use them for an eruv."

---

91 For variants see above in the body of this article.
92 For variants see above in the body of this article.
93 For variants see above in the body of this article.

TABLE 10.3 Palestinian sages (*cont.*)

R. Zera

[1] Berakhot 23a (through R. Ya'aqov b. Aha): referring to a baraita in Y. Berakhot 2:2 (4c)	[1] Berakhot 2:2 (4c, p. 16): R. Ya'aqov b. Aha in the name of R. Ze'ira: "And this is when ... but ..."
[2] Shabbat 65a: referring to Mishnah Shabbat 6:5	[2] Shabbat 6:5 (8c, p. 399): R. Mana said: "You heard a reason from R. Shmuel in the name of R. Ze'ira but I do not know what you heard."

TABLE 10.4 Babylonian Sages

Rav

[1] Yevamot 88a:[94] referring to Mishnah Yevamot 10:1	[1] Yevamot 15:4 (15a, p. 899): R. Nahman b. Ya'aqov said in the name of Rav: If she was married based on the testimony of two witnesses, even if he [the husband] comes. They said to him: We do not know you.[95]
[2] Nazir 7a: referring to Mishnah Nazir 1:3	[2] Nazir 1:3 (51c, p. 1099): Rav said: "[One who declares] 'Behold I will be a nazirite for thirty days and one day' has made two nazirite vows."
[3] Nazir 26a (through R. Huna):[96] referring to Mishnah Nazir 4:4	[3] Nazir 4:4 (53b, p. 1110): R. Ba said in the name of Rav: Coins are anonymous; an animal is not anonymous.

Shmuel

Niddah 11a (through R. Giddel): referring to Mishnah Niddah 10:1	Niddah 1:7 (49c, p. 1437): Shmuel said: A night and the following day count as a period; and part of a period counts as an entire one; if she stopped [bleeding] and then saw [a stain], she is impure; if the appearance of her blood changed, she is impure.

---

94 Oxford Opp. 248 (367) reads: "Rava."
95 On the reading of this source see: Friedman, "A Critical Study of Yebamot X," 332–333 [Hebrew].
96 Munich 95, Vatican 100 and Moscow, Ginzberg collection 1134 read: R. Huna said in the name of R. Hanina.

Bibliography

Abraham, David. (ed), Malakhi Ha-Cohen, *Sefer Yad Malakhi*, Vols. 1–2. Jerusalem: Makhon Yerushalayim, 2016

Albeck, Ḥanoch. *Shisha Sidrei Mishnah, Vols. 1–6*. Jerusalem and Tel Aviv: Mosad Bialik and Dvir, 1958

Albeck, Ḥanoch. *Introduction to the Talmud Babli and Yerushalmi*, Tel-Aviv: D'vir, 1969 [Hebrew]

Albeck, Ḥanoch. *Meḥkarim Babraita UvaTosefta Veyaḥasan LaTalmud*, Jerusalem: Mosad Harav Kuk, 1970

Albeck, Shalom. *The Law of Property and Contract in the Talmud*, Tel-Aviv: Dvir, 1976

Albeck, Shalom. *Introduction to Jewish Law in Talmudic Times*, Ramat-Gan: Bar-Ilan University Press, 1999

Albeck, Shalom. "Sof Ha-Hora'a Ve-Siyum Hatalmud," *Sinai* 50 (1957) 73–79

Aminoah, Noaḥ. *The Redaction of the Shabbat abd Eruvin Tractates of the Babylonian Talmud: Compilation, Redaction, Textual Readings, Parallel Sugyot*, Tel-Aviv: Tel-Aviv University Press, 2016 [Hebrew]

Amit, Aaron. "The Place of Yemenite Manuscripts in the Transmission—History of b. Pesaḥim," *Hebrew Union College Annual* 73 (2002) 31–77 [Hebrew]

Assis, Moshe. *A Concordance of Amoraic Terms Expressions and Phrases in the Yerushalmi*, Vols. 1–3. Jerusalem-New York: The Jewish Theological Seminary Press, 2010 [Hebrew]

Atzmon, Arnon. "Haggadah Dimegillat Esther: Towards the Anthologist's Methodology," *Iggud* 1 (2008) 277–291 [Hebrew]

Bacher, Willhelm. *Tradition und Tradenten in den Schulen Palästinas und Babyloniens*, Leipzig: Fock, 1914

Bokser, Baruch. *Shmuel's Commentary on the Mishna: Its Nature, Forms, and Content*, Leiden: Brill, 1975

Breuer, Yoḥanan. "On the Hebrew Dialect of the Amoraim in the Babylonian Talmud," *Language Studies* 2–3 (1987) 127–153 [Hebrew]

Brüll, Naḥum. "Die Agada der babylonischen Amoräer, ein Beitrage zur Geschichte der Agada und zur Ein. In den babylonischen Talmud von Prof. Dr. Wilhelm Bacher," *Jahrbücher für Jüdische Geschichte und Literatur*, 5 (1883) 163–164

Cohen, Avinoam. "Al Hitpalgut Haneti'ot Hahilkhatiot shel Ha'amoraim Lefi Askolot," *Asufot* 8 (1994) 107–129

Cohen, Barak. *For Out of Babylonia Shall Come Torah and the Word of the Lord from Nehar Peqod: The Quest for Babylonian Tannaitic Traditions*, Boston: Brill, 2017

Cohen, Barak. "'Shmuel said: Hilkheta': The Halakhic Rulings of Shmuel in the Two Talmudim," *Jewish Studies, An Internet Journal* 12 (2015) 1–32 [Hebrew]

Cohen, Barak. "Citation Formulae in the Babylonian Talmud: From Transmission to Authoritative Traditions," *Journal of Jewish Studies* 70 (2019) 24–44

De-Vries, Benjamin. *Studies in the Development of the Talmudic Halakah*, Tel-Aviv: Abraham Zioni, 1962

Efrati, J., and Itzhaki E. *Masekhet Yom Tov Perek Shelishi*, Petah-Tikva: Bne'i Asher, 1993

Epstein, Jacob Naḥum. *Introduction to the Mishnaic Text*, Vols. 1–2. Jerusalem: Magnes, 2000 [Hebrew]

Feldblum, Meyer. *Talmudic Law and Literature: Tractate Gittin*, New-York: Yeshiva University, 1969 [Hebrew]

Flursheim. Joel. "Rav Ḥisda as Exegetor of Tannaitic Sources," *Tarbiz* 42 (1972) 24–48 [Hebrew]

Frankel, Zecharias. *Darkhei Hamishnah HaTosefta, Mekhilta, Sifra Vesifre*, Warsaw: Zeilingold, 1923

Frankel, Zecharias. *Mavo HaYerushalmi*, Jerusalem: Omanim, 1967

Friedman, Shamma (ed.). *Halakhot Rabbati of R. Isaac Alfasi*, Jerusalem: Makkor, 1974

Friedman, Shamma (ed.). "A Critical Study of Yevamot x with A Methodological Introduction," *Texts and Studies* 1 (1977) 275–441 [Hebrew]

Friedman, Shamma (ed.). *Talmudic Studies: Investigating the Sugya, Variant Readings and Aggada*, New-York: The Jewish Theological Seminary, 2010 [Hebrew]

Gafni, Isaiah. "A Generation of Scholarship on Eretz-Israel in the Talmudic Era: Achievements and Reconsiderations," *Cathedra* 100 (2001) 199–226

Ginzberg, Louise. *A Commentary on the Palestinian Talmud: A Study of the Development of the Halaka and Haggadah in Palestine and Babylonia*, 4 Vols. 1–4. New-York: The Jewish Theological Seminary, 1941 [Hebrew]

Goldberg, Abraham. *Commentary to the Mishna Shabbat: Critical Edited and Provided with Introduction, Commentary and Notes*. Jerusalem: Jewish Theological Seminary of America, 1976 [Hebrew]

Goldberg, Abraham. *Literary Form and Composition in Classical Rabbinic Literature: Selected Literary Studies in Mishna, Tosefta, Halakhic and Aggadic Midrash and Talmud*, Jerusalem: Magnes, 2011 [Hebrew]

Goldsmith, Areye (ed.). *Maḥzor Vitri Lerabenu Simḥa Mivitri Talmid Rashi*, Vols. 1–2. Jerusalem: Otzar Haposkim, 2004

Goodblatt, David. *Rabbinic Instruction in Sasanian Babylonia*, Leiden: Brill, 1975

Gordis, David. "The Exegesis of Mishna and Baraita of Rav and Samuel," PhD diss., The Jewish Theological Seminary, 1980

Gray, Alyssa. *A Talmud in Exile: The Influence of Yerushalmi Avodah Zarah on the Formation of Bavli Avodah Zarah*. Providence, R.I.: Brown Judaic Studies, 2005

Halevi, Elimelekh. "Matter of Fact Pshitta Arguments in the Babylonian Talmud which Are Not So Matter of Fact," *Proceedings of the Seventh World Congress of Jewish Studies, Vol. 1: Studies in Talmud, Halakha and Midrash*, 129–140. Jerusalem: World Union of Jewish Studies, 1981 [Hebrew]

Elman, Yaakov. "How Should a Talmudic Intellectual History Be Written? A Response to David Kraemer's Responses," *Jewish Quarterly Review* 89 (1999) 361–386

Halivni, David. '"Whoever Studies Laws ..." The Apodictic and the Argumentational in the Talmud," *Proceedings of the Rabbinical Assembly* 41 (1979) 298–303

Halivni, David. *Sources and Traditions: A Source Critical Commentary on the Talmud Sources and Traditions Tractates Erubin and Pesaḥim*, Jerusalem: Jewish Theological Seminary, 1982

Halivni, David. *Introduction to "Sources and Traditions": Studies in the Formation of the Talmud*, Jerusalem: Magnes, 2009 [Hebrew]

Hame'iri, Menaḥem. *Sefer Beit Habeḥira al Masekhet Berakhot*, Jerusalem: Makhon Hatalmud Haisraeli Hashalem, 1960

Hayes, Christine. *Between the Babylonian and Palestinian Talmuds: Accounting for Halakhic Difference in Selected Sugyot from Tractate Avodah Zarah*, Oxford: Oxford University Press, 1997

Henshke, David. *The Original Mishna in the Discourse of Later Tanna'im*, Ramat-Gan: Bar-Ilan University Press, 1997

Herman, Geoffrey. "Table Etiquette and Persian Culture in the Babylonian Talmud," *Zion* 77 (2012) 149–188 [Hebrew]

Hilman, David Z'vi (ed.). *Perush Harashbatz al Masekhet Berakhot*, Jerusalem: Ahavat Shalom, 2002

Hoffmann, David Z'vi. *Mar Samuel: Rector der Jüdischen Akademie zu Nehardea in Babylonien: Lebensbild eines Talmudisch*, Leipzig: Leiner, 1873

Hoffmann, David Z'vi. *Hamishna Harishona Uflugta Detana'ei*, Berlin: Gard-Est, 1913

Hyman, Pinḥas. "From Tiberias to Mehoza: Redactorial and Editorial Processes in Amoraic Babylonia," *Jewish Quarterly Review* 93 (2002) 117–148

Kahana, Menaḥem. "Shalosh Maḥlokot Muḥlafot Bebattei Midrashotohem shel Rav Ushmuel," *Meḥqerei Talmud* 2 (1993) 302–333

Kalmin, Richard. "The Post—Rav Ashi Amoraim: Transition or Continuity? A Study of the Role of the Final Generations of Amoraim in the Redaction of the Talmud," *AJS Review* 11 (1986) 157–187

Kalmin, Richard. *The Redaction of the Babylonian Talmud: Amoraic or Saboraic?* Cincinnati: Hebrew Union College Press, 1989

Kalmin, Richard. "Rabbinic Literature of Late Antiquity as a Source for Historical Study," in *Judaism in Late Antiquity* edited by Jacob Neusner and Alan J. Avery-Peck, 187–199. Leiden: Brill, 1999

Kalmin, Richard. "The Formation and Character of the Babylonian Talmud", *The Cambridge History of Judaism* 4 (2006) 840–876

Kelman, Jonathan. "The Amoraic Oqimta 'Hacha B'Ma'i Assiqinan Relating to Tannaitic Sources" PhD diss., Bar—Ilan University, 2001 [Hebrew]

Kohut, Alexander (ed.). *Arukh Hashalem*, Vols. 1–9. New York: Pardes, 1955

Kosowsky, Ḥaim. *Otzar Leshon Hatalmud: Sefer Hamatimot Letalmud Bavli*, Vols. 1–42, New-York: Jewish Theological Seminary Press, 1954 [Hebrew]

Kraemer, David. *Responses to Suffering in Classical Rabbinic Literature*, Oxford: Oxford University Press, 1995

Kraemer, David. "Rabbinic Sources for Historical Studies," *Judaism in Late Antiquity* 3 (1999) 201–212

Kretzmer-Raziel, Yoel. "The Opening Sugya of Tractate Betzah in the Bavli and the Yeshushalmi and the Status of the Stam," *Sidra* 32 (2017) 59–109 [Hebrew]

Kretzmer-Raziel, Yoel. "Talmudic "Stam" as an Evolutionary Phenomenon: The Opening "Sugyot" of Tractate Nedarimin the Talmud Yerushalmi and the Talmud Bavli," *Tarbiz* 86 (2019) 611–661 [Hebrew]

Krauss, Samuel. *Talmudische Archäologie*, Vols. 1–3. Leipzig: Fock, 1910–1912

Lavee, Moshe. "Rabbinic Literature and The History of Judaism" in *Rabbinic Texts and the History of Late-Roman Palestine*, edited by M. Goodman and P. Alexander, 319–351. Oxford: Oxford University Press, 2010

Levine, David. "Is Talmudic Biography Still Possible?" *Jewish Studies* 46 (2009) 41–64 [Hebrew]

Levy, Israel. *Mavo Uferush LeTalmud Yerushalmi*, Jerusalem: Kedem, 1970

Levy, Jacob. *Wörterbuch über die Talmudim und Midraschim*, Vols. 1–4. Berlin: Harz, 1924

Lieberman, Saul. *Hayerushalmi Kifshuto: A Commentary Based on Manuscripts and of the Yerushalmi, and Works of the Rishonim in Mss. And Rare Editions*, Jerusalem-New-York: The Jewish Theological Seminary, 2008

Medini, Ḥaim Ḥizkiya. *Sde Ḥemed*, Vols. 1–2, New-York: Kehat, 1948

Melamed, Ezra Zion. *Milon Arami-Ivri Letalmud Bavli*, Jerusalem: Samuel and Odette Levy Foundation, 1992

Metzger, David (ed.). *Perushe'i Rabbenu Hanan'el Lemasekhet Berakhot*, Jeruslem: Lev Same'ḥ, 1990

Metzger, David (ed.). *Perushe'i Rabbenu Hanan'el Lemasekhet Shabbat*, Jerusalem: Vagshal, 1993

Milikowsky, Ḥaim. "On Parallels and Primacy: Seder 'Olam and Mekhilta d'Rabbi Shimon ben Yohai on the Israelites in Egypt," *Bar-Ilan University Annual* 26–27 (1995) 221–225 [Hebrew]

Miller, Stuart. *Sages and Commoners in Late Antique Erez Israel: A philological Inquiry into Local Traditions in Talmud Yerushalmi*, Tübingen: Mohr Siebeck, 2006

Mivina, R. Itzḥak. *Sefer Or Zaru'a Lerabbenu Hagadol Rabbi Itzḥak Mivina*, Hilkhor Keri'yat Shema, Vols. 1–3. Jerusalem: Makhon Yerushalaim, 2010

Sefer Or Zaru'a Lerabbenu Hagadol Rabbi Itzḥak Mivina, Hilkhor Keri'yat Shema, Vols. 1–3. Jerusalem: Makhon Yerushalaim, 2010

Moscovitz, Leib. "'The Holy One blessed be He … does not permit the righteous to stumble': Reflections on the Development of a Remarkable BT Theologoumenon," in *Creation and Composition: The Contribution of the Bavli Redactors (Stammaim) to the Aggada*, edited by J.L. Rubenstein, 125–179. Tübingen: Mohr Siebeck, 2005

Moscovitz, Leib. *The Terminology of the Yerushalmi: The Principal Terms*, Jerusalem: Magnes, 2009 [Hebrew]

Neusner, Jacob. "Evaluating the Attributions of Sayings to Named Sages in the Rabbinic Literature," *Journal for the Study of Judaism* 26 (1995) 93–111

Oppenheimer, Aaron. "'Those of the School of Rabbi Yannai'," in *Studies in the History of the Jewish People and the Land of Israel In Honour of Azriel Schochat on the Occasion of his Seventieth Birthday*, edited by M. Graetz, U. Rappaport and J. Shatzmiller, 137–145. Haifa: Haifa University Press, 1978 [Hebrew]

Ratner, Be'er. *Ahavat Tzion Virushalayim: Mesekhet Shabbat*, Jerusalem: Publisher Unknown, 1967

Rappaport, Shlomo Yehuda. *Erekh Milin*, Vols. 1–2. Jerusalem: Makkor, 1970

Rosenfeld, Ben-Zion. *Torah Centers and Rabbinic Activity in Palestine 70–400 C.E.* Leiden: Brill, 2010

Rosenthal, David. "The Transformation of Eretz Israel Traditions in Babylonia" *Cathedra* 92 (1999) 36–44 [Hebrew]

Rubenstein, Jeffrey. "The Talmudic Expression 'Rabbi X following his Reasoning, said,'" *Sidra* 10 (1994) 111–129 [Hebrew]

Rubenstein, Jeffrey. *The Culture of the Babylonian Talmud*, Baltimore and London: The Johns Hopkins University Press, 2003

Sabato, Mordechai. *Talmud Bavli, Sanhedrin Chapter 3: Critical Edition and Commentary*, Vols. 2. Jerusalem: Mosad Bialik, 2018 [Hebrew]

Safrai, Ze'ev. *Mishnat Eretz Israel: Tractate Shabbat with Historical and Sociological Commentary*, Vols. 1–2. Jerusalem: The E.M. Lipshitz Publishing House College, 2008

Schremer, Adiel. "Stammaitic Historiography," in *Creation and Composition: The Contribution of the Bavli Redactors (Stammaim) to the Aggada*, edited by J.L. Rubenstein, 219–135. Tübingen: Mohr Siebeck, 2005

Shelomo b. Aderett. *Ḥidushei Harashba: Masekhet Berakhot*, Jerusalem: Makhon Or, 1980

Silberg, Moshe. *The Writings of Moshe Silberg*, Jerusalem: Magnes, 1998 [Hebrew]

Shemesh, Aaron. *Punishments and Sins: From Scripture to the Rabbis*, Jerusalem: Magnes Press, 2003 [Hebrew]

Sokoloff, Michael. *A Dictionary of Jewish Babylonian Aramaic of the Talmudic and Geonic Periods*, Ramat-Gan & Baltimore: Bar-Ilan University Press, 2002

Steinfeld, Z'vi Arye. *A People Alone: Studies in Tractate 'Avoda Zara*, Ramat-Gan: Bar-Ilan University Press, 2008 [Hebrew]

Stern, Sacha. "Attribution and Authorship in the Babylonian Talmud," *Journal of Jewish Studies* 45 (1995) 28–51

Stollman, Aviad. *BT Eruvin Chapter X with Comprehensive Commentary*, Jerusalem: The Society for the Interpretation of the Talmud, 2008 [Hebrew]

Sussman, Jacob. "Veshuv Lirushalmi Nezikin," *Meḥqerei Talmud* 1 (1990) 55–133

Theodor, Julius. "W. Bacher, Die Agada der Babylonischen Amoräer," *Monatsschrift für die Geschichte und Wissenschaft des Judenthums*, 28 (1879) 43–47, 84–87

Weiss, Abraham. *The Talmud in Its Development*, New-York: Feldheim, 1954 [Hebrew]

Weiss, Iaac Hirsch. *Dor Dor Vedorshav*, Vols. 1–4. Jerusalem and Tel Aviv: Ziv, 1962

Wetheimer, A., and Liss A (eds.). *Piskei Harid: The Rulings of Rabbi Isaiah the Elder: Volume one: Tractates Berakhot and Shabbat*, Jerusalem: Mosad Harav Kuk, 1964

Zuri, Jacob. *Toldot Hamishpat Aziburi Ha'ivri: Shilton Hanesiut Vehava'ad*, Paris: Voltaire, 1931

CHAPTER 11

Cultural Attitudes towards Scent in the Interpretation of Isaiah 11:3

Meira Wolkenfeld

וַהֲרִיחוֹ בְּיִרְאַת יְהוָה וְלֹא לְמַרְאֵה עֵינָיו יִשְׁפּוֹט וְלֹא לְמִשְׁמַע אָזְנָיו יוֹכִיחַ׃

Isaiah 11:3 has been interpreted in different ways, reflecting the ambiguity of the word וַהֲרִיחוֹ. Scholarly treatments have especially dealt with the lexical ambiguity, particularly with regard to whether וַהֲרִיחוֹ should be understood in relation to the meaning of 'spirit' or 'scent.' This paper follows Ian D. Ritchie in suggesting that the translation choice reflects cultural attitudes towards the sense of smell.[1] In his paper, "The Nose Knows: Bodily Knowing in Isaiah 11:3," Ritchie contrasts the interpretation of the Septuagint with that of the Babylonian Talmud. In the Septuagint the phrase, וַהֲרִיחוֹ בְּיִרְאַת יְהוָה is translated as "The spirit of the fear of God will fill him," while in the Babylonian Talmud (henceforth: Bavli), Rava suggests that the verse means that the messiah will judge by smelling (b. Sanhedrin 93b). Ritchie contends that these divergent interpretations reflect different cultural contexts. The Bavli came together in the third through sixth centuries CE, in Sasanian Babylonia, while the Septuagint originated in the third through second centuries BCE in Ptolemaic Egypt. The Bavli's interpretation should be understood within a context where the sense of smell was treated as reliable, whereas the Septuagint reflects one where it was often considered suspect. My paper advances Ritchie's theory by further demonstrating that other Western interpretations also translate the verse away from the meaning of scent, while a range of sources from the Sasanian Empire treat scent as a reliable and admirable means of discernment.[2]

This paper is part of a larger project examining the role of the sense of smell in the cultural world of the Babylonian Talmud. I follow the example of historians of the senses, aiming to understand broad cultural trends. This type of scholarship is typified by Constance Classen, whose history of the rose traces a shift from a time when it was valued primarily for its fragrance, to modernity,

---

1 Ritchie, "Nose Knows," 59–73.
2 Ritchie's treatment does not address the Bavli's cultural context.

where it is more often prized for its appearance.³ She writes, "formerly potent religious concepts such as the odour of sanctity and the stench of sin are now regarded simply as quaint expressions of a more credulous age."⁴ I start with an analysis of the biblical verse and then turn to ancient interpretations, proposing that they reflect cultural differences. Western translations reflect contexts where the sense of smell was sometimes thought of as animalistic and unreliable, whereas Rava's interpretation befits a setting where scent was seen as spiritual and manifesting truth.

Ambiguity and Meaning of וַהֲרִיחוֹ

Scholars have long noted the ambiguity of the term וַהֲרִיחוֹ.⁵ וַהֲרִיחוֹ is a *hiphil* verb with a pronominal suffix. It can be interpreted as either an infinitive ("And his smelling will be with the fear of the Lord")⁶ or a converted perfect ("It will cause him to smell by means of the fear of the Lord").⁷ It also has a lexical ambiguity, which produces more significant differences in interpretation and has been expressed as whether וַהֲרִיחוֹ is formed from the root רוח, meaning 'spirit,' or ריח, 'scent.'⁸ Although this is a good statement of interpretive differ-

---

3 Classen, *Worlds of Sense*, 15–36.
4 Classen, *Worlds of Sense*, 15. The history of the sense of smell has often been told as a linear story of deodorization and diminished reliance on olfaction, from the stench of antiquity to the modern quest for hygiene. The study of the history of smell owes much to Annales scholar Lucien Febvre, who in his 1937 book *The Problem of Unbelief in the Sixteenth Century*, claims that smell was devalued after the sixteenth century. Febvre, *Problem of Unbelief*, 432. Norbert Elias contemporarily claimed that use of olfaction diminished and reliance on sight increased in his 1939 work *The Civilizing Process*. According to Mark Jenner, "Such thinking was strongly influenced by Freud's suggestion, first in his discussion of the Rat Man and then in *Civilization and Its Discontents*, that humankind's adoption of an erect posture led to the 'depreciation of his sense of smell.'" Some recent treatments have suggested that the past was not always more odoriferous, and when it was, it might not have been experienced that way as people become habituated to scents. Jenner, "Follow Your Nose," 342–344. Morley, "Urban Smells," 112.
5 From the ancient interpreters like the rabbis of the Bavli (b.Sanhedrin 93b), through medieval and modern commentators referenced below.
6 For example, see Shifman, "'A Scent' of the Spirit," 241–249, 242; Roberts, *First Isaiah*, 177; and Koehler and Baumgartner, *Hebrew and Aramaic Lexicon*, 1196.
7 While we might expect a *segol* and *hataf segol* in the vocalization of a converted perfect, similar verbs are attested both ways. For example, וְהֵשִׁיבְךָ (Genesis 40:13) and וֶהֱשִׁיבְךָ (Deuteronomy 28:68). I thank Moshe Bernstein for help with this point. The unstated subject would refer to the subject of the previous verse, the spirit of God, wisdom, and understanding.
8 For example, Shifman, "'A Scent' of Spirit," 242, and Unterman, "(Non)Sense of Smell," 17–23, 18–19.

ence, it obscures the relationship between the two meanings, which can both be derived from the root רוח.⁹

The overlapping sounds and meanings enhance the poetry of the verse. The word רוח is repeated four times in the previous verse, Isaiah 11:2, emphasizing that a godly spirit rests on the shoot of Jesse (usually understood as referring to the messiah),[10] suffusing him with wisdom and understanding. The end of verse 3 states that he will not be led astray by the report of his eyes or ears. A reference to smell in the first half of verse 3 contrasts the fallibility of sight and hearing mentioned in the second half of the verse. The word וַהֲרִיחוֹ echoes the sounds of the repeated word רוח, spirit, while simultaneously conveying the meaning of scent. Nonetheless, interpreters have had to choose whether to translate וַהֲרִיחוֹ in relation to the meaning of scent or spirit. Throughout the twentieth century, some have even suggested that the phrase be omitted as a dittography.[11] To my mind, a translation based on the meaning of 'scent' is most straightforward. As mentioned, it fits with the contrast set up by the verse. Furthermore, other *hiphil* attestations of the same root relate to scent.[12] The full verse can thus be rendered, "It will cause him to smell with the fear of the Lord. He will not judge by the sight of his eyes nor decide by the report of his ears."

---

9   Both BDB and the Koehler-Baumgartner lexicon understand וַהֲרִיחוֹ as a *hiphil* of the verb 'to smell,' derived from the root רוח. These meanings are also related in Middle Persian, where the word *bōy* can mean smell, scent, or spirit. MacKenzie, *Concise Pahlavi Dictionary*, s.v. "*Bōy*," 19. Moazami, *Wrestling with the Demons*, 493.

10 Ibn Ezra notes an alternative interpretation that suggests the passage refers to Hezekiah. Ibn Ezra, Isaiah 11:1.

11 For example, Marti, *Das Buch Jesaja*. For other references and discussion of this phenomenon see Roberts, *First Isaiah*, 178, Ritchie, "Nose Knows," 69, Shifman, "'A Scent' of Spirit," 242, and Unterman, "(Non)Sense of Smell," 20.

12 This is evident in Genesis 27:27, where Isaac smells Jacob's earthy scent. Other occurrences are often translated metaphorically, but reflect meaning related to 'scent,' and not 'spirit.' For example, in Genesis 8:21 and Amos 5:21, God's appreciation and reproof are responses to the scent of sacrifice. These verses can be understood literally, but are often translated metaphorically, perhaps precipitating the common translation of Isaiah 11:3 as, "he will delight in the fear of the Lord" (New International Version, New American Standard Bible, and others). Job 39:25 refers to smelling battle from afar as, "מֵרָחוֹק יָרִיחַ מִלְחָמָה." This is often translated loosely as "from afar he senses war," (The New Living Translation) though it could certainly refer to literal scent. Judges 16:9 describes Samson's breaking bonds like threads that incinerate when they merely smell fire, "כַּאֲשֶׁר יִנָּתֵק פְּתִיל הַנְּעֹרֶת בַּהֲרִיחוֹ אֵשׁ" (Judges 16:9). This attestation, also a *hiphil* infinitive, is often translated as, "as threads that come apart when they sense—'come close to' (New International Version, NET Bible) or even 'touch' (English Standard Version, Berean Study Bible, New American Standard Bible, King James Bible, Christian Standard Bible, and JPS Tanakh 1917)—fire." However, meaning and poetic imagery are lost in the metaphoric translations.

Instead, as in the Bavli's interpretation, the messiah follows his nose.

Judgment through scent can be interpreted literally or figuratively. Smell is often associated with immediate, visceral, and emotional response. David Kimhi, born in Provence in 1160, hints to this when he explains that the messiah "will feel (ירגיש)" who is good and who is bad.[13] Imbued with godly spirit and understanding, the messiah judges intuitively with his gut. Instilled with truthful perception, he judges based on divinely intuited knowledge, instead of being swayed by other reports. Eyes and ears can deceive, writes Abraham Ibn Ezra, born in Spain in 1089, but the nose is infallible.[14] Smelling with the fear of God implies judgment through divine insight and "a nose" for the truth. As Walter Ong writes, "Sight reveals only surfaces."[15] "Smell, on the other hand," writes Classen, "is by nature concerned with essences, with the life-giving breath which unites interiors and exteriors in a dynamic interchange ..."[16]

However, despite arguments for translating וַהֲרִיחוֹ in relation to scent, we find several alternatives in Western translations.

Western Non"Scent"ical Translations

I have already cited the Greek translation of the Septuagint, ἐμπλήσει αὐτὸν πνεῦμα φόβου θεοῦ, "The spirit of the fear of God will fill him."[17] The late fourth century Latin Vulgate translates similarly, *Et replebit eum spiritus timoris Domini*, "And he shall be filled with the spirit of the fear of the Lord."[18] This would seem to reflect an understanding of והריחו as a converted perfect built on the meaning of the root רוח as 'spirit.'[19] Reflecting Western origin,[20] Targum

---

13 Kimhi, Isaiah 11:3.
14 Ibn Ezra, Isaiah 11:3.
15 Ong, *Presence of the Word*, 74.
16 Classen, *Worlds of Sense*, 16.
17 Esias 11:3, trans. Silva, *New English Translation*, 833.
18 The Vulgate Bible IV: The Major Prophetical Works, trans. Douay-Theims, 47.
19 This reading was also later espoused by the 11th century biblical commentary Rashi, as it appears in most printed editions, which read, 'ימלא רוח יראת ה "He will be filled with the spirit of fear of God." This version can be found in several manuscripts, including MS Oxford 82. In some Rashi manuscripts this explanation is accompanied by an Old French gloss, rendered as, *éd énosmera il luy (et il l'animera)* or "he will be animated." Maarsen, *Parshandatha*, 37. Other manuscripts read 'ימלא ריח יראת ה. Cohen, *Mikra'ot Gedolot 'Haketer.'* According to Shifman these are Oxford 296, Parma 387, and New York 778. Shifman, "'A Scent' of the Spirit," 245. In this reading, the messiah himself smells like the fear of God. See Nissan and Shemesh, "Olfaction When Judging," 4. As Medel Gottesman librarian Moshe Schapiro pointed out to me, while the difference between ריח and רוח is striking in context, "ו" and "י" can be easily mistaken.
20 The historical background and formation of the Targum is somewhat uncertain. Churgin

Jonathan renders the verse, ²¹יויְ וִיקָרְבִינֵיהּ לִדְחַלְתֵּיהּ "And the Lord shall bring him near to his fear."²² This translation may be based on the idea that scents trigger God's approval and disdain in verses like Genesis 8:21 and Amos 5:21.²³ The Syriac translation in the Peshitta—which likely came together in second century Edessa, at the borders of the Roman Empire and became important for Eastern Christianity²⁴—reads, ܘܢܕܢܚ ܒܕܚܠܬܗ ܕܡܪܝܐ "He will shine forth in the fear of the Lord,"²⁵ perhaps based on the Hebrew והזריחו instead of והריחו,²⁶ or playing upon the nearness of those words in a Christological reworking.²⁷ Instead of "shine forth," a variant version of the Peshitta reads, ܘܢܕܥ, "and he will know" or "and he will be experienced with."²⁸ These sources all interpret the verse away from the meaning of scent, displaying what Ritchie terms, "olfaction avoidance syndrome."²⁹

Although this paper proposes an East-West distinction, the histories of the Targum and of the Peshitta are a good reminder that we should not oversimplify this dichotomy. Translations influenced each other. Communities, people, and ideas move. Attitudes towards senses are broad and can vary across individuals as much as societies; and of course, many factors influence translation choice. With that caveat, I nevertheless suggest that the lines fall in accord with general cultural differences.³⁰

---

suggested that it developed over a period of time, with a Tannaitic Palestinian origin and continued development in amoraic Babylonia. Churgin, *Targum Jonathan*. This remains the scholarly consensus.

21 MS Or. 2211. The Antwerp Polygot Bible has (ויקרבינה) בדחלתא דייי. Codex Reuchlinianus and MS p. 116 have לדחלתא דייי. Reuchlinianus also has a marginal addition, translated by Chilton as, "behold, the Messiah, who is about to come, will be teaching judgment, and will judge by the fear of the Lord." Sperber, *Bible in Aramaic*, 25. In contrast to MS Or. 2211, in these other versions, "the Lord" is not the subject of the verse, but a direct object in the phrase "fear of the Lord."

22 Trans. Chilton, *Isaiah Targum*, 28.

23 Another possibility is that it is, "derived as a causative verb being a corradical of the Aramaic noun *orḥa* 'road'." Nissan and Shemesh, "Olfaction When Judging," 4.

24 Greenberg, *Syriac Peshitta Bible*, XV.

25 "'Shine forth' or 'rise'." *Syriac Peshitta Bible*, trans. Greenberg and Walter, 57.

26 Shifman, "'A Scent' of the Spirit," 242.

27 Thank you to Binyamin Goldstein for this insight and for help with the Syriac translations. According to Goshen-Gottstein, this is an inner-Syriac reworking, and not based on an alternate Hebrew text. Goshen-Gottstein, *Hebrew University Bible*, 44.

28 This is the version in two eleventh-century lectionaries. Brock, *Old Testament in Syriac*, 20.

29 Ritchie, "Nose Knows," 71.

30 We should note as well, that recent scholarship has demonstrated the increasing Hellenization of the Sasanian Empire. For example, Elman and Moazami, "Ancient Legal Thought," 405–420. Nonetheless, there would still be cultural differences.

Hellenistic Attitudes towards Scent

As Ritchie suggests, the choice to translate without reference to the sense of smell may reflect a Hellenistic sensory sensibility. Writing in Greece in the fourth century BCE, Aristotle explained that humans are not as good at smelling as animals, and that human ability to smell is befuddled by pleasure and aversion.[31] Instead of aiding "rational" discernment, scent leads astray through pleasure and pain. Aristotle follows Plato in viewing sight as the most philosophical sense, followed by hearing. "Touch and taste are 'animal' senses, in his view ... the senses of the 'least honour'."[32] The sense of smell is ranked ambiguously between the upper "philosophical" senses, and the "lower," more base ones. However, in characterizing scent as swayed by pleasure and pain, Aristotle seems to associate it more closely with the lower, non-philosophical senses. Certainly, he sees smelling as inferior to seeing and hearing. In contrast, the author of Isaiah 11:3—if this verse relates to scent—treats seeing and hearing as more fallible than smelling.

Philo, in first century CE Alexandria, explicitly characterizes the sense of smell as non-philosophical. In *Questions On Genesis*, he describes four senses (though elsewhere he mentions five,[33] or seven[34]), considering touch an overarching sense involved in the function of each of the others.[35] In this, he likely follows Plato, who in *Timaeus* "deals systematically with the senses, in the [ascending hierarchical] order of taste, smell, hearing and vision."[36] These are Philo's four as well, and like Plato and Aristotle, he considers seeing and hearing particularly philosophical. Smell and taste, in contrast, are "servile" and engaged in supporting the physical body. Thus, in the Armenian *Questions and Answers on Genesis* we find, "Two of these, by which we see and hear, are philosophic, and through them a good life is attained by us. But the others, being non-philosophic, (namely) smell and taste, are servants and have been created only for the living ... Thus smell and taste strengthen the mortal body. But sight and hearing help the immortal mind."[37]

The belief in the irrationality of scent, and its ability to lead astray through pleasure, evident in Aristotle, is also expressed in later Roman attitudes towards

---

31   Aristotle, *On the Soul* II.9, trans. W.S. Hett, 118–119.
32   Synott, "Puzzling Senses," 63–64.
33   For example, Philo, *De Abrahamo* 29:147.
34   For example, Philo, *Quod Deterius Potiori Insidiari Soleat* 44 and 47.
35   Philo, *Questions on Genesis* 3:5 (Genesis 15:10).
36   Jütte, *History of the Senses*, 35.
37   Philo, *Questions on Genesis* 3:5 (Genesis 15:10), trans. Marcus, 187.

perfume. In the first century CE, Pliny the Elder, famously called perfume *materia luxus e cunctis maxume supervacui* or the "most superfluous luxury," writing, *summa commendatio eorum ut transeunte femina odor invitet etiam aliud agentes*, "The very highest recommendation of them is, that when a female passes by, the odour which proceeds from her may possibly attract the attention of those even who till then are intent upon something else."[38] He considers fragrance a distracting lure and claims that perfume was invented by the Persians who, "soaked themselves in it to quench the odor 'born from their unwashed state',"[39] deceptively using perfume to disguise fetor. His younger contemporary Martial similarly suggests that *"non bene olet qui bene semper olet,"* essentially, "anybody who smells good all the time is suspect."[40] The Church Father John Chrysostom, who studied Greek rhetoric under Libanius, wrote in the late fourth century, "Nothing is more unclean for the soul then when the body has such a fragrance [as perfume] ... Who will expect anything noble and good from one who smells of perfumes?"[41] Fragrance undoubtedly played a large role in Roman culture and religion, but as demonstrated, concurrently had negative associations.

Pliny's view that perfume distracts finds a complement in a Palestinian midrash which claims that perfume worn by women in the *shuk* entraps men, "like the venom of an aroused snake."[42] In one particularly misogynist statement, Genesis Rabbah, an early amoraic Palestinian midrashic collection, suggests, like Pliny, that perfume is used to disguise stench. According to Genesis Rabbah, that is why women need it, and not men.[43] Another anecdote from the tannaitic work the Tosefta praises the women of the house of Avtinos for

---

38   Pliny the Elder, *Natural History* 13.4, Rackham, 111, trans. Bostock and Riley, http://www.perseus.tufts.edu/hopper/text?doc=Perseus:abo:phi,0978,001:13.

39   Potter, "Odor and Power," 175. *"unguentum Persarum gentis esse debet; illi madent eo et accersita commendatione inluvie natum virus extingunt."* Pliny, *Natural History* 13.3.

40   Martial 2.12, Bradley, "Foul Bodies," 137.

41   Chrysostom, *On Wealth and Poverty*, trans. Roth quoted in Harvey, *Scenting Salvation*, 206, 314 n. 44.

42   Leviticus Rabbah Metsorah 19:1, Lamentations Rabbah 4:18, b.Yoma 9b, b.Shabbat 62b, and later citation in Yalkut Shimoni Isaiah 247:397. The versions in Lamentations Rabbah and Leviticus Rabbah have "the smell permeated into them like the venom of a snake," while b.Yoma 9b and b.Shabbat 62b have "the evil inclination entered them like the venom of a snake." Although this tradition is transmitted in the Bavli, the Bavli's version may somewhat dim some of the more grotesque aspects found in Palestinian versions, by stating simply that the women put spices in their shoes, instead of describing a perfuming practice involving stepping on eggshells and chicken goiters. I suggest that this reflects a more favorable attitude towards perfume in the Babylonian context.

43   Genesis Rabbah 17:8.

not wearing perfume, as their perfume could be mistaken for illicitly applied temple incense.[44] Andreas Lehnardt has argued that this source reflects a negative, Hellenistic attitude towards scent.[45] In all of these texts, perfume has the ability to disguise and foil rational judgment.

The tendency to consider scent irrationally affecting, particularly in contrast to the more philosophical senses of seeing and hearing, would make Isaiah 11:3 difficult to understand in relation to scent as the verse extolls the messiah's ability to judge justly based on the metaphor of judgment through scent, instead of being swayed by the report of eyes or ears. The implied superiority of the sense of smell would have been baffling for Western interpreters, directly contrasting attitudes towards the senses evidenced in different types of Greco-Roman texts, from Plato and Aristotle through Pliny and Martial, as well as rabbinic texts from Roman Palestine critiquing perfume use. This sensory sensibility may have prompted or predisposed interpreters towards alternative explanations.

וַהֲרִיחוֹ in the Bavli

While texts from the Greco-Roman world downplay the allusion to scent in Isaiah 11:3, in the Babylonian Talmud, the verse is understood as referring to literal smelling. As we will see, this accords with other Bavli texts, which portray smelling as a particularly praiseworthy and spiritual sense.

In b.Sanhedrin 93b, the fourth generation Babylonian amora Rava succinctly explains that, 'והריחו ביראת ה means, [46]שמריח ודן "that he smells and judges." Rava's interpretation is preceded by the more fanciful explanation of the Pales-

---

44   T.Yoma 2:5/6, Song of Songs Rabbah 3:5/4 20d, y.Yoma 3:9 41a, y.Sheqalim. 5:2 49a. This tradition is also transmitted in b.Yoma 38a, but in a more limited way. In all BT mss, it is not women of the House of Avtinos who do not wear perfume, but only brides: מעולם לא יצאת כלה מבושמת מבתיהן. The Bavli version may reflect a minimization of the baraita as Babylonian rabbis did not see the value or plausibility of abstaining from perfume use indefinitely; abstaining from perfume use on ones wedding day was already a great sacrifice. There is also another instance in which Babylonian rabbis qualify a Toseftan baraita in a way that minimizes a restriction on perfume use (t.Berakhot 5:29, y.Berakhot 8:5 12b:3, b.Berakhot 43b).

45   Lehnardt, "Scent of Women," 28–29.

46   MS Jerusalem, Yad Harav Herzog 1, as well as Munich 95. The Vilna, Barko Print (?) (1497), and Venice editions have דמורח ודאין. Throughout, manuscripts are selected according to the Historical Dictionary Project of the Academy of the Hebrew Language. Manuscript analysis is based on The Saul Lieberman Institute of Talmudic Research and The Friedberg Jewish Manuscript Society databases.

tinian amora R. Alexandri, who associates the word והריחו with the word for millstones, ריחיים,[47] explaining that the messiah experiences afflictions and mitsvot like millstones around his neck. Once again, the Western interpretation strays from the more obvious literal meaning, which is all the more striking when juxtaposed to Rava's rather straightforward and concise explanation.

Rava's formulation may express the immediacy of reactions to scent. The messiah smells and judges; no deliberation is necessary. Perhaps Rava intends his interpretation metaphorically, meaning that the messiah senses moral goodness and evil instantaneously. Even if that is so, he translates literally, displaying no hesitation in associating smelling with sound judgement and godliness.

Rava's position that the messiah can judge by smelling is advanced by the anonymous narrators of the Bavli, who explain that Bar Kokhba was proven a false messiah when it was shown that he lacked this ability (b.Sanhedrin 93b). This tradition lacks extent precedent and therefore seems to reflect a particularly Babylonian innovation and sensibility. Indeed, in a famous Palestinian tradition (y.Ta'anit 4:5 68d, Lamentations Rabbah 2:5), Rabbi Aqiva[48] proclaims Bar Kokhba a messiah while R. Yohanan b. Torta disagrees. However, it is only in the Bavli's account that Bar Kokhba pronounces himself a messiah, that this claim is tested, and that Bar Kokhba is condemned to death when he fails a smell test.[49] The smell test is predicated on Rava's exegesis (without attribution), further indicating that it is a late, Babylonian innovation. In understanding Rava's interpretation of Isaiah 11:3 literally, the Stammaitic storytellers express the view that a keen nose is a godly trait and that scent can be a reliable means of discernment. In the section that follows, I demonstrate that this view is evident in several other uniquely Babylonian *aggadot*.

Discernment through Scent in the Bavli

In addition to the story about Bar Kokhba, at least three other stories unique to the Bavli treat the ability to discern by smelling as a commendable, spiritual strength.

---

47 MS Jerusalem, Yad Harav Herzog has כריחים, but this may be a case of a dropped *yud*.
48 Peter Schäfer suggests that the attribution to Aqiva is not original. Schäfer, "Bar Kokhba," 3.
49 J.C. O'Neill suggests that this Bar Kokhba story derives from a Jesus tradition. He points to Matthew 26:67–68, Mark 14:65, and Luke 22:64, where after (possibly) professing himself a messiah, Jesus is blindfolded, commanded to prophesize, and condemned to death. O'Neill, "Mocking of Bar Kokhba," 39–41, 40. While this is an intriguing parallel, Jesus's ordeal does not explicitly entail a smell test.

B.Sotah 49a recounts an incident in which Rav Huna finds a fragrant date and wraps it in cloth. Although the date is hidden from view, when Rav Huna's son Rabbah enters, he is able to identify it by its scent. Rav Huna responds, בני[50] טהרה יש בך "My son, you have purity in you!" and then gifts the date to his son. When Rav Huna's grandson arrives soon after, Rav Huna's son gives the date to him. The anecdote concludes with a bittersweet aphorism: והיינו דאמרי אינשי רחמי דאבא אברא ורחמי דברא אבני דהוו ליה "That is what people say, the love of a father is for his son, the love of his son is for his own son." In this anecdote, a simple object, a date, is treated as a precious heirloom due to its scent. The father's desire to pass it on illustrates his affection. Rabbah bar Rav Huna's ability to discern fragrance and correctly identify it signifies his purity, making him worthy of the precious, aromatic gift.

The association between purity and fragrance is also found in the mishna which precedes this account, in which R. Simeon b. El'azar states, הטהרה נטלה את הטעם ואת הריח "[The loss of] purity takes away the taste and the scent" (m.Sotah 9:13). According to this view, the absence of holiness felt as a result of the destruction of the Temple entails the loss of taste and fragrance. This statement implies a universal loss of scent. However, the narrative of Rav Huna and his son contrasts the mishna, in its depiction of a fragrant date and the people who are able to perceive its aroma. Fragrance, according to the story, still persists and is perceived by those who are worthy. Rav Huna's suggestion that olfactory prowess denotes spirituality may be based on the inference that if loss of purity is associated with the loss of scent, then the ability to discern scent implies purity. Nonetheless, the explicit belief that an individual's ability to discern scent reflects spirituality is unique to the later Babylonian source. A similar view, intimating that the experience of smelling fragrance transcends physicality, is expressed in relation to a statement attributed to the first-generation Babylonian amora Rav:

אמ' מר זוטרא בר טוביה אמ' רב מנין שמברכין על ריח טוב[51] שנא' כל הנשמה תהלל יה אי זהו דבר שהנשמה ניהנית ממנו ולא הגוף הוי אומ' זה ריח טוב

Rav Zutra bar Tuviah said that Rav said: How do we know that we make a blessing on fragrant scent? Because it says, "all the soul (or 'everything

---

50   MS Oxford—Bodl. heb. d. 20 (2675). The other manuscripts are consistent, with the exception of Vatican 110–111, which has ריח טהרה יש בך. This interesting alternative may be a dittography.

51   MS Oxford Opp. Add. fol. 23, Bodleian Library (366). Munich 95 and Paris 671 also have על ריח טוב, while the Vilna, Venice, and Soncino editions simply state מנין שמברכין על הריח.

that breathes') praises God" [Psalms 150:6].[52] What gives enjoyment to the soul but not the body? I would say, that is fragrant scent. (b.Berakhot 43b)

The story of Rav Huna similarly venerates the experience of smelling and the individual attuned to that experience. While Philo considers smelling "servile" to the "mortal body," Rav and Rav Huna regard it as a spiritual gift.

Two stories on b.Niddah 20b also treat olfactory aptitude as a mark of distinction. In the second, King Shapur's mother, Ifra Hormiz, asks Rava to examine a sample of her vaginal discharge. Rava smells the sample and determines that it is "the blood of desire," which is not contaminating. Ifra Hormiz sings his praises to her son, the Persian king, who expresses skepticism. Spurred to prove Rava's skill, Ifra Hormiz sends Rava an additional sixty blood samples. Rava passes the test, successfully identifying all except for the last, which he does not recognize. He returns his answers with the present of a delousing comb. This ends up working in his favor as the last sample was, coincidentally, louse blood, and so Ifra Hormiz assumes that he correctly identified it. Shai Secunda has shown that this story is attentive to cultural resonance, evincing a reaction to Zoroastrian menstrual purity laws.[53] Secunda suggests that one goal of the story is to assert the superiority of the rabbis by demonstrating their ability to discern different types of emissions, in contrast to their Zoroastrian neighbors who did not distinguish between different colors of discharge.[54] I would add that the fact that the superiority of the rabbis is asserted through smelling is significant, reflecting the valuation of smell in society. The capability of the rabbis is demonstrated by Rava's discerning nose, as once again, the Stammaitic storytellers treat the ability to discern scent as venerable.

The narrative of Rava and Ifra Hormiz is built on the example of two other stories that also appear in the Bavli.[55] The second half, in which Rava correctly identifies sixty blood samples, parallels a similar account in which the second-century sage R. Elazar b. R. Shimon examines sixty blood samples (b.Bava Metsia 84b). However, R. Elazar b. R. Shimon is not depicted smelling the samples. The first half, in which Rava explicitly smells the blood, closely parallels another account immediately preceding it, in which R. Elazar b. Pedat smells a sample

---

52 Rav's statement may play off an earlier tradition in which Psalm 150:6 is used to suggest that one should make a blessing on every breath, found in Genesis Rabbah 14:9 on Gen 2:7 and Deuteronomy Rabbah 2:37 on Deuteronomy 6:5. The following line in the Bavli, "What gives enjoyment to the soul but not the body? I would say, that is fragrant scent," may be a Stammaitic interpolation.
53 Secunda, "Talmudic Text," 51–53, 63.
54 Secunda, "Talmudic Text," 59–63. *Pahlavi Widewdad* 16. Šāyest nē šāyest 3.19.
55 This has been demonstrated by Secunda, "Talmudic Text," 51–54.

of discharge and determines that it is "the blood of desire" (b.Niddah 20b). The image of a rabbi who smells blood is unique to the Babylonian Talmud, and particularly to these two juxtaposed Stammaitic accounts, the stories of R. Elazar b. Pedat and of Rava. The only earlier reference to a similar practice is the polemical claim of Jerome, that the wise men of the Pharisees, "if they are unable to discern by sight whether the blood of a virgin or menstruant is pure or impure, they test it by taste."[56] In Jerome, taste is meant to elicit disgust. In contrast, the stories of Rava and Ifra Hormiz and R. Elazar b. Pedat betray no hint of repugnance with smelling the substance. Instead, smelling is used to demonstrate rabbinic aptitude.

The significance of scent in these two stories is highlighted by the stories surrounding them, which discuss rabbis who **look** at blood samples or choose not to. B.Niddah 20b recounts a series of tales in which rabbis express uncertainty about their ability to perform visual examinations of menstrual blood. Variations of the root חזי, meaning to see, appear seventeen times on b. Niddah 20b alone. The analogous Hebrew root ראה appears an additional five times,[57] further demonstrating the importance of sight in the pericope. Discussions include rabbis who have bad eyesight and who examine samples in different conditions such as during the day or night, by light of a lamp, on a cloudy day, or with an eyesore. While the wider context, the second chapter of tractate Niddah, deals with the visual examination of discharge, this cluster of stories at the end of the chapter teases out the subjectivity of that practice and problematizes it. Thus, Yalta shows a sample to two different rabbis who give her opposite answers. Another rabbi wavers about the permissibility of a sample depending on whether he looks at it during the day or night. Reacting to his distress over his mistake, the anonymous redactors counsel, אין לו לדיין אלא מה שעיניו רואות, "he can only judge *what his eyes can see*."[58] To quote Ong once more, "Sight presents surfaces ... but it does not present all surfaces, only those in front of us."[59] In the middle of these stories about rabbis **looking** at blood samples—in shade, sun, and with different visual abilities—the two narratives about rabbis smelling the samples stand out. They are the only stories in the group which demonstrate the rabbinic ability to correctly assess blood samples, proving rabbinic capability, instead of problematizing it. R. Elazar b.

---

56   Jerome, Letter to Algasia (121), chapter 10, quoted in Schwartz, "Rabbinization," 63. See also Fonrobert, *Menstrual Purity*, 115–116.
57   These counts were taken in the Vilna text.
58   Compare b.Bava Batra 131a.
59   Ong, *The Presence of the Word*, 128.

Pedat and Rava do not judge by what their eyes can see, which the surrounding pericope implies is limited, but by their noses, which allows them to perceive beyond the surface.

In these stories, smelling may denote an almost magical intuition. R. Elazar b. Pedat smells the sample and determines that it is "the blood of desire." This is confirmed when the woman confides that she had desired her husband while he was away on a trip. Rava displays similar intuition when he sends Ifra Hormiz a delousing comb, despite his uncertainty about the last sample, which just so happens to be louse blood. Yael Avrahami suggests regarding Isaiah 11:3, that, "judgment through smell is reserved to a future leader, in a utopian time, when 'The wolf shall dwell with the lamb, the leopard lie down with the kid'," as the passage continues (Isaiah 11:6).[60] In these texts, judgment through scent might indicate clairvoyance.

In the series of stories on b.Niddah 20b, the intuitive, truthful nature of scent stands in contrast to sight, which is shown to be prone to subjective interpretation. Smell is distinct from sight in representing the capability of the rabbis, while the subjectivity of sight manifests their fallibility. In the discussed Babylonian *aggadot*, attunement to scent signifies perceptiveness.

Discernment through Scent in Middle Persian Texts

Sensing impurity through scent, as Rava does in the story, may have particular cultural resonance. According to the Middle Persian *Dēnkard* V 24, menstrual blood is particularly foul smelling:

> ud daštān kē az ān sūrāk-ē +āyēd pad wyšsyltkyh (?) ī ōy druz andar hamāg tan ud rēzišn ī-š xwēs gandagīh ud rēmanīh gētīgīg ⟨ud⟩ mēnōgīg ō-z bērōn bawēd ... ud daštān jud-gōnīh-iz ī az abārīg xūn ud garāy-gandīh ud āhōgēnīdārīh xwad-iz ōy tan kē padiš wināhīdārīh pad nazdīkīh ō-z āb ud urwar kāhišnīh ud xwarišnīhā a-mizag ud bōy-wardišnīh

> The menstrual matter that comes out of that one hole comes out also with the **vinegar-smelling** (?) poison of that demon and with all of her own **stench** and the pollution of both worlds that she pours out ... And because menstrual matter is also of different color from the other blood, because of its **grievous stench** and because it soils everything, the body

---

60 Avrahami, *The Senses of Scripture*, 105.

itself in which it has this destructive effect also causes water and plants to diminish and foods to lose their taste and **smells bad**.[61]

As Secunda points out, "the Zoroastrian priests did not devise a complex system of pure and impure discharges that led to a new kind of ecclesiastical expertise ... there is no indisputable mention in the Zand or in subsequent medieval responsa of women or priests checking the appearance of vaginal discharges."[62] There are no references to examinations by scent either. Nonetheless, in Pahlavi literature, impurity is often associated with foul odor, as evident in the passage above, which references the odor of menstruation at least three times. Corpse impurity is apparently similarly odoriferous:

> *ud tan ka murd abarwēzīhā abar madan ī druz ī margīh -kardār ud a-gārēnīdār Astwihād ud stōwēnīdan ī gyān aziš ud abāz grift⟨an⟩ ī-š brādarān gandēnīdārān ⟨ud⟩ +posēnīdārān ⟨ud⟩ abārīg an-abēdān-kardārān dēwān ō tan ud ānāftan ī-šān jud jud xwēš hambadīg čiyōn hu-bōyīh ud pākīh ud hu-burdīh ud hu-čihrīh ud abārīg ī abāyišnīg az tan ud mehmānīhā wālīdan ī-šān andar ham tan ōwōn frāyīha kū ō⟨h⟩-iz bē gand ud nasuš ⟨ud⟩ wisp wēmārīh damēnd ud ānōh kū dēwān mehmānīh damēnd pad ān ēwānag rēmānīh guftan abē-pahikār sazēd būd.*[63]

> when a body is dead, then the demon that causes death stops the body from functioning. That is, the Bone-untier comes upon it in supremacy, overcomes and chases the soul (*gyān*) from the body. Then it takes back the life in place after place and brings its brothers into the body to abide in it, producing stench and rot, as well as the other demons who render it useless. And each of them rejects from the body his own opponent, for instance, fragrance, cleanness, good behavior, beauty, and other decent things. And they prosper as inhabitants in the same body to such a great extent that they breathe to the outside, too, stench, dead matter, and all the illnesses. It hardly seems disputable that, where the demons inhabit in that manner, it should be called pollution.[64]

---

61   *Dēnkard* V 24:20–20a. Amouzgar, *Le Cinquième Livre*, 94–95. Trans. Skjærvø, *Spirit of Zoroastrianism*, 254, 136:20–20a. The last phrase is perhaps better translated, "and foods become tasteless and their scents change." I thank Mahnaz Moazami for all of her assistance with the Persian sources.
62   Secunda, "Talmudic Text," 62–63.
63   *Dēnkard* V 24:19a. Amouzgar, *Le Cinquième Livre*, 75, 91.
64   *Dēnkard* V 24, trans. Skjærvø, *Spirit of Zoroastrianism*, 252–253, 136:19a.

Elsewhere the *Dēnkard* states, *ud wizend madan andar gumēzišn ōwōn a-čārīg čiyōn nē-z šāyēd {ud} andar gumēzišn ī ō nasā +nē ōšmārdan ī gand,* "The fact that, in the Mixture, there would be damage was as inevitable as not to smell stench in something mingled with dead matter."[65] The claim that impurity is inevitably smelly is an expression of the truthfulness and reliability of scent. The story of Rava and Ifra Hormiz similarly treats odor as an indication of purity status.

In Middle Persian literature, the binary of fragrance and stench is an expression of dualism. As one text puts it, *ud az kē nēkīh ud az kē wadīh. ud az kē rōšnīh ud az kē tārīkīh. ud az kē hu-bōyīh ud az kē gandagīh,* "From whom is goodness and badness? From whom is light and darkness? From whom is fragrance and stench? From whom is right and wrong?"[66] Stench and fragrance parallel darkness and light. Fragrance is not ambiguous or deceptive, but grouped with light, right, goodness, and forgiveness. Stench is correspondingly evil. In fact, the evil power is often referred to as Gannāg Mēnōy, or Foul Spirit, "referring to the *stench* coming from evil beings."[67] According to the doctrine of anatomical dualism, the lower half of the body is also odorous:

> *pad hangōšīdag ēdōn harw čē azabar nēmag ī tan čiyōn āšnawišn ud hambōyišn gyāg ī xrad ud gyān ud ox menišn ud ōš ud wīr ud āsn-xrad ud gōšōsrūd-xrad gyāg ī yazdān ud amahrspandān ... ud azēr nēmag ast čiyōn gandagīh ud rēmanīh gyāg gōmēzdān ud sargēn ud gandagīh homānāg ud gilistag ī gyāg ī ahreman ud dēwān*

> In the same way, all that is in the upper half of the body, such as hearing and smell—the place of wisdom, the soul, the mind, thought, intelligence, perception, the inborn wisdom that acquired through hearing—is the place of the gods and the Amarspands ... The lower half is like a place of stench and pollution, the bladder and excrement. And the stench is like the lair and place of Ahreman and the demons.[68]

What is bad and impure is necessarily demonic and odoriferous. And yet, the act of smelling is itself part of the upper body, associated with wisdom, the soul,

---

65 *Dēnkard* v 24:8. Amouzgar, *Le Cinquième Livre,* 80. Trans. Skjærvø, *Spirit of Zoroastrianism,* 249, 136:8.
66 *Čīdag Andarz ī Pōryōtkēšān. The Book of Advice of Zarathustra* 92:1, trans. Skjærvø, *Spirit of Zoroastrianism,* 193.
67 Skjærvø, *Spirit of Zoroastrianism,* 9, 20.
68 *Dēnkard* v 22, trans. Skjærvø, 247.

thought, and perception. The ability to perceive scent, to discern foul from fragrant, is admirable and advantageous.

In fact, the capability of discerning scent is a boon to the exalted role of the dog in Zoroastrianism. In the ritual of *sagdīd*, meaning "seeing by a dog,"[69] a dog is brought to gaze at a corpse, helping purge the corpse demon. While this is accomplished through the dog's vision, the dog's superior sense of smell may also play a role, enabling the dog "to become aware of those presences invisible to humans."[70] The role of the dog's nose is perhaps evident in that even a blind dog can be used to perform the ritual, as the text *Šāyast-nē-Šāyast* explains, a blind dog can perform the ritual by putting its muzzle on the corpse.[71] In Aristotle's analysis, animals' superior senses of smell taint that sense.[72] In contrast, in Pahlavi literature the dog's discerning nose contributes to its esteemed role and status.

Much as the messiah is said to judge through scent in b.Sanhedrin 93b, in Middle Persian literature, the ability to discern through scent is a hallmark of the messianic age. According to the Zādspram, redacted in the 9th century, the resurrected bodies of the righteous *hu-bōytar hēnd kū mušk ud ambar ud +kāpūr*, "will be more fragrant than musk, ambergris, or camphor."[73] Rav Zutra bar Tuviah[74] similarly states in the name of Rav, עתידים בחורי ישראל (שלא טעמו טעם חטא)[75] שיתנו ריח טוב כלבנון, "In the future the young men of Israel (who have never tasted the taste of sin) will give off fragrant scent like the Lebanon" (b.Berakhot 43b, interpreting Hosea 14:7). The idea that a messiah could and would discern by smelling would cohere within this broader cultural context.

While Aristotle and Philo treat scent as a non-philosophical sense, oriented towards the needs of the body, the *Dēnkard* and statements in the Bavli associate scent with spiritual, and not physical, experience.

---

69 Moazami, *Wrestling with the Demons*, 145.
70 Moazami, "A Purging Presence," 22, 27.
71 *Šāyast-nē-Šāyast* 2.4, trans. Tavadia, *Šāyast-nē-Šāyast*, 32.
72 Aristotle, *On the Soul* II.9.
73 Zādspram 35:51, *Anthologie de Zādspram*, eds. Gignoux and Tafazzoli, 138–139, trans. King, *Scent from the Garden*, 128.
74 MSS Oxford Opp. Add. fol. 23, Bodleian Library (366), and Paris 671 have רב חסדא בר טוביה.
75 This qualifier appears in MSS Oxford Opp. Add. fol. 23, Bodleian Library (366), Munich 95, and Paris 671.

Scent and Emotion

Aristotle's claim that the sense of smell is "inseparably bound up with and so confused by pleasure and pain"[76] has biological basis. Scent is processed in ways that make it more closely tied to emotions than other senses.[77] This also explains the role scent plays in inculcating purity systems through disgust. Scents provoke immediate and visceral emotional responses. In describing the use of scent in rituals of transition, the anthropologist David Howes writes, "Recognizing the scent, we are at once 'transported'—as the poet (Baudelaire 1975: 42) would say—back to the event with which it is originally associated, and 'we live the moment over again with the full cord of its emotions vibrating our soul and startling our consciousness' (McKenzie 1923: 48)." In this context, he quotes "Barbara Lex (1977: 330) [who writes that] intense stimulation of the autonomic nervous system [including response to odor] 'retards or prohibits logical reasoning'."[78] While scent is often associated with memory, studies have shown that the "accuracy, detail, and vividness" of memories triggered by scent are equal to the accuracy, detail, and vividness of memories triggered by other senses. Memories triggered by scent differ only, "in one important way: their emotionality."[79]

Attitudes towards knowledge through scent may thus align with broader cultural trends, like attitudes towards the body and emotions. Isaiah 11:3 and its interpretation in the Bavli can be read as suggesting that the messiah will possess intuitive understanding, reacting viscerally to goodness and evil. Some

---

76   Aristotle, *On the Soul* II.9, trans. Smith, http://www.mesacc.edu/~barsp59601/text/philtext/aristotle/soul/bk2/9.html.
77   After scent chemicals connect with receptors on the olfactory epithelium, nerve impulses are sent to the olfactory bulbs and relayed onward to other parts of the limbic system and other regions of the brain. In addition to the olfactory bulbs, the limbic system contains the hippocampus and amygdala, areas of the brain responsible for processing memory and emotion. Scent signals have direct pathways to these functions. As the psychologist and cognitive scientist Rachel Herz writes, evolutionarily, "A primitive olfactory cortex was the first fabric of our brain and from this neural tissue grew the amygdala, where emotion is processed, and the parts of the brain that are responsible for basic memory and motivation." She explains that the function of olfaction and emotion are interconnected, "dysfunction in the amygdala alters the normal functioning of the olfactory cortex, and dysfunction in the olfactory cortex alters the normal functioning of the amygdala. The olfactory and emotion areas of our brain are dependent upon each other for their mutual health and integrity ... the experiences of emotion and olfaction are similarly primal, visceral, and removed from verbal semantic analysis." Herz, *The Scent of Desire*, 14–16.
78   Howes, "Olfaction and Transition," 132.
79   Herz, *The Scent of Desire*, 67.

audiences, oriented towards philosophical reasoning, might be generally skeptical of emotional knowledge, or the reliability of judgment through scent. Accordingly, translations of Isaiah 11:3 originating in the Greco-Roman world render the verse without reference to the sense of smell. In contrast, the idea that the messiah will literally judge by smelling is embraced in the Babylonian Talmud. Other *aggadot* unique to the Bavli also treat the ability to discern scent as a mark of superiority, purity, and godliness. This accords with the approach of Middle Persian literature, which treats smelling as a godly trait, associating fragrance and purity.

Attitudes towards discernment through scent may also relate to conceptions of the nature of scent. Ephemeral and invisible, scent, in some contexts, was considered spiritual instead of physical. According to one statement from the Bavli quoted above, smelling entails spiritual—and not physical—enjoyment (b. Berakhot 43b). In her work on scent in Late Antique Christianity, Susan Ashbrook Harvey writes that, due to their "invisibility and uncontainability … smells could mark human-divine interaction and relation precisely because they indicated a certain seepage between the divine and human domains in anticipation of what would come."[80] In addition to emotionally transporting the perceiver, anthropologists also explain the use of fragrance in rituals of transition, as related to the ability of scents to move from place to place.[81] Invisible and mobile, scent could be seen as enabling the messiah to perceive past the physical veneer, offering a whiff of essence.

Different cultural environments favor different attitudes towards scent and sensory experience. When considered animalistic, the sense of smell would be unbefitting a messiah. But when considered spiritual, the sense of smell would be a particularly godly gift, enabling the messiah "to smell and judge" forthwith. Translations and interpretations of Isaiah 11:3 reflect these divergent attitudes towards the sense of smell: considered, at times, animalistic, unreliable, and distracting in the Greco-Roman world, and more often than not, as spiritual and manifesting truth in the Sasanian Empire.

---

80 Harvey, *Scenting Salvation*, 224.
81 Howes, "Olfaction and Transition."

Bibliography

The Academy of the Hebrew Language. http://maagarim.hebrew-academy.org.il/.
Amouzgar, Jaleh and Ahmad Tafazzoli, trans. *Le Cinquième Livre du Dēnkard*. Paris: Association pour l'Avancement des Études Iraniennes, 2000.
Avrahami, Yael. *The Senses of Scripture: Sensory Perception in the Hebrew Bible*. New York: T & T Clark International, 2012.
Bradley, Mark. "Foul Bodies in Ancient Rome." In *Smell and the Ancient Senses*, edited by Mark Bradley, 133–145. London: Routledge, 2015.
Brock, Sebastian P. ed. *The Old Testament in Syriac: According to the Peshiṭta Version* III.1. Leiden: Brill, 1987.
Chilton, Bruce D. trans. *The Isaiah Targum: Introduction, Translation, Apparatus and Notes, The Aramaic Bible*, Volume 11. Project director Martin McNamara. Wilmington: Michal Glazier, 1987.
Churgin, Pinkhos. *Targum Jonathan to the Prophets*. New Haven: Yale University Press, 1927.
Classen, Constance. *Worlds of Sense: Exploring the Senses in History and Across Culture*. London: Routledge, 1993.
Cohen, Menahem, ed. *Mikra'ot Gedolot 'Haketer.'* Ramat Gan: Universiṭat Bar Ilan, 1992.
Douay-Theims, trans. *The Vulgate Bible IV: The Major Prophetical Works*. Edited by Angela M. Minney. Cambridge: Harvard University Press, 2012.
Elman, Yaakov and Mahnaz Moazami. "Some Aspects of Ancient Legal Thought: Functionalism, Conceptualism, and Analogy." In *Strength to Strength: Essays in Honor of Shaye J.D. Cohen*, edited by Michael L. Satlow, 405–420. Providence, Rhode Island: Brown Judaic Studies, 2018.
Evans, Craig A. *To See and Not Perceive: Isaiah 6.9–10 in early Jewish and Christian interpretation*. Sheffield: JSOT Press, 19 89.
Fonrobert, Charlotte Elisheva. *Menstrual Purity: Rabbinic and Christian Reconstructions of Biblical Gender*. Stanford: University of Stanford Press, 2000.
The Friedberg Jewish Manuscript Society. https://bavli.genizah.org/.
Gignoux, Ph. and A. Tafazzoli, trans. *Anthologie de Zādspram*. Paris: Association pour l'Avancement des Études Iraniennes, 1993.
Goshen-Gottstein, Moshe H., ed. *The Hebrew University Bible: The Book of Isaiah*. Jerusalem: Magnes, 1995.
Greenberg, Gillian and Donald M. Walter, trans. *The Syriac Peshiṭta Bible with English Translation: Isaiah*. Pascataway: Gorgias, 2012.
Harvey, Susan Ashbrook. *Scenting Salvation: Ancient Christianity and the Olfactory Imagination*. Berkeley: University of California Press, 2006.
Herz, Rachel. *The Scent of Desire: Discovering our Enigmatic Sense of Smell*. New York: Harper, 2007.

Hett, W.S., trans. Aristotle, *On the Soul*. Loeb Classical Library 288. Cambridge: Harvard University Press, 1957.

Howes, David. "Olfaction and Transition." In *The Varieties of Sensory Experience: A Sourcebook in the Anthropology of the Senses*, edited by David Howes, 398–416. Toronto: University of Toronto Press, 1991.

Jenner, Mark S.R. "Follow Your Nose? Smell, Smelling, and Their Histories." *AHR Forum* 116, no. 2 (2011) 335–351.

Jütte, Robert. *A History of the Senses: From Antiquity to Cyberspace*. Translated by James Lynn. Bonn: Polity, 2005.

King, Anya H. *Scent from the Garden of Paradise: Musk and the Medieval Islamic World*. Boston: Leiden, 2017.

Koehler, Ludwig and Walter Baumgartner. *The Hebrew and Aramaic Lexicon of the Old Testament*. New York: Brill, 1994–2000.

Lehnardt, Andreas. " 'The Scent of Women': Incense and Perfume in Talmud Yerushalmi Sheqalim 5:2." In *Introduction to Seder Qodashim: A Feminist Commentary on the Babylonian Talmud* v, eds. Tal Ilan, Monika Brockhaus, Tanja Hidde, 23–31. Mohr Siebeck: Tübingen, 2012.

Maarsen, Isaac. *Parshandatha: The Commentary of Rashi on the Prophets and Hagiographs*, Edited on the Basis of Several Manuscripts and Editions, Part II. Isajah. Jerusalem: Makor, 1971 or 1972.

MacKenzie, D.L. *A Concise Pahlavi Dictionary*. London: Oxford University Press, 1971.

Marcus, Ralph, trans. *Philo, Questions and Answers on Genesis: Translated from the Ancient Armenian Version of the Original Greek*. Loeb Classical Library 380 Suppl. I. Cambridge: Harvard University Press, 1953.

Marti, D. Karl. *Das Buch Jesaja*. KHC 10; Tübingen: Mohr Siebeck, 1900.

Moazami, Mahnaz. "A Purging Presence: The Dog in Zoroastrian Tradition." *Anthropology of the Middle East* 11, no. 1 (2016) 20–29.

Moazami, Mahnaz. *Wrestling with the Demons of the Pahlavi Widewdad: Transcription, Translation and Commentary*. Leiden: Brill, 2014.

Morley, Neville. "Urban Smells and Roman Noses." In *Smell and the Ancient Senses*, edited by Mark Bradley, 110–119. New York: Routledge, 2013.

Nissan, Ephraim, and Abraham Ofir Shemesh. "Olfaction When Judging, According to Isaiah 11:3–4." *Bibbia e Oriente* 59, no. 4 (2017) 1–28.

O'Neill, John Cochrane. "The Mocking of Bar Kokhba and of Jesus." *Journal for the Study of Judaism in the Persian, Hellenistic, and Roman Period* 31, no. 1 (2000) 39–41.

Ong, Walter. *The Presence of the Word: Some Prolegomena for Cultural and Religious History*. New Haven: Yale University Press, 1967.

Potter, David S. "Odor and Power in the Roman Empire." In *Constructions of the Classical Body*, edited by James I. Porter, 169–189. Ann Arbor: University of Michigan Press, 2002.

Ritchie, Ian D. "The Nose Knows: Bodily Knowing in Isaiah 11:3." *Journal for the Study of the Old Testament* 87 (2000) 59–73.

Roberts, Jim. *First Isaiah: A Commentary*. Edited by Peter Machinist. Minneapolis: Fortress, 2015.

Schäfer, Peter. "Bar Kokhba and the Rabbis." In *The Bar Kokhba War Reconsidered: New Perspectives on the Second Jewish Revolt Against Rome*, edited by Peter Schäfer, 1–22. Tübingen: Mohr Siebeck, 2003.

Schwartz, Seth. "Rabbinization in the Sixth Century." In *The Talmud Yerushalmi and Graeco-Roman Culture*, Volume 3, edited by Peter Schäfer, 55–69. Tübingen: Mohr Siebeck, 2002.

Secunda, Shai. "Talmudic Text and Iranian Context: On the Development of Two Talmudic Narratives." *AJS Review* 33 (2009) 45–69.

Shifman, Arie. "'A Scent' of the Spirit: Exegesis of an Enigmatic Verse (Isaiah 11:3)." *Journal of Biblical Literature* 131, no. 2 (2012): 241–249.

Silva, Moisés, trans. *A New English Translation of the Septuagint (NETS)*. Oxford University Press, 2009. http://ccat.sas.upenn.edu/nets/edition/.

Skjærvø, Prods Oktor, trans. and ed. *The Spirit of Zoroastrianism*. New Haven: Yale University Press, 2011.

Sperber, Alexander. *The Bible in Aramaic: Based on Old Manuscripts and Printed Texts*. Leiden: Brill, 1962.

Synott, Anthony. "Puzzling Over the Senses: From Plato to Marx." In *The Varieties of Sensory Experience: A Sourcebook in the Anthropology of the Senses*, edited by David Howes, 61–78. Toronto: University of Toronto Press, 1991.

Tavadia, Jehangir C., trans. *Šāyast-nē-Šāyast: A Pahlavi Text on Religious Customs*. Hamburg: De Gruyter & Co, 1930.

Unterman, Jeremiah. "The (Non)Sense of Smell in Isaiah 11:3." *Hebrew Studies* 33 (1992) 17–23.

CHAPTER 12

"And God Blessed Them": Procreation in Palestinian *Halakhah* and in Babylonian *Aggadah*

Shana Strauch Schick

> The mother is no parent of that which is called her child, but only nurse of the new-planted seed that grows. The parent is he who mounts. A stranger, she preserves a stranger's seed ... There can be a father without any mother.*[1]

Procreation is unique in requiring the participation of both a man and woman; this has therefore given rise to significant questions of agency from the ancient Greeks to today, and of course for the rabbinic sages. From the biological perspective, what does each parent contribute to the process of reproduction? From a halakhic one, who is actually commanded to have children and does one have the right to abstain or refuse to do so?

We will see that on these matters, rabbinic sages from Babylonia and the Land of Israel during the talmudic period diverge significantly, but they do so in different ways depending on whether the text is aggadic or halakhic. In aggadic texts describing the physical process of conception, traditions recorded in the Babylonian Talmud (hereon: Bavli) highlights women's material contribution where earlier parallels from the Land of Israel, notably those found in Leviticus Rabbah, disregard it. Yet when it comes to halakhic texts, we find the reverse: Works from the Land of Israel, including, the Tosefta and Palestinian Talmud (hereon: Yerushalmi), side with the mishnaic view that equates men's and women's obligation. By contrast, throughout the Bavli, the dissenting view which obligates men alone is unequivocally preferred. What is more, in both the halakhic and aggadic texts, the Bavli incorporates and reframes Palestinian traditions within its discourse; however, in the halakhic discussion of procreation, what appear as rulings and brief statements in the Tosefta

---

* My thanks to Steven Fine, Lynn Kay, Ilana Kurshan, Moshe Shoshan and Ari Schick for reading through this article and offering important insights. Unfortunately I never had the opportunity to discuss most of the ideas explored in this article with Yaakov Elman z"l, but his sensibilities and outlook are a constant guide.
1 Grene, *Aeschylus I*, 158 lines 658–666.

and Yerushalmi, are presented in the form of narratives in the corresponding Bavli text.

Drawing on recent work by Barry Wimpfheimer, which explores the relationship between *halakhah* and *aggadah* in the Bavli, I will argue that the Bavli aggadic texts and narratives serve to highlight potential problems with the accepted halakhic position and give voice to marginalized positions—the very views found in Palestinian texts. In this way, the Bavli provides a forum for presenting the variant opinions from *Erets Yisrael* as a multidiscursive contrast to its own discourse.

The Aggadic Discussion of Procreation: The Mother's Physical Contribution

Aggadic discussions of the physical process of procreation present conflicting opinions as to women's physical contributions, with those from the Land of Israel greatly reducing them while traditions found in the Bavli highlighting them. This is seen specifically in two texts which contain sustained discussions on the matter: a section of Leviticus Rabbah, an amoraic midrashic collection from the Land of Israel whose redaction has been dated between the mid-fourth to fifth centuries, and its Babylonian parallel found in the final unit of the third chapter of Bavli Niddah (30b–31b).[2]

In a recent article,[3] I suggested that Leviticus Rabbah 14, a homily on Leviticus 12:2, *'ishah ki-tazria'* (generally translated as "when a woman conceives"), largely disregards the role of the mother and rather depicts the father as the sole source of physical material. God is repeatedly praised for intervening at all stages of procreation. The Bavli, by contrast, contains several passages which view the mother as essential in conception and embryology, even as significant portions of the *sugya* conform to Leviticus Rabbah 14 in both content and form.

The primacy of the father's role is evident in Leviticus Rabbah 14:2, where R. Levi, a third-generation Palestinian amora,[4] describes the process of conception as a man placing a "drop of the whitest fluid in private" which God forms into an embryo.[5] Similarly, 14:5 states that God "gathers up every single of drop

---

2 Margulies, *Vayyikra Rabbah*, 2:311, to line 2.
3 Strauch Schick, "From Dungeon to Haven."
4 Babylonian sages do not generally appear in Leviticus Rabbah. Margulies, *Vayyikra Rabbah*, XXXI introduction.
5 Vayikra Rabbah, *Tazria, par. 14*, to Leviticus 12:2 (ed. Margulies, 2:301).
   For other Palestinian works containing similar depictions, see Bereshit Rabbah, *Bere'shit*,

that there is" and inseminates the woman. In 14:6 R. Yohanan and Reish Laqish discuss how God creates the embryo from the father's seed, drawing analogy from the process of winnowing to describe God's intimate involvement in forming the fetus from the "whitest drop."[6]

As Gwenn Kessler and Tamar Jacobowitz have observed, the mother's absence from Leviticus Rabbah 14 and its depictions of the fetus as generated solely from male seed correlates with Soranus's one seed theory.[7] This first-second-century Greek physician asserted that only men produce seed which enters the mother's body, where it develops into a fetus.[8] The mother makes no physical contribution. I further argued that the negation of the mother's role is consistent with the general tone of Greek literature, beginning with Hesiod and continuing to later Roman times.[9] Returning to the quote from Aeschylus's *Oresteia* cited at the beginning of this article, Apollo argues that Orestes was justified in killing his own mother, Clytemnestra, on the grounds that a mother is not active in the process of procreation and therefore not considered a true parent. A one-seed theory was not the dominant position among Greek theorists, but it seems clear that Leviticus Rabbah (mostly)[10] embraces this view.[11]

A different picture emerges from the Bavli in the concluding unit of b.Niddah 30b–31b, which consists of an aggadic cluster dealing with conception, embryology, pregnancy, and birth.[12] Although much of this *sugya* conforms to Leviticus Rabbah, it also includes traditions which include the mother in the

---

     par. 17 Genesis 2:21 (ed. Theodor-Albeck, 1:159); Mekhilta de'Rabbi Yishmael, *par. Be-Shalakh, mas. De'Shira* 8 (ed. Horotvitz-Rabin, 144); Mekhilta de'Rabbi Shimon b Yohai, *par. Be-Shalakh*, 15:11 (ed. Epstein-Melamed, 94).

6   While a shift occurs in the two final *gufa* passages which depict the mother as involved in fetal development, these still make no explicit mention of how the parents each physically contribute to fetal development or determining the sex of the child.

7   Kessler, *Conceiving Israel*, 92–93; Jacobowitz, "Leviticus Rabbah and the Spiritualization of the Laws of Impurity."

8   Temkin, *Soranus: Gynaecology*, 12, 1.12.

9   Semonides of Amorgos (seventh century BCE) deemed women "the worst plague Zeus has made." Lloyd-Jones, *Females of the Species*; Arthur, "Early Greece: The Origins of the Western Attitude toward Women." Studies that address this include Frymer-Kensky, *In the Wake of the Goddesses*, chap. 19; Dinnerstein, *The Mermaid and the Minotaur*; Pomeroy, *Women in Classical Antiquity*; Cantarella, *Pandora's Daughters*; Zeitlin, "The Dynamics of Misogyny: Myth and Mythmaking in the Oresteia."

10   Excepting 14:9.

11   As I demonstrate in another forthcoming article, this view is also evident in other aggadic and halakhic texts from the Land of Israel, including the Targumim on Leviticus 12:2, m.Niddah 2:1, and t.Niddah 2:8. See Strauch Schick, "Do Women Emit Seed?."

12   On aggadic clusters devoted to one topic see Friedman, "Historical Aggadah in the Talmud," 120; Weiss, *Al Ha-Yetsirah Ha-Sifrutit Shel Ha-Amoraim*, 171–174, 194–281.

physical process. They describe women discharging seed during intercourse and as contributing materially to conception and embryogenesis.

The first of these uniquely Bavli traditions, introduced as a baraita yet unknown from extant tannaitic literature,[13] describes "three partners in a person: The Holy One, blessed be He, his father, and his mother." It then lists the physical elements that each contribute to the developing fetus. Following a series of traditions paralleling Leviticus Rabbah, another set of uniquely Bavli traditions appears which again includes the mother. The first is attributed to R. Yitshaq b. R. Ami (third-generation Babylonian amora) and the second is introduced as a baraita.[14] These both assert that men and women emit seed and that the sex of the baby depends on who does so first. These are followed by a baraita containing proof-texts for this claim.[15]

Several studies have demonstrated that these Bavli traditions appear to be informed by a two-seed theory,[16] where—as opposed to the one-seed theory— both man and woman produce seed which together form the embryo.[17] The description of what each parent contributes to the developing embryo resonates particularly with the Aristotelian modified two-seed theory, which maintains that women supply menstrual blood, which is shaped by the male seed to create an embryo,[18] along with the Hippocratic concept of pangenesis

---

[13] Higger, *Ozar Ha-Baraitot in Ten Volumes*, 5:57; Higger, *Ozar Ha-Baraitot*, 6:448; Kiperwasser, "Three Partners in a Person."

[14] MS Paris, Bibliotheque Nationale-Heb. 671 attributes this statement to R. Yitshaq *in the name of* R. Ami, both Babylonian sages who emigrated to the Land of Israel and who appear together in the Bavli and Yerushalmi. This is likewise how the attribution appears in b.Niddah 31b. See Satlow, *Tasting the Dish*, 304. Joshua Levinson counters that R. Yitshaq b. R. Ami is the preferred version. Levinson, "Cultural Androgyny in Rabbinic Literature," 124, nt. 32.

  A similar statement is cited in b.Niddah 71a in the name of R. Hama b. R. Haninah, a Palestinian sage.

[15] This baraita appears with many similarities in Leviticus Rabbah 14:8 (and in y.Kilaim 8:4), however, there is a crucial difference. In the Bavli, this baraita garners proof for the fact that each parent's seed results in a child of the opposite sex, while in Leviticus Rabbah 14:8 (and y.Kilaim) there is no mention of seed or how the parents physically contribute to fetal formation. It may rather refer to how genealogy is ascribed in scripture and not a biological description. As such, only the tradition as presented in the Bavli expressly depicts females as emitting seed.

[16] Brodsky, *Bride Without a Blessing*, 160, nt. 104; Kessler, *Conceiving Israel*, 108; Kiperwasser, "Three Partners in a Person."

[17] Lloyd, *Science, Folklore and Ideology*, 88–94; Dean-Jones, *Women's Bodies in Classical Greek Science*, 149. I discuss parallels in Zoroastrian texts (*Bundahišn* 15:4), which demonstrate the prevalence of a two-seed theory in Sassanian Persia during the talmudic period. See also Kiperwasser, "Three Partners in a Person."

[18] *Generation of Animals*. Peck, *Aristotle*, 716a, 729b, 737a 5. Although some scholars argue

"that each part of the body of each parent renders up some aspect of itself."[19] The description of female seed having the same ability to determine gender as male seed also finds parallel in Hippocratic texts.[20]

The analysis of the Bavli sugya strongly suggests that it derives from Leviticus Rabbah 14 or an earlier shared source that served as its backbone.[21] However, it combines these traditions with those that present the mother as actively contributing to the development of the embryo in various ways. This redactional effort results in a multivocal sugya evincing a significantly more inclusive attitude toward the role of the mother. Thus, while material found in Leviticus Rabbah makes up much of the *sugya* and is placed at the center, the Bavli traditions expressing opposing ideas are arranged in a manner that frames them and therefore somewhat undermines them.[22]

In sum, Bavli Niddah presents a far more inclusive role with respect to women's material contribution in the physical act of procreation than that found in Palestinian aggadic texts. However, this apparently did not extend to its halakhic discourse. In the section that follows, we turn to texts which discuss the commandment of procreation and whether this obligation is incumbent upon women. In this context, texts from the Land of Israel prefer the inclusive position, while the Bavli excludes women altogether.

---

that Aristotle is more in line with one-seed theories, his view that women contribute menstrual blood in embryogenesis distinguishes him from the latter. See Connell, *Aristotle on Female Animals*, 100–106.

19   Laqueur, *Making Sex*, 39.
20   Hippocrates, *On the Generating Seed and the Nature of the Child*, 6–7. Furthermore, in Hippocratic theories, neither seed is inherently stronger than the other. Brodsky, *Bride Without a Blessing*, 141.
21   On citations of Leviticus Rabbah in the Bavli, see Margulies, *Vayyikra Rabbah*, XXXI in his introduction, and in his comments on p. 18 to line 9 and p. 75 to line 9.
22   As I demonstrate in the appendix, the traditions comprising this Bavli aggadic *sugya* is organized in a chiastic structure, with the uniquely Bavli traditions framing the Leviticus Rabbah material in the center. On the use of chiastic structures as a literary device in rabbinic texts, see Cohen, "Structural Analysis of a Talmudic Story," 161–177; Fraenkel, *Darkhe ha-'aggadah ve-ha-midrash*, 23–269, 307; Steinmetz, "Must the Patriarch Know 'Uqtzin?," 171.

The Halakhic Discussion of *Peru U'revu*: Are Women Included in the Obligation?

It has long been seen as the prevailing position that only men are obligated in procreation,[23] yet this is far from the only or even dominant view evinced among the range of rabbinic literature. Indeed, Mishna Yevamot 6:6 presents two opinions on the matter:

> לא יבטל אדם מפריה ורביה אלא אם כן יש לו בנים. בית שמאי אומרים שני זכרים ובית הלל אומרים זכר ונקבה שנאמר (בראשית ה') זכר ונקבה בראם נשא אשה ושהה עמה עשר שנים ולא ילדה אינו רשאי ליבטל גירשה מותרת לינשא לאחר ורשאי השני לשהות עמה עשר שנים ואם הפילה מונה משעה שהפילה האיש מצווה על פריה ורביה אבל לא האשה רבי יוחנן בן ברוקא אומר על שניהם הוא אומר (בראשית א') ויברך אותם אלהים ויאמר להם פרו ורבו:

> A person may not desist from procreating unless he has children. Beit Shammai says: "two sons." Beit Hillel says: "one son and one daughter, for it says, 'male and female He created them'." (Genesis 5:2)
> If he took a wife and remained with her for ten years and she did not give birth, he is not allowed to desist. If he divorced her, she is permitted to marry someone else. And the second husband is allowed to remain with her for ten years. But if she miscarried, she counts from the time she miscarried.
> A man is commanded concerning the duty of procreation but not a woman. Rabbi Yohanan ben Baroqa says: "Concerning both of them it is said, 'And God blessed them; and said to them … Be fruitful and multiply.'" (Genesis 1:28)

The mishnah begins with the divergent opinions of Beit Shammai and Beit Hillel regarding when one may cease procreating, then continues with what steps a man should take when a marriage is childless. As these first sections are directed solely at a man, they ostensibly assume that the duty rests on him alone. Nevertheless, the final section of this mishnah cites two opinions as to whether women are also included in the commandment. The first anonymous opinion (the Tanna Qamma) limits the obligation of procreation to men; R. Yohanan b. Baroqa counters that both men and women are equally obligated,

---

23   Cohen, *Jewish Women*, 203, observes how indisputable this assumption is.

which he supports with a citation of Genesis 1:28, where G-d directs the first people in the plural to "be fruitful and multiply," without signaling out Adam. This mishnah remains inconclusive, but other texts from *Erets Yisrael* side with the view of R. Yohanan b. Baroqa.

Palestinian Texts: Women Are Obligated in Procreation

The Tosefta contains a similar discussion to the Mishnah regarding the command to procreate, however it consistently portrays men and women as equally obligated (t.Yevamot 8:4, ed. Lieberman):

לא יבטל אדם מפריה ורביה אלא אם כן יש לו בנים. בני בנים הרי הן כבנים מת אחד מהן או שנעשה אחד מהן סריס אין רשיי לבטל
האיש אין רשאי לישב בלא אשה, ואשה אינה[24] רשאה לישב שלא באיש.
האיש אין רשיי לשתות עיקרין שלא יוליד. והאשה אין[25] רשאה לשתות עיקרין שלא תלד.
האיש אין רשיי לישא עקרה וזקינה אילונית וקטנה ושאין ראויה לילד, האשה אינה[26] רשאה להנשא אפי' לסריס ...

> A person may not desist from procreating unless he has children. Children's children are like children. If one [of his two children] dies or becomes castrated, he is not allowed to desist [from continuing to procreate].
>
> A man may not live without [being married to] a woman, and a woman may not live without [being married to] a man.
>
> A man is not allowed to drink a sterilizing potion to avoid producing children and a woman may not drink a sterilizing potion in order to avoid producing children.
>
> A man may not marry a barren woman, an old woman, an *aylonit* (one unable to bear children), a minor, or a woman who is not fit to have children. A woman may not marry a eunuch even.

---

24 Absent from MS Erfurt and the printed edition, which would seem to represent an attempt to conform the text to the Bavli, stating: ואשה רשאה לישב בלא איש. See Hauptman, *Rereading The Rabbis*, 134. Lieberman follows the Genizah fragments and MS Vienna. See his discussion in Lieberman, *Tosefta Kefshuta: Seder Nashim, Parts 6–7*, 67–68.

25 Absent from MS Erfurt and the printed edition. Lieberman, *Tosefta Kefshuta: Seder Nashim, Parts 6–7*, 68–69.

26 Absent from MS Erfurt and the printed edition. Lieberman, 69.

The first line of this Tosefta tradition, which states that a man may cease procreating only after he has had children, parallels the mishnah. This is followed by a clarification of what constitutes children that allows him to stop (i.e. grandchildren qualify as well).[27] The remainder, however, offers a new discussion, equating men and women in all laws pertaining to procreation: Both are commanded to have children, are encouraged to marry, and are prohibited from sterilizing themselves or marrying someone who is unable to conceive. Similarly, while Tosefta 8:5 requires a man to divorce his wife after ten years of barren marriage and remarry for "perhaps he did not merit being built up through her" (שמא לא זכה ליבנות ממנה), as Judith Hauptman observes, a similar directive is made regarding women in t.Yevamot 8:6 which likewise encourages women to remarry:[28]

גרשה תלך ותנשא לאחר שמא לא זכת ליבנות ממנה

> If he divorced her, she should go and marry another; perhaps she did not merit being built up through this man.

Both men and women should remarry so that each may attempt to have children if they were unable to in their first marriage.

This view is likewise advanced in the Yerushalmi's treatment of m.Yevamot 6:6 (y.Yevamot 6:6, 7d). The Yerushlami passage comprises several statements concerning the opinion of R. Yohanan b. Baroqa who includes women in the obligation:

(a) רבי לעזר בשם רבי יוסי בר זימרה טעמא דהן תנייא פרו ורבו ומלאו את הארץ וכבשוה וכבשה כתיב מי דרכו לכבוש האיש לא האשה.
(b) רבי ירמיה רבי אבהו רבי יצחק בר מריון בשם רבי חנינה: הלכה כרבי יוחנן בן ברוקה
(c) רבי יעקב בר אחא ורבי יעקב בר אידי רבי יצחק בר חקולה בשם רבי יודן נשייא: אם תובעת להינשא הדין עמה
(d) רבי לעזר בשם רבי חנינה: הלכה כרבי יוחנן בן ברוקה.
(e) אמר ליה רבי בא בר זבדא: 'עמד הייתי לא את אמרת אלא אם היתה תובעת להינשא הדין עמה הדא הוא דתנינן ...

---

27 This Tosefta appears to be elucidating what is found in the Mishnah, possibly indicating that in this instance, the Tosefta post-dates the Mishnah. On the relationship between the Mishnah and Tosefta, see the introduction in Friedman, *Tosefta Atikta*.
28 Hauptman, *Rereading the Rabbis*, 134.

a) R. L'azar in the name of R. Yose son of Zimra:[29] The reason for the tannaitic position is: "Be fruitful and multiply, and fill the land and conquer it" (Genesis 1:28) "Conquer it" it is written (as if in the singular). Whose manner is to conquer? It is the man, not the woman.
b) R. Yirmiya, R. Abbahu, and R. Yitshaq b. Merion in the name of R. Hanina: The law is like R. Yohanan b. Baroqa.
c) R. Ya'aqov b. Aha and R. Ya'aqov b. Idi, R. Yitshaq b. Haqola in the name of R. Yudan the patriarch: If the woman lay claims to be married, the law supports her position.
d) R. L'azar in the name of R. Hanina: The law is like R. Yohanan b. Baroqa
e) R. Ba b. Zabeda said to him: "I was with you. The statement that was made was only 'if she laid claim to be married, the law supports her position'." for it was taught .... (it now cites another dispute between R. L'azar and R. Ba b. Zebeda regarding a teaching of R. Hanina and what he actually said.)

Although the sugya begins with the exegetical basis for the first opinion of the mishnah (Tanna Qamma), which limits the obligation to men (a), the remainder of this passage consists of dicta by Palestinian sages mainly from the second to fourth generations stating either that the law follows R. Yohanan b. Baroqa (b, d), or the related rule that a wife has the right to demand a divorce from a childless marriage so that she may remarry (c, e). While her right to divorce appears to be a direct result of her equal obligation, section (e) is ambiguous on the matter. Nevertheless, the dominant approach of the Yerushalmi *sugya* is that women share an obligation to procreate and that the *halakhah* always grants a wife the right to sue for divorce in the case of a barren marriage. This passage contains no narratives, but rather short, apodictic statements.

---

29 R. El'azar b. Pedat, a third generation amora; originally from Babylonian where he learned under Rav and Samuel and later immigrated to Babylonia where he studied with R. Yohanan. He often transmits aggadic teachings of the first generation amora R. Yose b. Zimra. Strack and Stemberger, *Introduction to the Talmud and Midrash*, 84.

Bavli Yevamot 65b–66a: Women Are Exempt from Procreation

The parallel Bavli sugya to m.Yevamot 6:6 presents a different picture. B.Yevamot 65b–66a overwhelmingly follows the position of the first opinion of Mishna Yevamot 6:6, obligating only men in procreation. This is likewise reflected in several other sugyot throughout the Bavli (e.g. b.Shabbat 110, b.Gittin 43b, b.Qiddushin 34a, b.Eruvin 27a). Despite the clear dominance of this approach, however, b.Yevamot 65b–66a also includes several rulings and legal narratives, which echo elements of the parallel Yerushalmi as well as other texts from the Land of Israel.

The Opinion of the Tanna Qamma

A. מנא הני מילי? אמר ר׳ אילעא[30] משום ר׳ אלעזר בר׳ שמעון[31], אמר קרא: ומלאו את הארץ וכבשוה, איש דרכו לכבש, ואין אשה דרכה לכבש.
    1. אדרבה, וכבשוה תרתי משמע!
    2. אמר רב נחמן בר יצחק: "וכבשה" כתיב.
    3. רב יוסף אמר, מהכא: אני אל שדי פרה ורבה, ולא קאמר פרו ורבו.

A. From where are these matters (that a woman is not obligated in procreation)? R. Il'ai said in the name of R. El'azar b. R. Simeon: The verse states: "Be fruitful and multiply, and fill the land and conquer it" (Genesis 1:28). It is the manner of a man to conquer and it is not the manner of a woman to conquer.
    1. On the contrary: "And conquer it [*vekhivshuha*, i.e. in the plural form]," indicates two (that both are commanded)?
    2. R. Nahman b. Yitshaq said: It is written "And conquer it [*vekhivsha*]" (without a *vuv*, and hence in the singular).
    3. Rav Yosef said: From here: "I am God Almighty, be fruitful and multiply [*perei urvei*]" (Genesis 35:11), which is in singular, and it does not state: Be fruitful and multiply [*peru urevu* in the plural].

Like the Yerushalmi passage (a), the Bavli opens with the proof-text for the Tanna Qamma's position, obligating only men in the command to procreate, based on Genesis 1:28 "fill the land and conquer it" attributed to R. Il'ai in the

---

30 Munich 95] אלעזר. Vatican 110–111] אלעי.
31 Munich 95, Vatican 110–111, CUL: T-S F 2(2), St. Petersburg: Yevr.111 B 497–498] ר׳ יהודה ב״ר שמעון.

name of R' El'azar b. R. Simeon (A).³² Although this proof-text is initially challenged (1), Babylonian amoraim R. Nahman b. Yitshaq of the fifth generation and R. Yosef, of the third generation, defend R. Il'ai's reading of the verse as being directed at men alone (2, 3).

This section is followed by two more homilies taught by R. Il'ai in the name of R' El'azar b. R. Simeon. The first states that one should teach only what will be listened to and not that which will not be heeded. The second homily is linguistically related to the latter part of the sugya and I therefore cite it in full:

B. ‏וא״ר אילעא משום רבי אלעזר בר׳ שמעון: מותר לו לאדם לשנות בדבר השלום, שנאמר: אביך צוה וגו׳ כה תאמרו ליוסף אנא שא נא וגו׳ ...

1. ‏ר׳ נתן אומר: מצוה, שנאמר: ויאמר שמואל איך אלך ושמע שאול והרגני וגו׳.

2. ‏דבי רבי ישמעאל תנא: גדול השלום, שאף הקדוש ברוך הוא שינה בו, דמעיקרא כתיב: ואדוני זקן, ולבסוף כתיב: ואני זקנתי.

> B. R. Il'ai further stated in the name of R. El'azar b. R. Simeon: One may change a statement for a matter of peace; for it is said in Scripture, "Thy father did command etc. so shall ye say unto Joseph: Forgive, I pray thee now," etc. (Genesis 50:16–17).
>
>> 1. R. Nathan said: It is a commandment; for it is stated in Scripture, And Samuel said: "How can I go? If Saul hears it, he will kill me," etc (Samuel I 16:2).
>>
>> 2. It was taught at the School of R. Yishmael: Great is peace, as even the Holy One, Blessed be He, changed [a statement] for it. As, initially it is written [that Sarah said of Abraham]: "And my lord is old" (Genesis 18:12), and in the end it is written [that God told Abraham that Sarah said]: "And I am old" (Genesis 18:13).

At first glance, the connection between the homilies appears to be merely formal in their common attribution to R. Il'ai in the name of R' El'azar b. R. Simeon. However, as I discuss below, they are thematically related to a later section. In particular, the idea of "changing a statement" or lying for the sake of peace, and especially the School of R. Yishmael's tradition regarding maintaining marital

---

32   In the Yerushalmi, it is attributed to R. El'azar b. Pedat. However, given the many similarities between 'Ila'i' and 'El'azar'—their names, lifetimes, residences and their close association with R. Yohanan—and the general tendency for the Bavli and Yerushalmi to offer different attributions for a single statement, it is not unusual for ascriptions to these amoraim to be reversed. Moreover, some text witnesses of the Bavli contain an attribution of R. El'azar/ R. El'a' (*supra* n. 32).

harmony (B.2), become linguistically and thematically associated towards the end of the *sugya*.³³

Conforming Palestinian Traditions to the Opinion of the Tanna Qamma

The *sugya* continues with a discussion over whether the law follows R. Yohanan b. Baroqa, and affirming that it does not:

C. אתמר: רבי יוחנן ור' יהושע בן לוי, חד אמר: הלכה כרבי יוחנן בן ברוקה, וחד אמר: אין הלכה כרבי יוחנן בן ברוקה.

D. ותסתיים, דרבי יוחנן הוא דאמר אין הלכה, דיתיב ר' אבהו וקאמר משמיה דרבי יוחנן: הלכה, ואהדרינהו רבי אמי ורבי אסי לאפייהו. איכא דאמרי: רבי חייא בר אבא אמר, ואהדרינהו רבי אמי ורבי אסי לאפייהו.

1. אמר רב פפא: בשלמא למאן דאמר רבי אבהו אמרה, משום כבוד בי קיסר לא אמרו ליה ולא מידי, אלא למאן דאמר, רבי חייא בר אבא אמרה, לימרו ליה: לא אמר רבי יוחנן הכי
2. מאי הוה עלה?

E. ת"ש, דאמר ר' אחא בר חנינא³⁴ אמר ר' אבהו אמר ר' אסי:³⁵,³⁶ עובדא הוה קמיה דרבי יוחנן בכנישתא דקיסרי, ואמר: יוציא ויתן כתובה;

1. ואי ס"ד לא מפקדה, כתובה מאי עבידתה?
2. דלמא בבאה מחמת טענה;

C. It was stated: R. Yohanan and R. Yehoshua b. Levi, [disagreed]: One said that the law is like R. Yohanan b. Baroqa, and one said that the law is not like R. Yohanan b. Baroqa.

D. Conclude that it was R. Yohanan who said that the law is not [like R. Yohanan b. Baroqa], for R. Abbahu was sitting and said in the name of R. Yohanan that the law [is like R. Yohanan b. Baroqa], and R. Ami and

---

33   Esther Fischer suggests that all of the homilies by R. I'lai in the name of R. El'azar b. R. Simeon might be thematically linked to the entire *sugya* concerning whether women are included in the command. Fischer, "Women's Exemption from the Commandment of 'Peru u-Revu.'"

34   Third generation Palestinian amora.

35   First generation Babylonian amora.

36   Munich 95: דא"ר חייא בר חנינא א"ר אבהו א"ר אסי; MSS Moscow—Guenzburg 1017, Oxford Opp. 248 (367)—דא"ר אחא בר חני; MSS Munich 141, Moscow—Guenzburg 594, Cambridge—T-S F2 (2) 1—דא"ר אחא בר חנינא א"ר אמי א"ר אסי; Vatican 111—דא"ר אחא בר' חנינא א"ר אסי.

R. Asi, turned their faces (indicating that they disagreed). There are some who say, that R. Hiyya b. Abba said this, and R. Ami and R. Asi turned their faces.

1. R. Papa said: "Granted, according to the one who said that Rabbi Abbahu said it, due to the honor of Caesar's court,[37] Rabbi Ami and Rabbi Asi did not say anything to him. However, according to the one who said that Rabbi Hiyya bar Abba said it, let them say to him explicitly: Rabbi Yohanan did not say this."
2. What was reached about this issue?

E. Come and hear, as R. Aha b. Hanina said that R. Abbahu said that R. Asi said that there was an incident that came before Rabbi Yohanan in the synagogue of Caesarea (involving a woman who wanted to initiate a divorce after ten years of childless marriage), and he said [the husband must] divorce her and give her the payment for her marriage contract.

1. If it enters your mind to say that she is not commanded to be fruitful and multiply, what is the marriage contract doing here?
2. Perhaps it was where she came [to initiate a divorce] due to a [different] claim.

This Bavli *sugya* reflects the Babylonian rabbis' opposition to the position of R. Yohanan b. Baroqa, which includes women in the obligation, and hence the conflict caused by traditions from the Land of Israel suggesting otherwise. The discussion opens with competing opinions as to whether R. Yohanan b. Nappaha, the prominent second-generation Palestinian amora, followed the opinion of R. Yohanan b. Baroqa (C), thereby leaving open the possibility that he did. The anonymous redactors negate this suggestion: (D) cites two alternate accounts in which either R. Abbahu or R. Hiyya b. Abba reports that R. Yohanan maintained the view of R. Yohanan b. Baroqa (women are obligated), while Rabbi Ami and Rabbi Asi reject the tradition by turning their faces. The redactors thus conclude that R. Yohanan did *not* concur with R. Yohanan b. Baroqa. It is important to establish R' Yohanan's decision, for he often determines whom the *halakhah* follows.[38] Ensuring that he did not agree with R. Yohanan b. Baroqa gives credence to the opposing position of the Tanna Qamma which is favored in the Bavli. Nevertheless, evidence that R. Yohanan ruled in con-

---

37 Elsewhere R. Abbahu is also depicted as having relations with government officials (b.Hagigah 14a, b.Ketubbot 17a, b.Sanhedrin 14a).
38 See e.g. b.Berakhot 13b, 28a; b.Shabbat 35a, 39b, 44a b.Nedarim 20a along with the fact that the *halakhah* often follows R. Yohanan (b.Betsah. 4a as against Rav, b.Bava Qamma 104b as against Samuel).

sonance with R. Yohanan b. Baroqa is not eliminated but is rather bolstered by the report which concludes this section, (E) where R. Yohanan allows a woman to initiate a divorce from a childless marriage. This decision would ostensibly demonstrate that R. Yohanan held that women have an obligation to procreate and are therefore able to procure a divorce (E.1). This also correlates with the parallel Yerushalmi *sugya* and in all probability reflects the dominant *Erets Yisrael* position which deems women as possessing an equal obligation to reproduce. Nevertheless, the Bavli's redactors limit R. Yohanan's decision to an instance in which the woman made a different claim that would allow her to procure a divorce (E.2), thus indicating that he was motivated by other factors in granting her one.

Additional support for the supposition that R. Yohanan does not follow the opinion of R. Yohanan b. Baroqa is then garnered, by reporting two more incidents depicting women seeking divorces:

F. כי ההיא דאתאי לקמיה דר׳ אמי, אמרה ליה: הב לי כתובה, אמר לה: זיל, לא מיפקדת, אמרה ליה: מסיבו דילה מאי תיהוי עלה דהך אתתא? אמר: כי הא ודאי כפינן.

G. ההיא דאתאי לקמיה דרב נחמן, אמר לה: לא מיפקדת, אמרה ליה: לא בעיא הך אתתא חוטרא לידה ומרה לקבורה? אמר: כי הא ודאי כפינן.

F. Like the case of a woman who came before R. Ami and said to him, "Give me the payment of the marriage contract." He said to her: "Go, you are not commanded," she said to him: "What shall become of a woman like myself in her old age!" He said: "In such a case, we certainly compel [the husband]."

G. A woman came [with a similar plea] before R. Nahman. He told her: "You are not commanded." She said to him: "Does not a woman like myself require a staff in her hand and a hoe for digging her grave!" He said: "In such a case, we certainly compel [the husband]."

R. Ami and R. Nahman both declare that women are not obligated in procreation, per the law as determined in the first half of the Bavli *sugya* including by R. Ami himself (D), and that these women therefore have no grounds for forcing a divorce. Both are then confronted with challenges to their rulings by the women; if she cannot demand a divorce from her childless marriage, she will be left helpless in her old age, with no one to care for her. R. Ami and R. Nahman each respond by changing his decision and allowing the woman in question to divorce. While their final rulings effectively mirror the position of the Yerushalmi, there is a key difference: In the Yerushalmi, childlessness is always considered grounds for a wife to initiate a divorce, resulting from the assumption that women have an obligation to have children. In the Bavli, by contrast, these women's ability to divorce are exceptions and ad hoc remedies limited to their specific cases, since the law follows the Tanna Qamma's position that only men are obligated in procreation. Within the immediate context of the *sugya*, these cases demonstrate that it is possible for R. Yohanan to both rule that a wife could leave a childless marriage and still maintain that women are exempt from procreation. In this way, the Bavli preserves Yerushalmi traditions within the context of its own understanding of the law.

The Story of Yehudit: Proof and Implications of the Opinion of the Tanna Qamma

Echoes of traditions from *Erets Yisrael* continue in the account that follows, regarding Yehudit and her husband R. Hiyya:

H. (יהודה וחזקיה תאומים היו, אחד נגמרה צורתו לסוף תשעה, ואחד נגמרה צורתו לתחלת שבעה)39 יהודית דביתהו דר' חייא הוה לה צער לידה, שנאי מנא, ואתיא לקמיה דר' חייא, אמרה: אתתא מפקדא אפריה ורביה? אמר לה: לא. אזלא אשתיא סמא דעקרתא, לסוף איגלאי מילתא, אמר לה: איכו ילדת לי חדא כרסא אחריתא; דאמר מר: יהודה וחזקיה אחי, פזי וטוי אחוותא

    H.   (Yehudah and Hezeqiah were twins. The features of one were developed at the end of nine months, and those of the other were developed at the beginning of the seventh month.)[40] Yehudit, the wife of R. Hiyya, had painful childbirths. She changed her clothes and appeared before R. Hiyya. She said: "Is a woman commanded to propagate the race?" He told her: "No." She went and drank a sterilizing potion. When her action finally became known, he said to her, "Would that you bore me only one more issue of the womb!" For a Master stated: Yehudah and Hezeqiah were twin brothers and Pazi and Tavi were twin sisters.

---

39   Appearing only in ed. Vilna and at the conclusion of the account in Munich 95. It is absent from all other text witnesses. Other reference to Yehudah and Hezeqiah as twins appears only in the anonymous strata of the Bavli (b.Niddah 27a (which also references their being born in different months); ibid. 40a; b.Sanhedrin 38a; b. Mo'ed Qatan 25a).

40   See previous note.

PROCREATION IN PALESTINIAN HALAKHAH AND IN BABYLONIAN AGGADAH 275

In this anecdote, Yehudit has suffered from agonizing pregnancies in the past and wants to prevent any more from occurring.[41] She therefore disguises herself,[42] apparently so that her husband will not recognize her, and inquires whether women are included in the obligation to procreate. He replies in the negative, in line with the approach of the Bavli, and she responds by drinking a sterilizing potion. When he discovers what his wife has done, R. Hiyya bemoans the fact that she will not bear him any more children.

In the immediate context of the *sugya*, this story functions as yet another proof that the law follows the Tanna Qamma that only men are obligated. At the same time, it presents another implication of this ruling: Because women are not commanded in procreation, they may take measures to prevent pregnancy from occurring. Indeed, even as R. Hiyya is anguished by his wife's actions, he does not rescind his ruling exempting women from procreation.[43] The anonymous gloss which concludes this anecdote, however, might be meant to mitigate this broad inference: "Yehudah and Hezeqiah were twin brothers and Pazi and Tavi were twin sisters." Although it might merely be explaining what was so difficult about Yehudit's pregnancies and why she wanted a break—she was prone to conceiving twins—it might also be intended to diminish Yehudit's drastic act.[44] In other words, R. Hiyya already had children and hence he was halakhically permitted to stop procreating as delineated in the first part of m.Yevamot 6:6. By having twin sons and twin daughters, he even managed to satisfy both the views of Beit Shammai ("two sons") and Beit Hillel ("one son and one daughter"). Accordingly, it is possible that this addendum reflects a discomfort with Yehudit's action and its broad implication regarding women's

---

41 On the gender implications of this narrative and how it reflects gender power relations, see Raveh, "A Story of Women's Suffering"; Raveh, "Sippuro Shel Za'ar Nashi"; Fischer, "Women's Exemption from the Commandment of 'Peru u-Revu.'"

42 Raveh points to how Yehudit's act echoes a motif of women masquerading themselves in the biblical accounts of Leah and Tamar, in order to trick a man into getting her pregnant; though Yehudit disguises herself to prevent one. (Raveh, "A Story of Women's Suffering," 5, n. 9.) Raveh suggests that Yehudit disguised herself as a man, which "expresses the critical and subversive intent which is at the foundation of our narrative situation," and correlates with Yehudit's more "masculine" inquiry which addresses the *halakhah* as opposed to the subjective aspect of her personal suffering (Raveh, 6.) I would argue that she presents a halakhic as opposed to subjective inquiry for that is the normal form of discourse of the Bavli.

43 Fischer, "Women's Exemption from the Commandment of 'Peru u-Revu.'"

44 If the reference to multiple twins is meant to mitigate her action, this might be why the line describing Yehudah and Hezeqiah's birth as occurring multiple months apart was added to some text witnesses in order to explain what was difficult about her pregnancies.

reproductive freedom.[45] Granted, such an understanding contradicts the logic of the story itself, which describes the direct impetus for Yehudit drinking the sterilizing potion as her understanding that women are not commanded to procreate. This final line thus creates a tension within the text, which, as I discuss below, is evinced throughout this *sugya*.

Returning to our analysis of this account, as in the previous two anecdotes regarding R. Ami and R. Nahman (F,G), in the Yehudit anecdote (H), a woman raises a challenge to a rabbi in order to receive a ruling that suits her fertility needs though in (F,G), the women want to remarry in order to have children, while Yehudit wants to stop having children.[46] Also like the previous cases, the conclusion mirrors a Palestinian ruling. In (F,G), R. Ami and R. Nahman allow the women to divorce, paralleling the law cited in the Yerushalmi (c,e). Yehudit's response in drinking the sterilizing potion similarly recalls Tosefta Yevamot (Lieberman) 8:4:

.... האיש אין רשיי לשתות עיקרין שלא יוליד. והאשה אין רשאה לשתות עיקרין שלא תלד ...

A man is not allowed to drink a sterilizing potion to avoid producing children and a woman may not drink a sterilizing potion in order to avoid producing children.

The Tosefta prohibits men and women alike from drinking a sterilization potion since both are commanded in procreation. Yehudit's decision to drink this potion is a direct consequence of her perceived exemption from procreation. Yehudit's story thus offers a mirror image to the Palestinian ruling which it rejects.

This story appears to be of redactional original, as it is presented anonymously, almost entirely in Aramaic,[47] with variants among the test witnesses, and contains elements found elsewhere in the anonymous strata. Its redactional provenance is further reinforced by a similar anecdote concerning Yehudit and R. Hiyya and the former's painful births which appears in b.Qiddushin 12b:

---

45 Indeed R. Abraham Zvi Hirsh Eisenstad, in his commentary the *Pitchei Teshuva* to the *Shulchan Aruch Even HaEzer* 5:11, limits cases where a woman may drink a sterilizing potion to where she suffers greatly or already has had children (like Yehudit).
46 Hauptman, *Rereading the Rabbis*, 138.
47 The one Hebrew line in this account is absent from all text witnesses aside from ed. Vilna.

PROCREATION IN PALESTINIAN HALAKHAH AND IN BABYLONIAN AGGADAH 277

לאו הייט דיהודית דביתהו דרבי חייא, דהוית לה צער לידה,
אמרה ליה, אמרה לי אם: קיבל ביך אבוך קידושי כי זוטרת! אמר לה: לאו כל כמינה
דאימך דאסרת ליך עילואי.

> Is this not similar to the case of Yehudit, wife of Rabbi Hiyya, who had painful childbirths?
> She said to him: "My mother told me: 'When you were young your father accepted betrothal on your behalf [from another man, which would render you forbidden to Rabbi Hiyya]'." He said to her: "It is not in your mother's [power] to prohibit you to me."

This anecdote appears in a passage concerning whether a betrothal has occurred in a case where a man gives a woman an object whose value might be less than the minimum amount (a *peruta*) and if so, whether she requires a writ of divorce. When such a case came before the third-generation Babylonian amora R. Hisda, he ruled that no betrothal occurred and that the woman was therefore free to marry another man. The mother of the first man countered that on the day the first betrothal occurred, the object was in fact worth a *peruta*, and the betrothal is therefore valid. R. Hisda responds to her claim: "It is not in your power to prohibit her" to another man whom she wishes to marry. The anecdote concerning Yehudit and R. Hiyya follows, demonstrating another case where it was "not in your (the mother of one of the party's) power to prohibit" a woman to the (second) man she married.

It is unclear whether this account belongs to the redactional strata or is a continuation of R. Hisda's statement (Rashi *ad. loc.* s.v. *lav*, assumes the latter). However, the fact that it appears with variants among the textual witnesses and is easily detachable, able to stand independently from the first statement which is explicitly attributed to R. Hisda, would lend support to its redactional origins.[48]

It is possible that the two stories present different attempts on the part of Yehudit to relieve her suffering—the one in b.Qiddushin, an earlier failed one followed by her later success as reported in b.Yevamot—however, the two share many features and themes which suggest that they may rather be variations of a common account: Both begin with the same opening, describing her history of agonizing births, and depict Yehudit's attempt to prevent future pregnancies

---

48   Furthermore, the account does not align well with the first part of R. Hisda's statement, which ostensibly conforms with the wishes of the woman in marrying the second man. In the Yehudit account, by contrast, her wishes to extricate herself from her marriage to R. Hiyya are disregarded.

by approaching R. Hiyya in a deceitful manner (due to his apparent indifference),[49] where she invokes a halakhic principle. In both, he responds by maintaining the *halakhah* that corresponds with the surrounding *sugya*.

The main difference between the two Yehudit accounts is regarding the *halakha* that they relate to. However, this may be a result of the redactors' work in aligning them with the *sugya* in which each is found. Thus, in b.Qiddushin, where the topic is uncertain betrothals and whether a woman needs a writ of divorce before marrying another, Yehudit tries to extricate herself from her marriage to R. Hiyya by telling him that her father already contracted such a marriage thereby invalidating her second betrothal to R. Hiyya. B.Yevamot, which is concerned with women's exemption from procreation, reports Yehudit asking R. Hiyya whether women are commanded and acting on the basis of his response. Her decision to drink a sterilizing potion, as mentioned previously, seems to draw from t.Yevamot 8:4. Furthermore, Yehudit's ruse in "changing her clothes" recalls the homilies of section (B) where R. Il'ai in the name of R. El'azar b. R. Simeon states "One may change (לשנות) a statement for matters of peace" and more relevant, the School of R. Yishmael's teaching that "great is peace, as even the Holy One, Blessed be He, changed (שינה בו) [a statement] for it," in the case of maintaining marital harmony.[50] The account of Yehudit parallels these homilies both linguistically, using the same verb (שנאי מנא, "she change her clothes" paralleling לשנות and שינה בו), as well as thematically: she deceives her husband by disguising herself.

There are several possible ways to understand the thematic connection between the Yehudit account and the homilies in (B). Yehudit may be an example of one who is permitted to change a statement for peace—in this case, for her own peace of mind and protection[51]—or a perversion of it—her deceit destroys R. Hiyya's peace. Esther Fischer suggests that the message of the homilies might be directed at R. Hiyya; he should have "changed a statement for peace" by concealing the fact that the law follows the Tanna Qamma, thereby preventing Yehudit from choosing to not have children. Alternatively, it might be the opinion of R. Yohanan b. Beroqa that should be concealed.[52] Irrespec-

---

49 Two other references to the (nameless) wife of R. Hiyya appear in the Bavli, which portray R. Hiyya as a caring and thoughtful husband (b.Betsah 13; b.Yevamot 63a). B.Yevamot 63a rather presents his wife as uncaring and difficult.
50 Raveh, "Sippuro Shel Za'ar Nashi," 165, cites other rabbinic texts concerning the issue of lying for the sake of marital harmony.
51 Raveh, 166.
52 Fischer, "Women's Exemption from the Commandment of 'Peru u-Revu,'" 209. Fischer also shows how the other homily, encouraging teaching a statement only if it will be listened to, is also related.

Concluding Account: The Case of a Slave Woman

The Yevamot *sugya* (and chapter) concludes with one final account which again seems to challenge the Bavli position that the law follows the Tanna Qamma, exempting women:

I. ולא מיפקדי? והאמר רב אחא בר רב קטינא[53] א"ר יצחק[54]: מעשה באשה אחת שחציה שפחה וחציה בת חורין, וכפו את רבה ועשאה בת חורין!
1. אמר רב נחמן בר יצחק: מנהג הפקר נהגו בה.[55]

I. Are [women] really not commanded? But R. Aha b. R. Qatina said that R. Yitshaq said: There was an incident involving a woman who was half enslaved and half freed, and they forced [her owner] to free her!
1. Said R. Nahman: They were taking liberties with her.

The third to fourth-generation Babylonian amora, R. Huna/Hana b. Rav Qatina, describes the case of a female slave who was partially freed, and whose owner was forced to free the enslaved part of her. The implicit question is that the only reason to grant her full freedom would be if she had an obligation in procre-

---

53 הא׳ רב הונא בר רב קטינא] MS Munich 95
   והאמ׳ רב הונא בר רב קטינא] MS Munich 141
   והאמ׳ רב חנא בר רב קטינא] MSS Oxford Opp. 248 (367), Moscow—Guenzburg 594, Cambridge—T-S F2 (2) 1-
   והא׳ רב חנא בר רב קטינא] MS Moscow—Guenzburg 1017
   והאמ׳ רב חיננא] MS Vatican 111.
   This is a name which appears in different ways—both R. Aha, R. Hanina, R. Huna. Either way, he's a third-fourth generation Babylonian amora.

54 א"ר יצחק] MS Munich 95, MSS Oxford Opp. 248 (367), Moscow—Guenzburg 594, Cambridge —T-S F2 (2) 1. (R. Yitshaq is a second generation Babylonian amora.
   א"ר יצחק א"ר אלעז] MS MS Moscow—Guenzburg 1017
   א"ר אלע] MS Vatican 111
   R. El'azar refers to R. El'azar b. Pedat, who also appears in the parallel Yerushalmi *sugya*, citing the homily that defends the position of the Tanna Qamma (section a).

55 This account is also found in b.Gittin 38a–b; 43b. In those instances too, there are variants of the attributions.

ation, once more calling into question women's exemption.[56] As in the previous cases, this anecdote parallels a Palestinian tradition, specifically Mishnah Gittin 4:5 which discusses a male who is half enslaved. This mishnah makes the connection between his forced emancipation and an obligation to procreate explicit:

> **מִי שֶׁחֶצְיוֹ עֶבֶד וְחֶצְיוֹ בֶּן חוֹרִין**, עוֹבֵד אֶת רַבּוֹ יוֹם אֶחָד וְאֶת עַצְמוֹ יוֹם אֶחָד, דִּבְרֵי בֵית הִלֵּל. אָמְרוּ לָהֶם בֵּית שַׁמַּאי, תִּקַּנְתֶּם אֶת רַבּוֹ, וְאֶת עַצְמוֹ לֹא תִקַּנְתֶּם. לִשָּׂא שִׁפְחָה אִי אֶפְשָׁר, שֶׁכְּבָר חֶצְיוֹ בֶּן חוֹרִין. בַּת חוֹרִין אִי אֶפְשָׁר, שֶׁכְּבָר חֶצְיוֹ עָבֶד. יִבָּטֵל, וַהֲלֹא לֹא נִבְרָא הָעוֹלָם אֶלָּא לִפְרִיָּה וְלִרְבִיָּה, שֶׁנֶּאֱמַר (ישעיה מה) לֹא תֹהוּ בְרָאָהּ, לָשֶׁבֶת יְצָרָהּ. אֶלָּא מִפְּנֵי תִקּוּן הָעוֹלָם, **כּוֹפִין אֶת רַבּוֹ וְעוֹשֶׂה אוֹתוֹ בֶּן חוֹרִין**, וְכוֹתֵב שְׁטָר עַל חֲצִי דָמָיו. וְחָזְרוּ בֵית הִלֵּל לְהוֹרוֹת כְּדִבְרֵי בֵית שַׁמַּאי:

> **One who is half a slave and half free** works for his master one day and for himself one day, the words of Beit Hillel. Beit Shammai said to them: you have set things right for the master but you have not set things right for the slave. He cannot marry a female slave because he is already half free, and he cannot marry a free woman because he is half a slave. Shall he then decease [from having children]? But wasn't the world only made to be populated, as it says, "He did not create it as a waste, he formed it to be inhabited" (Isaiah 45:18)? Rather because of tikkun olam **we compel his master to emancipate him** and he writes a document for half his purchase price. Beit Hillel retracted [their opinion and] ruled like Beit Shammai.

Beit Shammai reasons that one who has partial ownership of a slave is compelled to free him, for otherwise the latter is unable to marry and have children. Beit Hillel ultimately concurs. The anecdote in section (1), which challenges the Bavli's position of following the Tanna Qamma, directly parallels the (bolded) language of m.Gittin 4:5.

The inconsistency is resolved by R. Nahman b. Yitshaq (I.1), who likewise appeared at the beginning of the *sugya* (A.2) where he defended the reading of Genesis 1:28 as being directed at men alone. Once again, R. Nahman b. Yitshaq maintains the Bavli position that women are exempt from procreation (I.1), by suggesting that there is another reason to free the slave woman; so liberties are not taken with her. As in the earlier anecdotes, this final story affirms the view that the law follows the Tanna Qamma that women are exempt, by re-interpreting a case which seems to indicate otherwise.

---

56 The question is made explicit in its parallel citation in b.Gittin 43b.

Erets Yisrael Material in a Bavli Sugya

As we saw in our previous discussion of b.Niddah and Leviticus Rabba, b.Yevamot is comprised of various Palestinian traditions, which have been combined with the Bavli material. This may be demonstrated in the following chart:

Bavli Yevamot 65b–66a	Land of Israel texts
	Yerushalmi Yevamot
A. מנא הני מילי? אמר ר׳ אילעא משום ר׳ אלעזר בר׳ שמעון, אמר קרא: ומלאו את הארץ וכבשוה, איש דרכו לכבש, ואין אשה דרכה לכבש. 1. אדרבה, וכבשוה תרתי משמע! 2. אמר **רב נחמן בר יצחק**: ״וכבשה״ כתיב. 3. רב יוסף אמר, מהכא: אני אל שדי פרה ורבה, ולא קאמר פרו ורבו	a) רבי לעזר בשם רבי יוסי בר זימרה טעמ׳ דהן תנייא פרו ורבו ומלאו את הארץ וכבשוה וכבשה כתי׳ מי דרכו לכבוש האיש לא האשה.
B. וא״ר אילעא משום רבי אלעזר בר׳ שמעון: מותר לו לאדם **לשנות** בדבר השלום, שנאמר: אביך צוה וג׳ כה תאמרו ליוסף אנא שא נא וג׳. 1. ר׳ נתן אומר: מצוה ... 2. דבי רבי ישמעאל תנא: גדול השלום, שאף הקדוש ברוך הוא **שינה** בו, דמעיקרא כתיב: ואדוני זקן, ולבסוף כתיב: ואני זקנתי.	b) רבי ירמיה רבי אבהו רבי יצחק בר מריון בשם רבי חנינה: **הלכה כרבי יוחנן בן ברוקה**.
C. אתמר: רבי יוחנן ור׳ יהושע בן לוי, חד אמר: **הלכה כרבי יוחנן בן ברוקה**, וחד אמר: אין הלכה כרבי יוחנן בן ברוקה.	c) רבי יעקב בר אחא ורבי יעקב בר אידי רבי יצחק בר חקולה בשם רבי יודן נשייא: **אם תובעת להינשא הדין עמה**
D. ותסתיים, דרבי יוחנן הוא דאמר אין הלכה, דיתיב ר׳ אבהו וקאמר משמיה דרבי יוחנן: **הלכה**, ואהדרינהו רבי אמי ורבי אסי לאפייהו. איכא דאמרי: רבי חייא בר אבא אמר, ואהדרינהו רבי אמי ורבי אסי לאפייהו. 1. אמר רב פפא: בשלמא למאן דאמר רבי אבהו אמרה ...	d) רבי לעזר בשם רבי חנינה: **הלכה כרבי יוחנן בן ברוקה**.
E. ת״ש, דאמר ר׳ אחא בר חנינא אמר ר׳ אבהו אמר ר׳ אסי: עובדא הוה קמיה דרבי יוחנן בכנישתא דקיסרי, ואמר: **יוציא ויתן כתובה**; 1. ואי ס״ד לא מפקדה, כתובה מאי עבידתה? 2. דלמא בבאה מחמת טענה.	e) אמר ליה רבי בא בר זבדא: ׳עמד הייתי לא את אמרת אלא אם היתה **תובעת להינשא הדין עמה** הדא הוא דתנינן ...
F. כי ההיא דאתאי לקמיה דר׳ אמי, אמרה ליה: הב לי כתובה, אמר לה: זיל, לא מיפקדת, אמרה ליה: מסיבו דילה מאי תיהוי עלה דהך אתתא? אמר: **כי הא ודאי כפינן**.	

(*cont.*)

Bavli Yevamot 65b–66a	Land of Israel texts
G. ההיא דאתאי לקמיה דרב נחמן, אמר לה: לא מיפקדת, אמרה ליה: לא בעיא הך אתתא חוטרא לידה ומרה לקבורה? אמר: **כי הא ודאי כפינן.**	
	Tosefta Yevamot 8:4
	... אין רשיי לבטל האיש אין רשאי לישב בלא אשה ואשה אינה רשאה לישב שלא באיש. האיש אין רשיי לשתות עיקרין שלא יוליד. **והאשה אין רשאה לשתות עיקרין שלא תלד.**
H ... יהודית דביתהו דר׳ חייא הוה לה צער לידה, שנאי מנא, ואתיא לקמיה דר׳ חייא, אמרה: אתתא מפקדא אפריה ורביה? אמר לה: לא. אזלא אשתיא סמא דעקרתא...	
	Mishnah Gittin 4:5
	מִי שֶׁחֶצְיוֹ עֶבֶד וְחֶצְיוֹ בֶן חוֹרִין, ... יִבָּטֵל, וַהֲלֹא לֹא נִבְרָא הָעוֹלָם אֶלָּא לִפְרִיָּה וְלִרְבִיָּה, שֶׁנֶּאֱמַר (ישעיה מה) לֹא תֹהוּ בְרָאָהּ, לָשֶׁבֶת יְצָרָהּ. אֶלָּא מִפְּנֵי תִקּוּן הָעוֹלָם, **כּוֹפִין אֶת רַבּוֹ וְעוֹשֶׂה אוֹתוֹ בֶן חוֹרִין**
I. ולא מיפקדי? והאמר רב אחא בר רב קטינא א"ר יצחק: מעשה באשה אחת שחציה שפחה וחציה בת חורין, **וכפו את רבה ועשאה בת חורין!**	
i. אמר **רב נחמן בר יצחק**: מנהג הפקר נהגו בה	

A close reading of the Bavli *sugya* shows that it has been arranged in a chiastic structure: (A.2) and (I.1) both cite R. Nahman b. Yitshaq resolving a challenge to the Bavli view that the law follows the Tanna Qamma, exempting women; (B) and (H) discuss altering the truth, using the same verb (שנה), as affecting marital harmony; (C) and (F,G) parallel rulings found in the Yerushalmi *sugya*, stating that the law follows R. Yohanan b. Baroqa (C) and that a wife may compel a divorce (F,G). Sections (D,E), the midpoint, both cite R. Asi and R. Abbahu, the latter attributing to R. Yohanan the view that women are obligated in procreation or the related rule that a woman may initiate a divorce from a childless marriage. Both are rejected/interpreted accordingly. The central section thus affirms that R. Yohanan did *not* maintain the position of R. Yohanan b. Beroqa and that women are not obligated in procreation, despite Palestinian traditions indicating otherwise.

We also see the degree to which this Bavli passage recalls the language of Palestinian texts throughout. Both the Bavli and Yerushalmi *sugyot* (A; a) begin with the same homily of Genesis 1:28, supporting the opinion of the Tanna Qamma. The statement "the law is like R. Yohanan b. Baroqa" appears repeatedly in both (C,D; b,d), as does the attribution to R. Abbahu citing an earlier Palestinian sage (D,E;b). Both contain rulings that a woman may force a divorce

(F,G; c,e). As already discussed, the story of Yehudit (H) mirrors t.Yevamot 8:4, and the case brought before R. Aha b. R. Qatina (I) parallels m.Gittin 4:5.

Despite these similarities and the likelihood that the Palestinian material served as sources for the Bavli sugya, there is a noticeable difference. All of the traditions in texts from the Land of Israel—the Yerushalmi, Tosefta, and Mishnah—are stated as short, apodictic rulings, issued as halakhic statements devoid of narrative context. In the Bavli, on the other hand, beginning with the central section of the chiastic structure (E), they are embedded as elements within narratives. Thus, the Yerushalmi and Bavli similarly rule that a woman may initiate a divorce, but in the Yerushalmi, this is stated as a general rule: "If the woman lay claims to be married, the law supports her position" (c,e). In the Bavli, by contrast, this ruling appears as decisions in actual cases brought before R. Yohanan (E), R. Ami (F) and R. Nahman (G). T.Yevamot 8:5's rule prohibiting one drinking a sterilizing potion (*"leshtot ikarin"*), is the action taken by Yehudit (H). Finally, the law of m.Gittin 4:5, is described as the details of a case that came before R. Aha b. Qatina and the decision he issued (I).

The inclusion of Palestinian traditions in a Bavli *sugya* is certainly not surprising. More notable is the way these various legal traditions have been incorporated into narratives in the second half of the *sugya*, and the effect of their new context in particular.

As mentioned, the overall aim of b.Yevamot 65b–66a is maintaining the position of the Tanna Qamma, obligating men alone in the commandment to procreate. The narratives challenge the Bavli position in one of two ways. They either report a case whose ruling seems to contradict women's exemption (E, I—the first and last cases of the second half of the chiasm), or they present the subjects of the decision—in all three instances women[57]—critiquing it (F,G,H). (Note that the second section has its own internal chiasm). Although the challenges are mainly resolved to conform to the Bavli position, the Palestinian traditions consistently present tensions with the accepted Babylonian *halakhah*, serving as counterpoints to it. As we will discuss in the section that follows, this correlates with the more general function of narratives within legal discourse.

---

57   *Infra* n. 60.

Law and Narrative

In his recent work on the relationship between halakhic and aggadic texts in the Bavli, Barry Wimpfheimer has pointed to the function of Talmudic narratives in showing the ways that the subjects of the *halakhah* interact with it.[58] Drawing from the work of Mikhail Bakhtin and from Robert Cover, Wimpfheimer argues that narratives often reflect the concerns of real people in the real world and the contexts in which the law was understood and practiced by them. He argues that "legal narrative reflects normative behavior" and in the process, imports significance to views that have been effectively marginalized by the codifiers of the law.[59]

I would argue that these stories in b.Yevamot accomplish both. Despite the *halakhah* following the Tanna Qamma, obligating only men in procreation, the narratives recorded in the Bavli *sugya* both show the conflict that the *halakhah* of the Tanna Qamma could cause for its adherents and give voice to the rejected view that was prevalent in the Land of Israel.

Sections (F,G) point to the problems that may result for women when they are not obligated in procreation and have no means to leave a childless marriage; they will have no one to care for them in their old age. The decision that infertility is grounds for a wife to demand a divorce is offered as the solution to the problems caused by the halakhic status quo and the tension between the prescribed ideal law and what people actually face in their lived realities. Although the immediate purpose of these anecdotes is to demonstrate that R. Yohanan could both exempt women from procreation and still rule that a wife may leave a childless marriage, they ultimately serve to demonstrate an actual problem generated by the ruling itself. The fact that the challenges are voiced by women correlates with a general trend found in the Bavli of attributing critiques to accepted rabbinic positions to non-rabbinic "Others" such as women.[60]

Another conflict resulting from the law is illustrated in the narrative describing Yehudit's attempts to avoid another agonizing pregnancy by disguising herself and asking her husband whether women are commanded in procreation (H). In this story, Yehudit's lack of obligation leads her to sterilize herself, which causes anguish to R. Hiyya by robbing him of the chance of having more chil-

---

58 Wimpfheimer, *Narrating the Law*.
59 Wimpfheimer, 60–61.
60 See Ilan, "Beruriah Has Spoken Well," 184–188; Valler, "Women's Talk—Men's Talk." Christine Hayes has demonstrated this tendency in regard to Romans and *minim*, Hayes, "Displaced Self-Perceptions."

PROCREATION IN PALESTINIAN HALAKHAH AND IN BABYLONIAN AGGADAH 285

dren. It is ambiguous with whom our sympathies are meant to lie; the anecdote opens by describing Yehudit's experience of pregnancy and her desperation to prevent any more from occurring, yet concludes with R. Hiyya voicing his loss. Furthermore, another anecdote recorded two folio earlier (b.Yevamot 63a), depicts R. Hiyya as being devoted to his unfeeling (nameless) wife, who constantly torments him.[61] These latter points coupled with the male authorship and perspective of the Bavli would suggest that the actions of Yehudit themselves are the conflict to the Bavli position. This story then demonstrates the logical extreme which results from exempting women from the obligation to procreate; there is nothing to prevent them from self-sterilization.

The narratives thus provide a thick description of life:[62] if women have no obligation, they have no recourse to leave a childless marriage, and they will be alone in old age (F,G). Moreover, even men will suffer for there will be nothing to prevent their wives from sterilizing themselves if they don't want to have children anymore (H).

But what we also see is how the rabbis of the Bavli negotiated this tension between law and narrative. Despite the strict *halakhah*, when deciding actual cases (albeit as recorded by them) they treated female subjects as if they were indeed commanded and hence granted them the power to leave their marriage. The Bavli *sugya* thus follows the first opinion of the Mishnah, obligating only men in procreation, but at the same time recognizes the costs for women and men in rejecting the Palestinian view following R. Yohanan b. Baroqa and therefore, in practice often followed it. In the stories of R. Ami and R. Nahman (F,G) there are costs to wives who lack grounds to sue for divorce. The solution was to rule in contrast to the actual Bavli position and in accordance with R. Yohanan b. Baroqa, per the law in the Land of Israel. The Yehudit story (H) demonstrates that by following the Bavli position alone there are even costs for men whose desire for more children are frustrated, yet clear benefits for women in granting them more reproductive freedom.[63] Ultimately the narratives reveal both the tensions between the divergent rulings of Babylonia and the Land of Israel, as

---

61 *Supra* n. 50.
62 Wimpfheimer, *Narrating the Law*, 5.
63 Esther Fischer suggests both the possible negative and positive implications of women's exemption, such as the autonomy that her lack of command entails in allowing her to choose whether to have children. Fischer, "Women's Exemption from the Commandment of 'Peru u-Revu,'" 199.

Although as noted, the addendum added to the story of Yehudit might be limiting the degree of freedom allowed to her by implying that she only resorted to sterilization after having two sets of twins, male and female, thus already enabling her husband to fulfill his obligation.

well as the tensions that may arise when a commandment that requires a man and woman to complete is not equally incumbent upon them both.

The difference between the "real world" reflected in aggadic texts and that which is mandated by *halakhah* comes into starker relief when we consider the passages from Leviticus Rabbah and Bavli Niddah regarding the mother's material contributions of conception, discussed above. In this case, the aggadic texts give voice to current biological theories that were prevalent in both milieus, though it was against each community's respective halakhic position. Thus, although the *halakhah* as determined in b.Yevamot rules that women are not obligated in procreation, the aggadic text in b.Niddah expresses women's actual physical involvement. In contrast, the prevailing position in the Land of Israel was that women are indeed included in the obligation, yet Leviticus Rabbah reveals competing positions which downplay women's physical involvement.

Conclusion

The Bavli exempts women from the formal obligation of procreation, however, in actual practice, the rabbis are recorded as acting as though women too had an obligation in certain cases. Likewise, in aggadic texts depicting the physical process of procreation, the Bavli includes traditions which depict women as active contributors, on par with the scientific theories that were prevalent in their day. The parallel Leviticus Rabbah passage, by contrast, disregards their physical contribution, which too resonates with Greco-Roman literature, despite the predominant law in Palestinian rabbinic texts obligating women in the command to procreate. This dissonance between the *halakhah* and the *aggadah* may well reflect the relationship between the law as it is prescribed on the one hand, and how it is practiced and perceived by its subjects on the other, showing the shades of gray and the range of possibilities in the lives of real people and thus the multi-vocal discourse embedded within rabbinic texts.[64] Although the Babylonian rabbis depart from their Palestinian counterparts in their official decision, aggadot and anecdotes reveal that the redactors of the Bavli nevertheless preserve their position within the discourse, both resolving the tension that arises from its rejection, and inverting it to depict a tension left unresolved.

---

64   Wimpfheimer, *Narrating the Law*, 165–166.

Appendix

The following chart illustrates both the use of Leviticus Rabbah 14 by the Bavli and how it has been worked into a sugya following a chiastic structure of A-B-C-D-C1-B1-A1:

	B. Niddah 30b–31a	Parallels in Leviticus Raba 14
	Introductory material, stands apart from chiasm: R. Simlai: The position of the fetus and the Torah it learns in the womb.	14:8, 14:1, 14:2
A	*Tanu rabbanan*: The position of the fetus; what causes labor pain; *Haynu detnan*: Females cause more pain than males because: "Each one emerges [from the womb] according to its position during intercourse [זה בא כדרך תשמישו וזה בא כדרך תשמישו]: [The female] must turn her face up, but [the male] does not turn his face [זו—הופכת פניה, וזה אין הופך פניו]."	14:5
B	*Tanu rabbanan*: The benefits of semen for mother and fetus during different trimesters. *Tanna*: The danger of intercourse on the ninetieth day. Abaye disagrees.[65]	
C	*Tanu rabbanan*: Three partners in conception: God, father, and mother. Support by R. Papa.	
D	R. Ḥinana b. Papa: (*derashah* on Job 9:10) God protects the fetus from falling out of womb; contrasted to a person holding a bundled parcel upside down.	14:3
	Davar 'aḥer: God ensures that the fetus does not fall out; though it increases in weight it moves upward; contrasted to a weight on a scale.	14:3
	R. Yose ha-Gelili: (*derashah* on Psalms 139:14) God forms the fetus in the womb; compared to winnowing. *Davar 'aḥer*: formation of the fetus compared to dyeing.	14:6
	R. Yosef: (*derashah* on Isaiah 12:1) Praise God even for suffering; support from R. Eleazar based on Psalms 82:18.	

---

65   This is one of several amoraic debates that are scattered throughout the aggadic cluster, which is a common phenomenon. See Rosenthal, "Bene ha-talmud hifsiku ve-kafzu le-hakshot be-tokh ha-baraita," 560–563.

(cont.)

B. Niddah 30b–31a	Parallels in Leviticus Raba 14
R. Ḥanina b. Papa: (*derashah* on Psalms 139:3) The fetus is formed from brightest part of the semen. *Tanna de'bei R. Yishmael*: compared to winnowing. Support from R. Abbahu from 2 Samuel 22:40, Psalms 18:33. Reference to David.	14:2, 6
R. Abbahu: (*derashah* on Numbers 23:10) God counts every seed of Israel. Support from R. Joḥanan based on Genesis 30:16: God intervenes and causes individuals to be born	14:5
C1 R. Yitshaq citing R. Ami: If a man emits seed first, a daughter is born; if woman emits seed first, a son is born. Proof from Leviticus 12:2. *Tanu rabbanan*: Same teaching as above, with additional proof texts.	14:8
B1 R. Katina: I could produce only male children. Rava: Guidance for how to have male children.	14:2–6
R. Yitshaq citing R. Ami: Woman only conceives close to her period (Psalms 51:7). R. Joḥanan: Close to her immersion.	14:5
R. Yitshaq b. R. Ami: The benefits of male babies.	14:2–6
Four questions posed to R. Simeon b. Yoḥai: 1. Why does a parturient bring a sacrifice?	
2. Why does birth of a girl cause more impurity? All rejoice over the birth of a boy.	14:4
3. Why is circumcision on day 8? 4. Why is a woman a menstruant for seven days?	14:7
A1 Four questions to R. Dostai: 1. Why do men pursue women? 2. Why do men face down and women face up [during intercourse]? 3. Why can men be appeased? 4. Why do women have sweet voices? 2–4 answer: "He faces the place from where he was created, and she faces the place where she was created."	

Bibliography

Arthur, Marilyn. "Early Greece: The Origins of the Western Attitude toward Women." *Arethusa* 6 (1973): 7–58.

Brodsky, David. *A Bride Without a Blessing: A Study in the Redaction and Content of Massekhet Kallah and Its Gemara*. Tübingen: Mohr Siebeck, 2006.

Cantarella, Eva. *Pandora's Daughters: The Role and Status of Women in Greek and Roman Antiquity*. Translated by Maureen Fant. Baltimore: Johns Hopkins University Press, 1986.

Cohen, Norman J. "Structural Analysis of a Talmudic Story: Joseph Who Honors the Sabbath," *Jewish Quarterly Review* 72 (1982): 161–177.

Cohen, Shaye J.D. *Why Aren't Jewish Women Circumcised?: Gender and Covenant in Judaism*. Berkeley, Los Angeles, London: University of California Press, 2005.

Connell, Sophia M. *Aristotle on Female Animals: A Study of the Generation of Animals*. Cambridge: Cambridge University Press, 2016.

Dean-Jones, Lesley. *Women's Bodies in Classical Greek Science*. Oxford: Clarendon Press, 1996.

Dinnerstein, Dorothy. *The Mermaid and the Minotaur: Sexual Arrangements and Human Malaise*. New York: Harper & Row, 1976.

Fischer, Esther. "Women's Exemption from the Commandment of 'Peru u-Revu.'" *Lehiyot Isha Yehudiyah* 3 (2005): 199–212.

Fraenkel, Jonah. *Darkhe ha-'aggadah ve-ha-midrash*. Jerusalem: Masada, 1991.

Friedman, Shamma. "Historical Aggadah in the Talmud." In *Saul Lieberman Memorial Volume*, edited by Shamma Friedman, 1–46. Jerusalem: Jewish Theological Seminary, 1993.

Friedman, Shamma. *Tosefta Atikta: Synoptic Parallels of Mishna and Tosefta Analyzed With Introduction*. Ramat Gan: Bar Ilan University Press, 2002.

Frymer-Kensky, Tikva Simone. *In the Wake of the Goddesses: Women, Culture, and the Biblical Transformation of Pagan Myth*. New York: Free Press, 1992.

Grene, David, ed. *Aeschylus I: Oresteia: Agamemnon, The Libation Bearers, The Eumenides*. Translated by Richmond Lattimore. 2 edition. Chicago, London: University Of Chicago Press, 1969.

Hauptman, Judith. *Rereading the Rabbis: A Woman's Voice*. Boulder, CO: Westview Press, 1998.

Hayes, Christine. "Displaced Self-Perceptions: The Deployment of Mînîm: And Romans in b. Sanhedrin 90b–91a." In *Religious and Ethnic Communities in Later Roman Palestine*, edited by Hayim Lapin, 249–289. Bethesda: University Press of Maryland, 1998.

Higger, Michael. *Ozar Ha-Baraitot*. Vol. 6. NY, 1943.

Higger, Michael. *Ozar Ha-Baraitot in Ten Volumes*. Vol. 5. NY, 1942.

Ilan, Tal. "Beruriah Has Spoken Well: The Historical Beruriah and Her Transformation in the Rabbinic Corpora." In *Integrating Women into Second Temple History*, 175–194. Tübingen: Mohr Siebeck, 1999.

Jacobowitz, Tamar. "Leviticus Rabbah and the Spiritualization of the Laws of Impurity." Ph.D, University of Pennsylvania, 2010.

Kessler, Gwynn. *Conceiving Israel: The Fetus in Rabbinic Narratives*. Philadelphia: University of Pennsylvania Press, 2009.

Kiperwasser, Reuven. "'Three Partners in a Person' The Genesis and Development of Embryological Theory in Biblical and Rabbinic Judaism." *Lectio Difficilior* 10 (2009).

Laqueur, Thomas. *Making Sex: Body and Gender from the Greeks to Freud*. Cambridge, MA: Harvard University Press, 1990.

Levinson, Joshua. "Cultural Androgyny in Rabbinic Literature." *From Athens to Jerusalem: Medicine in Hellenized Jewish Lore and in Early Christian Literature*, 2000, 119–140.

Lieberman, Saul. *Tosefta Kefshuta: Seder Nashim, Parts 6–7*. Third. New York; Jerusalem: Jewish Theological Seminary, 2007.

Lloyd, Geoffrey Ernest Richard. *Science, Folklore and Ideology: Studies in the Life Sciences in Ancient Greece*. Cambridge: Cambridge University Press, 1983.

Lloyd-Jones, Hugh, ed. *Females of the Species: Semonides on Women*. London: Duckworth, 1975.

Margulies, Mordecai. *Midrash Vayyikra Rabbah*. 3rd ed. New York; Jerusalem: Jewish Theological Seminary, 1993.

Peck, A.L., trans. *Aristotle: Generation of Animals*. Cambridge, MA: Harvard University Press, 1942.

Pomeroy, Sarah. *Goddesses, Whores, Wives, and Slaves: Women in Classical Antiquity*. New York: Schocken, 1995.

Raveh, Inbar. "A Story of Women's Suffering: A Gender Reading of the Story of Judith, Wife of Rabbi Hiyya." *Journal of Ancient Judaism* 3, no. 1 (2012): 68–76.

Raveh, Inbar. "Sippuro Shel Za'ar Nashi." *Akdamut* 26 (2011): 157–170.

Rosenthal, David. "Bene ha-talmud hifsiku ve-kafzu le-hakshot be-tokh ha-baraita." *Tarbiz* 60 (1991): 551–576.

Satlow, Michael L. *Tasting the Dish: Rabbinic Rhetorics of Sexuality*. Society of Biblical Literature, 1995.

Steinmetz, Devorah. "Must the Patriarch Know 'Uqtzin? The Nasi as Scholar in Babylonian *Aggada*," *AJS Review* 23, no. 2 (1998): 163–189.

Strack, Hermann, and Gunter Stemberger. *Introduction to the Talmud and Midrash*. Minneapolis: Fortress Press, 1992.

Strauch Schick, Shana. "Do Women Emit Seed?: Theories of Embryogenesis and the Regulation of Female Masturbation in Rabbinic Literature." In *Female Bodies, Female Practitioners: Proceedings from the 2014 Conference in Berlin*, edited by Lennart Lehmhaus, forthcoming.

Strauch Schick, Shana. "From Dungeon to Haven: Competing Theories of Gestation in Leviticus Rabbah and the Bavli." *AJS Review* 43, no. 1 (2019): 143–168.

Temkin, Owsei, trans. *Soranus: Gynaecology*. Baltimore: Johns Hopkins University Press, 1991.

Valler, Shulamit. "Women's Talk Men's Talk: Babylonian Talmud Erubin 53a–54a." *Revue Des Etudes Juives* 162 (2003): 421–445.

Weiss, Abraham. *Al Ha-Yetsirah Ha-Sifrutit Shel Ha-Amoraim*. NY: Horev Yeshiva University, 1962.

Wimpfheimer, Barry. *Narrating the Law: A Poetics of Talmudic Legal Stories*. Philadelphia: University of Pennsylvania Press, 2011.

Zeitlin, Froma. "The Dynamics of Misogyny: Myth and Mythmaking in the Oresteia." *Arethusa* 11 (1978): 149–184.

PART 3

Tributes to Yaakov Elman

∴

CHAPTER 13

Remembering Yaakov Elman ז״ל

Lawrence H. Schiffman

It is a great privilege to speak to you today about the colleague and friend whose memory we are here to honor, Professor Yaakov Elman, *zichrono livrakhah*.¹ I say colleague, but I had the privilege to be his teacher during his years at NYU and about him in those years I can truly say, מתלמידי יותר מכולן, "but I have learned more from my students than from anyone else" (b. Makkot 10a). That was an era in which academic business was conducted much more informally. I knew that the gentleman whom I had met in Rabinowitz's Hebrew Bookstore held a Master's degree from Columbia University in Assyriology but that he was not continuing there. I must admit that I did not shop very often in Rabinowitz, since my real home among the *sefarim* (Jewish book) stores on the Lower East Side was Biegeleisen, where I constantly stopped on the way home from NYU to our home in Great Neck. Thus, it took a while for me to get to know Yaakov Elman when I occasionally looked for something that only the more modern Rabinowitz store would have. It became clear to me that this incipient scholar, who wanted nothing more than to discuss scholarship with academic customers when they entered the store, could make an amazing contribution to Judaic Studies. In any conversation, one could see that his academic training and interest were already at this early stage integrated with his prodigious traditional learning. One night, therefore, I went to the store and, not wanting to have this conversation take place in front of Mrs. Rabinowitz, suggested that Yaakov join me at the kosher pizza store across the street for a few minutes. Out of nowhere I told him that I had secured for him the potential of a full tuition grant and a $2500 stipend—the maximum that we gave in those days. Happily for all of us, Yaakov made a decision to accept and enrolled in the Department of Near Eastern Languages and Literatures that was my home and that of Judaic Studies at NYU in those days.

It was not long before Mrs. Rabinowitz decided to close the store. However, somehow or another the powers above often provide for us just when we need

---

1 Memorial remarks delivered at the Yeshiva University conference, "Land and Spirituality in Rabbinic Literature: A day in memory of Professor Yaakov Elman ז״ל," February 19, 2019.

it. Bernie Scharfstein of Ktav Publishing called me up one day looking for an editor, and before you know it Yaakov was working at Ktav, where he would remain for many years, even while starting out his career at YU. Before long, Ktav's editor was now Dr. Elman, having completed a very important study of the relationship of Tosefta Pesaḥim to the Talmud Bavli. During his years as a graduate student, Yaakov was also successful in establishing relationships with Jacob Neusner and David Weiss Halivni. These relationships would stand him in good stead as his academic career flourished.

We can thank Leo Landman, then Dean of the Bernard Revel Graduate School and somehow making decisions about Stern College, for inviting Yaakov to teach at Stern part-time as a kind of *"probe,"* a try out for a full faculty position. Happily, he was, as expected, a great success, and before long was a full-time member of the faculty. He was able to reduce his workload at Ktav but his continued contribution there enabled the publication of numerous important scholarly works at a time when many of the present avenues of publication were not yet available.

It did not take long for Dr., now Professor, Elman to move uptown. But here is a curious fact. A scholar who had completed a degree in Talmudic studies was essentially being converted into a professor of Bible. Again, happily for us he maintained his research program in the field of rabbinics and produced numerous papers during those early years at YU. Gradually it became clear that he should be teaching graduate students and over time he was able to successfully shift his program into his real field—the academic study of rabbinic literature. One funny story from this intermediate period: I was at a conference somewhere with Professor Arthur Hyman, then serving as Dean of the Bernard Revel Graduate School of Jewish Studies. He told me that because of a leave of absence being taken by another faculty member it had been proposed that Yaakov Elman be asked to substitute in teaching graduate courses in biblical studies. Arthur wanted to know from me if Yaakov was qualified. I was frankly astounded that anybody who knew anything about his wide-ranging knowledge and his Master's degree in Assyriology would ask this ridiculous question. Instead of reacting that way to the question, I answered instead in a serious manner, describing his qualifications and indicating my own personal recommendation. Anyone who knew Professor Elman knows that he had acquired a wide-ranging knowledge of the various fields of Judaic Studies that has today become a rarity, unfortunately.

As we all know, at some point he began to move into the study of what we might call the Persian environment in which the Babylonian Talmud came into being. This is a subject that in the 19th century had attracted some attention but about which virtually nothing was being done. In some ways, I have always thought of the kindling of this new interest as a kind of return to his origins as a scholar in the Semitic languages program at Columbia where he specialized in Akkadian under Professor Moshe Held. There he had written one article attempting to tie an Akkadian expression to later Jewish usage. But, of course, what he was doing at Columbia was learning about the language, culture, and literature that influenced the rise of early Israelite literature. Thus, after entering Talmudic studies, this very same interest motivated him to study the language and literature of the Sasanian Persians who ruled over Babylonia in the Talmudic period. Interestingly, the only contemporary American Judaic scholar who earlier had had an idea of the value of these types of questions was indeed Jacob Neusner, as one can see scattered throughout his *History of the Jews of Babylonia*. In any case, we are all aware that Yaakov Elman went on essentially to create and build a new subfield in Talmudic studies, the study of the links between Iranian society, culture, and literature and the rabbinic tradition.

The Iranian/Persian period in his scholarship was also a period of tremendous personal satisfaction and attainment of a reputation beyond the usual bounds of rabbinic scholarship. He linked up with scholars of Middle Persian and spent a considerable amount of time at Harvard, and he derived tremendous satisfaction from his enthusiastic reception there. However, I think that one of the most important accomplishments of this period is that it was in these years that he trained doctoral students at YU. The students had the benefit of thorough technical training, encouragement of wide-ranging creativity, and the kind of devoted mentorship that I hope he learned from his teachers at NYU. We should mention that these accomplishments came for the most part during a period of difficult physical suffering resulting from his having been severely injured. His ability to continue in this difficult situation and, indeed, to overcome it, was admired by all of us.

One of the privileges I had during my tenure at YU some years ago was reading the citation at the event at which Professor Elman was invested in the Herbert S. and Naomi Denenberg Chair in Talmudic Studies. As you can imagine, this was a great privilege for me, having been his dissertation advisor.

Please allow me this personal note: today marks another of fortunately not too many occasions when I have joined in memorializing a student who has passed away. The rabbis have given us halakhic parameters to enable students to mourn their teachers, recognizing the special relationship, but as far as I know they have not codified the teacher's obligation to mourn the student. Perhaps this is because of the complexity of feeling that occurs. There is the sadness of seeing the former student pass into the next world but there is also the joy of knowing that that student has made enormous contributions to the understanding and transmission of our common heritage and of the academic approach to the study of that heritage.

Our emotions and feelings of gratitude can in no way parallel those of the family members who both sacrificed for and benefited from his illustrious career as a scholar. So we close with our continued expression of sympathy to them and with our thanks as well for making possible his work over so many years. Thank you.

CHAPTER 14

Perpetual Motion

Shai Secunda

One day many years ago, I returned home to a bewildering message scrawled on a Post-it note: "Dr. E. wants you to call him back immediately. Something about ... orangutans?!?!"[1] There was no question *who* had called. "Dr. E" was Yaakov Elman, my teacher, mentor, and, as we like to say in academe, *Doktorvater*. Yaakov was an expert and pioneer in the study of the Talmud in its Iranian context, and his career had been so capacious—spanning from meteorology to Assyriology, biblical interpretation, Dead Sea Scrolls, Hasidic thought, rabbinic literature, and Zoroastrianism—that for a moment I had to consider the possibility that this was no game of telephone and that my teacher had taken up primatology. As it turned out, Dr. E. had made progress not on *orangutans* but on the Nērangestān, a Middle Persian text devoted to the laws of Zoroastrian worship.

Professor Yaakov Elman passed away in Brooklyn, NY, on 17 Av 5778 (July 29, 2018). He left behind a towering scholarly legacy. Staggeringly fluent in Talmud, he was also one of the few truly voraciously hungry intellectuals left in a professionalized academia. He combined a Hasidic heart with a *litvishe kop*, a critical academic sense with the creativity of an original tosafist. Yaakov wrote copiously about times, people, and places distant from him and from each other—the fabled ruler of the ancient Persian Empire Darius the Great; the early 20th-century Reform German rabbi Benno Jacob; a medieval Catalan thinker known as the Meiri; a radical 19th-century Polish Hasidic master named Rabbi Tzadok Ha-kohen of Lublin; talmudic rabbis such as Rava and Abaye; and late antique Zoroastrian priests bearing names such as Sōšāns and Gogušnasp. With his black velvet yarmulke, white beard, and *payis*, Yaakov spoke excitedly of those long-buried and largely forgotten Zoroastrian sages as if they were close friends. The entire motley crew he studied was brought into endlessly fascinating conversations with one another in the vast halls of his brilliant mind, just as he cultivated an astoundingly diverse group of close, real-life companions that included yeshiva heads, professors, Christians, Muslims, atheists, Zoroastrians, and Jews of all denominations.

---

1 This tribute originally appeared in *The Jewish Review of Books*, August 21, 2018.

Yaakov's first day job, after he finished City College in 1966, was in meteorology. Eight years later, he moved on to the S. Rabinowitz Hebrew Book Store on New York City's Lower East Side, where, as manager for just more than a decade, he held court for a stream of traditional and academic scholars who sought his wisdom as much as they shopped for Hebrew books. From there he went on to publishing, serving as associate editor at Ktav for more than 15 years. During that time, he also pursued a doctorate at NYU, and then, well into middle age, he became a professor at Yeshiva University.

Even within the confines of his chosen area of academic study (Talmud) Yaakov's chief accomplishment was ambulatory. While his early work was strictly philological and focused on topics such as the relationship between the early rabbinic compilation known as the Tosefta and the Babylonian Talmud, he moved on to ingeniously combine Iranian and talmudic studies in a hybrid that became known as Irano-Talmudica. Yaakov was not the first scholar to realize that studying Babylonian Jewry's Persian context could illuminate the Babylonian Talmud, but he is the one who built it into a real movement of flesh-and-blood people from different fields, working in close relationships. These pairings proved fascinating, productive, and, at times, hilarious.

Yaakov began this Irano-Talmudic stage of his career at age 50, on a fellowship at Harvard. There he befriended professor Oktor Skjærvø, a tall, wry Norwegian master of Indo-Iranian languages. Oktor and Yaakov, the brilliant, *heimishe* patriarch of a large Orthodox family, soon became inseparable, spending many hours each day studying Middle Persian in Skjærvø's large, book-lined office. Occasionally attending faculty parties in the evening, they appeared as the ultimate odd couple. And Yaakov became close with his "fellow" graduate students, chiding one Harvard couple to tie the knot after many years of dating (they did not) and ensuring that a Zoroastrian student wore his *sudreh* and *kusti*—a ritual belt and shirt resembling Jewish *tsitsit*—on the day of his comprehensive exams (he did).

Traveling the world for Jewish and Iranian studies conferences, Yaakov became a tireless evangelist for reading the Talmud alongside Middle Persian texts, regularly launching into detailed discussions of Zoroastrian law and describing it, to the astonishment of many, as "halakhic," "rabbinic," and "strikingly parallel" to Jewish law. He became an ongoing associate at Harvard, and his reading group with Skjærvø expanded to include a growing cast of characters, such as a visiting University of Tehran professor and Yaakov's own Talmud students (including me). The tiny field of Old Iranian studies, which had been languishing due to lack of interest, gained tremendously from the sudden, unexpected infusion of these Talmud scholars.

Back in Washington Heights, Yaakov's Yeshiva University classes expanded with students who had come to hear a talmudic genius talk about Zoroastrianism and its significance for understanding the Talmud. And regular, nonacademic devotees of Jewish texts caught wind of what was happening and began to follow Yaakov's work from beyond the ivory tower. It is difficult to capture the exhilaration of that time, when one could feel the vibrations of a major shift taking place at the traditional, talmudic core of Jewish studies. One can now legitimately divide Talmud scholarship into two periods—BE, before Elman, when Talmud research focused on the text and its development, and AE, after Elman rewrote the curriculum of talmudists to include the languages and literatures of communities neighboring Babylonian Jewry, especially the Persian-speaking Zoroastrians, who ruled the powerful Sassanian Iranian Empire.

Yaakov's establishment of Irano-Talmudica also faced considerable trials and tribulations. He suffered a near fatal car crash in early 2004, which landed him in the hospital for the good part of a year. Soldiering on, he conducted class via conference call from a hospital bed flanked by teetering piles of books. (It took the Mount Sinai hospital staff some time to learn how to accommodate a patient whose uninjured work ethic made him function like a waylaid army general.)

The academic politics could be even more debilitating. Reluctant to retrain and retool, some classically trained talmudists argued loudly that the Greco-Roman language and culture they had studied in graduate school were somehow more important than Iranian languages and culture for understanding the Babylonian Talmud and its world—despite the fact that the Talmud was composed under Iranian rule, not Roman. And then there was the occasional, hard-hitting review attacking various claims and interpretations of the Irano-Talmudic school. Yaakov's strategy was always to fight fire with fire and to push ahead with more research. But the academic battles took their physical and emotional toll. In the end, a compelling scholarly movement built on human relationships could also be rocked by the inherent vulnerability of human relationships.

Yaakov was a man of limitless intellectual curiosity, ambitions, and passions. Like all creatures he was destined to die, as the rabbis have it, "with not even half his desires fulfilled." Still, that cup was nearly half full. Chief among his numerous accomplishments across Jewish (and non-Jewish) studies is the now-basic expectation that scholars of the Babylonian Talmud acknowledge the Talmud's Iranian context. What also remains is the lingering dynamism of a man who never ceased to learn and think and write and teach and grow. May his memory be a blessing to us all.

CHAPTER 15

Professor Yaakov Elman: A Talmud Scholar of Singular Depth and Scope

Shana Strauch Schick

It is hard to be reconciled to the fact that Professor Yaakov Elman has passed away.[1] I find myself with a profound sadness and loss, yet at the same time gratitude, to count myself among the small group of Yaakov Elman's doctoral students, with the distinct privilege of benefiting from his mentorship, and now the difficult task of trying to do justice to his memory—as a brilliant scholar, a selfless and ever supportive advisor, and one of the kindest, most sincere people I have ever known.

When I first met Professor Elman, he was in the hospital after a terrible car crash that left him partially paralyzed from the neck down. But this brush with death and devastating injury did not seem to faze him. From his bed he delivered an impromptu lecture on the Iranian practice of temporary marriage, which illuminated the peculiar stories of the Babylonian amoraim, Rav and Rav Nahman, marrying for one day—a topic he would touch on in several articles. His excitement over an insight into a deeply perplexing *sugya*, allowed him to push past the physical pain and uncertainty over his health, something he continued to do over the subsequent fifteen years.

His sincere love of pursuing and spreading knowledge was manifest in many other ways. He not only appreciated good scholarship; he enthusiastically promoted the work of others. In his writing and in person he was open and respectful to scholars from all disciplines and walks of life, Jew and gentile, male and female; and he extended this respect to his students as well. It was almost comical how much time he would spend photocopying articles to distribute in class, so that he could give his students the most up-to-date material instead of sending them to the library in search of it.

His dedication to, and respect for, his students came through in every aspect of his career at Yeshiva University. Not content to teach required courses and pursue his own work, he set about to revive a Talmud department that had long

---

1 This tribute originally appeared in thelehrhaus.com (https://www.thelehrhaus.com/timely-thoughts/professor-yaakov-elman-a-talmud-scholar-of-singular-depth-and-scope/) August 30, 2018.

been in a state of decline. His classes at the Bernard Revel Graduate School became a beacon to students who, like himself, brought a love of learning from the *beit midrash* but felt drawn toward critical approaches. Having revitalized the department, he set about to secure the necessary institutional resources to take on and support doctoral students, personally arranging for students to do additional coursework at Columbia, NYU, and Harvard, and always ensuring that we had the necessary funding to complete PhDs.

As an advisor he went above and beyond. He was ever supportive, always available, insightful, with the right amount of criticism during the dissertation process. And this continued throughout the years that followed. Even when he was once again confined to a hospital bed, he continued to be a devoted mentor; he still read our works, offered his insights and critiques, sent articles he thought would be of interest, and was there to help in any way he could—irrespective of the current state of his health. His devotion and pride in our work was like that of a father. I will always be grateful to him and try to live up to the standard he set for us.

He was an individual in the truest sense of the word; his varied career was an extension of an insatiable intellectual curiosity that took him from the "*beis medrish*" to college, a stint in weather forecasting, to Assyriology and of course academic Talmud study. In this realm he brought together diverse strands of scholarship to build an approach that I can best describe as holistic. For him, the Bavli, read carefully, yields a vivid picture of overlapping intellectual and cultural moments, populated by commanding legal minds, creative religious thinkers, and more than a few colorful or even roguish personalities. Rav Yosef, Rav Nahman, and of course Rava, whom Professor Elman would often remind us is the most oft-cited sage in the Bavli. These were not abstract names or literary constructs, but people who lived and died, and at some level struggled with the same problems that rabbinic Jews living within prosperous foreign cultures would face over the next 1500 years.

To understand the texts, the anonymous editors who constructed them, and the figures active within them, Professor Elman forged a unique path, drawing on studies as diverse as the orality of Scottish epic poetry, sociology of religion, legal theory, and the study of Middle Persian texts and cultures. As he often acknowledged, Shaul Shaked and Isaiah Gafni had demonstrated the importance of the Middle Persian texts, and he completely devoted himself to advancing this as a central aspect of modern talmudic scholarship. Collaborating with scholars of ancient Iran, he mastered Pahlavi and sought to read Zoroastrian religious works with the same rigor that he would bring to a Talmudic *sugya*. As he would often quip, unlike the Talmud, the Middle Persian works had not benefited from over a thousand years of continuous study and commentary.

Professor Elman's holistic approach was devoted to showing how the Bavli could be read critically as a source of intellectual and cultural history. He simultaneously accepted the serious challenges inherent in analyzing a vast compendium, compiled and redacted over the course of hundreds of years, while rejecting the idea that this compels us toward extreme skepticism. He had utmost respect for the work and skill that had gone into creating, transmitting, and interpreting the Talmudic corpus over two millennia, so he was confident that by using the tools of modern critical Talmud study it was possible to trace developments across generations, expose differences between regions and schools of thought, and even between the approaches of individual sages to law and communal policy. This is exemplified by his sustained interest in Rava. Through Professor Elman's work, we now have a picture of Rava that is neither a legendary hero of aggadic lore, nor a supposed kernel of truth derived from those tales, but a fleshed-out, cosmopolitan thinker and revolutionary jurist whose influence can be detected throughout the redacted layers of the Bavli.

One of the last articles he worked on, which I had the privilege to edit, reflects the scope of his interests as well as his ability to integrate different areas of scholarship. Drawing from recent studies as well as his own research, he points to parallel developments in Qumran, early Rabbinic, and Zoroastrian law, demonstrating that each system evinces a move toward greater abstraction and conceptualization, including quantification, analogical reasoning, and second-order interpretation. As always, he constructs a broad picture that might not otherwise have come into focus. Going over some of his last writings brings home how much more he could have done and how much we will not get to see.

Professor Elman wrote extensively about the final *sugya* of *Mo'ed Qatan*, which reflects the Babylonian Rabbis' concern with theodicy, the seeming arbitrariness of life, and their fear of death, topics that he, unfortunately, perhaps understood better than most. But it is the concluding words of the *masekhet* (29a) that suit him best. For someone who never stopped studying, writing, and expanding his horizons; someone who, to our great benefit, even in the most difficult times, did not rest, the teaching of R. Hiyya Bar Ashi in the name of Rav is most fitting:

> Rav Hiyya bar Ashi said that Rav said: Torah scholars have no rest, even in the World to Come, as it is stated: "They go from strength to strength, they will appear before God in Zion" (Psalm 84:8).

May his memory be a blessing and an inspiration to us all.

CHAPTER 16

A Tribute to Professor Yaakov Elman

Meira Wolkenfeld

I embarked on a doctorate in Talmud because of Dr. Elman's encouragement. He related to his students with an innate egalitarianism and an infectious love of learning; always interested in our feedback and ideas. His classes rarely stayed on topic. Instead, they strayed to whatever he was working on and what excited him. His ideas rose to the surface like the fizzy bubbles in the Cokes he drank while teaching.

Dr. Elman was insightful and dedicated to his students. When I was looking for a dissertation topic, he suggested that I work on the sense of smell (see my article in this volume), and he guided me with relevant reading recommendations. It was a fitting suggestion, engaging my interests in Middle Persian literature, the history of daily life, and the body. During the semester that I finished writing my research proposal, he was hospitalized and then, for some time, convalescing at a rehab center. He was having trouble with his eyes and couldn't see well, so he had me print out my proposal draft in an extra large font, then dictated his comments and notes, so that I could write them down when he could not. Now, as I write my dissertation, I feel a pang when I make a point that I think he might appreciate, quote a scholar he loved like Walter Ong, or spend time toiling over a research question that he could have answered instantaneously.

After hearing Dr. Elman passed away, I thought of a text that I learned from him. The last mishnah in tractate Sotah associates the death of different rabbis with the loss of different qualities. For example, "משמת רבי בטלה ענוה ויראת חטא, When Rabbi (Yehuda HaNasi) died, humility and fear of sin were nullified (ceased to exist)" (m. Sotah 9:15). According to the Babylonian Talmud, "אמר ליה רב יוסף לתנא לא תיתני ענוה דאיכא אנא, Rav Yosef said to the reciter of the mishnah, 'Don't teach (that there is no more) humility (in the world), after all, there's me!'" (b. Sotah 49b). I thought of these words, which I could hear Dr. Elman reciting with his characteristic delight. I thought of the relationships he had with the various personalities of the Talmud, and the joy he got from their wit. I thought of the feeling of bereft that the mishnah evokes, that there is a special quality missing from the world—a way of thinking and teaching—that was uniquely his.

He is missed.

Photographs

The Moshe and Madelaine Baumel Judaic Faculty Incentive Award, 1992

Interview photo, 2004

Portrait, 2004

Bibliography of Yaakov Elman's Publications

Monographs

Elman, Yaakov. Authority and Tradition: Toseftan Baraitot in Talmudic Babylonia. New York: Yeshiva University Press, 1994.

Edited Volumes

Elman, Yaakov and Jeffrey Gurock (ed.). Hazon Nahum: Studies in Jewish Law, Thought and History Presented to Dr. Norman Lamm in Honor of His Seventieth *Birthday*. New York: Yeshiva University Press, 1997.

Elman, Yaakov and Israel Gershoni. Transmitting Jewish Traditions: Orality, Textuality, *and Cultural Diffusion*. New Haven: Yale University Press, 2000.

Texts

Elman, Yaakov. *The Living Nach: Early Prophets*, Jerusalem: Moznaim, 1994.

Elman, Yaakov. *The Living Nach: Later Prophets*, Jerusalem: Moznaim, 1996.

Elman, Yaakov and Solomon Almoli. *Dream Interpretation from Classical Jewish Sources*, Hoboken, NJ: Ktav, 1998. Translation

Sperber, Daniel. Why Jews Do What They Do: A History of Jewish Customs Throughout the *Cycle of the Jewish Year*. Yakov Elman (trans). Hoboken, NJ: Ktav, 1999.

Articles

Elman, Yaakov. "Babylonian Echoes in a Late Rabbinic Legend," *Journal of the Ancient Near East Society* 4 (1972): pp. 13–19.

Elman, Yaakov. "Authoritative Oral Tradition in Neo-Assyrian Scribal Circles," *Journal of* the Ancient Near East Society 7 (1975): pp. 19–32.

Elman, Yaakov. "An Akkadian Cognate of Hebrew šeḥîn," *Journal of the Ancient Near East Society* 8 (1976): pp. 33–34.

Elman, Yaakov. "In the Margins of the Yerushalmi: Hagiga," *In the Margins of the Yerushalmi: Glosses on the English Translation*. Jacob Neusner ed., Chicago, California: Scholars Press, 1983, pp. 31–57.

Elman, Yaakov. "In the Margins of the Yerushalmi: Moed Qatan," *In the* Margins of the Yerushalmi: Glosses on the English Translation. J. Neusner ed. Chicago, California: Scholars Press, 1983, pp. 59–67

Elman, Yaakov. "Reb Zadok HaKohen of Lublin on Prophecy in the Halakhic Process," Jewish Law Association Studies I (1985): pp. 1–16.

Elman, Yaakov. "R. Zadok HaKohen of Lublin on the History of Halakha," *Tradition* 21 (1985): 1–26.

Elman, Yaakov. "The Order of Arguments in Kalekh-baraitot in Relation to the Conclusion," *Jewish Quarterly Review* 79 (1989): pp. 295–304.

Elman, Yaakov. "When Permission is Given: Aspects of Divine Providence," *Tradition* 24 (1989): pp. 24–45.

Elman, Yaakov. "Ha-mal'akh ha-Mashhit bi-Zeman ha-Ge'ulah" [Hebrew], *Rinat Yitzchak* 1 (1988–1989): pp. 109–113.

Elman, Yaakov. "The Suffering of the Righteous in Babylonian and Palestinian Sources," *Jewish Quarterly Review* 80 (1990): pp. 315–339.

Elman, Yaakov. "From the Pages of Tradition: Rabbi Moses Samuel Glasner: The Oral Torah," *Tradition* 25 (1990): pp. 63–69.

Elman, Yaakov. "Babylonian Baraitot in Tosefta and the 'Dialectology' of Middle Hebrew," Association for Jewish Studies Review 16 (1991): pp. 1–29.

Elman, Yaakov. "Righteousness as Its Own Reward: An Inquiry into the Theologies of the Stam," Proceedings of the American Academy for Jewish Research 57 (1991): pp. 35–67.

Elman, Yaakov. "The History of Gentile Wisdom According to R. Zadok Hakohen of Lublin," Journal of Philosophy and Jewish Thought 3 (1993): pp. 153–187.

Elman, Yaakov. "A Theological Reflection on Death, Resurrection, and the Age of the Universe: R. Israel Lipschitz' Derush Or ha-Hayyim," Aryeh Kaplan ed., *Immortality, Resurrection and the Age of the Universe*. Hoboken, NJ: Ktav, 1992, pp. 66–163.

Elman, Yaakov. "'It Is No Empty Thing': Nahmanides and the Search for Omnisignificance," *The Torah U-Madda Journal* 4 (1993): pp. 1–83.

Elman, Yaakov. "Le-Toledot ha-Ribbuy ba-Talmud ha-Bavli," *Proceedings of* the Eleventh World Congress of Jewish Studies. D. Assaf ed., Jerusalem: World Union of Jewish Studies, 1994, 87–94.

Elman, Yaakov. "Some Remarks on 4QMMT and the Rabbinic Tradition, Or, When Is a Parallel Not a Parallel?" Reading 4QMMT: New Perspectives *on Qumran Law and History*. M.J. Bernstein and J. Kampen ed., Atlanta, GA: Scholars Press, 1996, pp. 99–128.

Elman, Yaakov. "Progressive *Derash* and Retrospective *Peshat*: Non-Halakhic Considerations in Talmud Torah," *Modern Scholarship in the Study of Torah: Contributions and Limitations*. S. Carmy ed., Northvale, NJ: J. Aaronson, 1996, pp. 189–287.

Elman, Yaakov. "Moses ben Nahman / Nahmanides (Ramban)," *Hebrew Bible/Old Tes-*

tament: *History of Its Interpretation*. M. Sabo ed., Goettingen: Vandenhoeck & Ruprecht, 1996, vol. 1, pp. 416–432.

Elman, Yaakov. "The Status of Deuteronomy as Revelation: Nahmanides and Abarbanel," Hazon Nahum: Studies in Jewish Law, Thought and History Presented to Dr. Norman Lamm in Honor of His Seventieth Birthday. Y. Elman and J. Gurock ed. New York: Yeshiva University Press, 1997, pp. 229–250.

Elman, Yaakov. "The Contribution of Rabbinic Thought Towards a Theology of Suffering," *Jewish Perspectives on the Experience of Suffering*. S. Carmy ed. Northvale, NJ: J. Aaronson 1999, pp. 155–212.

Elman, Yaakov. "Orality and the Transmission of Tosefta Pisha in Talmudic Literature," Introducing Tosefta: Textual, Intratextual and Intertextual Studies. H. Fox and T. Meacham ed. Hoboken, NJ: Ktav, 1999, 117–174.

Elman, Yaakov. "Mishnah and Tosefta," *Encyclopedia of the Dead Sea Scrolls*. L.H. Schiffman and J.C. VanderKam ed., Oxford: Oxford University Press, 2000, vol. 1, pp. 117–174.

Elman, Yaakov. "Talmudim," *Encyclopedia of the Dead Sea Scrolls*. L.H. Schiffman and J.C. VanderKam ed., Oxford: Oxford University Press, 2000, vol. 2, pp. 913–915.

Elman, Yaakov. "Orality and the Redaction of the Babylonian Talmud," *Oral Tradition* 14 (1999) [published in 2000]: pp. 52–99.

Elman, Yaakov. "MMT B 3–5 and Its Ritual Context," *Dead Sea Discoveries* 6 (1999): pp. 148–156.

Elman, Yaakov and Daphna Ephrat. "The Institutionalization of Oral Tradition: From Study Circle to Yeshiva and Madrassa in Jewish and Islamic Babylonia," *Orality, Textuality and the Materiality of Jewish Tradition: Representations and Transformations*. Y. Elman and I. Gershoni ed., New Haven: Yale University Press, 2000, pp. 107–137.

Elman, Yaakov. "The Rebirth of Omnisignificant Biblical Exegesis in the Nineteenth and Twentieth Centuries," *JSIJ* 2 (2002): pp. 1–42. Elman, Yaakov. "The Small Scale of Things: The World Before the Genizah," *Proceedings* of the American Academy of Jewish Research 63 (1997–2001) [published in 2002]: pp. 49–86.

Elman, Yaakov. "Benno Jacob in Historical Context," *Die Exegese hat das erste Wort: Beiträge zu Leben und Werk Benno Jacobs*. W. Jacob and A. Juergensen ed., Stuttgart: Calwer Verlag, 2001 [published 2002], pp. 102–107.

Elman, Yaakov. "Derekh ha-GRA u-Magamato be-Ferush Midrash Halakhah be-'Aderet Eliyahu' al Sefer Vayiqra" [Hebrew] *Ha-GR"A u-Veit Midrasho*. M. Halamish, et al, Ramat Gan: Bar-Ilan University Press, 2003, pp. 63–80.

Elman, Yaakov. "Classic Rabbinic Interpretation," *Jewish Study Bible*, A. Berlin and M.Z. Brettler ed. New York: Oxford University Press, 2003, pp. 1844–1862.

Elman, Yaakov. "Marriage and Marital Property in Rabbinic and Sasanian Law," *Rabbinic Law in Its Roman and Near Eastern Context*. C. Hezser ed., Tübingen: Mohr-Siebeck, 2003, pp. 227–276.

Elman, Yaakov. "Rava ve-Darkei ha-Iyyun ha-Eretz Yisraeliyyot be-Midrash ha-Halakhah" [Hebrew], *Merkaz u-Tefutzah: Eretz Yisrael veha-Tefutzot bi-Ymei Bayit Sheni, ha-Mishnah veha-Talmud*. Y. Gafni ed. Jerusalem: Merkaz Shazar, 2004, pp. 217–242.

Elman, Yaakov. "Acculturation to Elite Persian Norms in the Babylonian Jewish Community of Late Antiquity," *Neti'ot David*. E. Halivni, Z.A. Steinfeld, and Y. Elman ed., Jerusalem: Orhot, 2004, pp. 31–56.

Elman, Yaakov. "Order, Sequence, and Selection: The Mishnah's Anthological Choices," *The Anthology in Jewish Literature*. D. Stern ed., New York: Oxford University Press, 2004, pp. 53–80.

Elman, Yaakov. "'Up to the Ears' in Horses' Necks: On Sasanian Agricultural Policy and Private 'Eminent Domain',"*JSIJ* 3 (2004), pp. 95–149.

Elman, Yaakov. "Midrash Halakhah in Its Classic Formulation," *Recent Developments in Midrashic Research*. L.M. Teugels and R. Ulmer ed., Piscataway, NJ: Gorgias Press, 2005, pp. 3–16.

Elman, Yaakov. "Cultural Aspects of Post-Redactional Additions to the Bavli," *Creation and Composition: The Contribution of the Bavli Redactors (Stammaim) to the Aggadah* [*TSAJ* 114], Jeffrey Rubenstein ed., Tübingen: Mohr-Siebeck, 2005, pp. 383–416.

Elman, Yaakov. "The Babylonian Talmud in Its Historical Context," *Printing the Talmud: From Bomberg to Schottenstein*. S. Lieberman-Mintz and G.M. Goldstein ed., New York: Yeshiva University Museum, 2005, pp. 19–28.

Elman, Yaakov. "Torah va-Avodah as Competing Values in Hazal," *Jewish Spirituality and Divine Law*. A. Mintz and L. Schiffman ed., New York: Yeshiva University Press, 2005, 61–124.

Elman, Yaakov. "Scripture Versus Contemporary Needs: A Sasanian/Zoroastrian Example," *Cardozo Law Review* 28 (2006): pp. 153–169.

Elman, Yaakov. "Yeshivot Bavliyot ke-Vatei Din" [Hebrew], *Yeshivot u-Vatei Midrash*. E. Etkes ed., Jerusalem: Merkaz Shazar, 2006, pp. 31–55. Elman, Yaakov. "R. Yosef be-cIdan Ritha," *Bar Ilan Annual* 30–31 Memorial Volume for Prof. M.S. Feldblum (2006): pp. 93–104.

Elman, Yaakov. "Middle Persian Culture and Babylonian Sages: Accommodation and Resistance in the Shaping of Rabbinic Legal Tradition," *Cambridge Companion to Rabbinic Literature*. C.E. Fonrobert and M.S. Jaffe ed., Cambridge: Cambridge University Press, 2007, pp. 165–197.

Elman, Yaakov. "'He in His Cloak and She in Her Cloak': Conflicting Images of Sexuality in Sasanian Mesopotamia," Discussing Cultural Influences: Text, Context, and Non-Text in Rabbinic Judaism: Proceedings of a Conference on Rabbinic Judaism at Bucknell University. Rivka Ulmer ed., Lanham, MD: University Press of America, 2007, pp. 129–164.

Elman, Yaakov. "Ma'aseh be-Shtei Ayarot: Mahoza u-Pumbedita Ke-Metzayygot Shtei Tarbuyot Hilkhatiyyot" [Hebrew], *Torah li-Shemah: Mehqarim be-Madacei ha-Yahadut li-khvod Prof. Shamma Yehudah Friedman. D. Golinkin ed., Ramat Gan: Bar Ilan University Press, 2007, pp. 3–38.

Elman, Yaakov. "The Socioeconomics of Babylonian Heresy," *Jewish Law Association Studies* 17 (2007): pp. 80–126.

Elman, Yaakov. "Who Were the Kings of East and West in Ber 7a?: Roman Religion, Syrian Gods and Zoroastrianism in the Babylonian Talmud," *Studies in Josephus and the Varieties of Ancient Judaism: Louis H. Feldman Jubilee Volume*. S.J.D. Cohen and J. Schwartz ed., Leiden: E.J. Brill, 2007, pp. 43–80.

Elman, Yaakov. "Hercules Within the Halakhic Tradition: A Response to Ronald Dworkin," *Dinei Yisrael* 25 (2008): pp. 7*–42*.

Elman, Yaakov. "Tsadok ha-Kohen of Lublin," YIVO *Encyclopedia of Eastern Europe*. G.D. Hundert ed., New Haven: Yale University Press, 2008, vol. 2, p. 1909.

Elman, Yaakov. "Returnable Gifts in Rabbinic and Sasanian Law," *Irano-Judaica*. S. Shaked ed., Jerusalem: Yad Izhak Ben Zvi, 2008, vol. 6, pp. 150–195.

Elman, Yaakov. "The Other in the Mirror: Iranians and Jews View One Another. Questions of Identity, Conversion, and Exogamy in the Fifth-Century Iranian Empire. Part One," *Bulletin of the Asian Institute* 19 (2005; publ. 2009): pp. 15–25.

Elman, Yaakov. "Why Study Talmud: Wellsprings of Torah and the Individual Soul," *Why Study Talmud in the Twenty-first Century?: The Relevance of the Ancient Jewish Text to Our World*. P. Socken ed., Lanham, MD: Rowman and Littlefield Publishing Group, 2010, pp. 135–150.

Elman, Yaakov. "The Halakhah Follows Rava ... Except When It Doesn't: A Mediation on Halakhic Decision-making," Vixens Disturbing Vineyards: Embarrassment and Embracement of Scriptures: Festschrift in Honor of Harry Fox. T. Yoreh, et al ed., Boston: Academic Studies Press, 2010, pp. 272–307.

Elman, Yaakov. "Zekhuyot ha-Ishah bi-Nekahsaha be-Askolat Mahoza" [Hebrew], *Sidra* 24–25 (2010): pp. 17–48.

Elman, Yaakov. "Toward an Intellectual History of Sasanian Law: An Intergenerational Dispute in Hērbedestān 9 and Its Rabbinic Parallels," *The Talmud in Its Iranian Context*. C. Bakhos and R. Shayegan ed., Tübingen: Mohr-Siebeck, 2010, pp. 21–57.

Elman, Yaakov. "Why Is There No Central Zoroastrian Temple?: A Thought Experiment," The Temple of Jerusalem: From Moses to the Messiah: Studies in Honor of Professor Louis H. Feldman. Steven Fine ed., Leiden: E.J. Brill, 2011, pp. 151–170.

Elman, Yaakov. "Zoroastrianism and Qumran," *The Dead Sea Scrolls at Sixty* [*Studies on the Texts of the Desert of Judah, vol. 89*]. L.H. Schiffman and S. Tzoref ed., Leiden: E.J. Brill, 2010, pp. 91–98.

Elman, Yaakov. "Resh Pesahim ba-Bavli uvi-Yerushalmi—Inyanei Arikhah ve-Hithavvut," *Melekhet Mahshevet*, C. Milikowsky ed., Ramat Gan: Bar Ilan University Press, 2011, pp. 9–25.

Elman, Yaakov. "Meiri and the Non-Jew: A Comparative Investigation," *New Perspec-*

tives on Jewish-Christian Relationships In Honor of David Berger. E. Carlebach and J.J. Schachter ed. Boston: E.J. Brill, 2012, pp. 265–296.

Elman, Yaakov. "Jewish Acculturation to Persian Norms at the End of the Parthian Period," *The Parthian Empire and its Religions: Studies in the Dynamics of Religious Diversity*. Peter Wick, Markus Zehnder and Jan Schäfer ed., Gutenberg: Computus Druck Satz & Verlag, 2012, pp. 151–161.

Elman, Yaakov. "The Emotional Palette of the Grodno School: Ye'ush and Hefker," *Rav Shalom Banayikh: Essays Presented to Rabbi Shalom Carmy by Friends and Students in Celebration of Forty Years of Teaching*. Hayyim Angel and Yitzchak Blau ed., Jersey City: Ktav, 2012, pp. 95–128.

Elman, Yaakov. "Law in the Crisis of Empire: A Sasanian Example," *Journal of Persianate Studies* 6 (2013): pp. 101–114.

Elman, Yaakov. "Levirate Marriage, Sturih and Zikkah in the Talmuds" [Hebrew], *Ke-Tavor Be-Harim: Studies in Rabbinic Literature Presented to Joseph Tabory*. Arnon Atzmon and Tzur Shafir, ed., Alon Shvut: Tevunot, 2013, pp. 139–163.

Elman, Yaakov. "Commercial Law in Rome and Ctesiphon: Roman Jurisconsults, Rabbis and Sasanian Dastwars on Risk," *Rabbinic Traditions between Palestine and Babylonia*. Ronit Nikolsky and Tal Ilan ed., Leiden: Brill, 2014, pp. 250–283.

Elman, Yaakov. "Saffron, Spices, and Sorceresses: Magic Bowls and the Bavli," *Daughters of Hecate: Women and Magic in the Ancient World*. Kimberly B. Stratton and Dayna Kalleres ed., Oxford: Oxford University Press, 2014, pp. 365–385.

Elman, Yaakov. "Autonomy and Its Discontents: A Meditation on Pahad Yitshak," *Tradition* 47:2 (Summer 2014): pp. 7–40.

Elman, Yaakov. "Striving for Meaning: A Short History of Rabbinic Omnisignificance," *World Philology*. Sheldon Pollock, Benjamin A. Elman, and Ku-ming Kevin Chang ed., Cambridge: Harvard University Press, 2014, pp. 62–91, 343–345, 394–398.

Elman, Yaakov. "Contrasting Intellectual Trajectories: Iran and Israel in Mesopotamia," *Encounters by the Rivers of Babylon: Scholarly Conversations Between Jews, Iranians and Babylonians in Antiquity*. Uri Gabbay and Shai Secunda ed., Tübingen: Mohr Siebeck, 2014, pp. 7–105.

Elman, Yaakov and Prods Oktor Skjaervo. "Concepts of Pollution in Late Sasanian Iran: Does Pollution Need Stairs, and Does It Fill Space?" *ARAM* 26:1–2 (2014): pp. 21–45.

Elman, Yaakov. "Pahad Yitzhak: A Joyful Song of Affirmation," *Hakirah* 20 (Winter 2015): pp. 25–64.

Elman, Yaakov. "Shopping in Ctesiphon: A Lesson in Sasanian Commercial Practice," *The Archaeology and Material Culture of the Babylonian Talmud*. Markham J. Geller ed., (Leiden: Brill, 2015), 225–244. Elman, Yaakov, and Shai Secunda. "Judaism," *The Wiley Blackwell Companion to Zoroastrianism*. Yuhan Vevaina and Michael Stausberg ed., Oxford: Wiley-Blackwell, 2015, pp. 423–435.

Elman, Yaakov. "Some Aspects of Interreligious Polemic in the Babylonian Talmud,"

Bridging between Sister Religions: Studies of Jewish and Christian Scriptures Offered in Honor of Prof. John T. Townsend. Isaac Kalimi ed., Leiden: Brill, 2016, pp. 175–194.

Elman, Yaakov. "Rav Isaac Hutner's Pahad Yitzhak: A Torah Map of the Human Mind and Psyche in Changing Times," *Books of the People: Revisiting Classic Works of Jewish Thought*. Stuart Halpern ed., Jerusalem: Maggid Books, 2017, pp. 301–343.

Elman, Yaakov and Mahnaz Moazami. "PV 5.1–4 in the Context of Late Antique Intellectual History," *Bulletin of the Asia Institute* 27 (2017): pp. 13–41.

Elman, Yaakov and Mahnaz Moazami. "The Quantification of Religious Obligation in Second Temple Judaism-And Beyond," HĀ-'ÎSH MŌSHE: *Studies in Scriptural Interpretation in the Dead Sea Scrolls in Honor of Moshe J. Bernstein*. Binyamin Y. Goldstein et al. ed., Leiden: Brill, 2018, pp. 96–135.

Elman, Yaakov. "Dualistic Elements in Babylonian Aggadah," *Aggadah of the Bavli and its Cultural World*. Geoffrey Herman and Jeffrey L. Rubenstein ed., Providence: Brown Judaic Studies, 2018, pp. 273–311.

Elman, Yaakov and Mahnaz Moazami. "Some Aspects of Ancient Legal Thought: Functionalism, Conceptualism, and Analogy," *Strength to Strength: Essays in Honor of Shaye J.D. Cohen*. Michael L. Satlow ed., Providence, Rhode Island: Brown Judaic Studies, 2018, pp. 405–420. Elman, Yaakov. "The Torah of Temporary Marriage: A Study in Cultural History," *A Thousand Judgements: Festschrift for Maria Macuch*. Almut Hintze et al. ed., Wiesbaden: Harrassowitz Verlag, 2019, pp. 83–107.

Elman, Yaakov. "Samuel's Scythe-handle: Sasanian Mortgage Law in the Bavli," *Irano-Judaica*, vol. 7 (2019): pp. 129–143.

Elman, Yaakov. "The Hērbedestān in the Hērbedestān: Priestly Teaching from the Avesta to the Zand," *Irano-Judaica*, vol. 7 (2019): pp. 267–294.

Elman, Yaakov. "Digestion as a Means of Purification in Fourth and Fifth-Century Sources: A Rabbinic Conundrum and an Avestan Problem," *Iran, Israel, and the Jews: Symbiosis and Conflict*. Aaron Koller and Daniel Tsadik ed., Eugene, OR: Pickwick; New York: Yeshiva University, 2019, pp. 59–107

Elman, Yaakov and Mahnaz Moazami. "The Scholasticization of Religion: From Qumran to Ctesiphon," *From Scrolls to Traditions: A Festschrift Honoring Lawrence H. Schiffman*. Stuart Miller, Michael Swartz, Steven Fine, Naomi Grunhaus, Alex Jassen ed., Leiden: Brill, 2020, pp. 66–98.

Reviews

Elman, Yaakov. "The Judaism of the Mishna: What Evidence?" [Review of J. Neusner, Judaism: The Evidence of the Mishna], *Judaica Book News* 12 (1982): pp. 17–25.

Elman, Yaakov. "R. Polzin, Moses and the Deuteronomist: A Literary Study of the Deuteronomic History," *Judaica Book News* 12 (1982): pp. 69–70.

Elman, Yaakov. "B. Greenberg, On Women and Judaism: A View from Tradition," *Judaica Book News* 12 (1982): p. 72.

Elman Yaakov. "L. Jacobs, Teyku: The Unsolved Problem in the Babylonian Talmud," Judaica Book News 12 (1982): pp. 82–83.

Elman, Yaakov. "Election Without Faith, Judaism Without Mitzvot" [Review of Michael Wyschogrod, Body of Faith: Judaism as Corporal Election], Judaica Book *News* 15 (1984), pp. 8–10, 56–58.

Elman, Yaakov. "Structure, Movement, and Tension" [Review of Robert Alter, *The Art of Biblical Poetry*], Judaica Book News 16 (1986): pp. 20–21.

Elman, Yaakov. "A Humanistic Wolf in Covenantal Clothing: Covenant as a Bill of Divorce" [review of David Hartman, A Living Covenant.], Judaica Book News 17 (1986–1987): pp. 20–25.

Elman, Yaakov. "Rejoinder [to David Hartman]." *Judaica Book News* 18 (1987–1988), pp. 6–8, 66–67.

Elman, Yaakov. "Poetics of Biblical Narrative: A Review Essay" [Review of M. Sternberg, Poetics of Biblical Narrative], Judaica Book News 18 (1987–1988): pp. 13–16.

Elman, Yaakov. "J. Neusner, *Tosefta*," *Jewish Quarterly Review* 78 (1987): pp. 130–136.

Elman, Yaakov. "N. Aminoah, Arikhat Masekhtot Betzah, Rosh Hashanah, Ta`anit Ba-Talmud Ha-Bavli," Journal of Jewish Studies 39 (1988), pp. 124–125.

Elman, Yaakov. "J. Levenson, *Sinai and Zion*," *Tradition* 24, (1988): pp. 99–104.

Elman, Yaakov. "S. Safrai, ed. The Literature of the Sages, First Part: Oral Tora, Halakha, Mishna, Tosefta, Talmud, External Tractates," Judaica Book News 18 (1988): pp. 52–53.

Elman, Yaakov. "Recreating the Mind of the Genizah: Goitein's *Mediterranean Society*," *Judaica Book News*, 19 (1988–1989): pp. 16–21.

Elman, Yaakov. "American Jewry: Where Are We Going?" [Review of Charles S. Liebman, Deceptive Images: Toward a Redefinition of American Judaism], Judaica *Book News* 19/ (1989): pp. 25–28.

Elman, Yaakov. "H.C. Schimmel and A. Carmell, *Encounter: Essays on Torah and Modern Life*," *Jewish Action* 50 (1990): pp. 79–82.

Elman, Yaakov. "A.J. Avery-Peck, New Perspectives on Ancient Judaism, Volume 4: The Literature of Early Rabbinic Judaism: Issues in Talmudic Redaction and Interpretation," Religious Studies Review 17 (1991): pp. 177–178.

Elman, Yaakov. "D. Kraemer, The Mind of the Talmud: An Intellectual History of the Babylonian Talmud, Religious Studies Review," Jewish Quarterly Review 84 (Oct 1993–Jan 1994): pp. 261–282.

Elman, Yaakov. "H.L. Strack and G. Stemberger, *Introduction to the Talmud and Midrash*," Shofar: An Interdisciplinary Journal 10 (1992): pp. 121–122.

Elman, Yaakov. "Review of Pseudo-Rabad Commentary to Sifre Deuteronomy, edited and annotated according to manuscripts and citations by Herbert W. Basser," *Religious Studies Review* 21 (1995): pp. 157–158.

Tributes

https://www.yu.edu/sites/default/files/inline-files/Professor_Yaakov_Elman_Dr_Koller.pdf

https://www.yu.edu/sites/default/files/inline-files/Rabbi_Ari_Lamm.pdf

https://www.thelehrhaus.com/timely-thoughts/lo-alman-yisrael-reflections-on-the-legacy-of-yaakov-elman/?fbclid=IwAR3zFxbWBV1QnTrQSCfC5D7KUDx4VrSR7jnxjUjxdK84JyOIqegCDfdJLhc

https://www.thelehrhaus.com/timely-thoughts/a-tribute-to-yaakov-elman/

https://www.thelehrhaus.com/timely-thoughts/life-children-and-sustenance-personal-reflections-on-the-legacy-of-a-torah-scholar/

https://www.thelehrhaus.com/timely-thoughts/yaakov-elman-and-the-history-of-halakha/

Prof. Yaakov Elman z"l publications can be accessed at: https://yeshiva.academia.edu/Elman

Index

Abaye   194–197, 198, 199, 201, 299
Abba Shaul   17–18, 21, 24, 28
Abraham (biblical)   11, 16, 21, 99, 128, 145, 270
The Academy of R. Yannai   214–216
Adik bVa'u al Zion (poem)   152–170
Aelian   14
Aeschylus   262
Ahreman   253
Akbara   215
Akkadian   297
'Ammei haarets ("commoners")   53
Amemar   199, 201
Ammonite   8, 67, 203
Amram ben Solomon   151
Amram Dare   147, 151–153
Anaqim   see Rephaites
Aramaic poetry   IX, 151, 159–170
Aristotle   244, 246, 254–255
Astrology   see Mazal
Augustus Caesar   14, 78
Augustine of Hippo   25–26

Baba Rabba   149–150
Babylonian Aramaic   225
Babylonian Gaonate   51, 206
Barbaria   99, 101
Bar Kokhba   55, 247
Bar Qappara   197–198, 211, 227
Basilosaurus   19
Benjamin of Tudela   30–31
Bet Shearim   29
Bezalel (biblical)   180–181

Categories of Jewish Lineage   63–64, 69–76, 79
Chrysostom, John   245
Converts   VIII, 63–66, 68–70, 72–88

Dayumeset   193
dei Rossi, Azariah   26
Dēnkard   251–254
Divre Sofrim   38, 40–49
Divre Torah   38, 40–49

Elizur, Shulamit   161–166

Elman, Yaakov   VII, X–XI, XVI, 32, 60, 176, 226, 295–318
Ezra (biblical)   57, 186–187, 189–191

Forbidden Marriages   67–77, 79–87
Forgetting and Restoration of Law motif
   in BT   175–179, 181–206
   in JT   175–185, 198
Fossils   VII–VIII, 5, 10, 14, 18–20, 31
Fraade, Steven   40, 46–47
Frigidaria   58
Furstenberg, Yair   40, 88

Garden of Eden   see Shabbat Gan Eden
Gezerah shavah   188
Giants in antiquity   VII, 3–11, 13–19, 21, 24–26, 28, 30–31
Gigantomachy   16, 29–30
Goliath Ossuaries   7–8

Hadrian   26, 28–30
ḥalal   66, 69–70, 75–77, 80, 82–85, 87
Halakhah le-Moshe mi-Sinai   175, 177, 180, 183–184, 186, 188, 191, 200, 202–205
Hananiah b. Hezeqiah b. Gurion   182
Havdalah   184–185
Hayes, Christine   65, 175–176, 202
Hebron   8–17, 30
Hesiod   262
Hidary, Richard   205
Hillel the Elder   40, 42–43, 186–187, 189–195
House of Hillel   38, 182, 265–266, 275, 280
House of Shammai   38, 43, 182, 265, 275, 280

Ifra Hormiz   249–251, 253
Ishmaelite   93–102
Ivory Beds   22–23

Jabez   see Othniel b. Kenaz
Jacob, Benno   299
Josephus   VII, 5–6, 8–16, 20, 30
Joshua (biblical)   9–10, 16, 40, 70–71, 180–181, 188,

Klawans, Jonathan   106, 130–134

Lamentations 160
Leprosy   *see Nega* and *Tsara'at*
Lo shanu ela traditions   208–221, 224–226

Ma'aseh Tuvia   4
Machpellah Tomb   12, 15–16
Maimonides   100
Mamre   11–12, 16
Manilius   14
Mayor, Adrienne   5, 13, 19, 22
Mazal   176
Meiri   98, 299
The *Menatzpach*   190–191
Menstrual Discharge   55–56, 249–252, 263, 288
The Messiah   X, 239, 241–242, 246–247, 254–256
Middle Persian   X, 251–254, 256, 297, 299–300, 305
Minhag
    in Roman Palestine   51–60
    in medieval Ashkenaz   51
Miriam (biblical)   108, 113–116, 121, 123, 134
Moabite   67, 203
Mount Gerizim   148–150,
Mos maiorum (custom of the ancestors)   52
Moses (biblical)   16, 40, 55, 70, 108–109, 114–115, 122–124, 143, 175, 177, 180, 183–184, 186, 188, 191, 200, 202–205

Naeh, Shlomo   39
Nahote   197
Nazarite   219–221, 232
Nega   107, 113, 116–119, 125, 127–128
The Ninth of Av   IX, 159–161, 166
Nisibis   193

Og king of Bashan   3, 8, 21, 27–28
One seed theory   262–263,
Onqelos
    Proselyte   191–192
    Targum   191
Othniel b. Qenaz   188–190, 197, 203
Ovid   13

Palestinian Aramaic   IX, 159
Pausanias   15
Perugita   193
Peshitta   243

Philo   244, 249, 254
Philostratus   15
Pinhas b. Yair   223
Pirqoi ben Baboi   51–52, 206
Piyutei Harachva (poetic genre)   161, 167
Plato   244, 246
Pliny the Elder   13, 19, 26, 142, 245–246
Prehistoric Elephant teeth   4–6, 18–19, 22
Proboscideans   4
Procreation
    Obligation of   X, 260–261, 265–288
    in Babylonian sources   262–264, 269–273, 276–288
    in Palestinian sources   261–262, 265–265, 273–276, 281–288
    in Greco-Roman sources   262
    Mother's contribution to   262–264
    Father's contribution to   261–262

Qal v'homer   188
Qerova (poetic genre)   160
Qillirian tradition   159–160, 162
Qinot   159–160, 165–166
Qiryat Sefer   188
Qumran   VII, 111–112, 130, 304

R. Abbahu   183–184, 190, 228–229, 268, 271–272, 282, 288,
R. Aqiva   23–24, 182, 184, 193, 200, 202, 219, 247
R. Avdimi of Haifa   199–201
R. Eleazar b. Arakh   193–195
R. Eleazar b. Azariah   124, 186, 193
R. Hiyya   24, 26, 128, 183, 186–187, 189–190, 197–198, 218, 272
R. Hiyya b. Abba   97, 190, 274–278, 284–285
R. Levi   179, 181, 261
R. Meir   24, 72–73, 75, 81, 116–120
R. Shimon b. Eleazar   114, 116, 118–119
R. Shimon ben Laqish   179–180, 187, 194, 197, 227–229, 262
R. Shmuel b. Nahman   215–216, 227
R. Yannai   53, 57, 193, 214–216
R. Yehoshua   191
R. Yohanan   181, 183–185, 188, 190, 193, 204, 217–220, 223–224, 227–228, 230–231, 262, 271–274, 282–285
R. Yohanan b. Baroqa   265–268, 271–273, 282, 285

INDEX

R. Yehudah b. Ilai   26, 72–77, 80, 82–84, 86–87, 116, 125–128
R. Yehudah b. Beteyra   193
R. Yehudah ben Hanina   179–180, 193
R. Yeshebab   179–180, 182
R. Yose b. Ḥalafta   56, 75, 81–87, 211
R. Yose bar Hanina   221–222, 229
R. Yose b. R. Bun   179–180, 182, 227
Rabban Gamliel   179–180, 191–192
Rabban Yoḥanan b. Zakai   26–30, 39
Rabbinic units of measure   188–189
Rav   24, 186, 188, 191, 184, 219–221, 229, 230, 232, 248, 249, 254, 304
Rav Ashi   196, 200, 202–204
Rav Huna   181, 248–249
Rav Yehuda   24–25, 186–188
Rav Yosef   194–195, 198, 269–270, 303, 305
Rava   195–196, 200–202, 204, 239–240, 246–247, 249–251, 253, 288, 299, 303–304
Rahit style   164
Rand, Michael   159–160, 165–166, 169
Renewal of Jerusalem (poetic motif)   162–165
Rephaites   3, 8
Ritchie, Ian D.   239, 243–244
Ritual Baths   55–58, 140
Ritual Impurity   54–57, 107, 109–110, 117, 130–131, 133, 182–183, 232, 250–253, 288
Roman Freedman   66, 75, 77–79, 87–88
Roman Law   52, 64–66, 79, 81, 85, 87

Samaritan
    Sukkot   IX, 137–156
    Pentateuch   141
    liturgy   147–148, 151–156
Sasanian Empire   25, 30, 205, 239, 256, 297
Saracens   98, 100–101
School of R. Yishmael   270, 278, 288
Schremer, Adiel   40, 42–43, 46–47
Sense of Smell
    In Greco-Roman sources   244–246, 255–256
    in Bavli   246–251, 255–256
    in Middle Persian sources   251–256
Sevara   196
Shammai   40, 42–43
Shabbat Gan Eden   141, 143–144, 147–148
Shapur, Sasinian king   249
Shemini Atseret   150, 152–153
Shimon b. Shatah   92–103

Shimon HaPequli   192
Slaves   66, 69, 71–72, 77–88
Sokoloff, Michael   159–160
Soloveitchik, Hayim   51
Soranus   262
Stam   223, 247, 249
Suetonius   14
Sukkah
    Rabbinic   137–138, 142–143
    Samaritan   137–138, 141–148, 150, 152–153, 155–156
    Karaite   143
    in Nehemiah   143
Sukkot   IX, 137–156
Synagogue   29–30, 56, 58, 138–139, 166, 184, 272

Ta-Shma, Israel   51
Targum   191, 242–243
Te'sof Nefutzot Zion (poem)   161–169
Tibat Marqe   144, 147–148, 153, 155
Throne of Maximianus   22–23
Tobius Cohen   see Ma'aseh Tuvia
Tosefta Eduyot   VIII, 38–49
Tsara'at
    in Qumran   110
    ritual discussions of   IX, 106, 108–109, 130–134
    as a punishment   IX, 106, 108–109, 112–124, 126–127, 130–134
    as a reward   124–126, 128–129, 134
Two seed theory   262–264

Usha   179–183
Uzziah (biblical)   108, 114–115, 121, 123, 134

Water-libation   183

Yannai   30
Yavneh   38–40, 42, 44, 46–47, 49, 180, 191–192
Yehudai Gaon of Sura   51
Yehudit, wife of R. Hiyya   274–279, 283–285

The Zādspram   254
Zoar Tombstone   XII
Zoroastrianism   VII, X, 205, 249, 252–254, 299–301, 303–304
Zulay, Menahem   161

Printed in the United States
by Baker & Taylor Publisher Services